Great Cases in Psychotherapy

Great Cases in Psychotherapy

edited by
Dan Wedding &
East Tennessee State University
Raymond J. Corsini

F. E. PEACOCK PUBLISHERS, INC.
ITASCA, ILLINOIS 60143

Copyright © 1979
All rights reserved
Printed in the United States
F.E. Peacock Publishers, Inc., Itasca, IL
Library of Congress Catalog Card No. 78-61878
ISBN 0-87581-234-1
Fifth Printing, 1983

To Leonard P. Ullmann and William C. Schutz
Pioneers in Psychotherapy

Example is always more efficacious than precept.
Samuel Johnson

Contents

Foreword

As a student, therapist, and researcher I have always felt that there is more to be learned from what psychotherapists do than what they say they do, and that psychotherapy must be studied on the basis of the transactions between a therapist and a patient rather than the theoretical formulations by which "systems of psychotherapy" are generally known. It is also true that compared to the plethora of theoretical writings in the clinical literature there is a striking dearth of case histories, particularly verbatim accounts. Prior to the advent of sound recordings, primary data were impossible to obtain and case histories of necessity had to be reconstructed from a therapist's notes and memory. Sound film, and more recently, videotape recordings have ushered in a new era in which for the first time it has become feasible to study in detail the actual interchanges between patients and therapists.

The lack of adequate technology, however, has been only one of the reasons for the relative dearth of primary data. Issues of confidentiality have always been real and our collective awareness of protecting a patient's identity has been significantly sharpened during recent years. However, there is reason to believe that therapists have been the more reluctant party. Carl Rogers, perhaps more than any other prominent therapist, deserves the credit for breaking with the tradition of secrecy, and many other experienced therapists have followed his lead. This is both a welcome and a necessary change because in order for students to learn they have to be in a position to study the masters, not residents or graduate students taking their first faltering steps. Until fairly recently, the situation was analogous to what might be the case if virtuosos like Heifetz, Stern, Szigeti and others had never performed in public and our knowledge of what expert violin playing is like had been restricted to listening to the scratching noises of novices.

As all therapists privately acknowledge, there is a vast hiatus between the printed exposition of a theory and its practical application. A theory, by definition, is an abstraction, and at times it has only a vague resemblance to clinical reality. In order to understand the therapeutic process and how therapeutic change occurs, we must study what goes on between a therapist and a patient. There is an apocryphal story that Freud said many things to patients between the time they rose from the couch and left the office, and for all we know these seemingly casual comments, suggestions, recommendations, or whatever may have played as important, or more important, a part in their therapy than the formal interpretations Freud advanced when the patient was in a recumbent position. Yet Freud and all other theoretical writers chose to conceptualize their operations in particular terms, often leaving out of account elements that might have been of far greater significance than the operations to which therapeutic change was attributed by the theory. What needs to be understood about psychotherapy is what works and how it works, which is not necessarily the same thing as the theory. All a theory can ever be is an approximation.

However, even with verbatim accounts, sound tapes, or films, we still have a hard time divining the nature of the patient's *experience*. We cannot look into the patient; we do not know the *meanings* he or she attributes to the therapist's questions, comments, interpretations, gestures, smiles, frowns, hesitations, and so forth, nor can we adequately describe internal, structural changes that may occur. We are always dealing with an exceedingly complex process involving two (or more) people, and we can never go beyond inferences concerning the interactions. The dilemma is this: if we arrest the process, as one might in stopping a film, we destroy its living quality; if we immerse ourselves in the process we are left to struggle with multitudinous variables whose single effects we cannot isolate. We cannot observe how the grass grows; we can only discern that after a period of time *something* has happened that produced the change. A case history, therefore, no matter how detailed or perspicacious will still remain only a pale replica of the astounding richness of any human relationship.

In recent years a body of literature has concerned itself with the question of "specific" versus "nonspecific" factors in psychotherapy. The former set of variables pertains to the techniques purported to produce therapeutic change, the latter to such variables as the therapist's kindliness, warmth, empathy, understanding, respect, commitment, and so forth. The distinction is artificial: there is no such thing as a "nonspecific" factor—only factors we do not fully understand. It may well turn out to be the case that the weight of the therapeutic influence is carried by these so-called nonspecific factors, but they are clearly as much in need of specification as a technique which might be described by its originator as unique.

The collection of case histories assembled in this volume is an excellent cross-section of contemporary psychotherapy and its antecedents. All therapists and students of therapy can learn much from these exemplars. To be sure, psychotherapy, like any practical art, cannot be learned from a book, but the case histories included here can be of great help to the serious student. In studying these fascinating accounts, I would urge the reader to keep in mind such questions as the following:

How and to what extent did the patient change as a result of his or her psychotherapeutic experience? Was the change real and lasting?

To what qualities in the therapist's attitudes, demeanor, techniques, or charismatic qualities can the change be attributed?

Could another therapist, using different techniques and having different personality attributes, have produced comparable changes? Could you use the same approach and expect comparable results?

To what extent can a particular approach be used by another therapist who inevitably is a person whose style, personality attributes, values, and convictions differ from the therapist portrayed in the case history?

Can the case history be considered a faithful and valid account of what actually transpired? To what extent has the therapist edited or slanted the report? To what extent do the therapist's biases and theoretical predilections color the printed account?

Were the idiosyncrasies of the patient and the circumstances surrounding the therapy a significant factor in the change he or she experienced? Is it possible to generalize from a particular case history to other patients, therapists, and circumstances?

Are there common elements in the various case histories transcending their apparent diversity?

No conclusive answers to any of these questions will be forthcoming, but they will provide food for thought to the critical reader. It may also be well to remember that psychotherapy as practiced by many fine clinicians is often less dramatic but no less valuable on that account.

Hans H. Strupp
Vanderbilt University

Preface

While formal psychotherapy is perhaps no more than one hundred years old, beginning probably with the innovations of Paul Dubois, today no fewer than one hundred different psychotherapies exist. They range, alphabetically, from Active Psychotherapy to Will Therapy and include—just to give the ABCs—such well-known approaches as Autogenic Training, Bioenergetics, and Conditioned Reflex Therapy. In addition, a wide variety of innovative therapies exist such as Breakthrough Dreaming, Cognitive Behavior Modification, Eidetics, Fixed Role Therapy, Implosive Therapy, Multimodal Behavior Therapy, Open Encounter, Primal Therapy, and Transpersonal Therapy.

In the extensive literature of psychotherapy—consisting of over ten thousand items—practically every innovator, proponent or adherent of a particular "school" of psychotherapy attests to the efficacy of his or her particular system by citing case examples, some very short and some taking up a whole book.

It was our intention to make a judicious selection of previously published papers to demonstrate various psychotherapeutic systems in action. Our guidelines included the following:

(1) To cover all systems included in *Current Psychotherapies* so that *Great Cases* would be an extension of this text,
(2) To include a balanced presentation of selections, each of which on its own would be an example of good therapy,
(3) To pay special attention to "breakthrough" cases in which the therapist/ theorist discovered some new aspect of psychotherapy,
(4) To locate items that were well written with dramatic impact.

Our steps in collecting and selecting cases were:

(1) All authors of chapters in *Current Psychotherapies* and *Current Personality Theories* were asked for "nominations" of cases which in their opinion represented the very best examples of psychotherapy known to them.
(2) An independent search was conducted through the *Psychological Abstracts* from 1943 to 1977 for case examples that appeared to meet the criteria we had established.
(3) Further cases from other authorities, listed later in this preface, were solicited.

The result was a pool of approximately five hundred published cases, each of which was read by one of us and rated as A (excellent), B (good), or C (poor). These ratings, we hasten to add, referred only to our conception of this book. Any item rated A or B by either of us was then read by the other for an independent rating. Once a pool of items rated AA, BA, and AB had been collected, we began to make selections in terms of our criterion of representativeness.

The major purpose of this book is to advance psychotherapy as an art through presentation of cases that we felt were "great" and could serve as examples of what could be done and as inspiration for creative work in this challenging profession. In the process of selection, we became more tolerant of the views of others and less dogmatic about our own therapeutic predilections (Behavior Therapy and Adlerian Psychotherapy). Editing *Great Cases in Psychotherapy* has been a growth experience for us and we believe that reading this book will be a similar experience for students of psychotherapy who will share the excitement, the joy, the anguish, and the pleasure found in these cases.

In addition to the chapter authors of *Current Psychotherapies* and *Current Personality Theories* we wish to express our appreciation to the following who were of help in a variety of ways: Heinz Ansbacher, Alexander Bassin, Fred Binder, Nathaniel Branden, Joseph R. Cautela, Joseph Chassell, Viktor Frankl, Glen A. Holland, Arthur Janov, Rita Knipp, W. Scott MacDonald, Salvatore Maddi, Renaldo Maduro, Donald Meichenbaum, Harold Mosak, Henri Niedzielski, E. Lakin Phillips, Annette Sproul, Thomas Szasz, Cynthia Townsend, Carter Umbarger, and Paul Watzlawick. We wish to especially note the helpful comments and advice of Arnold A. Lazarus and Albert Ellis. Janet Terner helped us locate difficult-to-find items and Elizabeth Stickney assisted in the technical preparation of this book.

The student of psychotherapy who wishes to extend his readings will find in the Appendix a list of cases we found excellent but which could not be included due to lack of space; these should be considered an extension of this book, and the serious student will find them rewarding.

Dan Wedding
Raymond J. Corsini

Case 1

Editors' Introduction

We are pleased to have located this selection from the writings of Pierre Janet. According to Janet Terner of the Library of Congress, who was able to provide us with a copy of this item, it has never before been translated into English. We have excerpted the case; what is here presented amounts to about 30 percent of the original material.

We must not think of exorcism as a relic of the past. While the witch trials of Salem and the torturing of those considered possessed by the devil are long gone, there are still reported cases of religious exorcisms of the devil.

Pierre Janet was a link between the pioneers of psychiatry, such as Ambrose Liebeault, Hippolyte Bernheim, August Forel, Paul Dubois, and Jean-Martin Charcot and the modern exponents of dynamic psychology such as Sigmund Freud, Alfred Adler, and Carl Jung. His dramatic account of the treatment of Achille, which we here report, well demonstrates the difference between pre-dynamic thinking and modern trends. In this engaging selection there is at the same time a curious old-fashioned air and yet a most exciting hint of coming revelations. Janet felt he deserved more credit than was generally given to him for his innovations. Perhaps the reader can see why after reading this selection.

PIERRE JANET

A Case of Possession and Modern Exorcism

The Society of the Friends of Lyons University has honored me with an invitation to discuss before you some of my recent research in the domain of moral and psychological sciences. I am happy and proud to be able to discuss matters that interest me very much in a city which has contributed so brilliantly to the progress of medical and philosophical sciences.

The mind, in effect, is subject to diseases like the body, and the diseases of the mind permit us to establish certain psychological phenomena that are very interesting from many points of view. These illnesses show certain exaggerations of normal phenomena and permit us to study these facts of the mind in an expanded form just as the microscope permits us to do this for physical objects. It is not useless to hope that the study of pathological psychology shall develop someday into a treatment of the mind which will permit soothing and curing. The results of the psychological studies even though they are practical should not be disdained. On the contrary, they should be considered an achievement, the compensation of all the work of students.

It is this important role of objective psychology from the point of view of science and the point of view of practice that I would like to explicate through a single example. The case to be presented has general interest, since it deals with a kind of madness which has played a rather important role in history, possession by the devil. The case concerns a sick man seized by this delirium, one possessed by the devil that we have been able to study some years ago at La Salpètrière. The analysis of his mental state has been done in a small, psychological laboratory which my excellent and much-missed master, Charcot, helped to install in his department at La Salpètrière, and in which my eminent teacher, Professor Raymond, directed me. This examination of a sick mind can give a general idea of certain objective psychological research and of the possibilities it brings for soothing the mentally ill.

These insanities of possession by the devil were formerly very frequent and appeared in a variety of forms so that one has considered them until today as

Pierre Janet, "Un Cas de Possession et L'exorcisme Moderne." Reprinted from *Néuroses et Idée Fixes* (Paris: Ancienne Librarie Germer Baillière et Cie., 1898), R. J. Corsini, translator.

3

different kinds of mental disease. Frequently these illnesses occurred simultaneously to a great number of persons in the same area and actually formed veritable epidemics. One knows, to take one of several examples, of the possessions of the religious members of the monastery of Kintrop in 1550, whom the devil forced to leap about, to scream, and to cry; one knows the history so horrible and so shameful of the *Ursulines* of Loudun and of the pastor Urbain Grandier. The more recent epidemics of Morzine, 1860, and of Verzeguies, 1880, have often been well described.

All the experts who have discussed this issue are today well convinced that these possessions are nothing but simple mental diseases and that the exorcisms, when they succeed, play a role analogous to that of suggestion in hypnotic research.

The sick person who will serve us in this study is a man of thirty-three, who, four years ago, was brought to La Salpètrière to Charcot's clinic. I was able, with care, to examine this person who had been put in my charge, and I was happy to render him completely cured in a few months. This cure has happily maintained itself for more than three years, and the illness has been followed long enough so that we can now study the insanity, examine the procedure through which he has been cured which can be called *modern exorcism,* and finally, to extract from these observations the lessons contained. Besides, without any difficulty, I can tell of the misadventures of this poor man. I shall give him another name and I shall change his locale and his social situation; only the psychological and medical facts will be accurate, and they are of an abstract and impersonal nature which permits us to disclose them.

Achille, we shall call him, belonged to a modest peasant family of central France; his environment was simple and people therein evidently uneducated. This confirms the comment of Esquirol that the madness of possession does not occur in our era except in the lower classes of society. His parents and the inhabitants of the village were rather superstitious and unusual legends were current in his family. His father had been accused of formerly communicating with the devil, and of going every Saturday to an old tree trunk to talk with Satan who would then give him a sack of money. Achille's father laughed at these accusations, but he was, nevertheless, tormented and obsessed with superstitious fears. On top of that, his own father, the grandfather of Achille, was not completely sane: at various times, he had, without any motive, periodically left his home, and no one was able to explain these periods completely. It is difficult today to interpret them accurately.

It was about the same with the mother of our hero; she was healthy enough physically, but had a weak intelligence, and she was not able to resist a vice which is again a mental illness, drunkenness. . . Without a doubt, alcoholism in parents predisposes their children to all sorts of physical and mental diseases.

Achille had a normal infancy; he showed himself to be studious and applied himself well even though he had an average intelligence: he had, above all, a good memory and he read enormously without much discrimination. He was impressionable, took everything seriously, and he would be upset by fear of punishment for a long time for the least misadventure. He did not share the superstitions of his village and he had very few religious beliefs. One could have declared him almost normal were it not for frequent migraines—and if one did not observe some small facts which seemed important to me. Although he was very sensible and quite affectionate, he really didn't make many friends; he lived alone and he was somewhat ridiculed by his friends. Without exaggerating the importance of the fact which can sometimes be insignificant, I expect trouble with those children, those young people who are "butts" of ridicule of others in school. There is something amiss which puts them in this position, and these conditions are not favorable for the development of their personalities.

But Achille left his schooling at the proper age, and he became occupied in a business where he seemed to do fairly well. A rather happy circumstance for him was that he was married fairly early, about the age of twenty-two, to a woman who was affectionate and devoted, and who tried to straighten out certain elements of his imagination and make him comfortable and happy, for a number of years. He had one child, a little girl, whom he brought up in an absolutely normal fashion, and everything went for the best for our subject for about ten years. Achille was thirty-three when he experienced a number of accidents which were to bring him within a few months to La Salpêtrière.

Near the end of the winter of 1890, Achille had to make a business trip, and he came back home after several weeks. Although he stated he felt well and made an effort to appear lighthearted, his wife noticed a great change: he was preoccupied, he hardly kissed his wife and his child, and he spoke very little. After a few days, this lack of communication became worse, and the poor man had trouble speaking even a few words during the day. But his silence took on a special aspect: it stopped being voluntary as it had been originally; Achille was not silent because he didn't wish to speak but because he could no longer speak. He made unsuccessful efforts to produce sounds, but he couldn't succeed; he had become mute. The doctor who was consulted shook his head and found the case very serious, he listened to our man's chest, examined his urine, and concluded that there was a general weakness, a maladjustment, diabetes perhaps, etc., etc. These fears so upset Achille that he began to complain of all sorts of symptoms. He no longer had any strength, he ached all over, he couldn't eat, and he was tormented by an intense thirst. Without doubt, it was the diabetes diagnosed by the doctor. All the cures, all the treatments were tried. As one saw no improvement at the end of a long month, Achille went to consult another doctor. This eminent practitioner refuted a great deal of the diagnosis of his colleague, he concentrated on the heart beat, the wheezing of the sick person, and he asked if he didn't have strong pains in the left arm and in the last fingers of the hand. Achille hesitated a bit, then he remembered perfectly having these symptoms. Without hesitation, it was a question of angina of the chest, of a hypertrophic cardiac condition, and the greatest precautions were necessary. The diagnosis was further confirmed by a series of symptoms which the doctor had described, and which Achille evidenced on the following days.

The poor man went to bed and was overcome by the blackest sorrow. He did not go to work anymore, and he seemed to comprehend nothing that he read, and often seemed unable even to comprehend words addressed to him. To all the questions of his wife, he responded that he didn't know why he was so desolated, that he still had confidence, but despite himself, he still had all kinds of somber premonitions. He slept from time to time, but despite his sleep, his lips twitched and he murmured incomprehensible words, his eyes were filled with tears. Finally, his premonitions were realized. One day when he was more downcast than usual, he called his wife and his child, embraced them desperately, then stretched himself out on his bed and did not move. He remained immobile this way for two days while those who were around him expected that at any moment he would draw his last breath.

All of a sudden one morning, after two days of apparent death, Achille recovered, sat up, opened his eyes wide and began a frightening laugh. This convulsive laugh shook all his limbs, an exaggerated laugh which twisted his mouth, a lugubrious laugh which lasted more than two hours, truly satanic.

From this moment, everything was changed; Achille jumped out of his bed and refused any care. To all questions, he answered: "Don't do anything, it is useless, let's drink champagne, it is the end of the world." He uttered horrible cries: "I am being burned, someone is cutting me into pieces." These cries and these disjointed movements lasted until evening, and finally, our poor man fell into an agitated sleep.

The next day was not much better. Achille recounted to his family a thousand frightening things. "The demon," he said, "was in the room, surrounded by a pack of little devils with horns and grimacing; even more, the demon himself is in me and he forces me to pronounce all kinds of horrible blasphemies." Achille insulted God and the saints, and repeated at random all kinds of insults of the worst kind against religion. And what was even more grave and more cruel, the demon contorted his arms and his legs, and had him experience cruel sufferings which tore horrible cries from the unhappy man. One could have thought of a high fever, a passing delirium, but the state continued. Achille rarely had moments more calm than those in which he kissed his wife, crying and deploring his sad destiny which had made him the prey of demons. At no time did he have the slightest doubt that he was possessed by the devil. "I haven't believed enough of our sainted religion, only of the devil," said he, "He is well revenged, he holds me, he is in me, and he will never leave."

Once when he was not watched, Achille escaped from the house, ran across some fields, hid himself in some woods where he was found the next day thoroughly frightened. He kept attempting to go into the cemetery where they would find him lying asleep on a tomb. He seemed to be searching for death, for he began to swallow poisons. He drank laudanum, and other noxious substances;

he tied his feet together, and so bound, threw himself into the water. He rose, however, and on being rescued, he said sadly, "You can see that I am possessed by the devil, for I can't even die. I have used the proof demanded by religion, I threw myself into the water with my feet tied together and I did not drown. Ah! The devil is in me." It became necessary to keep him in his room under strict surveillance. After three months of this insanity which frightened his poor family, it was finally decided, on the advice of a physician who was consulted, to bring him to La Salpêtrière as the most proper place to exorcise the possessed person and to chase out the demons.

When Charcot and my friend, Monsieur Dutil, who was the chief of the clinic, gave me this interesting sick person, I ascertained immediately all the classic signs of possession which had been described in the epidemics of the Middle Ages. Eginhard expresses himself thus on the subject of a person possessed by demons: "It was an extraordinary spectacle that we who were present could see this evil spirit express itself through the mouth of this poor woman and to hear at the same time, the male voice as well as the sound of a female voice, but so distinct one from the other that one could not believe that this woman was speaking alone, and one imagined hearing two people arguing spiritedly and mutually insulting one another. It was, in effect, two people, two different wills, on the one side a demon who wants to break the body in which he is in possession, and the other the woman who desires to be delivered of this enemy who inhabits her."

This poor man, shrunken, his eyes haggard, with a sad appearance, presented to us the same spectacle; he murmured blasphemies in a somber voice: "Damn be God; Damn be the Trinity; Damn be the Virgin"; then with a voice more agitated and with tears in his eyes, "It is not my fault if my mouth says these horrible things, it is not me . . . it is not me . . . I close my lips so the words will not escape, will not be heard out loud but it doesn't succeed, the devil says these words despite me. I know that he makes me say them and he makes my tongue speak them despite me. . . ."

When he twisted his arms in convulsive movements, one could pinch him or stick a needle in him without his noticing. It has been noted in epidemics of possession that this anesthesia occurs in those parts of the body which are in convulsion. If the agitation is in the arms, the person can feel pinches in the legs, but not in the arms. Besides that, often Achille would strike himself, he would tear at his face with his nails and he experienced no pain. All the signs of possession were there.

When I attempted to console this poor man and to calm him a bit, I was very badly received: all my attempts were in vain. I tried, without success, to gain some authority over Achille to force him to obey me; I tried, as a last resort, to see if it was possible to get him to sleep, to have control over him while he was in a hypnotic state. Everything was useless; by no means was I able to succeed by using suggestions nor by hypnosis. He answered me with all kinds of insults and blasphemies, and the devil, speaking through his voice, railed at my failure. Just as it had been before: when the doctor said to the demon to keep quiet, the demon answered brutally, "You asked me to shut up, and I don't want to shut up."

On my request, the chaplain of La Salpètrière came to see the sick man, also tried to console him and tried to have him distinguish the true religion from these diabolical superstitions. He was not able to succeed, and he told me that the poor man was insane and needed the help of medicine more than the help of religion. It was necessary to return to work.

I then observed that the sick person did make various movements without being aware of them, and that, preoccupied with his hallucinations and his delirium, that he was totally distracted. It was easy to profit by this distraction in order to determine the movements that accompanied his unawareness. One knows of these distracted people who search for their umbrella everywhere while holding it in their hands, not realizing it. I was able to put a pencil into the fingers of his right hand and Achille grasped it and held it without being aware of it. I gently directed the hand which held the pencil and I had him write several dashes, several letters, and the hand directed by the movement of the sick person, who was constantly preoccupied with his delirium and who was unaware of what he was doing, continued to repeat these letters and even to sign his first name without being aware of it. These movements, so accomplished without the awareness of the person who can control them, are called automatic movements, and they were very numerous and quite varied in this sick man.

Having determined this, I decided to see if I could control these movements by simple command. Instead of addressing myself directly to the sick person, who, I knew all too well, would only respond with insults, I let him continue at his own pace in his delirium and in his exclamations, but I put myself behind him when I suggested certain movements in a low voice. These movements were not executed; however, to my great surprise, the hand which was holding the pencil began to write rapidly on the paper placed in front of him, and I read a certain little phrase that this man had written without awareness, just as he had signed his name without knowing it. The hand had written: "I don't want to." This seemed to be an answer to my order, and therefore, it was necessary to continue, "And why don't you want to?" I asked of him very quietly in the same tone; the hand immediately wrote: "Because I am stronger than you." "Who are you?"—"I am the devil"—"Ah! very well, very well, now we can talk."

Few people have had an occasion to talk with the devil so it is necessary to take advantage of this situation. To force the devil to obey me, I took advantage of the besetting sin of devils, vanity. "I don't believe in your power," I said to him, "and I will not believe unless you give me a proof."—"What?" asked the devil, borrowing as usual the hand of Achille who didn't hesitate at all. "Raise the left arm of this poor man without his knowing it." The left arm of Achille went up immediately.

I moved around toward Achille so that I could get his attention on me, and I remarked that his left hand was raised. He was quite surprised and he had some trouble bringing it down. "The devil is having fun with me," he said. It was accurate, but this time, the devil was doing this at my command.

By the same procedure, I was able to make the devil do a series of different acts, he always obeyed perfectly. He made Achille dance, made him put out his tongue, made him kiss a piece of paper, and so on . . .

All the preceding facts are identical in their details to those which have been observed by the ancient exorcists.

The difference between these old experiences with the devils and ours is that the exorcists used to speak in Latin or, perhaps, in Greek. But it was evident that that devil and I preferred to discuss in French. This is a matter which changes with the times and the locations. The other elements of possession, the commandments made to the devil, the resistance of the demon, his final obedience, the movements which he executed in the body of the possessed against the will of that person, and even his unawareness, the sensations and hallucinations that the devil, under order from the exorcist, had the patient experience, all these elements were exactly the same [as reported by ancient exorcists].

Thanks to these historical precedents, I was able somewhat later to do something that the exorcists did not think of doing. I demanded that the devil, as a last proof of his strength, would have Achille sleep on the couch and sleep completely without resistance. I had already attempted, but in vain, to hypnotize this sick man while talking to him directly; all was in vain, but this time, profiting from his distraction and addressing myself to the devil directly, I succeeded very easily. Achille tried in vain to fight against sleep which overtook him; he fell heavily on his back and soon was completely asleep.

The devil did not know what a trap I had established. Achille, who had gone to sleep because of me, was now in my power. Very gently, I ordered him to answer me without awakening, to tell me of his sufferings, and I learned, therefore, a series of events which no one was aware of, which Achille, himself, when he awakened, did not remember, and which threw an entirely new light on his sickness.

Before studying these new facts and the role which they played in the cure of this sick person, it is necessary to remember certain facts which we understand today, certain theories of pathological psychology which will now permit us to understand better the history of this unhappy, possessed person.

[Janet here has seven pages of discussion about the unconscious.]

Despite the sleep in which Achille was apparently plunged, he heard our questions and could respond to them; he was in a somnambulistic state.

This state presents great practical value: one knows, in effect, when one is in this condition, that during the somnambulism, a sick person recovers his memory singularly more than while awake. He can, at this moment—it is a point on which I have often insisted—retrace the memory of the delirium to find out what prompted and filled these attacks, the subconscious phenomena which have provoked a number of bad accidents and of which he is ignorant when he is awake.

It was exactly the same with Achille, for, once asleep, he could divulge a whole series of details of which he was ignorant or which he did not understand before. In this state of somnambulism, he now was able to recount his illness in an entirely different manner than he had done previously. That which he told us since then is very simple and can be summarized in a few words: for six months, he had been in a long reverie which unfolded itself more or less unconsciously during the day as well as at night. In the same manner of people who are distracted, as I have mentioned before, relative to looking for their umbrellas when they still had them in their hands, he had told himself a story, a long and lamentable story, but this reverie had assumed control over his weak spirit with special characters and had been of terrible consequences. In a word, his whole illness was nothing but a dream.

The origin of the sickness had been a peccadillo that he had committed in the spring during his trip. For a moment, he had forgotten his home and his wife. We need not be too angry with him, for he was cruelly punished. The memory of this mistake had tormented him on his return and had provoked the sadness, the distraction which has already been described. Above all, he was preoccupied with the thought of hiding from his wife his misadventure, and this thought caused him to examine carefully every one of his words. He thought that after a few days, he would forget and lose his disturbance, but it persisted constantly in himself, and it was that which bothered him when he wanted to speak.

Achille overwhelmed himself with reproaches and waited for all the sufferings which were in his mind only legitimate punishments. He dreamed of all the physical disorders, all of the most frightening diseases. These were the dreams of illness, which provoked fatigue, thirst, feelings of being suffocated, the sufferings that the doctor and the patient had successively taken for diabetes and for a heart condition. Achille, sick and open to suggestion, made real his dreams. Therefore, we see him saying goodbye to his wife and his child and lying down immobile. This more or less complete lethargy which lasted two days was but an episode, a chapter in this great dream.

When one has dreamed that one is dead, what else can one dream? What will be the end of the story that Achille recounted to himself for six months? The end is very simple, it is hell. Immobile, Achille dreamt better than ever. He dreamt that his death was complete. A devil came out of the abyss to claim him. This sick person, who during his somnambulism told us of his dreams, remembered perfectly the exact moment during which these lamentable events took place. At this moment, about eleven o'clock in the morning, a dog barked in the yard, without doubt bothered by the odor of hell; flames filled the room: innumerable demons beat this miserable person with whips of thongs, amusing themselves by pushing tacks into his eyes, by tearing his body. Satan took possession of his head and of his heart.

A knowledge of pathological psychology can today explain the details of this delirium. The blasphemies which Achille uttered in his unconscious state or against himself constitute a very interesting and very well-understood phenomenon. Language is not composed only of auditory images of words, of visual images, of written letters; it also includes images of movements, of articulations that we make when we pronounce the words. These images of a muscular sense, these kinesthetic verbal images, can separate from the personality and can develop against our will.

If we wish to exorcise our unfortunate Achille, it is completely useless to speak to him of hell, of demons, and of death. Even though he speaks of them endlessly, these are secondary matters and only psychological accessories. Although the sick person seems to be one who is possessed, his illness is not the possession, it is the emotion of remorse. It can be that the same was true for those who were possessed, the devil is nothing for them but the incarnation of their regrets, their remorse, their terrors, or their vices. It is the remorse of Achille, it is the memory of his mistake which was the cause of his losing his mind.

Achille was finally completely cured, the devil had been chased by a modern exorcism more delicate and less infallible, perhaps, than the old one, but not without interest and not without usefulness. It is good to add that this sick person has returned to his little town and frequently sent me news, and for three years, he has preserved his physical and mental health perfectly.

Case 2

Editors' Introduction

Of the thirteen case studies that Sigmund Freud published, the one generally known as the *Ratman,* here reprinted with its correct title of "A Case of Obessional Neurosis," is perhaps his most complete and the most satisfying. Even though this case history is the longest in this book, we have cut it down by about one-third, eliminating many of the asides and digressions, not to speak of several long footnotes. However, the essential story is retained, and the reader who may want to go into the fine details of the case may readily obtain the full-length version in practically any large library.

In this case presentation we see Freud at his best. He can be likened to a psychic detective, on the hunt for the cause of the crime—the neurosis. If the reader can get into the proper mood, this case should be as exciting as any mystery novel—with the added fillip that it is real.

Of all the great students of the human mind, Freud was the most engaging as a pure writer. Perhaps only Carl Rogers equals him in his intensity of writing and in his ability to give the reader the feeling of actually being present in therapy.

This report, written and published in 1909 when Freud was fifty-three and at the height of his intellectual powers, shows psychoanalysis at the zenith of its expression. While it may be true that many, perhaps most, of Freud's theories are unproven and perhaps unprovable, it cannot be doubted by anyone who reads this account carefully that the whole complex story makes good sense.

Freud was a great man, a dogged investigator into areas that were ordinarily forbidden, and he suffered the fate of many a pioneer—public scorn and ridicule which later turned practically to adulation.

SIGMUND FREUD

A Case of Obsessional Neurosis

A youngish man of university education introduced himself to me with the statement that he had suffered from obsessions ever since his childhood, but with particular intensity for the last four years. The chief features of his disorder were *fears* that something might happen to two people of whom he was very fond—his father and a lady whom he admired. Besides this he was aware of *compulsive impulses*—such as an impulse, for instance, to cut his throat with a razor; and further he produced *prohibitions,* sometimes in connection with quite unimportant things. He had wasted years, he told me, in fighting against these ideas of his, and in this way had lost much ground in the course of his life. He had tried various treatments, but none had been of any use to him except a course of hydrotherapy at a sanatorium near —; and this, he thought, had probably only been because he had made an acquaintance there which had led to regular sexual intercourse. Here he had no opportunities of the sort, and he seldom had intercourse and only at irregular intervals. He felt disgust at prostitutes. Altogether, he said, his sexual life had been stunted; onanism had played only a small part in it, in his sixteenth or seventeenth year. His potency was normal; he had first performed coitus at the age of twenty-six.

He gave me the impression of being a clear-headed and shrewd person. When I asked him what it was that made him lay such stress upon telling me about his sexual life, he replied that that was what he knew about my theories. Actually, however, he had read none of my writings, except that a short time before he had been turning over the pages of one of my books and had come across the explanation of some curious verbal associations which had so much reminded him of some of his own "efforts of thought" in connection with his ideas that he had decided to put himself in my hands.

Excerpted from "Notes Upon a Case of Obsessional Neurosis," in *The Collected Papers of Sigmund Freud,* edited by Ernest Jones, M.D. (Volume 3), authorized translation by Alix and James Strachey, published by Basic Books, Inc., Publishers, New York, by arrangement with The Hogarth Press Ltd. and The Institute of Psycho-Analysis, London.

The Beginning of the Treatment

The next day I made him pledge himself to submit to the one and only condition of the treatment—namely, to say everything that came into his head, even if it was *unpleasant* to him, or seemed *unimportant* or *irrelevant* or *senseless*. I then gave him leave to start his communications with any subject he pleased, and he began as follows:

He had a friend, he told me, of whom he had an extraordinarily high opinion. He used always to go to him when he was tormented by some criminal impulse, and ask him whether he despised him as a criminal. His friend used then to give him moral support by assuring him that he was a man of irreproachable conduct, and had probably been in the habit, from his youth onwards, of taking a dark view of his own life. At an earlier date, he went on, another person had exercised a similar influence over him. This was a nineteen-year-old student (he himself had been fourteen or fifteen at the time) who had taken a liking to him, and had raised his self-esteem to an extraordinary degree, so that he appeared to himself to be a genius. This student had subsequently become his tutor, and had suddenly altered his behaviour and begun treating him as though he were an idiot. At length he had noticed that the student was interested in one of his sisters, and had realized that he only taken him up in order to gain admission into the house. This had been the first great blow of his life.

He then proceeded without any apparent transition:

Infantile Sexuality

"My sexual life began very early. I can remember a scene out of my fourth or fifth year. (From my sixth year onwards I can remember everything.) This scene came into my head quite distinctly, years later. We had a very pretty young governess called Fräulein Peter.[1] One evening she was lying on the sofa lightly dressed, and reading. I was lying beside her, and begged her to let me creep under her skirt. She told me I might, so long as I said nothing to any one about it. She had very little on, and I fingered her genitals and the lower part of her body which struck me as very queer. After this I was left with a burning and tormenting curiosity to see the female body. I can still remember the intense excitement with which I waited at the Baths (which I was still allowed to go to with the governess and my sisters) for the governess to undress and get into the water. I can remember more things from my sixth year onwards. At that time we had another governess, who was also young and good-looking. She had abscesses on her buttocks which she was in the habit of expressing at night. I used to wait eagerly for that moment, to appease my curiosity. It was just the same at the Baths—though Fräulein Lina was more reserved than her predecessor." (In reply to a question which I threw in, "As a rule," the patient told me, "I did not sleep in her room, but mostly with my parents.") "I remember a scene which must have taken place when I was seven years old. We were sitting together one evening— the governess, the cook, another servant-girl, myself and my brother, who was eighteen months younger than me. The young women were talking, and I suddenly became aware of Fräulein Lina saying: 'It could be done with the little one; but Paul' (that was I) 'is too clumsy, he would be sure to miss it.' I did not understand clearly what was meant, but felt the slight and began to cry. Lina comforted me, and told me how a girl, who had done something of the kind with a little boy she was in charge of, had been put in prison for several months. I do not believe she actually did anything wrong with me, but I took a great many liberties with her. When I got into her bed I used to uncover her and touch her, and she made no objections. She was not very intelligent, and clearly had very strong sexual cravings. At twenty-three she had already had a child. She afterwards married its father, so that to-day she is a Frau Hofrat. Even now I often see her in the street.

"When I was six years old I already suffered from erections, and I know that once I went to my mother to complain about them. I know too that in doing so I had some misgivings to get over, for I had a feeling that there was some connection between this subject and my ideas and inquisitiveness, and at that time I used to have a morbid idea *that my parents knew my thoughts; I explained this to myself by supposing that I had spoken them out loud, without having heard myself do it.* I look on this as the beginning of my illness. There were certain people, girls, who pleased me very much, and I had a very strong wish *to see them naked.* But in wishing this I had *an uncanny feeling, as though something must happen if I thought such things, and as though I must do all sorts of things to prevent it.*"

(In reply to a question he gave an example of these fears: "For instance, *that my father might die.*") "Thoughts about my father's death occupied my mind from a very early age and for a long period of time, and greatly depressed me."

At this point I learnt with astonishment that the patient's father, with whom his obsessional fears were still occupied at that actual time, had died several years previously.

The Great Obsessive Fear

"I think I shall begin to-day with the experience which was the direct occasion of my coming to you. It was in August during the manoeuvres at —. I had been suffering before, and tormenting myself with all kinds of obsessional thoughts, but they had quickly passed off during the manoeuvres. I was keen to show the regular officers that people like me had not only learnt a good deal but could stand a good deal too. One day we started from — on a short march. During a halt I lost my pince-nez, and, although I could easily have found them, I did not want to delay our start, so I gave them up. But I wired to my opticians in Vienna to send me another pair by the next post. During that same halt I sat between two officers, one of whom, a captain with a Czech name, was to be of no small importance to me. I had a kind of dread of him, *for he was obviously fond of cruelty.* I do not say he was a bad man, but at the officers' mess he had repeatedly defended the introduction of corporal punishment, so that I had been obliged to disagree with him very sharply. Well, during this halt we got into conversation, and the captain told me he had read of a specially horrible punishment used in the East . . ."

Here the patient broke off, got up from the sofa, and begged me to spare him the recital of the details. I assured him that I myself had no taste whatever for cruelty, and certainly had no desire to torment him, but that naturally I could not grant him something which was beyond my power. He might just as well ask me to give him the moon. The overcoming of resistances was a law of the treatment, and on no consideration could it be dispensed with. (I had explained the idea of "resistance" to him at the beginning of the hour, when he told me there was much in himself which he would have to overcome if he was to relate this experience of his.) I went on to say that I would do all I could, nevertheless, to guess the full meaning of any hints he gave me. Was he perhaps thinking of impalement?—"No, not that; . . . the criminal was tied up . . . "—he expressed himself so indistinctly that I could not immediately guess in what position—" . . . a pot was turned upside down on his buttocks . . . some *rats* were put into it . . . and they . . ."—he had again got up, and was showing every sign of horror and resistance—". . . *bored their way in* . . ."—Into his anus, I helped him out.

At all the more important moments while he was telling his story his face took on a very strange, composite expression. I could only interpret it as one of *horror at pleasure of his own of which he himself was unaware.* He proceeded with the greatest difficulty: "At that moment the idea flashed through my mind *that this was happening to a person who was very dear to me.*" In answer to a direct question he said that it was not he himself who was carrying out the punishment, but that it was being carried out as it were impersonally. After a little prompting I learnt that the person to whom this "idea" of his related was the lady whom he admired.

He broke off his story in order to assure me that these thoughts were entirely foreign and repugnant to him, and to tell me that everything which had followed in their train had passed through his mind with the most extraordinary rapidity. Simultaneously with the idea there always appeared a "sanction," that is to say, the defensive measure which he was obliged to adopt in order to prevent the phantasy from being fulfilled. When the captain had spoken of this ghastly punishment, he went on, and these ideas had come into his head, by employing his usual formulas (a "But" accompanied by a gesture of repudiation, and the phrase "Whatever are you thinking of?") he had just succeeded in warding off *both* of them.

This "both" took me aback, and it has no doubt also mystified the reader. For so far we have heard only of one idea—of the rat punishment being carried out upon the lady. He was now obliged to admit that a second idea had occurred to him simultaneously, namely, the idea of the punishment also being applied to his father. As his father had died many years previously, this obsessive fear was much more nonsensical even than the first, and accordingly it had attempted to escape being confessed to for a little while longer.

That evening, he continued, the same captain had handed him a packet that had arrived by the post and had said: "Lieutenant A. has paid the charges for you. You must pay him back." The packet had contained the pince-nez that he had wired for. At that instant, however, a "sanction" had taken shape in his mind, namely, *that he was not to pay back the money* or it would happen—(that is, the phantasy about the rats would come true as regards his father and the lady). And immediately, in accordance with a type of procedure with which he was familiar, to combat this sanction there had arisen a command in the shape of a vow: *"You must pay back the 3.80 crowns to Lieutenant A."* He had said these words to himself almost half aloud.

Two days later the manoeuvres had come to an end. He had spent the whole of the intervening time in efforts at repaying Lieutenant A. the small amount in question: but a succession of difficulties of an apparently *external* nature had arisen to prevent it. First he had tried to effect the payment through another officer who had been going to the post office. But he had been much relieved when this officer brought him back the money, saying that he had not met Lieutenant A. there, for this method of fulfilling his vow had not satisfied him, as it did not correspond with the wording, which ran: *"You* must pay back the money to Lieutenant A." Finally, he had met Lieutenant A., the person he was looking for; but he had refused to accept the money, declaring that he had not paid anything for him, and had nothing whatever to do with the post, which was the business of Lieutenant B. This had thrown my patient into great perplexity, for it meant that he was unable to keep his vow, since it had been based upon false premises. He had excogitated a very curious means of getting out of his difficulty, namely, that he should go to the post office with both the men, A. and B., that A. should give the young lady there the 3.80 crowns, that the young lady should give them to B., and that then he himself should pay back the 3.80 crowns to A. according to the wording of his vov.

It would not surprise me to hear that at this point the reader had ceased to be able to follow. For even the detailed account which the patient gave me of the external events of these days and of his reactions to them was full of self-contradictions and sounded hopelessly confused. It was only when he told the story for the third time that I could get him to realize its obscurities and could lay bare the errors of memory and the displacements in which he had become involved. I shall spare myself the trouble of reproducing these details, the essentials of which we shall easily be able to pick up later on, and I will only add that at the end of this second sitting the patient behaved as though he were dazed and bewildered. He repeatedly addressed me as "Captain," probably because at the beginning of the hour I had told him that I myself was not fond of cruelty like Captain M., and that I had no intention of tormenting him unnecessarily.

The only other piece of information that I obtained from him during this hour was that from the very first, on all the previous occasions on which he had had a fear that something would happen to people he loved no less than on the present one, he had referred the punishments not only to our present life but also to eternity—to the next world. Up to his fourteenth or fifteenth year he had been devoutly religious, but from that time on he had gradually developed into the free-thinker that he was to-day. He reconciled the contradiction between his beliefs and his obsessions by saying to himself: "What do you know about the next world? Nothing *can* be known about it. You're not risking anything—so do it." This form of argument seemed unobjectionable to a man who was in other respects particularly clear-headed, and in this way he exploited the uncertainty of reason in the face of these questions to the benefit of the religious attitude which he had outgrown.

Initiation into the Nature of the Treatment

The reader must not expect to hear at once what light I have to throw upon the patient's strange and senseless obsessions about the rats. The true technique of psycho-analysis requires the physician to suppress his curiosity and leaves the patient complete freedom in choosing the order in which topics shall succeed each other during the treatment. At the fourth sitting, accordingly, I received the patient with the question: "And how do you intend to proceed to-day?"

"I have decided to tell you something which I consider most important and which has tormented me from the very first." He then told me at great length the story of the last illness of his father, who had died of emphysema nine years previously. One evening, thinking that the condition was one which would come to a crisis, he had asked the doctor when the danger could be regarded as over. "The evening of the day after to-morrow," had been the reply. It had never entered his head that his father might not survive that limit. At half-past eleven at night he had lain down for an hour's rest. He had woken up at one o'clock, and had been told by a medical friend that his father had died. He had reproached himself with not having been present at his death; and the reproach had been intensified when the nurse told him that his father had spoken his name once during the last days, and had said to her as she came up to the bed: "Is that Paul?" He had thought he noticed that his mother and sisters had been inclined to reproach themselves in a similar way; but they had never spoken about it. At first, however, the reproach had not tormented him. For a long time he had not realized the fact of his father's death. It had constantly happened that, when he heard a good joke, he would say to himself: "I must tell Father that." His imagination, too, had been occupied with his father, so that often, when there was a knock at the door, he would think: "Here comes Father," and when he walked into a room he would expect to find his father in it. And although he had never forgotten that his father was dead, the prospect of seeing a ghostly apparition of this kind had had no terrors for him; on the contrary, he had greatly desired it. It had not been until eighteen months later that the recollection of his neglect had recurred to him and begun to torment him terribly, so that he had come to treat himself as a criminal. The occasion of this happening had been the death of an aunt by marriage and of a visit of condolence that he had paid at her house. From that time forward he had extended the structure of his obsessional thoughts so as to include the next world. The immediate consequence of this development had been that he became seriously incapacitated from working. He told me that the only thing that had kept him going at that time had been the consolation given him by his friend, who had always brushed his self-reproaches aside on the ground that they were grossly exaggerated. Hearing this, I took the opportunity of giving him a first glance at the underlying principles of psycho-analytic therapy. When there is a *mésalliance,* I began, between an affect and its ideational content (in this instance, between the intensity of the self-reproach and the occasion for it), a layman will say that the affect is too great for the occasion—that it is exaggerated—and that consequently the inference following from the self-reproach (the inference, that is, that the patient is a criminal) is false. On the contrary, the physician says: "No. The affect is justified. The sense of guilt cannot in itself be further criticized. But it belongs to another content, which is unknown *(unconscious),* and which requires to be looked for. The known ideational content has only got into its actual position owing to a mistaken association. We are not used to feeling strong affects without their having any ideational content, and therefore, if the content is missing, we seize as a substitute upon another content which is in some way or other suitable, much as our police, when they cannot catch the right murderer, arrest a wrong one instead. Moreover, this fact of there being a mistaken association is the only way of accounting for the powerlessness of logical processes in combating the tormenting idea." I concluded by admitting that this new way of looking at the matter gave immediate rise to some hard problems; for how could he admit that his self-reproach of being a criminal towards his father was justified, when he must know that as a matter of fact he had never committed any crime against him?

At the next sitting he began by saying that he must tell me an event in his childhood. From the age of seven, as he had already told me, he had had a fear that his parents guessed his thoughts, and this fear had in fact persisted all through his life. When he was twelve years old he had been in love with a little girl, the sister of a friend of his. (In answer to a question he said that his love had not been sensual; he had not wanted to see her naked for she was too small.) But she had not shown him as much affection as he had desired. And thereupon the idea had come to him that she would be kind to him if some misfortune were to befall him; and as an instance of such a misfortune his father's death had forced itself upon his mind. He had at once rejected the idea with energy. And even now he could not admit the possibility that what had arisen in this way could have been a "wish"; it had clearly been no more than a "connection of thought."—By way of objection I asked him why, if it had not been a wish, he had repudiated it.—Merely, he replied, on account of the content of the idea, the notion that his father might die.—I remarked that he was treating the phrase as though it were one that involved *lèse-majesté;* it was well known, of course, that it was equally punishable to say "The Emperor is an ass" or to disguise the forbidden words by saying "If any one says, etc., . . . then he will have me to reckon with." I added that I could easily insert the idea which he had so energetically repudiated into a context which would exclude the possibility of any such repudiation: for instance, "If my father dies, I shall kill myself upon his grave."—He was shaken, but did not abandon his objection. I therefore broke off the argument with the remark that I felt sure this had not been the first occurrence of his idea of his father's dying; it had evidently originated at an earlier date, and some day we should have to trace back its history.—He then proceeded to tell me that a precisely similar thought had flashed through his mind a second time, six months before his father's death. At that time he had already been in love with his lady, but financial obstacles made it impossible to think of an alliance with her. The idea had then occurred to him that *his father's death might make him rich enough to marry her.* In defending himself against this idea he had gone to the length of wishing that his father might leave him nothing at all, so that he might have no compensation for his terrible loss. The same idea, though in a much milder form, had come to him for a third time, on the day before his father's death. He had then thought: "Now I may be going to lose what I love most"; and then had come the contradiction: "No, there is some one else whose loss would be even more painful to you." These thoughts surprised him very much, for he was quite certain that his father's death could never have been an object of his desire but only of his fear.—After his forcible enunciation of these words I thought it advisable to bring a fresh piece of theory to his notice. According to psychoanalytical theory, I told him, every fear corresponded to a former wish which was now repressed; we were therefore obliged to believe the exact contrary of what he had asserted. This would also fit in with another theoretical requirement, namely, that the unconscious must be the precise contrary of the conscious.—He was much agitated at this and very incredulous. He wondered how he could possibly have had such a wish, considering that he loved his father more than any one else in the world; there could be no doubt that he would have renounced all his own prospects of happiness if by so doing he could have saved his father's life.—I answered that it was precisely such intense love as his that was the condition of the repressed hatred. In the case of people to whom he felt indifferent he would certainly have no difficulty in maintaining side by side inclinations to a moderate liking and to an equally moderate dislike: supposing, for instance, that he were an official, he might think that his chief was agreeable as a superior, but at the same time pettifogging as a lawyer and inhuman as a judge.

Shakespeare makes Brutus speak in a similar way of Julius Caesar: "As Caesar loved me, I weep for him; as he was fortunate, I rejoice at it; as he was valiant, I honour him; but as he was ambitious, I slew him." But these words already strike us as rather strange, and for the very reason that we had imagined Brutus's feeling for Caesar as something deeper. In the case of someone who was closer to him, of his wife for instance, he would wish his feelings to be unmixed, and consequently, as was only human, he would overlook her faults, since they might make him dislike her—he would ignore them as though he were blind to them. So it was precisely the intensity of his love that would not allow his hatred—though to give it such a name was to caricature the feeling—to remain conscious. To be sure, the hatred must have a source, and to discover that source was certainly a problem; his own statements pointed to the time when he was afraid that his parents guessed his thoughts. On the other hand, too, it might be asked why this intense love of his had not succeeded in extinguishing his hatred, as usually happened where there were two opposing impulses. We could only presume that the hatred must flow from some source, must be connected with some particular cause, which made it indestructible. On the one hand, then, some connection of this sort must be keeping his hatred for his father alive, while on the other hand, his intense love prevented it from becoming conscious. Therefore nothing remained for it but to exist in the unconscious, though it was able from time to time to flash out for a moment into consciousness.

He admitted that all of this sounded quite plausible, but he was naturally not in the very least convinced by it. He would venture to ask, he said, how it was that an idea of this kind could have remissions, how it could appear for a moment when he was twelve years old, and again when he was twenty, and then once more two years later, this time for good. He could not believe that his hostility had been extinguished in the intervals, and yet during them there had been no sign of self-reproaches.—To this I replied that whenever any one asked a question like that, he was already prepared with an answer; he needed only to be encouraged to go on talking.—He then proceeded, somewhat disconnectedly as it seemed, to say that he had been his father's best friend, and that his father had been his. Except on a few subjects, upon which fathers and sons usually hold aloof from one another—(What could he mean by that?)—there had been a greater intimacy between them than there now was between him and his best friend. As regards the lady on whose account he had slighted his father in that idea of his, it was true that he had loved her very much, but he had never felt really sensual wishes towards her, such as he had constantly had in his childhood. Altogether, in his childhood his sensual impulses had been much stronger than during his puberty.—At this I told him I thought he had now produced the answer we were waiting for, and had at the same time discovered the third great characteristic of the unconscious. The source from which his hostility to his father derived its indestructibility was evidently something in the nature of *sensual desires,* and in that connection he must have felt his father as in some way or other an *interference.* A conflict of this kind, I added, between sensuality and childish love was entirely typical. The remissions he had spoken of had occurred because the premature explosion of his sensual feelings had had as its immediate consequence a considerable diminution of their violence. It was not until he was once more seized with intense erotic desires that his hostility reappeared again owing to the revival of the old situation. I then got him to agree that I had not led him on to the subject either of childhood or of sex, but that he had raised them both of his own free will.—He then went on to ask why he had not simply come to a decision, at the time he was in love with the lady, that his father's interference with that love could not for a moment weigh against his love of his father.—I replied that it was scarcely possible to destroy a person *in absentia*. Such a decision would only have been possible if the wish that he took objection to had made its first appearance on that occasion; whereas, as a matter of fact, it was *a long-repressed wish*, towards which he could not behave otherwise than he had formerly done, and which was consequently immune from destruction. This wish (to get rid of his father as being an interference) must have originated at a time when circumstances had been very different—at a time, perhaps, when he had not loved his father more than the person whom he desired sensually, or when he was incapable of making a clear decision. It must have been in his very early childhood, therefore, before he had reached the age of six, and before the date at which his memory became continuous; and things must have remained in the same state ever since.—With this piece of construction our discussion was broken off for the time being.

At the next sitting, which was the seventh, he took up the same subject once more. He could not believe, he said, that he had ever entertained such a wish against his father. He remembered a story of Sudermann's, he went on, that had made a deep impression upon him. In this story there was a woman who, as she sat by her sister's sick-bed, felt a wish that her sister should die so that she herself might marry her husband. The woman thereupon committed suicide, thinking she was not fit to live after being guilty of such baseness. He could understand this, he said, and it would be only right if his thoughts were the death of him, for he deserved nothing less.—I remarked that it was well known to us that patients derived a certain satisfaction from their sufferings, so that in reality they all resisted their own recovery to some extent. He must never lose sight of the fact that a treatment like ours proceeded to the accompaniment of a *constant resistance;* I should be repeatedly reminding him of this fact.

Some Obsessional Ideas and Their Explanation

Obsessional ideas, as is well known, have an appearance of being either without motive or without meaning, just as dreams do. The first problem is how to give them a sense and a status in the mental life of the individual, so as to make them comprehensible and even obvious. The problem of translating them may seem insoluble; but we must never let ourselves be misled by that illusion. The wildest and most eccentric obsessional or compulsive ideas can be cleared up if they are investigated deeply enough. The solution is effected by bringing the obsessional ideas into temporal relationship with the patient's experiences, that is to say, by inquiring when a particular obsessional idea made its first appearance and in what external circumstances it is apt to recur. When, as so often happens, an obsessional idea has not succeeded in establishing itself permanently, the task of clearing it up is correspondingly simplified. We can easily convince ourselves that, when once the interconnections between an obsessional idea and the patient's experiences have been discovered, there will be no difficulty in obtaining access to whatever else may be puzzling or worth knowing in the pathological structure we are dealing with—its meaning, the mechanism of its origin, and its derivation from the preponderant motive forces of the patient's mind.

As a particularly clear example I will begin with one of the *suicidal impulses* which appeared so frequently in our patient. This instance almost analysed itself in the telling. He had once, he told me, lost some weeks of study owing to his lady's absence: she had gone away to nurse her grandmother, who was seriously ill. Just as he was in the middle of a very hard piece of work the idea had occurred to him: "If you received a command to take your examination this term at the first possible opportunity, you might manage to obey it. But if you were commanded to cut your throat with a razor, what then?" He had at once become aware that this command had already been given, and was hurrying to the cupboard to fetch his razor when he thought: "No, it's not so simple as that. You must go and kill the old woman." Upon that, he had fallen to the ground, beside himself with horror.

In this instance the connection between the compulsive idea and the patient's life is contained in the opening words of his story. His lady was absent, while he was working very hard for an examination so as to bring the possibility of an alliance with her nearer. While he was working he was overcome by a longing for his absent lady, and he thought of the cause of her absence. And now there came over him something which, if he had been a normal man, would probably have been some kind of feeling of annoyance against her grandmother: "Why must the old woman get ill just at the very moment when I'm longing for *her* so frightfully?" We must suppose that something similar but far more intense passed through our patient's mind—an unconscious fit of rage which could combine with his longing and find expression in the exclamation: "Oh, I should like to go and kill that old woman for robbing me of my love!" Thereupon followed the command: "Kill yourself, as a punishment for these savage and murderous passions!" The whole process then passed into the obsessional patient's consciousness accompanied by the most violent affect and *in a reverse order*—the punitive command coming first, and the mention of the guilty outburst afterwards. I cannot think that this attempt at an explanation will seem forced or that it involves many hypothetical elements.

Another impulse, which might be described as indirectly suicidal and which was of longer duration, was not so easily explicable. For its relation to the patient's experiences succeeded in concealing itself behind one of those purely external associations which are so repellent to our consciousness. One day while he was away on his summer holidays the idea suddenly occurred to him that he was too fat [German *"dick"*] and that he must *make himself thinner.* So he began getting up from table before the pudding came round and tearing along the road without a hat in the blazing heat of an August sun. Then he would dash up a mountain at the double, till, dripping with perspiration, he was forced to come to a stop. On one occasion his suicidal intentions actually emerged without any disguise from behind this mania for getting thinner: as he was standing on the edge of a steep precipice he suddenly received a command to jump over, which would have been certain death. Our patient could think of no explanation of this senseless obsessional behaviour until it suddenly occurred to him that at that time his lady had also been stopping at the same resort; but she had been in the company of an English cousin, who was very attentive to her and of whom the patient had been very jealous. This cousin's name was Richard, and, according to the usual practice in England, he was known as *Dick.* Our patient, then, had wanted to kill this Dick; he had been far more jealous of him and enraged with him than he could admit to himself, and that was why he had imposed on himself this course of banting by way of a punishment. This obsessional impulse may seem very different from the directly suicidal command which was discussed above, but they have nevertheless one important feature in common. For they both arose as reactions to a tremendous feeling of rage, which was inaccessible to the patient's consciousness and was directed against some one who had cropped up as an interference with the course of his love.

Some other of the patient's obsessions, however, though they too were centred upon his lady, exhibited a different mechanism and owed their origin to a different instinct. Besides his banting mania he produced a whole series of other obsessional activities at the period during which the lady was stopping at his summer resort; and, in part at least, these directly related to her. One day, when he was out with her in a boat and there was a stiff breeze blowing, he was obliged to make her put on his cap, because a command had been formulated in his mind that *nothing must happen to her.* This was a kind of *obsession for protecting,* and it bore other fruit besides this. Another time, as they were sitting together during a thunderstorm, he was obsessed, he could not tell why, with the necessity *for counting* up to forty or fifty between each flash of lightning and its accompanying thunder-clap. On the day of her departure he knocked his foot against a stone lying in the road, and was *obliged* to put it out of the way by the side of the road, because the idea struck him that her carriage would be driving along the same road in a few hours' time and might come to grief against this stone. But a few minutes later it occurred to him that this was absurd, and he was *obliged* to go back and replace the stone in its original position in the middle of the road. After her departure he became a prey to an *obsession for understanding,* which made him a curse to all his companions. He forced himself to understand the precise meaning of every syllable that was addressed to him, as though he might otherwise be missing some priceless treasure. Accordingly he kept asking: "What was it you said just then?" And after it had been repeated to him he could not help thinking it had sounded different the first time, so he remained dissatisfied.

Compulsive acts like this, in two successive stages, of which the second neutralizes the first, are a typical occurrence in obsessional neuroses. The patient's consciousness naturally misunderstands them and puts forward a set of secondary motives to account for them—*rationalizes* them, in short. But their true significance lies in their being a representation of a conflict between two opposing impulses of approximately equal strength: and hitherto I have invariably found that this opposition has been one between love and hate. Compulsive acts of this sort are theoretically of special interest, for they show us a new type of symptom-formation. What regularly occurs in hysteria is that a compromise is arrived at which enables both the opposing tendencies to find expression simultaneously—which kills two birds with one stone; whereas here each of the two opposing tendencies finds satisfactions singly, first one and then the other, though naturally an attempt is made to establish some sort of logical connection (often in defiance of all logic) between the antagonists.

The conflict between love and hatred showed itself in our patient by other signs as well. At the time of the revival of his piety he used to make up prayers for himself, which took up more and more time and eventually lasted for an hour and a half. The reason for this was that he found, like an inverted Balaam, that something always inserted itself into his pious phrases and turned them into their opposite. For instance, if he said, "May God protect him," an evil spirit would hurriedly insinuate a "not." On one such occasion the idea occurred to him of cursing instead, for in that case, he thought, the contrary words would be sure to creep in. His original intention, which had been repressed by his praying, was forcing its way through in this last idea of his. In the end he found his way out of his embarrassment by giving up the prayers and replacing them by a short formula concocted out of the initial letters or syllables of various prayers. He then recited this formula so quickly that nothing could slip into it.

The Exciting Cause of the Illness

One day the patient mentioned quite casually an event which I could not fail to recognize as the exciting cause of his illness, or at least as the immediate occasion of the attack which had begun some six years previously and had persisted to that day. He himself had no notion that he had brought forward anything of importance; he could not remember that he had ever attached any importance to the event; and moreover he had never forgotten it.

After his father's death the patient's mother told him one day that she had been discussing his future with her rich relations, and that one of her cousins had declared himself ready to let him marry one of his daughters when his education was completed; a business connection with the firm would offer him a brilliant opening in his profession. This family plan stirred up in him a conflict as to whether he should remain faithful to the lady he loved in spite of her poverty, or whether he should follow in his father's footsteps and marry the lovely, rich, and well-connected girl who had been assigned to him. And he resolved this conflict, which was in fact one between his love and the persisting influence of his father's wishes, by falling ill; or, to put it more correctly, by falling ill he avoided the task of resolving it in real life.

The proof that this view was correct lies in the fact that the chief result of his illness was an obstinate incapacity for work, which allowed him to postpone the completion of his education for years. But the results of such an illness are never unintentional; what appears to be the consequence of the illness is in reality the cause or motive of falling ill.

As was to be expected, the patient did not, to begin with, accept my elucidation of the matter. He could not imagine, he said, that the plan of marriage could have had any such effects: it had not made the slightest impression on him at the time. But in the further course of treatment he was forcibly brought to believe in the truth of my suspicion, and in a most singular manner. With the help of a transference phantasy, he experienced, as though it were new and belonged to the present, the very episode from the past which he had forgotten, or which had only passed through his mind unconsciously. There came an obscure and difficult period in the treatment; eventually it turned out that he had once met a young girl on the stairs in my house and had on the spot promoted her into being my daughter. She had pleased him, and he pictured to himself that the only reason I was so kind and incredibly patient with him was that I wanted to have him for a son-in-law. At the same time he raised the wealth and position of my family to a level which agreed with the model he had in mind. But his undying love for his lady fought against the temptation. After we had gone through a series of the severest resistances and bitterest vituperations on his part, he could no longer remain blind to the overwhelming effect of the perfect analogy between the transference phantasy and the actual state of affairs in the past. I will repeat one of the dreams which he had at this period, so as to give an example of his manner of treating the subject. He dreamed that *he saw my daughter in front of him with two patches of dung instead of eyes.* No one who understands the language of dreams will find much difficulty in translating this one: it declared that *he was marrying my daughter not for her "beaux yeux" but for her money.*

The Father Complex and the Solution of the Rat Idea

From the exciting cause of the patient's illness in his adult years there was a thread leading back to his childhood. He had found himself in a situation similar to that in which, as he knew or suspected, his father had been before *his* marriage; and he had thus been able to identify himself with his father. But his dead father was involved in his recent attack in yet another way. The conflict at the root of his illness was in essentials a struggle between the persisting influence of his father's wishes and his own amatory predilections. If we take into consideration what the patient reported in the course of the first hours of his treatment, we shall not be able to avoid a suspicion that this struggle was a very ancient one and had arisen as far back as in his childhood.

By all accounts our patient's father was a most excellent man. Before his marriage he had been a non-commissioned officer, and, as relics of that period of his life, he had retained a straightforward soldierly manner and a *penchant* for using downright language. Apart from those virtues which are celebrated upon every tombstone, he was distinguished by a hearty sense of humour and a kindly tolerance towards his fellow-men. That he could be hasty and violent was certainly not inconsistent with his other qualities, but was rather a necessary complement to them; but it occasionally brought down the most severe castigation upon the children, while they were young and naughty. When they grew up, however, he differed from other fathers in not attempting to exalt himself into a sacrosanct authority, but in sharing with them a knowledge of the little failures and misfortunes of his life with good-natured candour. His son was certainly not exaggerating when he declared that they had lived together like the best friends, except upon a single point. And it must no doubt have been in connection with that very point that thoughts about his father's death had occupied his mind when he was a small boy with unusual and undue intensity, and that those thoughts made their appearance in the wording of the obsessional ideas of his childhood; and it can only have been in that same connection that he was able to wish for his father's death, in order that a certain little girl's sympathy might be aroused and that she might become kinder towards him.

There can be no question that there was something in the sphere of sexuality that stood between the father and son, and that the father had come into some sort of opposition to the son's prematurely developed erotic life. Several years after his father's death, the first time he experienced the pleasurable sensations of copulation, an idea sprang into his mind: "This is glorious! One might murder one's father for this!" This was at once an echo and an elucidation of the obsessional ideas of his childhood. Moreover, his father, shortly before his death, had directly opposed what later became our patient's dominating passion. He had noticed that his son was always in the lady's company, and had advised him to keep away from her, saying that it was imprudent of him and that he would only make a fool of himself.

To this unimpeachable body of evidence we shall be able to add fresh material, if we turn to the history of the onanistic side of our patient's sexual activitites.

Our present patient's behaviour in the matter of onanism was most remarkable. He did not indulge in it during puberty to any extent worth mentioning, and therefore, according to one set of views, he might have expected to be exempt from neurosis. On the other hand, an impulsion towards onanistic practices came over him in his twenty-first year, *shortly after his father's death*. He felt very much ashamed of himself each time he gave way to this kind of gratification, and soon foreswore the habit. From that time onwards it reappeared only upon rare and extraordinary occasions.

We must also consider in the same connection his curious behaviour at a time when he was working for an examination and toying with his favourite phantasy that his father was still alive and might at any moment reappear. He used to arrange that his working hours should be as late as possible in the night. Between twelve and one o'clock at night he would interrupt his work, and open the front door of the flat as though his father were standing outside it; then, coming back into the hall, he would take out his penis and look at it in the looking-glass. This crazy conduct becomes intelligible if we suppose that he was acting as though he expected a visit from his father at the hour when ghosts are abroad. He had on the whole been idle at his work during his father's lifetime, and this had often been a cause of annoyance to his father. And now that he was returning as a ghost, he was to be delighted at finding his son hard at work. But it was impossible that his father should be delighted at the other part of his behaviour; in this therefore he must be defying him. Thus, in a single unintelligible obsessional act, he gave expression to the two sides of his relation with his father, just as he did subsequently with regard to his lady by means of his obsessional act with the stone.

Starting from these indications and from other data of a similar kind, I ventured to put forward a construction to the effect that when he was a child of under six he had been guilty of some sexual misdemeanour connected with onanism and had been soundly castigated for it by his father. This punishment, according to my hypothesis, had, it was true, put an end to his onanism, but on the other hand it had left behind it an ineradicable grudge against his father and had established him for all time in his role of an interferer with the patient's sexual enjoyment. To my great astonishment the patient then informed me that his mother had repeatedly described to him an occurrence of this kind which dated from his earliest childhood and had evidently escaped being forgotten by her on account of its remarkable consequences. He himself, however, had no recollection of it whatever. The tale was as follows. When he was very small—it became possible to establish the date more exactly owing to its having coincided with the fatal illness of an elder sister—he had done something naughty, for which his father had given him a beating. The little boy had flown into a terrible rage and had hurled abuse at his father even while he was under his blows. But as he knew no bad language, he had called him all the names of common objects that he could think of, and had screamed: "You lamp! You towel! You plate!" and so on. His father, shaken by such an outburst of elemental fury, had stopped beating him, and had declared: "The child will be either a great man or a great criminal!" The patient believed that the scene made a permanent impression upon himself as well as upon his father. His father, he said, never beat him again; and he also attributed to this experience a part of the change which came over his own character. From that time forward he was a coward—out of fear of the violence of his own rage. His whole life long, moreover, he was terribly afraid of blows, and used to creep away and hide, filled with terror and indignation, when one of his brothers or sisters was beaten.

The patient subsequently questioned his mother again. She confirmed the story, adding that at the time he had been between three and four years old and that he had been given the punishment because he had *bitten* some one. She could remember no further details, except for a very uncertain idea that the person the little boy had hurt might have been his nurse. In her account there was no suggestion of his misdeed having been of a sexual nature.

A discussion of this childhood scene will be found in a footnote, and here I will only remark that its emergence shook the patient for the first time in his refusal to believe that at some prehistoric period in his childhood he had been seized with fury (which had subsequently become latent) against the father whom he loved so much. I must confess that I had expected it to have a greater effect, for the incident had been described to him so often—even by his father himself—that there could be no doubt of its objective reality. But, with that capacity for being illogical which never fails to bewilder one in such highly intelligent people as obsessional neurotics, he kept urging against the evidential value of the story the fact that he himself could not remember the scene. And so it was only along the painful road of transference that he was able to reach a conviction that his relation to his father really necessitated the postulation of this unconscious complement. Things soon reached a point at which, in his dreams, his walking phantasies, and his associations, he began heaping the grossest and filthiest abuse upon me and my family, though in his deliberate actions he never treated me with anything but the greatest respect. His demeanour as he repeated these insults to me was that of a man in despair. "How can a gentleman like you, sir," he used to ask, "let yourself be abused in this way by a low, good-for-nothing wretch like me? You ought to turn me out: that's all I deserve." While he talked like this, he would get up from the sofa and roam about the room,—a habit which he explained at first as being due to delicacy of feeling: he could not bring himself, he said, to utter such horrible things while he was lying there so comfortably. But soon he himself found a more cogent explanation, namely, that he was avoiding my proximity for fear of my giving him a beating. If he stayed on the sofa he behaved like some one in desperate terror trying to save himself from castigations of boundless dimensions; he would bury his head in his hands, cover his face with his arm, jump up suddenly and rush away, his features distorted with pain, and so on. He recalled that his father had had a passionate temper, and sometimes in his violence had not known where to stop. Thus, little by little, in this school of suffering, the patient won the sense of conviction which he had lacked—though to any disinterested mind the truth would have been almost self-evident. And now the path was clear to the solution of his rat idea. The treatment had reached its turning-point, and a quantity of material information which had hitherto been withheld became available, and so made possible a reconstruction of the whole concatenation of events.

In my description I shall, as I have already said, content myself with the briefest possible summary of the circumstances. Obviously the first problem to be solved was why the two speeches of the Czech captain—his rat story, and his request to the patient that he should pay back the money to Lieutenant A.— should have had such an agitating effect on him and should have provoked such violently pathological reactions. The presumption was that it was a question of "complexive sensitiveness," and that the speeches had jarred upon certain hyperaesthetic spots in his unconscious. And so it proved to be. As always happened with the patient in connection with military matters, he had been in a state of unconscious identification with his father, who had seen many years' service and had been full of stories of his soldiering days. Now it happened by chance—for chance may play a part in the formation of a symptom, just as the wording may help in the making of a joke—that one of his father's little adventures had an important element in common with the captain's request. His father, in his capacity as non-commissioned officer, had control over a small sum of money and had on one occasion lost it at cards. He would have found himself in a serious position if one of his comrades had not advanced him the amount. After he had left the army and become well-off, he had tried to find this friend in need so as to pay him back the money, but had not managed to trace him. The patient was uncertain whether he had ever succeeded in returning the money. The recollection of this sin of his father's youth was painful to him, for, in spite of appearances, his unconscious was filled with hostile strictures upon his father's character. The captain's words, "You must pay back the 3.80 crowns to Lieutenant A.," had sounded to his ears like an allusion to this unpaid debt of his father's.

But the information that the young lady at the post office at Z— had herself paid the charges due upon the packet, with a complimentary remark about himself, had intensified his identification with his father in quite another direction. At this stage in the analysis he brought out some new information, to the effect that the landlord of the inn at the little place where the post office was had had a pretty daughter. She had been decidedly encouraging to the smart young officer, so that he had thought of returning there after the manoeuvres were over and of trying his luck with her. Now, however, she had a rival in the shape of the young lady at the post office. Like his father in the tale of his marriage, he could afford now to hesitate upon which of the two he should bestow his favours when he had finished his military service. We can see at once that his singular indecision whether he should travel to Vienna or go back to the place where the post office was, and the constant temptation he felt to turn back while he was on the journey, were not so senseless as they seemed to us at first. To his conscious mind, the attraction exercised upon him by Z—, the place where the post office was, was explained by the necessity for seeing Lieutenant A. and fulfilling the vow with his assistance. But in reality what was attracting him was the young lady at the post office, and the lieutenant was merely a good substitute for her, since he lived at the same place and had himself been in charge of the military postal service. And when subsequently he heard that it was not Lieutenant A. but another officer, B., who had been on duty at the post office that day, he drew him into his combination as well; and he was then able to reproduce in his deliria in connection with the two officers the hesitation he felt between the two girls who were so kindly disposed towards him.

In elucidating the effects produced by the captain's rat story we must follow the course of the analysis more closely. The patient began by producing an enormous mass of associative material, which at first, however, threw no light upon the circumstances in which the formation of his obsession had taken place. The idea of the punishment carried out by means of rats had acted as a stimulus to a number of his instincts and had called up a whole quantity of recollections; so that, in the short interval between the captain's story and his request to him to pay back the money, rats had acquired a series of symbolical meanings, to which, during the period which followed, fresh ones were continually being added. I must confess that I can only give a very incomplete account of the whole business. What the rat punishment stirred up more than anything else was his *anal erotism,* which had played an important part in his childhood and had been kept in activity for many years by a constant irritation due to worms. In this way rats came to have the meaning of *"money."* The patient gave an indication of this connection by reacting to the word *"Ratten"* ["rats"] with the association *"Raten"* ["installments"]. In his obsessional deliria he had coined himself a regular rat currency. When, for instance, in reply to a question, I told him the amount of my fee for an hour's treatment, he said to himself (as I learned six months later), "So many florins, so many rats." Little by little he translated into this language the whole complex of money interests which centered round his father's legacy to him; that is to say, all his ideas connected with that subject were, by way of the verbal bridge *"Raten–Ratten,"* carried over into his obsessional life and became subjected to his unconscious. Moreover, the captain's request to him to pay back the charges due upon the packet served to strengthen the money significance of rats, by way of another verbal bridge *"Spielratte,"* which led back to his father's gambling debt.

But the patient was also familiar with the fact that rats are carriers of dangerous infectious diseases; he could therefore employ them as symbols of his dread (justifiable enough in the army) of *syphilitic infection.* This dread concealed all sorts of doubts as to the kind of life his father had led during his term of military service. Again, in another sense, the *penis* itself is a carrier of syphilitic infection; and in this way he could consider the rat as a male organ of sex. It had a further title to be so regarded; for a penis (especially a child's penis) can easily be compared to a *worm,* and the captain's story had been about rats burrowing in some one's anus, just as the large round-worms had in his when he was a child. Thus the penis significance of rats was based, once more, upon anal erotism. And apart from this, the rat is a dirty animal, feeding upon excrement and living in sewers. It is perhaps unnecessary to point out how great an extension of the rat delirium became possible owing to this new meaning. For instance, "So many rats, so many florins," could serve as an excellent characterization of a certain female profession which he particularly detested. On the other hand, it is certainly not a matter of indifference that the substitution of a penis for a rat in the captain's story resulted in a situation of intercourse *per anum*, which could not fail to be especially revolting to him when brought into connection with his father and the woman he loved. And when we consider that the same situation was reproduced in the compulsive threat which had formed in his mind after the captain had made his request, we shall be forcibly reminded of certain curses in use among the Southern Slavs. Moreover, all of this material, and more besides, was woven into the fabric of the rat discussions behind the screen-association *"heiraten"* ["to marry"].

The story of the rat punishment, as was shown by the patient's own account of the matter and by his facial expression as he repeated the story to me, had fanned into a flame all of his prematurely suppressed impulses of cruelty, egoistic and sexual alike. Yet, in spite of all this wealth of material, no light was thrown upon the meaning of his obsessional idea until one day the Rat Wife in Ibsen's *Little Eyolf* came up in the analysis, and it became impossible to escape the inference that in many of the shapes assumed by his obsessional deliria rats had another meaning still—namely, that of *children*. Inquiry into the origin of this new meaning at once brought me up against some of the earliest and most important roots. Once when the patient was visiting his father's grave he had seen a big beast, which he had taken to be a rat, gliding along over the grave. He assumed that it had actually come out of his father's grave, and had just been having a meal off his corpse. The notion of a rat is inseparably bound up with the fact that it has sharp teeth with which it gnaws and bites. But rats cannot be sharp-toothed, greedy and dirty with impunity: they are cruelly persecuted and mercilessly put to death by man, as the patient had often observed with horror. He had often pitied the poor creatures. But he himself had been just such a nasty, dirty little wretch, who was apt to bite people when he was in a rage, and had been fearfully punished for doing so. He could truly be said to find "a living likeness of himself" in the rat. It was almost as though Fate, when the captain told him his story, had been putting him through an association test: she had called out a "complex stimulus-word," and he had reacted to it with his obsessional idea.

According, then, to his earliest and most momentous experiences, rats were children. And at this point he brought out a piece of information which he had kept away from its context long enough, but which now fully explained the interest he was bound to feel in children. The lady, whose admirer he had been for so many years, but whom he had nevertheless not been able to make up his mind to marry, was condemned to childlessness by reason of a gynaecological operation which had involved the removal of both ovaries. This indeed—for he was extraordinarily fond of children—had been the chief reason for his hesitation.

It was only then that it became possible to understand the inexplicable process by which his obsessional idea had been formed. With the assistance of our knowledge of infantile sexual theories and of symbolism (as learnt from the interpretation of dreams) the whole thing could be translated and given a meaning. When, during the afternoon halt (upon which he had lost his pince-nez), the captain had told him about the rat punishment, the patient had only been struck at first by the combined cruelty and lasciviousness of the situation depicted. But immediately afterwards a connection had been set up with the scene from his childhood in which he himself had bitten someone. The captain—a man who could defend such punishments—had been substituted by him for his father, and had thus drawn down upon himself a part of the reviving exasperation which had burst out, upon the original occasion, against his cruel father. The idea which came into his consciousness for a moment, to the effect that something of the sort might happen to some one he was fond of, is probably to be translated into a wish such as "You ought to have the same thing done to you!" aimed at the teller of the story, but through him at his father. A day and a half later, when the captain had handed him the packet upon which the charges were due and had requested him to pay back the 3.80 crowns to Lieutenant A., he had already been aware that his "cruel superior" was making a mistake, and the only person he owed anything to was the young lady at the post office. It might easily, therefore, have occurred to him to think of some derisive reply, such as, "Will I, though?" or "Pay your grandmother!" or "Yes! You bet I'll pay him back the money!"—answers which would have been subject to no compulsive force. But, instead, out of the stirrings of his father-complex and out of his memory of the scene from his childhood, there formed in his mind some such answer as: "Yes! I'll pay back the money to A. when my father or the lady have children!" or "As sure as my father or the lady can have children, I'll pay him back the money!" In short, a derisive asseveration coupled with an absurd condition which could never be fulfilled.

But now the crime had been committed; he had insulted the two persons who were dearest to him—his father and his lady. The deed had called for punishment, and the penalty had consisted in his binding himself by a vow which it was impossible for him to fulfil and which entailed literal obedience to his superior's ill-founded request. The vow ran as follows: *"Now you must really pay back the money to A."* In his convulsive obedience he had repressed his better knowledge that the captain's request had been based upon erroneous premises: "Yes, you must pay back the money to A., as your father's surrogate has required. Your father cannot be mistaken." So too the king cannot be mistaken; if he addresses one of his subjects by a title which is not his, the subject bears that title ever afterwards.

Only vague intelligence of these events reached the patient's consciousness. But his revolt against the captain's order and the sudden transformation of that revolt into its opposite were both represented there. First had come the idea that he was *not* to pay back the money, or it (that is, the rat punishment) would happen; and then had come the transformation of this idea into a vow to the opposite effect, as a punishment for his revolt.

Let us, further, picture to ourselves the general conditions under which the formation of the patient's great obsessional idea occurred. His libido had been increased by a long period of abstinence coupled with the friendly welcome which a young officer can always reckon upon receiving when he goes among women. Moreover, at the time when he had started for the manoeuvres, there had been a certain coolness between himself and his lady. This intensification of his libido had inclined him to a renewal of his ancient struggle against his father's authority, and he had dared to think of having sexual intercourse with other women. His loyalty to his father's memory had grown weaker, his doubts as to his lady's merits had increased; and in that frame of mind he let himself be dragged into insulting the two of them, and had then punished himself for it. In doing so he had copied an old model. And when at the end of the manoeuvres he had hesitated so long whether he should travel to Vienna or whether he should stop and fulfil his vow, he had represented in a single picture the two conflicts by which he had from the very first been torn—whether or no he should remain obedient to his father and whether or no he should remain faithful to his beloved.

I may add a word upon *the interpretation of the "sanction"* which, it will be remembered, was to the effect that "otherwise the rat punishment will be carried out on both of them." It was based upon the influence of two infantile sexual theories, which I have discussed elsewhere. The first of these theories is that babies come out of the anus; and the second, which follows logically from the first, is that men can have babies just as well as women. According to the technical rules for interpreting dreams, the notion of coming out of the rectum can be represented by the opposite notion of creeping into the rectum (as in the rat punishment), and *vice versa.*

We should not be justified in expecting such severe obsessional ideas as were present in this case to be cleared up in any simpler manner or by any other means. When we reached the solution that has been described above, the patient's rat delirium disappeared.

Notes

1 Dr. Alfred Adler, who was formerly an analyst, once drew attention in a privately delivered paper to the peculiar importance which attaches to the *very first* communications made by patients. Here is an instance of this. The patient's opening words laid stress upon the influence exercised over him by men, that is to say, upon the part played in his life by homosexual object-choice; but immediately afterwards they touched upon a second *motif*, which was to become of great importance later on, namely, the conflict between man and woman and the opposition of their interests. Even the fact that he remembered his first pretty governess by her surname, which happened to be a man's Christian name, must be taken into account in this connection. In middle-class circles in Vienna it is more usual to call a governess by her Christian name, and it is by that name that she is more commonly remembered.

Case 3

Editors' Introduction

As is well known to every beginning student of psychology, the original big three of psychotherapy were Freud, Adler, and Jung. Adler, for a variety of reasons, has been slower to receive recognition and is often considered of less importance in the history of psychotherapy than either of the other two. However, history, which has a tendency to straighten matters out, indicates that Individual Psychology has begun to emerge as a strong force in recent years, primarily through the efforts of Heinz and Rowena Ansbacher and Rudolf Dreikurs, who is included in a later selection.

Incredibly, Adler—and this is also true of Jung—never wrote a full-length case study of any patient that he treated. Freud, in contrast, wrote sixteen. This selection is quite unusual in that it shows a master therapist in action, analyzing a woman, sentence by sentence, working from a case history. It is an example of high art, and reading this account should challenge the reader to check his/her own interpretation of the data to see if it agrees with Adler's.

ALFRED ADLER

The Case of Mrs. A.

General Introductory Statements

I have first to thank you all for your attention and for your eagerness to look into the workroom of Individual Psychology. My purpose is to approach it in this way: As you are partly trained and accustomed as doctors, I asked to receive an analysis of a sick, neurotic or psychotic person, knowing nothing about it. So you see this really is a clinic and you know what you have to do. You have to use general diagnosis and special diagnosis and so on. So you see we are in the general field of medicine. We do not act in any other way. We know that in general medicine we have to use all our means, all our tools, because otherwise we would not feel justified in going on to therapy.

Now in this case we have to deal with mental conditions and we must have an idea, a conception of mind. We are looking for mind as for a part of life. I do not believe we can go further. We do not know more, but we are satisfied, because we see that in other sciences also they cannot explain more. What are electricity, gravitation, and so on? Probably for a long time, or forever, nobody can contribute any more to our knowledge of mind than that it is a faculty of life, a part of life. Therefore, if life can be understood, we shall find that mind also wants to grow up and develop towards an ideal final goal.

This means that we have to consider at least two points. One is the point from which the symptom expression takes its rise. We shall find that wherever we can lay our finger on a complaint there will be a lack, the *feeling of a minus*. The second point is that mind always wants to overcome this minus, and strive for an ideal final form. We say that wherever there is life there is a striving for an ideal final form.

I cannot explain today all the finer features and characteristics of this growing up. It is enough if I remind you that in Individual Psychology we are looking for the situation in which a person feels confronted, and does not feel able to

Alfred Adler, "The Case of Mrs. A." reprinted from H. L. Ansbacher and R. R. Ansbacher (eds.), *Superiority and Social Interest* (Evanston, Ill.: Northwestern University Press, 1970), pp. 160–190.

overcome a certain problem or difficulty. Therefore, we have to look for the direction in which such a person is striving.

In this direction we meet with a million varieties, and these varieties can be measured to a certain degree if we have an idea of what *cooperation* means, and *social interest.* Very often we are able to calculate how far away from a right degree of cooperation we find this kind of patient striving. Therefore it is necessary—and each good analysis has to bring it about—to find on which point a person proves not to be prepared rightly for the solution of social problems, not to be prepared rightly because he cannot afford what is expected of him—the right degree of courage, of self-confidence, of social adjustment, the right type of cooperation, and so on. These things must be understood because you will see how the patient cannot pay, how he declares himself not to be able to solve his problem, and how he shows what I call the *hesitating attitude,* the stopping attitude. He begins to evade and wants to secure himself against a solution of the necessary problem.

On this point you will find him in the state of mind I have described as the *inferiority complex,* and because of that he is always striving to go ahead, to feel superior, to feel that he has overcome his difficulties in the present situation. You must look for this point where the patient feels satisfied on account of feeling superior. Now he cannot feel superior in regard to the solution of his present problem in a useful way and therefore his superiority is proved in the line of uselessness. In his own imagination he has reached his goal of superiority and perhaps satisfied himself, but it cannot be valued as a goal of usefulness.

This is the first description we would expect in each case history, in each analysis of a mental case; it belongs to the *general diagnosis.* Again belonging to the general diagnosis, we have to find some explanation of why this person has not been prepared. This is difficult to understand and to recognize. We have to delve back into the past of this person, to find out in what circumstances he has grown up, how he has behaved towards his family, and to ask questions resembling very much the questions we ask in general medicine. We ask: "What were your parents like?" The patients do not know that in their answers they express their whole attitude—if they felt pampered and the center of attention, or if they resented one or the other of their parents—but *we* see it. And especially on this point always give "empty" questions! You will then be sure that you do not insinuate and give a hint to the patient to speak as you want him to speak.

At this point you will see the origin of the lack of preparation for the present situation, which is like a test examination. Why the patient has not been prepared for it must be seen and explained in the case history.

That is the general diagnosis, but you must not believe that when you have done this you have understood the patient. Now begins the *special diagnosis.* In the special diagnosis you must learn by testing. It is the same kind of testing as you need, for example, in internal medicine. You must note what the patient says but, as in general medicine, you must not trust yourself. You must prove it, and not believe—if you find, for example, a certain frequency of the palpitations of the heart—that it necessarily means a particular cause. In medicine and surgery, as in Individual Psychology, you have to *guess,* but you have to prove it by other signs which agree. If you have guessed and the other signs do not agree, you have to be hard and cruel enough against yourself to look for another explanation.

What I want to do today is to take an analysis such as we might have in a clinic, for example. The doctor makes an analysis of a patient he has not seen before and tries to explain. We, perhaps, may work in this way, for then the whole audience is forced, willingly or unwillingly, to think it over.

Individual Psychology expects you to prove every rule. You must reject each rule and try to understand, and at last you will feel justified in your general views. Of course, you cannot help being influenced in your inquiries by those general views, but it is the same as in other sciences and especially in medicine. You must get rid of your understanding, for instance, of period, of constitution, of the work of the endocrine glands, and so on. But it is very worth while, because you have a hint, and you can go on what you find in this way. It is really the result of your thinking, and shows whether you are thinking rightly or not, if you are experienced or not, and so on. It is the same with Individual Psychology and, therefore, so far as I can see, Individual Psychology agrees wholly with the fundamental views of medicine.

The Case of Mrs. A.

Marital Situation

Now here is the case of Mrs. A. What we can see is that she is a married woman—perhaps a widow—we do not know more. You must fix each word and turn it over in your mind so that you may get everything that is in it.

The patient A., who forms the subject of this paper, was thirty-one years old at the time she came for treatment.

Thirty-one years old and a married woman! Now we know circumstances in which a woman, thirty-one years old, and married, might find herself. There could be a problem of marriage, of children, perhaps also a problem of income in these times. We are very careful. We would not presuppose anything, but we feel sure that—unless we are surprised later—there is something wrong in one of these ways. Now we go ahead.

She had been married eight years . . .

That carries us further—she had married at twenty-three years of age.

. . . and had two children, both boys, aged eight and four years respectively.

Now she had a child very soon. Eight years married and the child eight years old! What you think about that is your own affair. Perhaps we have to correct a recollection. You see the sharp eye of Individual Psychology!

Her husband was a lift man in a store.

Then they are probably in poor circumstances.

An ambitious man, he suffered considerable humiliation from the fact that, unlike his brother, he was prevented, he felt, from obtaining a better type of employment because during the war his right arm had been disabled.

If we can trust this description that he is an ambitious man and does not feel happy in his employment, this must reflect in his married life. He cannot satisfy his ambition outside the family. Perhaps he tries to satisfy it inside; tries to rule his wife and children and to "boss" them. We are not sure and we must be careful enough not to believe it and to be convinced, but we have a view. Perhaps we shall find something in this way. An ambitious husband!

His wife, however, had little sympathy with his trouble . . .

Now if we are right that this man wants to prove himself superior in his family life and his wife does not agree and give in, if she has little sympathy with his style of life, there must probably be some dissension in the family. This man wants to rule; his wife does not agree and does not give him a chance. Therefore, there must be trouble in the family.

Fear of Death and Cleanliness Compulsion

. . . being far too occupied with the compulsive thoughts and fears of death from which she suffered.

Compulsive thoughts and fear of death! It does not look like a compulsion neurosis; it looks more like an anxiety neurosis. Now on this point I should like to give you a rule out of our experience which can be used. I like to ask: What happens in these cases? What are the results if a married woman is suffering from fears of death and perhaps from other fears? What would it mean? She is occupied too much with it, as we can see, and so many of her necessary tasks would not be fulfilled. We see that she is much more occupied with her own person. She is not interested, as we have heard, in the troubles of the man.

We are, therefore, in agreement on these points, but we are not far ahead. We can understand that such a person cannot cooperate rightly if she is interested in the fear of death and other fears, and we understand that there must be many dissensions in this family.

These fears, indeed, occupied her mind to such an extent that she found difficulty at the time she came for treatment in thinking of anything else.

At this point we are justified in answering our question as to what happens: She cannot think of anything else. Now I want to tell you that this is what you will always find and, if in any cases it appears not to be so for a time, you will find confirmation later in the description. This shows that it is worth while, and encourages us because we know we are not right off the mark but have predicted what will be later.

We read that she is thinking only of her fears.

> Thus a careful housewife—she had previously been governed by an almost obsessional hatred of dirt and love of tidiness . . .

This gives another picture—a compulsion neurosis in regard to cleanliness, probably a wash-compulsion neurosis. If she was afraid of dirt she must make it clean always. She must wash and clean everything and herself. In the same way she is suffering from fear of death. There must be a mixed neurosis. This is really very rare. In our general experience the wash-compulsion neurotics do not suffer from fear of death. They may combine the two ideas and say: "If I do not wash this desk, or these shoes and so on, my husband will die," or whatever it may be. But that is not the fear of death as we find it in many anxiety neuroses. As I explained in a lecture in this room on "Obsessions and Compulsion in the Compulsion Neuroses," there is always an underlying idea. Here the idea is that of cleaning away the dirt.

Now we understand more on this point. We see that this woman is occupied in another place than that in which she is expected to be. She does not cooperate; she is interested only in her own sufferings, making everything clean, and perhaps the wash-compulsion. Therefore, we can judge: This is a type that can solve the social problems of life; but she is not prepared in cooperation, but much more prepared in thinking of herself. We know out of our general experience that we find such a style of life mostly in children suffering from imperfect organs, and in the great majority of pampered, petted, and dependent children. More rarely we find it in neglected children, because probably a child wholly neglected would die. The great majority of these neurotic children have been pampered, made dependent, and given such an idea of themselves that they are more interested in themselves than in others.

This woman is striving for a high ideal—to be cleaner than all the others. You can understand that she does not agree with our life; she wants it to be much cleaner. Now cleanliness is a very nice characteristic and we like it very much. But if a person focuses life on cleanliness she is not able to live our life, and there must be another place for such a person; because if you have really inquired into cases of wash-compulsion neurosis, you will be convinced that it is not possible to arrive at such an ideal of cleanliness as these people want to arrive at. You will always find some dirt and dust. You cannot carry on life by pointing to one part only—cleanliness, for instance—because it disturbs the harmony of life.

So far as I can see there is only one part of our emotions and life that can never be overstrained and that is social interest. If there is social interest you cannot overstrain it in such a degree that the harmony of life can be disturbed; but all other things can do so. If you point to health and think only of it, you ruin your life; if you think only of money, you ruin your life, in spite of the fact that, as we know, it is unfortunately necessary to think of it. If you turn to family life and exclude all the other relations, you ruin your life. It seems an unwritten law that we cannot turn only to one point without risking many damages!

Now we will see more.

> . . . hatred of dirt and love of tidiness, both with regard to her home and to her own person—she now began to show neglect in both these particulars.

This also is not usual, for we mostly receive such persons, with their care for cleanliness and avoidance of dirt, in this frame of mind. But this woman has broken down, so she gives up. We do not know how she appears now in this state of mind, but it is very probable that she did not succeed in her imagination with this compulsion neurosis and, therefore, she has made one step forward, coming—if I have read and understood rightly—to a state in which she begins to neglect herself and to be dirty.

Now here is an interesting point. I have never seen persons so dirty as those suffering from a wash-compulsion neurosis. If you enter the home of such a person there is a terrible fume. You find papers lying about, and dirt everywhere. The hands and the whole body are dirty, all the clothes are dirty, and they do not touch anything. I do not know if it is so here, but this is the usual condition among people with a wash-compulsion neurosis, and it is funny that all these persons experience some adventures that others never experience. Always, where there is dirt, they are mixed in it. Probably it is because they are always looking around for dirt and are not so clever as others in avoiding it. I have had a very queer experience with such persons who are always soiled where other people can avoid it. It is like a fate hanging over such people, that they must always find their way to dirt.

We do not know what the breakdown means in this case—perhaps a step nearer to psychosis. That happens sometimes in persons suffering from compulsion neurosis.

> Her fear of death referred to above was related to a definite knife phobia . . .

You can call a knife phobia also a compulsion idea, a very frequent one which persons suffer from if they see a knife. They feel that they could kill a person. But they never do. They stop at the idea. The meaning behind such an idea is hidden; we must find out its whole coherence and what it means. Now I have explained what it means. It is nearly the same as a person wanting to curse, "I could kill you," and such things.

Uncooperativeness and Hostility

We spoke before of dissensions. The husband is ambitious. She, as we know from our general diagnosis of neurotic persons, is ambitious. She wants to rule, to be the head. She wants to be the cleanest person, and we can understand how she avoids her husband, his personal approach, his sexual approach, because of his lack of cleanliness. She calls everything dirty. She can call a kiss dirt. We cannot commend her. We must find how far she is going to look for this dirt. She has two children and we must believe that this had not been at her own wish. Here we see the lack of cooperation. If you look a little nearer you may be sure this is a frigid woman. Do you see why? She is always thinking of herself, and the sexual functions among men and women can be right only if they are fulfilled as a task for two persons. If a person is interested only in self the sexual feelings are not right. Thus you have frigidity. More rarely you may have vaginismus, but it is mostly frigidity, and you can be sure that this is a woman who does not cooperate. This can be seen in the form of her sexual urge, which is sexuality. We must remember the difference—sexuality is a form and sexual urge is a movement. Therefore we can be sure and can predict—though we must not allow ourself to do so, but should wait and be patient—that she resents sexual intercourse.

We next read that this knife phobia was

> . . . connected with tendencies both suicidal and homicidal.

In the discussion of suicide, I have explained that this is always a sign of a person who is not trained in cooperation. He is always looking after himself, and when he is confronted with a social problem for which he is not prepared, he has such a feeling of his own worth and value that he is sure that, in killing himself, he hurts another person. If you have seen such cases in this connection, you have understood them. Therefore we can say in a certain way that suicide is always an accusation and a revenge, an attacking attitude. Sometimes it is an attack of revenge. Therefore, we must look for the person against whom this phobia is directed. There is no question that it is her husband. It may be guessed very surely—the husband with whom, as we have seen, she must be in dissension. He wants to rule and she is interested only in her own person, and therefore if there is revenge or attack or aggression against somebody, it must be against the husband. You can guess it, but please wait to see if we can prove it.

> Her aggressive thoughts and feelings towards other people were shown in other ways.

We see "other people." We do not know who they are, but it contradicts in a certain way our view that the husband is meant.

> She experienced at times an impulsive wish to hit her husband . . .

That is what I said before. It is as in general medicine. If you have guessed before, you may find a proof. If you have rapidly diagnosed pneumonia, for instance, you may find signs later that will prove it and which you can predict; when we find such proofs we feel that we are on terra firma.

> . . . her husband or . . .

We know what must follow—her husband or the children. There are no other persons she could accuse. She would not like children. If you asked her: "Do you like children?" she would say "Yes; my children are my all!" In Individual Psychology we learn from experience that if we want to understand a person we have to close our ears. We have only to look. In this way we can see as in a pantomime. Perhaps there are other persons. Perhaps there is a mother-in-law. It is possible. We would not be astonished. But, so far as we know the situation, we expect the children to follow.

> . . . her husband or anybody else who happened to have annoyed her.

Who are the persons who can have annoyed her? We can see that this woman is very sensitive, and if we look for what sensitiveness means in general diagnosis we find that it means a feeling of being in a hostile country and being attacked from all sides. That is the style of life of the person who does not cooperate and feel at home, who is always experiencing and sensing enmity in the environment; and, therefore, we can understand that she reacts in such a strong manner with emotion.

If I felt that I was in a hostile country and always expected attacks, expected to be annoyed and humiliated, I would behave in the same way. I also would be sensitive. This is a very interesting point. We cannot explain these persons only by looking to their emotion; we must look to their mistaken meaning of life and to their bringing up. She really believes she lives in a hostile country and is expecting always to be attacked and humiliated. She is thinking only of herself and her own salvation, her own superiority in overcoming the difficulties of life. These emotional persons must be understood from this point of view. If I believe an abyss is before me, whether there is an abyss or not, it is all the same: I am suffering from my meaning, not from reality. If I believe that there is a lion in the next room, it is all the same to me whether there is one or not. I shall behave in the same way. Therefore, we must look for the meaning of this person. It is "I must be safe"—a selfish meaning.

Now we read:

> These characteristics had of late extended in two directions. On the one hand she experienced at times a strong desire to hit any casual stranger she happened to pass in the street.

Is it not as I have described? She is living in a hostile country, where everybody is an enemy. To want to hit any stranger she meets in the street means to be impossible, to compromise herself. It means: "I must be watched; someone must take care of me." She forces other persons—or one other person—to take care of her. Whether she says it in words or not she speaks by her attitude in life and forces other persons to take care of her if she behaves in this way. But we must also look for the impression the husband has of it. His wife wants to hit every stranger in the street and he is living with her in social relations. Therefore, whatever she does affects him. He must do something. What can he do in such a case? We suppose this husband is not a fool or feeble-minded and we can predict what he has to do. He has to take care of her as far as possible, watch her and accompany her and so on. She is giving him the rules for his behavior in so doing. You see, this ambitious woman, with an ambitious husband, has conquered. He must do what she wants and commands. She behaves in such a way that other persons must feel responsible. She exploits him and is the commander and, therefore, we can understand that on this point she rules.

Wanting to Enslave Her Husband

Now let us see more:

> On the other hand she entertained homicidal feelings toward her younger son, a child of four . . .

This we have not seen before, but we have guessed it—that the attacks would be against the children. Here we have the second child specially pointed out, and it gives us a chance to guess that she wanted to avoid this child, that it was an unwanted child; and it finds expression in this way, that she is afraid she will kill him, that she does not treat him rightly, and so on. These feelings are sometimes so intense that the husband must watch her. The husband now becomes a slave, and probably this woman had nothing more in her meaning and imagination long ago but to make him a prisoner and slave. She would have been satisfied if her husband had submitted in a general way, as sometimes husbands do submit. But we have heard that this husband was ambitious; he wanted her to submit, wanted to subjugate her. He has lost and she has conquered. She could not conquer in a usual way, convincing him, or perhaps taking part in all his interests; therefore she came to a point that we can understand. She is right; she acts intelligently. If her goal is to be conqueror, to subjugate her husband, she has acted absolutely rightly. She has accomplished a creative work, a masterpiece of art, and we have to admire this woman!

Now I want to tell you something of how I go on with such cases. I explain it in short words. I say: "I admire you; you have done a masterpiece of art. You have conquered." I put it pleasantly.

Now we want to establish a coherence. This woman is looking for a fear that she will kill somebody. We have to look for the whole coherence. She is leaning on one point and is not looking for the others. Other psychologists will say she is surprised, but she is not surprised. I see it clearly. She does not want to see it, because if she did, her remainder of social interest would rise up and contradict it. No person who is not feebleminded or crazy would agree that he wanted to rule other persons in such a way and, therefore, she is not permitted to look. But we must make her look and, therefore, I prefer to have such a nice talk and to praise her for her cleverness: "You have done rightly."

Then there is the question whether, even before, she had no other meaning or goal in her mind but to rule everybody. On this point we have to find out whether in childhood also she was "bossing" and wanted to command everybody. If we can prove it as the next backward step in our understanding, what shall we say of all the skepticism, all the criticisms that we do not know anything about this woman and how she was as a child? If we can show that as a child she was "bossing," in what other science can you be so sure that you can postulate something which happened twenty-five or twenty-eight years before? If you ask her for her earliest recollections, I am sure she will tell you something in which you will find a "bossing" attitude, because we are soon to grasp the whole style of life of this woman. She is a "bossing" woman, but she could not conquer in a normal way. She had no chance—poverty, an ambitious husband, two children very soon, not cooperative, as we have seen. She had to be defeated in a normal way and she is looking for her conquest in another way that we could not agree with or call a useful or social way.

> Sometimes the idea of killing the boy was so intense that she feared that she might carry the intention into execution.

The more she was afraid she would execute it, the more her husband must watch her.

> She stated that these symptoms had been in existence for one and a half years.

If this is right we should be interested to find out what happened one and a half years ago, when this child was two and a half years old. I should understand it better if it had happened before the second child came, but if it be true that the symptoms originated one and a half years ago we must know in what situation the woman was at that time and what has affected her. We shall find that she had to offer cooperation and could not, that she was afraid she would be subjugated, and resisted, and wanted to conquer. But we must know.

> More careful examination, however, seemed to show that definite neurotic traits had been in existence many years, and had been accentuated since marriage. She herself indeed volunteered the information that she "had not been the girl she was since she had been married."

"Since marriage!" This is very interesting, because from our general experience we know there are three situations which are like test examinations to show whether a person is socially interested or not: the social problem—how to behave to others; the occupation problem—how to be useful in work; the marriage problem—how to converse with a person of the other sex. These are the test examinations for how far a person is prepared for social relations. If her symptoms have been worse since marriage it is a sign that she was not prepared for marriage because she was too much interested in her own person.

The Example of Her Parents

Now what of the family history? Many family histories I have read do not say very much. We Individual Psychologists are used to hearing of some situations and facts that involve the child in a way we can understand, but we would reject

Alfred Adler47

all descriptions in which we are referred to heredity only, such as that an aunt was crazy or a grandmother a drunkard. These do not say anything. It does not contribute to our understanding. We are very interested in imperfect organs, if we are to grasp a case, because we find very often children out of a family tree where persons have suffered in some organs, and we may suspect that they suffer from some lack of validity in those organs; but mostly we do not get much information from these descriptions.

The family history showed signs of neurosis on both sides.

This is worthwhile, because we can see that the family history of the child had been a bad one. Neurotic means that the parents were fighting for things, to boss, to rule, to subjugate others, to utilize and to exploit others, and so on, and therefore the children in such an atmosphere are really endangered. On this point, however, I have to say that although they are endangered, we are not sure that they must really suffer. They can overcome these dangers and get success and advantage out of them. But a certain probability gives us the right to expect that the danger is that the whole makeup and style of life will be in some way selfish.

At the same time it must be remembered that the informant on this matter was the patient, whose attitude to her parents, at least, was not without personal bias.

We want to see what her attitude was and this probably means that it was a hostile attitude to the parents; she has struggled against them.

For example, she felt aggrieved that both her father and mother were only children—for, as she pointed out, this meant that she had no uncles or aunts and could not receive presents as did other children.

This is a woman who is always expecting to be presented and here she betrays a good deal of her style of life. She is the type that wants to receive, not to give. We understand that this type is in danger and must have difficulties in life, especially if she meets an ambitious man.

The father was a laborer. The mother was a hardworking woman who did everything to keep the home together. She avoided responsibility, however, in one important particular. If her children needed correction, she preferred to leave that matter to her husband.

This means that she did not feel strong enough, and utilized her husband for punishments, as happens very often in families. It is a bad thing for the children, because they begin to disesteem and ridicule the mother and to make a joke of her, because they see her express herself as a weak person who cannot do the right thing.

This fact was unfortunate—since the latter was very sadistic.

I do not think "sadistic" here is to be interpreted as meaning that he had sexual satisfaction when he slapped the children, but that he was rough and ruling and bossing, and subjugated the children. Now we can understand that she has put her goal in the subjugation of others. I have known many cases where the child who has been beaten hard has gone round with the idea: "When I am grown up I will do the same with others—rule them and boss them." The father in his roughness has given this child a goal. What does superiority mean? What does it mean to be the most powerful person in the world? This poor girl, as a child who is always suppressed and maltreated, could have no other idea than that it is much better to be above and not down, to maltreat others and not to be maltreated. Now we see her from this standpoint and on this level.

> When he learnt from his wife that his children had misbehaved in any way— especially with reference to anything that touched his purse—for instance, if they wore out the soles of their boots quickly—he would beat them almost unmercifully.

This is a point where we can learn something in regard to corporal punishment.

> The consequence was that the children lived in dread of their father, at the same time that for obvious reasons they did not confide in their mother.

Where should they learn cooperation if neither with the father nor the mother? Some little degree of cooperation there must have been in this girl's mind, because she could get married. She may have learned it from other children, comrades perhaps, but not from father or mother.

> Nevertheless she maintained that he was a good father, except on Saturday nights, when he frequently came home drunk.

This would mean that she preferred the father. I am impressed, when I read this, with the idea that she was the oldest child. Mostly the oldest child, whether boy or girl, turns towards the father. When another child comes, relations with the mother are interrupted and the throne is vacant, which gives the father his chance. But this is only a guess and we have to prove it.

> He would then strike his wife as well as his children and openly threaten to cut their throats.

She imitates the father in her compulsion idea: to kill somebody with the knife—child, or husband. Did I not say that the father gave her the chance to put her goal of superiority in this way?
Notice that the father cursed only; he did not cut the throats of his children. Therefore I believe I am right in thinking that when she says she could kill somebody it is just a curse, an idea—"I could kill you!"

> This latter point is possibly of interest in view of a similar symptom exhibited by A. Indeed in many respects her neurotic symptom formation tended towards an imitation of her father's characteristics.

The writer, who is a doctor, goes on to say:

> She was apt in the same way to hit her own children without adequate provocation.

With this we do not agree. She has a provocation. She wants to be superior, as the father wanted to be superior. That is a provocation—she was provoked: "If I want to boss I shall use my children, because they are the weaker ones and cannot hit back."

Though it is true she afterwards regretted her cruelty . . .

This reminds me that we very often hear something said about regretting, feeling of guilt, and so on. Now we Individual Psychologists are skeptical in this matter. We do not judge this regret and feeling of guilt very highly. We say it is absolutely empty and useless. After a child is beaten hard, the regret does not matter. It is too much. Either one of these two things would be enough—the regret or the hit—but both! I would resent it very much if somebody hit me and then regretted it. I have seen that this feeling of guilt is a trick so that we shall not see this cruel attitude in bossing others. It means: "I am a noble woman and I regret it." I believe modern society should be warned not to take very seriously this regret. We find it among problem children very often. They commit some act, cry, and ask pardon very much, and then do it again. Why? Because, if they did not regret, but only continued doing it, they would be put out. Nobody could bear it always. They make a sort of hinterland where others will not interfere with them; they have a feeling that they are being smart children or people. So there is this woman, she is cruel and regrets it, but what does that matter? The facts are all the same.

. . . this feeling had little or no power to prevent similar outbursts on a subsequent occasion.

We expected that, because it is a trick. Where you find the feeling of guilt it is in cases of melancholia and is always a trick. It doesn't work. You see we guessed rightly.

Other Childhood and Youth Situations

A. was the second child and girl of a family of eight—four girls being followed by four boys.

In regard to second children, we know they are generally—though there are no rules, and we speak only of majorities—much more striving. It is like a race, and they want always to overcome the first child. The reason why I said I believed she was a first child was that she turned to the father, but there are circumstances in which the second child may do so, especially if she has been pampered and a third child comes and she is in a situation which draws her towards him.

We find second children striving to be first; there is a very good picture of this in the Bible picture of Jacob and Esau. It is very interesting, too, to see from statistics in America that, among juvenile delinquents, second children are in a majority. An inquiry into children of one and two years and younger has been started by Individual Psychologists, and there is a big field, which can be used for some understanding of their whole style of life. There will be something good or something wrong about second children. It is like a race; they try to overcome the first. Perhaps it was so in this case, but we do not want to say more.

As a child, she said, she had been on the whole happy-go-lucky, cheerful, and healthy . . .

If so, she had been in the center of the stage and favored. She was perhaps the favorite.

. . . very different from her oldest sister, whom she described as being silent and reserved, characteristics which A. interpreted as selfishness.

Now, surely, it is selfish to be reserved because it means to think of one's self. We can see that she had been lucky in her striving, and the older girl had the aspect of a defeated child and was overcome. We find this feature in her whole makeup—how to overcome. She is able to succeed in her goal to be mother and father and to boss, in an easy way, because the older sister has given way and been conquered.

The parents seemed to have held a somewhat similar opinion, and treated their oldest child with special severity.

Now the parents help her in her race, by suppressing the oldest child.

She was frequently in trouble, and the severe beatings which she received from her father filled A. with terror.

She had been scared because the oldest child had been beaten so severely.

The rest of the family A. regarded with considerable affection, with the exception, significantly enough, of her oldest brother.

That is, the first boy, who when he came was probably worshipped and appreciated in a way she did not like; and therefore we can conclude—though we must really prove it—that her position in the family was endangered by this boy.

As with her sister, so with him, she considered that he was selfish and inconsiderate, "so different from the rest of us, except, of course, T." (the oldest sister).

That she agreed with the other children means that she could rule them; they did not make difficulties. This boy and the oldest sister made difficulties and therefore she did not agree with them.

Personal History. As already mentioned A. had been a healthy child and prided herself on her robust health. From the age of fourteen to seventeen inclusive, however, she had some degree of goiter from which she subsequently recovered.

We see here a certain organic imperfection, as we find very often among neurotic patients. How far this influenced her we could learn only from the first child, of whom we have not many remarks.

Though she had no return of the trouble, yet, from time to time in the course of treatment she had considerable difficulty in times of stress in getting her breath—a symptom which caused her considerable anxiety.

This probably was not due to pressure of the thyroid, or it would have been recognized and treated. It probably was a psychological problem; she could not breathe when she became emotional under the treatment, or it may have appeared when she was wishing to pose, or felt she was unjustly treated. All this may have affected her breathing, but it could have been seen clearly if the thyroid was causing pressure.

Her school attainments were quite good and she had at that time no difficulty in making friends.

Do not forget that such persons, selfish from the beginning and striving to be in a favorable situation, do not lack all degrees of cooperation. Therefore, we are not astonished that she, who probably succeeded in the beginning and wanted to be ahead and lead the school, found it easier to make friends. Probably they were friends who were willing to submit to her, but that is a point we could find out in an interview.

She left school at the age of fourteen, but continued to live at home for some months, going from there to daily work, which she enjoyed.

In that case she probably fell on a good place, where she could express her opinion and perhaps also rule others.

But as soon as she entered domestic service away from home, new troubles began.

Now domestic service means to submit, and this woman cannot submit. She cannot submit in any way that can be accepted as cooperation. She must be ruling and here we have a new proof. She is not prepared to a situation in which others are ruling. We find many girls who have to do domestic work and cannot submit. For instance, I remember a governess who, when the woman who employed her asked her to clean the cage of the parrot, said: "You should ask what I want to do this afternoon, and I will say that I would like to clean the cage of the parrot." Thus it appeared to be her own idea; she was commanding. You meet the same thing in the exercises of the army, where the soldier, after he is commanded, must repeat the command in such a way as if it were his own. "I shall go on this parade." You see the wisdom of that rule in the army.

Within a week of her arrival she was attacked by such bad carbuncles on her back that the doctor ordered her home again.

I do not go so far as to say that those carbuncles were the result of her dislike, but is is a fact that is a person does not feel well in a certain place, something may happen. My daughter, who is a psychiatrist and has made researches into accidents, found that half of them occur among persons who do not like the job in which they are working. When people are run over, fall down from certain places and hurt themselves, or touch something, it is as though they would say: "It is because my father forced me to go to this job, and I wanted another job." Half of all the accidents! Therefore, I am quite sure that things like carbuncles can occur if a person does not like a certain situation. I would not go further.

This she did with considerable trepidation because she knew that her eldest sister, who had once similarly returned, owing to illness, had had a very bad reception.

She had learned how not to behave!

For a time, however, everything went well. But soon her father became openly dissatisfied at having to keep his daughter "eating her head off" as he put it. Matters came to a climax when, one morning as A. entered the kitchen to have breakfast, her father, without a word of warning, rushed at her with a shovel, obviously intending to hit her over the head.

It was in the morning, so he was not drunk!

She rushed from the house in terror and hid from the family for the rest of the day. It is possibly of significance, in view of her later fear of coffins, undertakers, and all matters relating to the subject of death, that she spent most of this time in the churchyard.

Now a new idea appears. In a certain way we can see that the illness and the neurotic symptoms of this woman are an accusation against the father whether she knows it or not. We are studying the natural history, the biology, of behavior. Now if we find one bone—such as this neurotic symptom represents—we can relate it to the father. The father is guilty and it is an accusation against him. She might put it in these words; "My father has tortured me so much that it is because of his treatment that I am as I am." Now the father had not been right, but does it follow that the daughter also must not be right? Is it really like cause and effect? Is she forced to be sick and to make mistakes because the father has made a mistake? The importance of this question is very great because that is what this woman, if we read her aright, is really saying—that because the father has made a mistake, she also must do so. But there is no causality in mind; only the causality *she* has effected. She has made something into a reason which must not be a reason, and I have seen other children who have been tortured by their parents go through this compulsion neurosis. It is not like the causality we find among dead things; and even among dead things causality is now beginning to be doubted.

In the evening, however, she was found by her mother, who persuaded her to return home. Her father treated the incident as a joke, and laughed at her for "being such a silly." His daughter, however, did not treat the matter so lightly and vowed that she would never return home to live again, a resolution which she kept for a long time.

Another resolution she had made, as I said before: "I must never be in a situation where another person can rule me." In the childish fashion which we always find in neurotic patients, she knows only contradiction and antithesis: to rule or to be ruled. This is very interesting that among all the failures in life, and not only among neurotic persons, you will find that they know only contradiction. They call it sometimes "ambivalence" or "polarity" but always they are forming judgments of contradiction—down, above; good, bad; normal, not normal; and so on. In children and neurotic persons, and in the old Greek philosophy, you find always this looking for contradiction.

She has concluded, in this way, never to be ruled.

After this affair she went once more into domestic service and appears to have worked hard and diligently. She showed, however, a preference for rough work. Her dislike for doing "fiddly work," such as dusting, she distinctly stated to be due to her dread that she would break ornaments and so on.

What is in her mind is that she is a girl of strong health, who values strength and does not like housekeeping. When we remember her contradiction towards the oldest boy, because a boy had been preferred, she probably did not want to be a woman at all. She disliked doing such things, being occupied with dusting and such little matters. This would explain why she was not prepared to be a married woman. This would be what I have called the *masculine protest*. In such a case, if you force a person to do things she does not like, she tries to exaggerate. There is a certain anger and rage and exaggeration.

This fact is of interest as being the possible forerunner of her later openly destructive wishes and feelings . . .

Premarital Difficulties

At the age of eighteen she was engaged to a young man whom she appears to have dominated.

We find the writer of this case history has been on the same track as we have, and she describes this domineering symptom when she points out that she dominated this man.

In course of time, however, she came to dislike him for what she considered his "stingy ways" and, after two or three years, dramatically broke off the engagement by throwing the ring in his face.

That is not what we expect from a girl; we expect milder processes!

She related, however, with pride, that he still maintained a somewhat doglike devotion to her, and even at the time she came for treatment still continued to ask after her. In spite of this manifestation of devotion she never showed any regret with reference to her behavior in the whole matter.

In this case she does not regret because there is no reason for her to do so.

During the war she entered a munitions factory in a provincial town, and it was then she met the man who is now her husband.

We now remember this man. He is a cripple, and sometimes you find among men and women who want to dominate that they are very fond of cripples and people who are weak in some way—sometimes alcoholics whom they want to save, and people of a lower social status than their own. I would warn people—girls especially, but also the men—against choosing in this way, because no person in love or marriage can safely be looked down on. They will revolt, as this man revolted.

He was quartered in hospital at the time, invalided home from the war. He fulfilled her ideal of a possible husband in two most important respects—he was tall and he was not an alcoholic.

We can understand that the father had been strong with his drunkenness, and the reason many persons, especially girls, are afraid of alcoholics is that they cannot rule them. Alcoholics and creeping things, like mice and insects, they fear sometimes. You find very often that this fright is because they cannot rule them and can be surprised by them. We can understand why she would resent an alcoholic, but why she preferred a tall man we do not know. It may have been the remains of her admiration of the father, or she may have been tall, or have thought it was more worthwhile to rule a tall man than a short one. This could be found out only by asking her.

It is also possible that his injuries appealed to her love of power—her wish to assume the dominant role was a notable trait in her character.

The writer has taken the line which I explained. We would underline this and say her style of life was characterized by a very domineering and bossing attitude.

For a time all went well. But when her fiancé went to London, he then, for reasons best known to himself, wrote letters well calculated to rouse her jealousy.

If we understand that she wanted to rule him, to be alone with him and the center of his attention, we know that jealousy is very near at hand. She has to look to it that she is not dethroned as she was when the other children came in the family, and when the boy came.

Unhappy and suspicious, A. followed him to London, obtained work as a waitress in a restaurant, and did all in her power to hold her fiancé.

You see how she is striving to keep him.

With this the attitude of the two lovers towards each other seems to have undergone a change. Not only did the woman assume the more active part in their relations . . .

We note this in proof of her meaning—she took the active part!

. . . but the man, from being attentive and kindly, now became careless and inconsiderate.

We saw in the beginning that she had forced him to be careful. At this point we read he had become careless.

They made appointments for which he either came late or did not keep at all. A. became suspicious, tearful, and "quite different from her former bright self."

She was afraid of losing her former ruling position.

Matters came to a head when he failed for a second time to keep an appointment with her—she having in the meanwhile waited for him for hours in the cold and fog of a November night.

This is a hard thing, and there is no question the man also was not adapted for such a marriage. Any girl would be right to look upon such negligence as an injury. This girl could find no other way than the creation of a compulsion idea with which she could again conquer him.

When she learned from him next day that he had not kept his appointment because he had gone out with some friends, she angrily told him she did not wish to see him again.

She would feel defeated. Perhaps we should be glad to get rid of such a partner, but this person does not want to be defeated. She wants to keep him.

Her attempt to break off the engagement, however, did not take place—a fact for which she felt thankful when, three weeks later, she discovered that she was pregnant.

Here is a good chance to speak of relations before marriage. It may seem in some cases to be an advantage, but I have found that it is a disadvantage and as doctors we should advise to wait. It always causes trouble.

Marital Difficulties

She felt desperate at this finding and entertained now for the first time definite suicidal feelings. Her fiancé endeavored to comfort her and promised to marry her as soon as possible—which he did three or four weeks after. The question of her residence for the next few months now arose. She dreaded to return home because her father had said that he would have nothing to do with any of his daughters if they got into trouble. Though his threat proved to be unfounded, and she was allowed by her parents to return home, she felt very unhappy during this time.

Really, she felt defeated.

Her misery was accentuated by the birth of a son; for both she and her husband had hoped for a daughter.

This is something we should not expect. We should expect that if a child was coming they would hope for a son. Why they wanted a daughter could be explained only by these two persons. But perhaps if they had had a daughter, she would have been disappointed.

It may be pointed out in passing that A.'s desire for a daughter and subsequent disappointment were connected with her later hostility towards her sons.

As we cannot verify her statements without asking her, we must assume she had disliked the men in her environment, her father, then her brother. Probably, too, she was looking for the antithesis man-woman, because these neurotic people look on men and women as *opposite* sexes. You know the widespread notion—the opposite sex. If you exaggerate this you will get an opposition against the opposite sex, which is very often to be found, both in men and women, and especially among neurotic persons.

After this event she then returned to London to live in two rooms with her husband. Matters, however, went badly from the first. It is true that to begin with she got on well with her neighbors, but soon feelings of inferiority began to assert themselves. These seem to have been connected with a certain jealousy of her husband, who was popular and well liked generally. She interpreted passing words and looks of those around her as criticisms directed against herself.

She looked on the neighbors, probably, as subjects she could rule, and therefore good relations never existed.

As a conscious reaction formation against the sensation that she was despised, she not only avoided making friendships, "keeping herself to herself" as she described it, but she also used to sing hymns in a loud voice to show her neighbors firstly, that she was not afraid, and secondly, that she at any rate had been well brought up. Unfortunately her criticisms of her neighbors were not without justification, quarrels and drunken brawls not being infrequent. In addition she and her husband found constant cause for disagreement. The methods she employed to gain his sympathy were characteristic. Thus after a quarrel she would retire to bed and threaten to kill herself and the child unless matters improved.

You see how she wanted to use force!

So matters continued, going from bad to worse until A.'s neurotic symptoms became so manifest that her husband took her to see a doctor. The diagnosis of nervous dyspepsia was made, and the recommendation given that all her teeth should be extracted.

I presume this was meant as a punishment, not as medical treatment.

After some hesitation she decided to take this advice, and with this end in view went to hospital accompanied by a friend. The latter was then considerably annoyed when A., after an hysterical outburst in front of the doctor and nurses, refused to have her mouth touched.

This suggests that she really understood the situation better!

Not unnaturally this same friend refused to accompany her a second time to hospital. On the second occasion, therefore, A. went alone, when it is noteworthy that, though nervous, she was able to have three or four teeth extracted without trouble. On the next occasion, however, matters did not go so smoothly. She had an hysterical outburst following the extraction of twelve teeth, due, she maintained, to the fact that she felt the whole operation although under an anesthetic. The fantastic nature of these "memories" was obvious. In accord also with her sadistic tendencies it is hardly surprising that these "remembrances," to which she had not infrequently referred, made a deep impression on her.

Now, imagine this woman: thirty years of age! They extracted, as far as I can count, sixteen teeth! I think a woman who had no "sadistic tendencies" would not look on this fact in a humorous spirit! It makes a deep impression. If you know what it means to a woman or a man to lose the first tooth, you will appreciate that this woman has lost sixteen. And she is jealous of her husband! She explained how she had suffered. I hope I am explaining it rightly, but this may have another explanation. This woman likes to explain how much she has suffered. Probably she had some dreams, as happens in narcosis, and she tells these things to impress others how she has suffered.

I do not think we should speak of sadistic tendencies in the way that has become common in our time, because we should use it only when the person has a sexual gratification. If we call all forms of attack "sadism" everything disappears in darkness.

The Final Exogenous Situation

Shortly after this her second child was born.

We see that is was a time of distress, when she was fighting hard for her superior position.

The fact that he was a boy caused her great disappointment—she had been quite certain that the infant would be a girl. The impotence of her wishes in the face of reality severely wounded her vanity—and from now on her neurotic tendency became more and more evident. The resentment she felt toward her infant was the obvious prelude to her later consciously felt wish to kill the child.

You will remember that in speaking of the first symptoms and when they occurred, I said I could have understood it if it had been when the second child came, because her importance would weaken and become less since she now has to share with two children, and she wants herself to be the center, not the children. She will feel resentment more strongly, and a desire to kill.

At the same time her pursuit by a drunken neighbor, who with a knife in his hand threatened to take her life, gave her a reason for an exacerbation of her symptoms. It also gave her a reasonable excuse for refusing to stay in the house where they were living although it was impossible to obtain any other room at the moment in the neighborhood.

Now really this house had not been very well fitted for a bossing woman. The neighbors did not like her. In this case you can find also that a paranoiac symptom appears and you can see that in a certain way the manner in which this woman behaves is in the neighborhood of paranoia—as if the others would pursue her and be interested in her and look at her. But even a compulsion neurosis reaches further and touches some symptoms which are generally described under another title. There are mixtures in this way.

In addition—by this means she was able to leave her husband for a time, she and her children finding a temporary home with her mother-in-law, her husband remaining alone in London. The arrangement, however, did not prove happy.

The mother-in-law probably also did not submit!

This position was partly due to the critical attitude of the mother-in-law towards her daughter-in-law, and partly to the fact that A. felt hostile towards her mother-in-law from the start, owing to the unfavorable comparisons which her husband was accustomed to draw between her and his mother.

The usual fact!

By mutual consent, therefore, the arrangement was terminated and A. and her children went to stay with her parents. From there she was recalled to London, owing to the fact that her husband had had a "nervous breakdown" in her absence and wanted her to nurse him.

We do not know the husband. Perhaps he also wanted to dominate somebody.

It seems improbable that it was only a coincidence that at the same time he had been able to find rooms for the family.

Probably he worked with nervous symptoms and wanted to impress her in this way by a "nervous breakdown."

Shortly after her return to London she was overcome by the obsessive thoughts and feelings which gradually came to occupy her attention more and more—to the exclusion of almost all else. She dated this phase of her illness back to a terrifying dream of angels surrounding a coffin.

This is the thought of death, but you see what it means. It affects the husband. He has to take care of her; so she has a dream of angels surrounding a coffin.

Of significance is her constant association of this dream with a picture of her old home, at which she frequently gazed when pregnant with her first child.

We understand that at this time she played with the idea of suicide. She looked round and the picture was there, and the other members of the family would be impressed. She would get the idea: "What would make me the master of the game would be if the others were afraid that I would commit suicide."

The rest of the case-paper deals with treatment, which is not part of my lecture. I have simply wanted to show you the *coherence of a life style*.

Case 4

Editors' Introduction

As in the case of Alfred Adler, Carl Jung never published any in-depth case histories of patients he had treated. Most of his writings were theoretical rather than clinical. However, we were fortunate to locate this fragment which shows how he interpreted dreams, and dreams are a primary focus of the clinical work of Jungian therapists.

This selection was originally a speech (as was the selection by Adler). It should have considerable appeal in that we are in effect watching a great master at work, step by step, so that we can think along with him to determine whether his views of human nature and of the intricacies of the mind agree with our own conceptions. For this reason, we suggest that this case be read dynamically. That is, instead of just reading to see what Jung does with a dream, think along with him and try to make your own interpretations. This should take longer than passive reading, but we suspect you will find it more fulfilling.

CARL G. JUNG

An Analysis of a Patient's Dreams

Ladies and gentlemen, we are now going to step over the border into dreams. I
do not want to give you any particular introduction to dream analysis. I think the
best way is just to show you how I proceed with a dream, and then it does not
need much explanation of a theoretical kind, because you can see what are my
underlying ideas. Of course, I make great use of dreams, because dreams are an
objective source of information in psychotherapeutic treatment. When a doctor
has a case, he can hardly refrain from having ideas about it. But the more one
knows about cases, the more one should make an heroic effort not to know in
order to give the patient a fair chance. I always try not to know and not to see. It is
much better to say you are stupid, or play what is apparently a stupid role, in
order to give the patient a chance to come out with his own material. That does
not mean that you should hide altogether.

This is a case of a man forty years old, a married man who has not been ill
before. He looks quite all right; he is the director of a great public school, a very
intelligent fellow who has studied an old-fashioned kind of psychology, Wundt
psychology,[1] that has nothing to do with details of human life but moves in the
stratosphere of abstract ideas. Recently he had been badly troubled by neurotic
symptoms. He suffered from a peculiar kind of vertigo that seized upon him from
time to time, palpitation, nausea, and peculiar attacks of feebleness and a sort of
exhaustion. This syndrome presents the picture of a sickness which is well
known in Switzerland. It is mountain sickness, a malady to which people who are
not used to great heights are easily subject when climbing. So I asked, "Is it not
mountain sickness you are suffering from?" He said, "Yes, you are right. It feels
exactly like mountain sickness." I asked him if he had dreams and he said that
recently he had had three dreams.

I do not like to analyze one dream alone, because a single dream can be
interpreted arbitrarily. You can speculate anything about an isolated dream; but if
you compare a series of, say, twenty or a hundred dreams, then you can see

From *Analytical Psychology: Its Theory and Practice,* by C. G. Jung. Copyright © 1968 by the
Heirs of C. G. Jung. Reprinted by permission of Pantheon Books, a Division of Random House, Inc.,
and Routledge & Kegan Paul Ltd.

interesting things. You see the process that is going on in the unconscious from night to night, and the continuity of the unconscious psyche extending through day and night. Presumably we are dreaming all the time, although we are not aware of it by day because consciousness is much too clear. But at night, when there is that *abaissement du niveau mental,* the dreams can break through and become visible.

In the first dream *the patient finds himself in a small village in Switzerland. He is a very solemn black figure in a long coat; under his arm he carries several thick books. There is a group of young boys whom he recognizes as having been his classmates. They are looking at him and they say: "That fellow does not often make his appearance here."*

In order to understand this dream you have to remember that the patient is in a very fine position and has had a very good scientific education. But he started really from the bottom and is a self-made man. His parents were very poor peasants, and he worked his way up to his present position. He is very ambitious and is filled with the hope that he will rise still higher. He is like a man who has climbed in one day from sea level to a level of 6,000 feet, and there he sees peaks 12,000 feet high towering above him. He finds himself in the place from which one climbs these higher mountains, and because of this he forgets all about the fact that he has already climbed 6,000 feet and immediately he starts to attack the higher peaks. But as a matter of fact though he does not realize it he is tired from his climbing and quite incapable of going any further at this time. This lack of realization is the reason for his symptoms of mountain sickness. The dream brings home to him the actual psychological situation. The contrast of himself as the solemn figure in the long black coat with thick books under his arm appearing in his native village, and of the village boys remarking that he does not often appear there, means that he does not often remember where he came from. On the contrary he thinks of his future career and hopes to get a chair as professor. Therefore the dream puts him back into his early surroundings. He ought to realize how much he has achieved considering who he was originally and that there are natural limitations to human effort.

The beginning of the second dream is a typical instance of the kind of dream that occurs when the conscious attitude is like his.

He knows that he ought to go to an important conference, and he is taking his portfolio. But he notices that the hour is rather advanced and that the train will leave soon, and so he gets into that well-known state of haste and of fear of being too late. He tries to get his clothes together, his hat is nowhere, his coat is mislaid, and he runs about in search of them and shouts up and down the house, "Where are my things?" Finally he gets everything together, and runs out of the house only to find that he has forgotten his portfolio. He rushes back for it, and looking at his watch finds how late it is getting; then he runs to the station, but the road is quite soft so that it is like walking on a bog and his feet can hardly move any more. Pantingly he arrives at the station only to see that the train is just leaving. His attention is called to the railway track, and it looks like this:

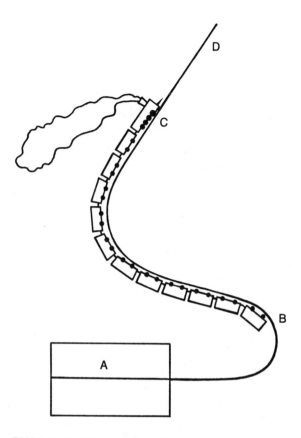

FIGURE 4.1. Dream of the train

He is at A, the tail end of the train is already at B and the engine is at C. He watches the train, a long one, winding round the curve, and he thinks, "If only the engine driver, when he reaches point D, has sufficient intelligence not to rush full steam ahead; for if he does, the long train behind him which will still be rounding the curve will be derailed." Now the engine driver arrives at D and he opens the steam throttle fully, the engine begins to pull, and the train rushes ahead. The dreamer sees the catastrophe coming, the train goes off the rails, and he shouts, and then he wakes up with the fear characteristic of nightmare.

Whenever one has this kind of dream of being late, of a hundred obstacles interfering, it is exactly the same as when one is in such a situation in reality, when one is nervous about something. One is nervous because there is an unconscious resistance to the conscious intention. The most irritating thing is that consciously you want something very much, and an unseen devil is always working against it, and of course you are that devil too. You are working against this devil and do it in a nervous way and with nervous haste. In the case of this dreamer, that rushing ahead is also against his will. He does not want to leave home, yet he wants it very much, and all the resistance and difficulties in his way are his own doing. He is that engine driver who thinks, "Now we are out of our trouble; we have a straight line ahead, and now we can rush along like anything." The straight line beyond the curve would correspond to the peaks 12,000 feet high, and he thinks these peaks are accessible to him.

Naturally, nobody seeing such a chance ahead would refrain from making the utmost use of it, so his reason says to him, "Why not go on, you have every chance in the world." He does not see why something in him should work against it. But this dream gives him a warning that he should not be as stupid as this engine driver who goes full steam ahead when the tail end of the train is not yet out of the curve. That is what we always forget; we always forget that our consciousness is only a surface, our consciousness is the avant-garde of our psychological existence. Our head is only one end, but behind our consciousness is a long historical "tail" of hesitations and weaknesses and complexes and prejudices and inheritances, and we always make our reckoning without them. We always think we can make a straight line in spite of our shortcomings, but they will weigh very heavily and often we derail before we have reached our goal because we have neglected our tail ends.

I always say that our psychology has a long saurian's tail behind it, namely the whole history of our family, of our nation, of Europe, and of the world in general. We are always human, and we should never forget that we carry the whole burden of being only human. If we were heads only we should be like little angels that have heads and wings, and of course they can do what they please because they are not hindered by a body that can walk only on the earth. I must not omit to point out, not necessarily to the patient but to myself, that this peculiar movement of the train is like a snake. Presently we shall see why.

The next dream is the crucial dream, and I shall have to give certain explanations. In this dream we have to do with a peculiar animal which is half lizard and half crab. Before we go into the details of the dream, I want to make a few remarks about the method of working out the meaning of a dream. You know that there are many views and many misunderstandings as to the way in which you get at dreams.

You know, for instance, what is understood by free association. This method is a very doubtful one as far as my experience goes. Free association means that you open yourself to any amount and kind of associations and they naturally lead to your complexes. But then, you see, I do not want to know the complexes of my patients. That is uninteresting to me. I want to know what the *dreams* have to say about complexes, not what the complexes are. I want to know what a man's unconscious is doing *with* his complexes, I want to know what he is preparing himself for. *That* is what I read out of the dreams. If I wanted to apply the method of free association I would not need dreams. I could put up a signboard, for instance "Footpath to So-and-so," and simply let people meditate on that and add free associations, and they would invariably arrive at their complexes. If you are riding in a Hungarian or Russian train and look at the strange signs in the strange language, you can associate all your complexes. You have only to let yourself go and you naturally drift into your complexes.

I do not apply the method of free association because my goal is not to know the complexes; I want to know what the dream is. Therefore I handle the dream as if it were a text which I do not understand properly, say a Latin òr a Greek or a Sanskrit text, where certain words are unknown to me or the text is fragmentary, and I merely apply the ordinary method any philologist would apply in reading such a text. My idea is that the dream does not conceal; we simply do not understand its language. For instance, if I quote to you a Latin or a Greek passage some of you will not understand it, but that is not because the text dissimulates or conceals; it is because you do not know Greek or Latin. Likewise, when a patient seems confused, it does not necessarily mean that he is confused, but that the doctor does not understand his material. The assumption that the dream wants to conceal is a mere anthropomorphic idea. No philologist would ever think that a difficult Sanskrit or cuneiform inscription conceals. There is a very wise word of the Talmud which says that the dream is its own interpretation. The dream is the whole thing, and if you think there is something behind it, or that the dream has concealed something, there is no question but that you simply do not understand it.

Therefore, first of all, when you handle a dream you say, "I do not understand a word of that dream." I always welcome that feeling of incompetence because then I know I shall put some good work into my attempt to understand the dream. What I do is this. I adopt the method of the philologist, which is far from being free association, and apply a logical principle which is called *amplification*. It is simply that of seeking the parallels. For instance, in the case of a very rare word which you have never come across before, you try to find parallel text passages, parallel applications perhaps, where that word also occurs, and then you try to put the formula you have established from the knowledge of other texts into the new text. If you make the new text a readable whole, you say, "Now we can read it." That is how we learned to read hieroglyphics and cuneiform inscriptions and that is how we can read dreams.

Now, how do I find the context? Here I simply follow the principle of the association experiment. Let us assume a man dreams about a simple sort of peasant's house. Now, do I know what a simple peasant's house conveys to that man's mind? Of course not; how could I? Do I know what a simple peasant's house means to him in general? Of course not. So I simply ask, "How does that thing appear to you?"—in other words, what is your context, what is the mental tissue in which that term "simple peasant's house" is embedded? He will tell you something quite astonishing. For instance, somebody says "water." Do I know what he means by "water"? Not at all. When I put that test word or a similar word to somebody, he will say "green." Another one will say "H_2O," which is something quite different. Another one will say "quicksilver," or "suicide." In each case I know what tissue that word or image is embedded in. That is *amplification*. It is a well-known logical procedure which we apply here and which formulates exactly the technique of finding the context.

Of course, I ought to mention here the merit of Freud, who brought up the whole question of dreams and who has enabled us to approach the problem of dreams at all. You know his idea is that a dream is a distorted representation of a secret incompatible wish which does not agree with the conscious attitude and therefore is censored, that is, distorted, in order to become unrecognizable to the conscious and yet in a way to show itself and live. Freud logically says then: Let us redress that whole distortion; now be natural, give up your distorted tendencies and let your associations flow freely, then we will come to your natural facts, namely, your complexes. This is an entirely different point of view from mine. Freud is seeking the complexes, I am not. That is just the difference. I am looking for what the *unconscious is doing* with the complexes, because that interests me very much more than the fact that people have complexes. We all have complexes; it is a highly banal and uninteresting fact. Even the incest complex which you can find anywhere if you look for it is terribly banal and therefore uninteresting. It is only interesting to know what people do with their complexes; that is the practical question which matters. Freud applies the method of free association and makes use of an entirely different logical principle, a principle which in logic is called *reductio in primam figuram,* reduction to the first figure. The *reductio in primam figuram* is a so-called syllogism, a complicated sequence of logical conclusions, whose characteristic is that you start from a perfectly reasonable statement, and, through surreptitious assumptions and insinuations, you gradually change the reasonable nature of your first simple or prime figure until you reach a complete distortion which is utterly unreasonable. That complete distortion, in Freud's idea, characterizes the dream; the dream is a clever distortion that disguises the original figure, and you have only to undo the web in order to return to the first reasonable statement, which may be "I wish to commit this or that; I have such-and-such an incompatible wish." We start, for instance, with a perfectly reasonable assumption, such as "No unreasonable being is free"—in other words, has free will. This is an example which is used in logic. It is a fairly reasonable statement. Now we come to the first fallacy, "Therefore, no free being is unreasonable." You cannot quite agree because there is already a trick. Then you continue, "All human beings are free"—they all have free will. Now you triumphantly finish up, "Therefore no human being is unreasonable." That is complete nonsense.

Let us assume that the dream is such an utterly nonsensical statement. This is perfectly plausible because obviously the dream is something like a nonsensical statement; otherwise you could understand it. As a rule you cannot understand it; you hardly ever come across dreams which are clear from beginning to end. The ordinary dream seems absolute nonsense and therefore one depreciates it. Even primitives, who make a great fuss about dreams, say that ordinary dreams mean nothing. But there are "big" dreams; medicine men and chiefs have big dreams, but ordinary men have no dreams. They talk exactly like people in Europe. Now you are confronted with that dream-nonsense, and you say, "This nonsense must be an insinuating distortion or fallacy which derives from an originally reasonable statement." You undo the whole thing and you apply the *reductio in primam figuram* and then you come to the initial undisturbed statement. So you see that the procedure of Freud's dream interpretation is perfectly logical, if you assume that the statement of the dream is really nonsensical.

But do not forget when you make the statement that a thing is unreasonable that perhaps you do not understand because you are not God; on the contrary, you are a fallible human being with a very limited mind. When an insane patient tells me something, I may think: "What that fellow is talking about is all nonsense." As a matter of fact, if I am scientific, I say "I do not understand," but if I am unscientific, I say "That fellow is just crazy and I am intelligent." this argumentation is the reason why men with somewhat unbalanced minds often like to become alienists. It is humanly understandable because it gives you a tremendous satisfaction, when you are not quite sure of yourself, to be able to say "Oh, the others are much worse."

But the question remains: Can we safely say that a dream is nonsense? Are we quite sure that we know? Are we sure that the dream is a distortion? Are you absolutely certain when you discover something quite against your expectation that it is a mere distortion? Nature commits no errors. Right and wrong are human categories. The natural process is just what it is and nothing else—it is not nonsense and it is not unreasonable. We do not understand: that is the fact. Since I am not God and since I am a man of very limited intellectual capacities, I had better assume that I do not understand dreams. With that assumption I reject the prejudiced view that the dream is a distortion, and I say that if I do not understand a dream, it is my mind which is distorted, I am not taking the right view of it.

So I adopted the method which philologists apply to difficult texts, and I handle dreams in the same way. It is, of course, a bit more circumstantial and more difficult; but I can assure you that the results are far more interesting when you arrive at things that are human than when you apply a most dreadful monotonous interpretation. I hate to be bored. Above all we should avoid speculations and theories when we have to deal with such mysterious processes as dreams. We should never forget that for thousands of years very intelligent men of great knowledge and vast experience held very different views about them. It is only quite recently that we invented the theory that a dream is nothing. All other civilizations have had very different ideas about dreams.

Now I will tell you the big dream of my patient:

"I am in the country, in a simple peasant's house, with an elderly, motherly peasant woman. I talk to her about a great journey I am planning: I am going to walk from Switzerland to Leipzig. She is enormously impressed, at which I am very pleased. At this moment I look through the window at a meadow where there are peasants gathering hay. Then the scene changes. In the backgound appears a monstrously big crab-lizard. It moves first to the left and then to the right so that I find myself standing in the angle between them as if in an open pair of scissors. Then I have a little rod or a wand in my hand and I lightly touch the monster's head with the rod and kill it. Then for a long time I stand there contemplating that monster."

Before I go into such a dream I always try to establish a sequence, because this dream has a history before and will have a history afterwards. It is part of the psychic tissue that is continuous, for we have no reason to assume that there is no continuity in the psychological processes, just as we have no reason to think that there is any gap in the processes of nature. Nature is a continuum, and so our psyche is very probably a continuum. This dream is just one flash or one observation of psychic continuity that became visible for a moment. As a continuity it is connected with the preceding dreams. In the previous dream we have already seen that peculiar snakelike movement of the train. This comparison is merely a hypothesis, but I have to establish such connections.

After the train dream the dreamer is back in the surroundings of his early childhood; he is with a motherly peasant woman—a slight allusion to the mother, as you notice. In the very first dream, he impresses the village boys by his magnificent appearance in the long coat of the Herr Professor. In this present dream too he impresses the harmless woman with his greatness and the greatness of his ambitious plan to walk to Leipzig—an allusion to his hope of getting a chair there. The monster crab-lizard is outside our empirical experience; it is obviously a creation of the unconscious. So much we can see without any particular effort.

Now we come to the actual context. I ask him, "What are your associations to 'simple peasant's house'?" and to my enormous astonishment, he says "It is the lazar house of St. Jacob near Basel." This house was a very old leprosery, and the building still exists. The place is also famous for a big battle fought there in 1444 by the Swiss against the troops of the Duke of Burgundy. His army tried to break into Switzerland but was beaten back by the avant-garde of the Swiss army, a body of 1,300 men who fought the Burgundian army consisting of 30,000 men at the lazar house of St. Jacob. The 1,300 Swiss fell to the very last man, but by their sacrifice they stopped the further advance of the enemy. The heroic death of these 1,300 men is a notable incident in Swiss history, and no Swiss is able to talk of it without patriotic feeling.

Whenever the dreamer brings such a piece of information, you have to put it into the context of the dream. In this case it means that the dreamer is in a leprosery. The lazar house is called "Siechenhaus," sick house, in German, the "sick" meaning the lepers. So he has, as it were, a revolting contagious disease; he is an outcast from human society, he is in the sick house. And that sick house is characterized, moreover, by that desperate fight which was a catastrophe for the 1,300 men and which was brought about by the fact that they did not obey orders. The avant-garde had strict instructions not to attack but to wait until the whole Swiss army had joined up with them. But as soon as they saw the enemy they could not hold back and, against the commands of their leaders, made a headlong rush and attacked, and of course they were all killed. Here again we come to the idea of this rushing ahead without establishing a connection with the bulk of the tail end, and again the action is fatal. This gave me a rather uncanny feeling, and I thought, "Now what is the fellow after, what danger is he coming to?" The danger is not just his ambition, or that he wishes to be with the mother and commit incest, or something of the kind. You remember, the engine driver is a foolish fellow too; he runs ahead in spite of the fact that the tail end of the train is not yet out of the curve; he does not wait for it, but rushes along without thinking of the whole. That means that the dreamer has the tendency to rush ahead, not thinking of his tail; he behaves as if he were his head only, just as the avant-garde behaved as if it were the whole army, forgetting that it had to wait; and because it did not wait, every man was killed. This attitude of the patient is the reason for his symptoms of mountain sickness. He went too high, he is not prepared for the altitude, he forgets where he started from.

You know perhaps the novel by Paul Bourget, *L'Étape*. Its motif is the problem that a man's low origin always clings to him, and therefore there are very definite limitations to his climbing the social ladder. That is what the dream tries to remind the patient of. That house and that elderly peasant woman bring him back to his childhood. It looks, then, as if the woman might refer to the mother. But one must be careful with assumptions. His answer to my question about the woman was "That is my landlady." His landlady is an elderly widow, uneducated and old-fashioned, living naturally in a milieu inferior to his. He is too high up, and he forgets that the next part of his invisible self is the family in himself. Because he is a very intellectual man, feeling is his inferior function. His feeling is not at all differentiated, and therefore it is still in the form of the landlady, and in trying to impose upon that landlady he tries to impose upon himself with his enormous play to walk to Leipzig.

Now what does he say about the trip to Leipzig? He says, "Oh, that is my ambition, I want to go far, I wish to get a Chair." Here is the headlong rush, here is the foolish attempt, here is the mountain sickness; he wants to climb too high. This dream was before the war, and at that time to be a professor in Leipzig was something marvelous. His feeling was deeply repressed; therefore it does not have right values and is much too naive. It is still the peasant woman; it is still identical with his own mother. There are many capable and intelligent men who have no differentiation of feeling, and therefore their feeling is still contaminated with the mother, is still in the mother, identical with the mother, and they have mothers' feelings; they have wonderful feelings for babies, for the interiors of houses and nice rooms and for a very orderly home. It sometimes happens that these individuals, when they have turned forty, discover a masculine feeling, and there is trouble.

The feelings of a man are so to speak a woman's and appear as such in dreams. I designate this figure by the term *anima*, because she is the personification of the inferior functions which relate a man to the collective unconscious. The collective unconscious as a whole presents itself to a man in feminine form. To a woman it appears in masculine form, and then I call it the *animus*. I chose the term anima because it has always been used for that very same psychological fact. The anima as a personification of the collective unconscious occurs in dreams over and over again. I have made long statistics about the anima figure in dreams. In this way one establishes these figures empirically.

When I ask my dreamer what he means when he says that the peasant woman is impressed by his plan, he answers, "Oh, well, that refers to my boasting. I like to boast before an inferior person to show who I am; when I am talking to uneducated people I like to put myself very much in the foreground. Unfortunately I always have to live in an inferior milieu."When a man resents the inferiority of his milieu and feels that he is too good for his surroundings, it is because the inferiority of the milieu *in himself* is projected into the outer milieu and therefore he begins to mind those things which he should mind in himself. When he says, "I mind my inferior milieu," he ought to say, "I mind the fact that my own inner milieu is below the mark." He has no right values, he is inferior in his feeling life. That is his problem.

At this moment he looks out of the window and sees the peasants gathering hay. That, of course, again is a vision of something he has done in the past. It brings back to him memories of similar pictures and situations; it was in summer and it was pretty hard to get up early in the morning to turn the hay during the day and gather it in the evening. Of course, it is the simple honest work of such folk. He forgets that only the decent simple work gets him somewhere and not a big mouth. He also asserts which I must mention, that in his present home he has a picture on the wall of peasants gathering hay, and he says, "Oh, that is the origin of the picture in my dream." It is as though he said, "The dream is nothing but a picture on the wall, it has no importance, I will pay no attention to it." At that moment the scene changes. When the scene changes you can always safely conclude that a representation of an unconscious thought has come to a climax, and it becomes impossible to continue that motif.

Now in the next part of the dream things are getting dark; the crab-lizard appears, apparently an enormous thing. I asked, "What about the crab, how on earth do you come to that?" He said, "That is a mythological monster which walks backwards. The crab walks backwards. I do not understand how I get to this thing—probably through some fairytale or something of that sort." What he had mentioned before were all things which you could meet with in real life, things which do actually exist. But the crab is not a personal experience, it is an archetype. When an analyst has to deal with an archetype he may begin to think. In dealing with the *personal* unconscious you are not allowed to think too much and to add anything to the associations of the patient. Can you add something to the personality of somebody else? You are a personality yourself. The other individual has a life of his own and a mind of his own inasmuch as he is a person. But inasmuch as he is not a person, inasmuch as he is also myself, he has the same basic structure of mind, and there I can begin to think, I can associate for him. I can even provide him with the necessary context because he will have none, he does not know where that crab-lizard comes from and has no idea what it means, but I know and can provide the material for him.

I point out to him that the hero motif appears throughout the dreams. He has a hero fantasy about himself which comes to the surface in the last dream. He is the hero as the great man with the long coat and with the great plan; he is the hero who dies on the field of honour at St. Jacob; he is going to show the world who he is; and he is quite obviously the hero who overcomes the monster. The hero motif is invariably accompanied by the dragon motif; the dragon and the hero who fights him are two figures of the same myth.

The dragon appears in his dream as the crab-lizard. This statement does not, of course, explain what the dragon represents as an image of his psychological situation. So the next associations are directed round the monster. When it moves first to the left and then to the right the dreamer has the feeling that he is standing in an angle which could shut on him like open scissors. That would be fatal. He has read Freud, and accordingly he interprets the situation as an incest wish, the monster being the mother, the angle of the open scissors the legs of the mother, and he himself, standing in between, just born or just going back into the mother.

Strangely enough, in mythology, the dragon *is* the mother. You meet that motif all over the world, and the monster is called the mother dragon. The mother dragon eats the child again, she sucks him in after having given birth to him. The "terrible mother," as she is also called, is waiting with wide open mouth on the Western Seas, and when a man approaches that mouth it closes on him and he is finished. That monstrous figure is the mother sarcophaga, the flesh eater; it is, in another form, Matuta, the mother of the dead. It is the goddess of death.

But these parallels still do not explain why the dream chooses the particular image of the crab. I hold—and when I say I hold I have certain reasons for saying so—that representations of psychic facts in images like the snake or the lizard or the crab or the mastodon or analogous animals also represent organic facts. For instance, the serpent very often represents the cerebrospinal system, especially the lower centers of the brain, and particularly the medulla oblongata and spinal cord. The crab, on the other hand, having a sympathetic system only, represents chiefly the sympathicus and parasympathicus of the abdomen; it is an abdominal thing. So if you translate the text of the dream it would read: if you go on like this your cerebrospinal system and your sympathetic system will come up against you and snap you up. That is in fact what is happening. The symptoms of his neurosis express the rebellion of the sympathetic functions and of the cerebro-spinal system against his conscious attitude.

The crab-lizard brings up the archetypical idea of the hero and the dragon as deadly enemies. But in certain myths you find the interesting fact that the hero is not connected with the dragon only by his fight. There are, on the contrary, indications that the hero is himself the dragon. In Scandinavian mythology the hero is recognized by the fact that he has snake's eyes because he is a snake. There are many other myths and legends which contain the same idea. Cecrops, the founder of Athens, was a man above and a serpent below. The souls of heroes often appear after death in the form of serpents.

Now in our dream the monstrous crab-lizard moves first to the left, and I ask him about this left side. He says, "The crab apparently does not know the way. Left is the unfavourable side, left is sinister." Sinister does indeed mean left and unfavorable. But the right side is also not good for the monster, because when it goes to the right it is touched by the wand and is killed. Now we come to his standing in between the angle of the monster's movement, a situation which at first glance he interpreted as incest. He says, "As a matter of fact, I felt surrounded on either side like a hero who is going to fight a dragon." So he himself realizes the hero motif.

But unlike the mythical hero he does not fight the dragon with a weapon, but with a wand. He says, "From its effect on the monster it seems that it is a magical wand." He certainly does dispose of the crab in a magical way. The wand is another mythological symbol. It often contains a sexual allusion, and sexual magic is a means of protection against danger. You may remember, too, how during the earthquake at Messina[2] nature produced certain instinctive reactions against the overwhelming destruction.

The wand is an instrument, and instruments in dreams mean what they actually are, the devices of man to concretize his will. For instance, a knife is my will to cut; when I use a spear I prolong my arm, with a rifle I can project my action and my influence to a great distance; with a telescope I do the same as regards my sight. An instrument is a mechanism which represents my will, my intelligence, my capability, and my cunning. Instruments in dreams symbolize an analogous psychological mechanism. Now this dreamer's instrument is a magic wand. He uses a marvelous thing by which he can spirit away the monster, that is, his lower nervous system. He can dispose of such nonsense in no time, and with no effort at all.

What does this actually mean? It means that he simply thinks that the danger does not exist. That is what is usually done. You simply think that a thing is not and then it is no more. That is how people behave who consist of the head only. They use their intellect in order to think things away; they reason them away. They say, "This is nonsense, therefore it cannot be and therefore it is not." That is what he also does. He simply reasons the monster away. He says, "There is no such thing as a crab-lizard, there is no such thing as an opposing will; I get rid of it, I simply think it away. I think it is the mother with whom I want to commit incest, and that settles the whole thing, for I shall not do it." I said, "You have killed the animal—what do you think is the reason why you contemplate the animal for such a long time?" He said, "Oh, well, yes, naturally it is marvelous how you can dispose of such a creature with such ease." I said, "Yes, indeed it is very marvelous!"

Then I told him what I thought of the situation. I said, "Look here, the best way to deal with a dream is to think of yourself as a sort of ignorant child or ignorant youth, and to come to a two-million-year-old man or to the old mother of days and ask, 'Now, what do you think of me?' She would say to you, 'You have an ambitious plan, and that is foolish, because you run up against your own instincts. Your own restricted capabilities block the way. You want to abolish the obstacle by the magic of your thinking. You believe you can think it away by the artifices of your intellect, but it will be, believe me, matter for some after-thought'." And I also told him this: "Your dreams contain a warning. You behave exactly like the engine driver or like the Swiss who were foolhardy enough to run up against the enemy without any support behind them, and if you behave in the same way you will meet with a catastrophe."

He was sure that such a point of view was much too serious. He was convinced that it is much more probable that dreams come from incompatible wishes and that he really had an unrealized incestuous wish which was at the bottom of this dream; that he was conscious now of this incestuous wish and had got rid of it and now could go to Leipzig. I said, "Well then, bon voyage." He did not return, he went on with his plans, and it took him just about three months to lose his position and go to the dogs. That was the end of him. He ran up against the fatal danger of that crab-lizard and would not understand the warning. But I do not want to make you too pessimistic. Sometimes there are people who really understand their dreams and draw conclusions which lead to a more favourable solution of their problems.

Notes

1 The reference is to Wilhelm Wundt, of Leipzig (1832–1920).
2 The reference is to the disaster of 1908, when 90 percent of the Sicilian city was destroyed, with a loss of 60,000 lives.

Case 5

Editors' Introduction

Carl Rogers is *sui generis* in the field of counseling and psychotherapy as well as in personality theory. In doing *Current Personality Theories,* the junior editor of this book surveyed the number of references and the amount of space given to all theorists, and Rogers came in second after Sigmund Freud, just before Alfred Adler.

Rogers is that rare combination of a sensitive therapist, a master teacher, and a superb hard-nosed researcher. He is also a gifted writer, and for those who know him, a wonderful friend.

This version of "The Case of Mrs. Oak" is, unfortunately, the shorter of two, but space limitations precluded the longer and more detailed selection which can be found in Rogers' and Dymond's book *Psychotherapy and Personality Change* (1954).

This selection should be read closely and slowly, since the reader will be experiencing a complex analysis of an analysis. In a way it is similar to the Ard/Ellis selection which follows, but with Rogers examining himself as well as dealing with patient material.

CARL R. ROGERS

The Case of Mrs. Oak

One aspect of the process of therapy which is evident in all cases, might be termed the awareness of experience, or even "the experiencing of experience." I have here labeled it as the experiencing of the self, though this also falls short of being an accurate term. In the security of the relationship with a client-centered therapist, in the absence of any actual or implied threat to self, the client can let himself examine various aspects of his experience as they actually feel to him, as they are apprehended through his sensory and visceral equipment, without distorting them to fit the existing concept of self. Many of these prove to be in extreme contradiction to the concept of self, and could not ordinarily be experienced in their fullness, but in this safe relationship they can be permitted to seep through into awareness without distortion. Thus they often follow the schematic pattern, "I am thus and so, but I experience this feeling which is very inconsistent with what I am"; "I love my parents, but I experience some surprising bitterness toward them at times"; "I am really no good, but sometimes I seem to feel that I'm better than everyone else." Thus at first the expression is that "I am a self which is different from a part of my experience." Later this changes to the tentative pattern, "Perhaps I am several quite different selves, or perhaps my self contains more contradictions than I had dreamed." Still later the pattern changes to some such pattern as this: "I was sure that I could not be my experience—it was too contradictory—but now I am beginning to believe that I can be *all* of my experience."

Perhaps something of the nature of this aspect of therapy may be conveyed from two excerpts from the case of Mrs. Oak. Mrs. Oak was a housewife in her late thirties, who was having difficulties in marital and family relationships when she came in for therapy. Unlike many clients, she had a keen and spontaneous interest in the processes which she felt going on within herself, and her recorded interviews contain much material, from her own frame of reference, as to her perception of what is occurring. She thus tends to put into words what seems to be implicit, but unverbalized, in many clients. For this reason, most of the excerpts in this chapter will be taken from this one case.

From an early portion of the fifth interview comes material which describes the awareness of experience which we have been discussing.

> CLIENT: It all comes pretty vague. But you know I keep, keep having the thought occur to me that this whole process for me is kind of like examining pieces of a jigsaw puzzle. It seems to me I, I'm in the process now of examining the individual pieces which really don't have too much meaning. Probably handling them, now even beginning to think of a pattern. That keeps coming to me. And it's interesting to me because I, I really don't like jigsaw puzzles. They've always irritated me. But that's my feeling. And I mean I pick up little pieces *(She gestures throughout this conversation to illustrate her statements.)* with absolutely no meaning except I mean the, the feeling that you get from simply handling them without seeing them as a pattern, but just from the touch, I probably feel, well it is going to fit someplace here.
>
> THERAPIST: And that at the moment that, that's the process, just getting the feel and the shape and the configuration of the different pieces with a little bit of background feeling of, yeah they'll probably fit somewhere, but most of the attention's focused right on, "What does this feel like? And what's its texture?"
>
> C: That's right. There's almost something physical in it. A, a—
>
> T: You can't quite describe it without using your hands. A real, almost a sensuous sense in—
>
> C: That's right. Again it's, it's a feeling of being very objective, and yet I've never been quite so close to myself.
>
> T: Almost at one and the same time standing off and looking at yourself and yet somehow being closer to yourself that way than—
>
> C: M-hm. And yet for the first time in months I am not thinking about my problems. I'm not actually, I'm not working on them.
>
> T: I get the impression you don't sort of sit down to work on "my problems." It isn't that feeling at all.
>
> C: That's right. That's right. I suppose what I, I mean actually is that I'm not sitting down to put this puzzle together as, as something, I've got to see the picture. It, it may be that, it may be that I am actually enjoying this feeling process. Or I'm certainly learning something.
>
> T: At least there's a sense of the immediate goal of getting that feel as being the thing, not that you're doing this in order to see a picture, but that it's a, a satisfaction of really getting acquainted with each piece. Is that—
>
> C: That's it. That's it. And it still becomes that sort of sensuousness, that touching. It's quite interesting. Sometimes not entirely pleasant, I'm sure, but—
>
> T: A rather different sort of experience.
>
> C: Yes. Quite.

This excerpt indicates very clearly the letting of material come into awareness, without any attempt to own it as part of the self, or to relate it to other material held in consciousness. It is, to put it as accurately as possible, an awareness of a wide range of experiences, with, at the moment, no thought of their relation to self. Later it may be recognized that what was being experienced may all become a part of self. Thus the heading of this section has been termed "The Experiencing of the Potential Self."

The fact that this is a new and unusual form of experience is expressed in a verbally confused but emotionally clear portion of the sixth interview.

C: Uh, I caught myself thinking that during these sessions, uh, I've been sort of singing a song. Now that sounds vague and uh—not actually singing—sort of a song without any music. Probably a kind of poem coming out. And I like the idea, I mean it's just sort of come to me without anything built out of, of anything. And in— following that, it came, it came this other kind of feeling. Well, I found myself sort of asking myself, is that the shape that cases take? Is it possible that I am just verbalizing and, at times kind of become intoxicated with my own verbalizations? And then uh, following this, came, well, am I just taking up your time? And then a doubt, a doubt. Then something else occurred to me. Uh, from whence it came, I don't know, no actual logical kind of sequence to the thinking. The thought struck me: We're doing bits, uh, we're not overwhelmed or doubtful, or show concern or, or any great interest when, when blind people learn to read with their fingers, Braille. I don't know—it may be just sort of, it's all mixed up. It may be that's something that I'm experiencing now.

T: Let's see if I can get some of that, that sequence of feelings. First, sort of as though you're, and I gather that first one is a fairly positive feeling, as though maybe you're kind of creating a poem here—a song without music somehow but something that might be quite creative, and then the, the feeling of a lot of skepticism about that. "Maybe I'm just saying words, just being carried off by words that I, that I speak, and maybe it's all a lot of baloney, really." And then a feeling that perhaps you're almost learning a new type of experiencing which would be just as radically new as for a blind person to try to make sense out of what he feels with his fingertips.

C: M-hm. M-hm. *(Pause)* . . . And I sometimes think to myself, well, maybe we could go into this particular incident or that particular incident. And then somehow when I come here, there is, that doesn't hold true, it's, it seems false. And then there just seems to be this flow of words which somehow aren't forced and then occasionally this doubt creeps in. Well, it sort of takes form of a, maybe you're just making music . . . Perhaps that's why I'm doubtful today of, of this whole thing, because it's something that's not forced. And really I'm feeling that what I should do is, is sort of systematize the thing. Oughta work harder and—

T: Sort of a deep questioning as to what am I doing with a self that isn't, isn't pushing to get things *done, solved? (Pause)*

C: And yet the fact that I, I really like this other kind of thing, this, I don't know, call it a poignant feeling, I mean—I felt things that I never felt before. I *like* that, too. Maybe that's the way to do it. I just don't know today.

Here is the shift which seems almost invariably to occur in therapy which has any depth. It may be represented schematically as the client's feeling that "I came here to solve problems, and now I find myself just experiencing myself." And as with this client this shift is usually accompanied by the intellectual formulation that it is wrong, and by an emotional appreciation of the fact that it "feels good."

We may conclude this section saying that one of the fundamental directions taken by the process of therapy is the free experiencing of the actual sensory and visceral reactions of the organism without too much of an attempt to relate these experiences to the self. This is usually accompanied by the conviction that this material does not belong to, and cannot be organized into, the self. The end point of this process is that the client discovers that he can *be* his experience, with all of its variety and surface contradiction; that he can formulate himself out of his experience, instead of trying to impose a formulation of self upon his experience, denying to awareness those elements which do not fit.

The Full Experiencing of an Affectional Relationship

One of the elements in therapy of which we have more recently become aware is the extent to which therapy is a learning, on the part of the client, to accept fully and freely and without fear the positive feelings of another. This is not a phenomenon which clearly occurs in every case. It seems particularly true of our longer cases, but does not occur uniformly in these. Yet it is such a deep experience that we have begun to question whether it is not a highly significant direction in the therapeutic process, perhaps occurring at an unverbalized level to some degree in all successful cases. Before discussing this phenomenon, let us give it some body by citing the experience of Mrs. Oak. The experience struck her rather suddenly, between the twenty-ninth and thirtieth interview, and she spends most of the latter interview discussing it. She opens the thirtieth hour in his way.

C: Well, I made a very remarkable discovery. I know it's—*(laughs)* I found out that you actually *care* how this thing goes. *(Both laugh.)* It gave me the feeling, it's sort of well—"maybe I'll let you get in the act," sort of thing. It's—again you see, on an examination sheet, I would have had the correct answer, I mean—but it suddenly dawned on me that in the—client-counselor kind of thing, you *actually care* what happens to this thing. And it was a revelation, a—not that. That doesn't describe it. It was a—well, the closest I can come to it is a kind of relaxation, a—not a letting down, but a—*(pause)* more of a straightening out without tension if that means anything. I don't know.

T: Sounds as though it isn't as though this was a new idea, but it was a new *experience* of really *feeling* that I did care and if I get the rest of that, sort of a willingness on your part to let me care.

C: Yes.

This letting the counselor and his warm interest into her life was undoubtedly one of the deepest features of therapy in this case. In an interview following the conclusion of therapy she spontaneously mentions this experience as being the outstanding one. What does it mean?

The phenomenon is most certainly not one of transference and counter-transference. Some experienced psychologists who had undergone psychoanalysis had the opportunity of observing the development of the relationship in another case than the one cited. They were the first to object to the use of the terms transference and countertransference to describe the phenomenon. The gist of their remarks was that this is something which is mutual and appropriate, where transference or countertransference are phenomena which are characteristically one-way and inappropriate to the realities of the situation.

Certainly one reason why this phenomenon is occurring more frequently in our experience is that as therapists we have become less afraid of our positive (or negative) feelings toward the client. As therapy goes on the therapist's feeling of acceptance and respect for the client tends to change to something approaching awe as he sees the valiant and deep struggle of the person to be himself. There is, I think, within the therapist, a profound experience of the underlying commonality—should we say brotherhood—of man. As a result he feels toward the client a warm, positive, affectional reaction. This poses a problem for the client who often, as in this case, finds it difficult to accept the positive feeling of another. Yet once accepted the inevitable reaction on the part of the client is to relax, to let the warmth of liking by another person reduce the tension and fear involved in facing life.

But we are getting ahead of our client. Let us examine some of the other aspects of this experience as it occurred to her. In earlier interviews she had talked of the fact that she did *not* love humanity, and that in some vague and stubborn way she felt she was right, even though others would regard her as wrong. She mentions this again as she discusses the way this experience has clarified her attitudes toward others.

C: The next thing that occurred to me that I found myself thinking and still thinking, is somehow—and I'm not clear why—the same kind of a caring that I get when I say "I don't love humanity." Which has always sort of—I mean I was always convinced of it. So I mean, it doesn't—I knew that it was a good thing, see. And I think I clarified it within myself—what it has to do with this situation, I don't know. But I found out, no, I don't love, but I do *care* terribly.

T: M-hm. M-hm. I see . . .

C: . . . It might be expressed better in saying I care terribly what happens. But the caring is a—takes form—its structure is in understanding and not wanting to be taken in, or to contribute to those things which I feel are false and—It seems to me that in—in loving, there's a kind of *final* factor. If you do that, you've sort of done *enough.* It's a—

T: That's *it,* sort of.

C: Yeah. It seems to me this other thing, this caring, which isn't a good term—I mean, probably we need something else to describe this kind of thing. To say it's an impersonal thing doesn't mean anything because it isn't impersonal. I mean I feel it's very much a part of a whole. But it's something that somehow doesn't stop . . . It seems to me you could have this feeling of loving humanity, loving people, and at the same time—go on contributing to the factors that make people neurotic, make them ill—where, what I feel is a resistance to those things.

T: You care enough to want to understand and to want to avoid contributing to anything that would make for more neuroticism, or more of that aspect in human life.

C: Yes. And it's—(pause). Yes, it's something along those lines. . . . Well, again, I have to go back to how I feel about this other thing. It's—I'm not really called upon to give of myself in a—sort of on the auction block. There's nothing final . . . It sometimes bothered me when I—I would have to say to myself, "I don't love humanity," and yet, I always knew that there was something positive. That I was probably right. And—I may be all off the beam now, but it seems to me that, that is somehow tied up in the—this feeling that I—I have now, into how the therapeutic value can carry through. Now, I couldn't tie it up, I couldn't tie it in, but it's as close as I can come to explaining to myself, my—well, shall I say the learning process, the follow through on my realization that—yes, you *do care* in a given situation. It's just that simple. And I hadn't been aware of it before. I might have closed this door and walked out, and in discussing therapy, said, yes, the counselor must feel thus and so, but, I mean, I hadn't had the dynamic experience.

In this portion, though she is struggling to describe her own feeling, it would seem that what she is saying would be characteristic of the therapist's attitude toward the client as well. His attitude, at its best, is devoid of the *quid pro quo* aspect of most of the experiences we call love. It is the simple outgoing human feeling of one individual for another, a feeling, it seems to me, which is even more basic than sexual or parental feeling. It is a caring enough about the person that you do not wish to interfere with his development, nor to use him for any self-aggrandizing goals of your own. Your satisfaction comes in having set him free to grow in his own fashion.

Our client goes on to discuss how hard it has been for her in the past to accept any help or positive feeling from others, and how this attitude is changing.

C: I have a feeling . . . that you have to do it pretty much yourself, but that somehow you ought to be able to do that with other people. (She mentions that there have been "countless" times when she might have accepted personal warmth and kindliness from others.) I get the feeling that I just was afraid I would be devastated. (She returns to talking about the counseling itself and her feeling toward it.) I mean there's been this tearing through the thing myself. Almost to—I mean, I felt it—I mean I tried to verbalize it on occasion—a kind of—at times almost not wanting you to restate, not wanting you to reflect, the thing is *mine*. Course all right, I can say it's resistance. But that doesn't mean a damn thing to me now . . . The—I think in—in relationship to this particular thing, I mean, the—probably at times, the strongest feeling was, it's mine, it's *mine*. I've got to cut it down myself. See?

T: It's an experience that's awfully hard to put down accurately into words, and yet I get a sense of difference here in this relationship, that form the feeling that "this is mine," "I've got to do it," "I am doing it," and so on, to a somewhat different feeling that—"I could let you in."

C: Yeah. Now. I mean, that's—that it's—well, it's sort of, shall we say, volume two. It's—it's a—well, sort of, well, I'm still in the thing alone, but I'm *not*—see—I'm—

T: M-hm. Yes, that paradox sort of sums it up, doesn't it?

C: Yeah.

T: In all of this, there is a feeling, it's still—every aspect of my experience is mine and that's kind of inevitable and necessary and so on. And yet that isn't the whole picture either. Somehow it can be shared or another's interest can come in and in some ways it is new.

C: Yeah. And it's—it's as though, that's how it should be. I mean, that's how it —has to be. There's a—there's a feeling, "and this is good." I mean, it expresses, it clarifies it for me. There's a feeling—in this caring, as though—you were sort of standing back—standing off, and if I want to sort of cut through to the thing, it's a—a slashing of—oh, tall weeds, that I can do it, and you can—I mean you're not going to be disturbed by having to walk through it, too. I don't know. And it doesn't make sense. I mean—

T: Except there's a very real sense of rightness about this feeling that you have, hm?

C: M-hm.

May it not be that this excerpt portrays the heart of the process of socialization? To discover that it is *not* devastating to accept the positive feeling from another, that it does not necessarily end in hurt, that it actually "feels good" to have another person with you in your struggles to meet life—this may be one of the most profound learnings encountered by the individual whether in therapy or not.

Something of the newness, the nonverbal level of this experience is described by Mrs. Oak in the closing moments of this thirtieth interview.

C: I'm experiencing a new type, a—probably the only worthwhile kind of learning, a—I know I've—I've often said what I know doesn't help me here. What I meant is, my acquired knowledge doesn't help me. But it seems to me that the learning process here has been—so dynamic, I mean, so much a part of the—of everything, I mean, of me, that if I just get that out of it, it's something, which, I mean—I'm wondering if I'll ever be able to straighten out into a sort of acquired knowledge what I have experienced here.

T: In other words, the kind of learning that has gone on here has been something of quite a different sort and quite a different depth; very vital, very real. And quite worthwhile to you in and of itself, but the question you're asking is: Will I ever have a clear intellectual picture of what has gone on at this somehow deeper kind of learning level?

C: M-hm. Something like that.

Those who would apply to therapy the so-called laws of learning derived from the memorization of nonsense syllables would do well to study this excerpt with care. Learning as it takes place in therapy is a total, organismic, frequently nonverbal type of thing which may or may not follow the same principles as the intellectual learning of trivial material which has little relevance to the self. This, however, is a digression.

Let us conclude this section by rephrasing its essence. It appears possible that one of the characteristics of deep or significant therapy is that the client discovers that it is not devastating to admit fully into his own experience the positive feeling which another, the therapist, holds toward him. Perhaps one of the reasons why this is so difficult is that essentially it involves the feeling that "I am worthy of being liked." This we shall consider in the following section. For the present it may be pointed out this aspect of therapy is a free and full experiencing of an affectional relationship which may be put in generalized terms as follows: "I can permit someone to care about me, and can fully accept that caring within myself. This permits me to recognize that I care, and care deeply, for and about others."

The Liking of One's Self

In various writings and researches that have been published regarding client-centered therapy there has been a stress upon the acceptance of self as one of the directions and outcomes of therapy. We have established the fact that in successful psychotherapy negative attitudes toward the self decrease and positive attitudes increase. We have measured the gradual increase in self-acceptance and have studied the correlated increase in acceptance of others. But as I examine these statements and compare them with our more recent cases, I feel they fall short of the truth. The client not only accepts himself—a phrase which may carry the connotation of a grudging and reluctant acceptance of the inevitable—he actually comes to *like* himself. This is not a bragging or self-assertive liking; it is rather a quiet pleasure in being one's self.

Mrs. Oak illustrates this trend rather nicely in her thirty-third interview. Is it significant that this follows by ten days the interview where she could for the first time admit to herself that the therapist cared? Whatever our speculations on this point, this fragment indicates very well the quiet joy in being one's self, together with the apologetic attitude which, in our culture, one feels it necessary to take toward such an experience. In the last few minutes of the interview, knowing her time is nearly up she says:

C: One thing worries me—and I'll hurry because I can always go back to it—a feeling that occasionally I can't turn out. Feeling of being quite pleased with myself. Again the Q technique.[1] I walked out of here one time, and impulsively I threw my first card, "I am an attractive personality"; looked at it sort of aghast but left it there, I mean, because honestly, I mean, that is exactly how it felt—a—well, that bothered me and I catch that now. Every once in a while a sort of pleased feeling, nothing superior, but just—I don't know, sort of pleased. A neatly turned way. And it bothered me. And yet—I wonder—I rarely remember things I say here, I mean I wondered why it was that I was convinced, and something about what I've felt about being hurt that I suspected in—my feelings when I would hear someone say to a child, "Don't cry." I mean, I always felt, but it isn't right; I mean, if he's hurt, let him cry. Well, then, now this pleased feeling that I have. I've recently come to feel, it's—there's something almost the same there. It's—We don't object when *children* feel pleased with themselves. It's—I mean, there really isn't anything vain. It's—maybe that's how people *should* feel.

T: You've been inclined almost to look askance at yourself for this feeling, and yet as you think about it more, maybe it comes close to the two sides of the picture, that if a child wants to cry, why shouldn't he cry? And if he wants to feel pleased with himself, doesn't he have a perfect right to feel pleased with himself? And that sort of ties in with this, what I would see as an appreciation of yourself that you've experienced every now and again.

C: Yes. Yes.

T: "I'm really a pretty rich and interesting person."

C: Something like that. And then I say to myself, "Our society pushes us around and we've lost it." And I keep going back to my feelings about children. Well, maybe they're richer than we are. Maybe we—it's something we've lost in the process of growing up.

T: Could be that they have a wisdom about that that we've lost.

C: That's right. My time's up.

Here she arrives, as do so many other clients, at the tentative, slightly apologetic realization that she has come to like, enjoy, appreciate herself. One gets the feeling of a spontaneous relaxed enjoyment, a primitive *joie de vivre*, perhaps analogous to the lamb frisking about the meadow or the porpoise gracefully leaping in and out of the waves. Mrs. Oak feels that it is something native to the organism, to the infant, something we have lost in the warping process of development.

Earlier in this case one sees something of a forerunner of this feeling, an incident which perhaps makes more clear its fundamental nature. In the ninth interview Mrs. Oak in a somewhat embarrassed fashion reveals something she has always kept to herself. That she brought it forth at some cost is indicated by the fact that it was preceded by a very long pause, of several minutes duration. Then she spoke.

C: You know this is kind of goofy, but I've never told anyone this *(nervous laugh)* and it'll probably do me good. For years, oh, probably from early youth, from seventeen probably on, I, I have had what I have come to call to myself, told myself were "flashes of sanity." I've never told anyone this *(another embarrassed laugh)*, wherein, in, really I feel sane. And, and pretty much aware of life. And always with a terrific kind of concern and sadness of how far away, how far astray that we have actually gone. It's just a feeling once in a while of finding myself a whole kind of person in a terribly chaotic kind of world.

T: It's been fleeting and it's been infrequent, but there have been times when it seems the whole you is functioning and feeling in the world, a very chaotic world to be sure—

C: That's right. And I mean, and knowing actually how far astray we, we've gone from, from being whole healthy people. And of course, one doesn't talk in those terms.

T: A feeling that it wouldn't be *safe* to talk about the singing you[2]—

C: Where does that person live?

T: Almost as if there was no place for such a person to, to exist.

C: Of course, you know, that, that makes me—now wait a minute—that probably explains why I'm primarily concerned with feelings here. That's probably it.

T: Because that whole you does exist with all your feelings. Is that it, you're more aware of feelings?

C: That's right. It's not, it doesn't reject feelings and—that's *it*.

T: That whole you somehow lives feelings instead of somehow pushing them to one side.

C: That's right. *(Pause)* I suppose from the practical point of view it could be said that what I ought to be doing is solving some problems, day-to-day problems. And yet, I, I—what I'm trying to do is solve, solve something else that's a great, that is a great deal more important than little day-to-day problems. Maybe that sums up the whole thing.

T: I wonder if this will distort your meaning, that from a hard-headed point of view you ought to be spending time thinking through specific problems. But you wonder if perhaps maybe you aren't on a quest for this whole you and perhaps that's more important than a solution to the day-to-day problems.

C: I think that's it. That's probably what I mean.

If we may legitimately put together these two experiences, and if we are justified in regarding them as typical, then we may say that both in therapy and in some fleeting experiences throughout her previous life, she has experienced a healthy satisfying enjoyable appreciation of herself as a whole and functioning creature; and that this experience occurs when she does not reject her feelings but lives them.

Here it seems to me is an important and often overlooked truth about the therapeutic process. It works in the direction of permitting the person to experience fully, and in awareness, all of his reactions including his feelings and emotions. As this occurs, the individual feels a positive liking for himself, a genuine appreciation of himself as a total functioning unit, which is one of the important end points of therapy.

The Discovery That the Core of Personality Is Positive

One of the most revolutionary concepts to grow out of our clinical experience is the growing recognition that the innermost core of man's nature, the deepest layers of his personality, the base of his "animal nature," is positive in nature—is basically socialized, forward-moving, rational, and realistic.

This point of view is so foreign to our present culture that I do not expect it to be accepted, and it is indeed so revolutionary in its implications that it should not be accepted without thoroughgoing inquiry. But even if it should stand these tests, it will be difficult to accept. Religion, especially the Protestant Christian tradition, has permeated our culture with the concept that man is basically sinful, and only by something approaching a miracle can his sinful nature be negated. In psychology, Freud and his followers have presented convincing arguments that the id, man's basic and unconscious nature, is primarily made up of instincts which would, if permitted expression, result in incest, murder, and other crimes. The whole problem of therapy, as seen by this group, is how to hold these untamed forces in check in a wholesome and constructive manner, rather than in the costly fashion of the neurotic. But the fact that at heart man is irrational, unsocialized, destructive of others and self—this is a concept accepted almost without question. To be sure there are occasional voices of protest. Maslow (1949) puts up a vigorous case for man's animal nature, pointing out that the antisocial emotions—hostility, jealousy, etc.—result from frustration of more basic impulses for love and security and belonging, which are in themselves desirable. And Montagu (1950) likewise develops the thesis that co-operation, rather than struggle, is the basic law of human life. But these solitary voices are little heard. On the whole the viewpoint of the professional worker as well as the layman is that man as he is, in his basic nature, had best be kept under control or under cover or both.

As I look back over my years of clinical experience and research, it seems to me that I have been very slow to recognize the falseness of this popular and professional concept. The reason, I believe, lies in the fact that in therapy there are continually being uncovered hostile and antisocial feelings, so that it is easy to assume that this indicates the deeper and therefore the basic nature of man. Only slowly has it become evident that these untamed and unsocial feelings are neither the deepest nor the strongest, and that the inner core of man's personality is the organism itself, which is essentially both self-preserving and social.

To give more specific meaning to this argument, let me turn again to the case of Mrs. Oak. Since the point is an important one, I shall quote at some length from the recorded case to illustrate the type of experience on which I have based the foregoing statements. Perhaps the excerpts can illustrate the opening up of layer after layer of personality until we come to the deepest elements.

It is in the eighth interview that Mrs. Oak rolls back the first layer of defense, and discovers a bitterness and desire for revenge underneath.

C: You know over in this area of, of sexual disturbance, I have a feeling that I'm beginning to discover that it's pretty bad, pretty bad. I'm finding out that, that I'm bitter, really. Damn bitter. I—and I'm not turning it back in, into myself . . . I think what I probably feel is a certain element of "I've been cheated." *(Her voice is very tight and her throat chokes up.)* And I've covered up very nicely, to the point of consciously not caring. But I'm, I'm sort of amazed to find that in this practice of, what shall I call it, a kind of sublimation that right under it—again words—there's a, a kind of passive force that's, it's pas—it's very passive, but at the same time it's just kind of *murderous.*

T: So there's the feeling, "I've really been cheated. I've covered that up and seem not to care and yet underneath that there's a kind of a, a latent but very much present *bitterness* that is very, very strong."

C: It's very strong. I—that I know. It's terribly powerful.

T: Almost a dominating kind of force.

C: Of which I am rarely conscious. Almost never . . . Well, the only way I can describe it, it's a kind of murderous thing, but without violence . . . It's more like a feeling of wanting to get even . . . And of course, I won't pay back, but I'd like to. I really would like to.

Up to this point the usual explanation seems to fit perfectly. Mrs. Oak has been able to look beneath the socially controlled surface of her behavior, and find underneath a murderous feeling of hatred and a desire to get even. This is as far as she goes in exploring this particular feeling until considerably later in therapy. She picks up the theme in the thirty-first interview. She has had a hard time getting under way, feels emotionally blocked, and cannot get at the feeling which is welling up in her.

C: I have the feeling it isn't guilt. *(Pause. She weeps.)* Of course I mean, I can't verbalize it yet. *(Then with a rush of emotion)* It's just being *terribly hurt!*

T: M-hm. It isn't guilt except in the sense of being very much wounded somehow.

C *(Weeping)*: It's—you know, often I've been guilty of it myself but in later years when I've heard parents say to their children, "stop crying," I've had a feeling, a hurt as though, well, why should they tell them to stop crying? They feel sorry for themselves, and who can feel more adequately sorry for himself than the child. Well, that is sort of what—I mean, as though I mean, I thought that they should let him cry. And—feel sorry for him too, maybe. In a rather objective kind of way. Well, that's—that's something of the kind of thing I've been experiencing. I mean, now— just right now. And in—in—

T: That catches a little more the flavor of the feeling that it's almost as if you're really weeping for yourself.

C: Yeah. And again you see there's conflict. Our culture is such that—I mean, one doesn't indulge in self-pity. But this isn't—I mean, I feel it doesn't quite have that connotation. It may have.

T: Sort of think that there is a cultural objection to feeling sorry about yourself. And yet you feel the feeling you're experiencing isn't quite what the culture objected to either.

C: And then of course, I've come to—to see and to feel that over this—see, I've covered it up. *(Weeps.)* But I've covered it up with so much *bitterness,* which in turn I had to cover up. *(Weeping) That's* what I want to get rid of! I almost don't *care* if I hurt.

T *(Softly, and with an empathic tenderness toward the hurt she is experiencing):* You feel that here at the basis of it as you experience it is a feeling of real tears for yourself. But *that* you can't show, mustn't show, so that's been covered by bitterness that you don't like, that you'd like to be rid of. You almost feel you'd rather absorb the hurt than to—than to feel the bitterness. *(Pause)* And what you seem to be saying quite strongly is, I do *hurt,* and I've tried to cover it up.

C: I didn't *know* it.

T: M-hm. Like a new discovery really.

C *(Speaking at the same time)*: I never really did know. But it's—you know, it's almost a physical thing. It's—it's sort of as though I were looking within myself at all kinds of—nerve endings and bits of things that have been sort of mashed. *(Weeping)*

T: As though some of the most delicate aspects of you physically almost have been crushed or hurt.

C: Yes. And you know, I do get the feeling, "Oh, you poor thing." *(Pause)*

T: Just can't help but feel very deeply sorry for the person that is you.

C: I don't think I feel sorry for the whole person; it's a certain aspect of the thing.

T: Sorry to see that hurt.

C: Yeah.

T: M-hm. M-hm.

C: And then of course there's this damn bitterness that I want to get rid of. It's—it gets me into trouble. It's because it's a tricky thing. It tricks me. *(Pause)*

T: Feel as though that bitterness is something you'd like to be rid of because it doesn't do right by you.

C *(Weeps. Long pause)*: I don't know. It seems to me that I'm right in feeling, what in the world good would it do to term this thing guilt. To chase down things that would give me an interesting case history, shall we say. What *good* would it do? It seems to me that the—that the key, the real thing is in this feeling that I have.

T: You could track down some tag or other and could make quite a pursuit of that, but you feel as though the core of the whole thing is the kind of experience that you're just having right here.

C: That's right. I mean if—I don't know what'll happen to the feeling. Maybe nothing. I don't know, but it seems to me that whatever understanding I'm to have is a part of this feeling of hurt, of—it doesn't matter much what it's called. *(Pause)* Then I—one can't go—around with a hurt so openly exposed. I mean this seems to me that somehow the next process has to be a kind of healing.

T: Seems as though you couldn't possibly expose yourself if part of yourself is so hurt, so you wonder if somehow the hurt mustn't be healed first. *(Pause)*

C: And yet, you know, it's—it's a funny thing *(pause)*. It sounds like a statement of complete confusion or the old saw that the neurotic doesn't want to give up his symptoms. But that isn't true. I mean, that isn't true here, but it's—I can just hope that this will impart what I feel. I somehow don't mind being hurt. I mean, it's just occurred to me that I don't mind terribly. It's a—I mind more the—the feeling of bitterness which is, I know, the cause of this frustration, I mean the—I somehow mind that more.

T: Would this get it? That, though you don't like the hurt, yet you feel you can accept that. That's bearable. Somehow it's the things that have covered up that hurt, like the bitterness, that you just—at this moment, can't stand.

C: Yeah. That's just about it. It's sort of as though, well, the first, I mean, as though, it's—well, it's something I can cope with. Now, the feeling of, well, I can still have a hell of a lot of fun, see. But that this other, I mean, this frustration—I mean, it comes out in so many ways, I'm beginning to realize, you see. I mean, just this sort of, this kind of thing.

T: And a hurt you can accept. It's a part of life within a lot of other parts of life, too. You can have lots of fun. But to have all of your life diffused by frustration and bitterness, that you don't like, you don't want, and are now more aware of.

C: Yeah. And there's somehow no dodging it now. You see, I'm much more aware of it. *(Pause)* I don't know. Right now, I don't know just what the next step is. I really don't know. *(Pause)* Fortunately, this is a kind of development, so that it—doesn't carry over too acutely into—I mean, I—what I'm trying to say, I think, is that I'm still functioning. I'm still enjoying myself and—

T: Just sort of want me to know that in lots of ways you carry on just as you always have.

C: That's it. *(Pause)* Oh, I think I've got to stop and go.

In this lengthy excerpt we get a clear picture of the fact that underlying the bitterness and hatred and the desire to get back at the world which has cheated her, is a much less antisocial feeling, a deep experience of having been hurt. And it is equally clear that at this deeper level she has no desire to put her murderous feelings into action. She dislikes them and would like to be rid of them.

The next excerpt comes from the thirty-fourth interview. It is very incoherent material, as verbalizations often are when the individual is trying to express something deeply emotional. Here she is endeavoring to reach far down into herself. She states that it will be difficult to formulate.

C: I don't know whether I'll be able to talk about it yet or not. Might give it a try. Something—I mean, it's a feeling—that—sort of an urge to really get out. I know it isn't going to make sense. I think that maybe if I can get it out and get it a little, well, in a little more matter of fact way, that it'll be something that's more useful to me. And I don't know how to—I mean, it seems as though I want to say, I want to talk about my *self*. And that is of course as I see, what I've been doing for all these hours. But, no, this—it's my *self*. I've quite recently become aware of rejecting certain statements, because to me they sounded—not quite what I meant, I mean, a little bit too idealized. And I mean, I can remember always saying it's more selfish than that, more selfish than that. Until I—it sort of occurs to me, it dawns, yeah, that's exactly what I mean, but the selfishness I mean, has an entirely different connotation. I've been using a word "selfish." Then I have this feeling of—I— that I've never expressed it before of selfish—which means nothing. A—I'm still going to talk about it. A kind of pulsation. And it's something aware all the time. And still it's there. And I'd like to be able to utilize it, too—as a kind of descending into this thing. You know, it's as though—I don't know, damn! I'd sort of acquired someplace, and picked up a kind of acquaintance with the structure. Almost as though I knew it brick for brick kind of thing. It's something that's an awareness. I mean, that—of a feeling of not being fooled, of not being drawn into the thing, and a critical sense of knowingness. But in a way—the reason, it's hidden and—can't be a part of everyday life. And there's something of—at times I feel almost a little bit terrible in the thing, but again terrible not as terrible. And why? I think I know. And it's—it also explains a lot to me. It's—it's something that is *totally* without hate. I mean, just *totally*. Not with love, but *totally without hate*. But it's—it's an exciting thing, too . . . I guess maybe I am the kind of person that likes to, I mean, probably even torment myself, or to chase things down, to try to find the whole. And I've told myself, now look, this is a pretty strong kind of feeling which you have. It isn't constant. But you feel it sometimes, and as you let yourself feel it, you feel it yourself. You know, there are words for that kind of thing that one could find in abnormal psychology. Might almost be like the feeling that is occasionally, is attributed to things that you read about. I mean, there are some elements there—I mean, this pulsation, this excitement, this knowing. And I've said—I tracked down one thing, I mean, I was very, very brave, what shall we say—a sublimated sex drive. And I thought, well, *there* I've got it. I've really solved the thing. And that there is nothing more to it than that. And for awhile, I mean, I was quite pleased with myself. That was it. And then I had to admit, no, that wasn't it. 'Cause that's something that had been with me long before I became so terribly frustrated sexually. I mean, that wasn't—and, but in the thing, then I began to see a little, within this very core is an acceptance of sexual relationship, I mean, the only kind that *I* would think would be possible. It was in this thing. It's not something that's been—I mean, sex hasn't been sublimated or substituted there. No. Within this, within what I know there—I mean, it's a different kind of sexual feeling to be sure. I mean, it's one that is stripped of all the things that have happened to sex, if you know what I mean. There's no chase, no pursuit, no battle, no—well, no kind of hate, which I think, seems to me, has crept into such things. And yet, I mean, this feeling has been, oh, a little bit disturbing.

T: I'd like to see if I can capture a little of what that means to you. It is as you've gotten very deeply acquainted with yourself on kind of a brick-by-brick experiencing basis, and in that sense have become more *self*-ish, and the notion of really,—in the discovering of what is the core of you as separate from all the other aspects, you come across the realization, which is a very deep and pretty thrilling realization, that the core of that self is not only without hate, but is really something more resembling a saint, something really very pure, is the word I would use. And that you can try to depreciate that. You can say, maybe it's a sublimation, maybe it's an abnormal manifestation, screwball and so on. But inside of yourself, you knew that it isn't. This contains the feelings which could contain rich sexual expression, but it sounds bigger than, and really deeper than that. And yet fully able to include all that could be a part of sex expression.

C: It's probably something like that . . . It's kind of—I mean, it's a kind of descent. It's a going down where you might almost think it should be going up, but no, it's—I'm sure of it; it's kind of going down.

T: This is a going down and immersing yourself in your self almost.

C: Yeah. And I—I can't just throw it aside. I mean, it just seems, oh, it just *is*. I mean, it seems an awfully important thing that I just had to say.

T: I'd like to pick up one of those things too, to see if I understand it. That it sounds as though this sort of idea you're expressing is something you must be going up to capture, something that *isn't* quite. Actually though, the feeling is, this is a going down to capture something that's more deeply there.

C: It is. It really—there's something to that which is—I mean, this—I have a way, and of course sometime we're going to have to go into that, of rejecting almost violently, that which is righteous, rejection of the ideal, the—as—and that expressed it; I mean, that's sort of what I mean. One is a going up into I don't know. I mean, I just have a feeling, I can't follow. I mean, it's pretty thin stuff if you ever start knocking it down. This one went—I wondered why—I mean, has this awfully definite feeling of descending.

T: That this isn't a going up into the thin ideal. This is a going down into the astonishingly solid reality, that—

C: Yeah.

T: —is really more surprising than—

C: Yeah. I mean, a something that you don't knock down. That's there—I don't know—seems to me after you've abstracted the whole thing. That lasts . . .

Since this is presented in such confused fashion, it might be worth while to draw from it the consecutive themes which she has expressed.

> I'm going to talk about myself as *self*-ish, but with a new connotation to the word.
> I've acquired an acquaintance with the structure of myself, know myself deeply.
> As I descend into myself, I discover something exciting, a core that is totally without hate.
> It can't be a part of everyday life—it may even be abnormal.
> I thought first it was just a sublimated sex drive.
> But no, this is more inclusive, deeper than sex.
> One would expect this to be the kind of thing one would discover by going up into the thin realm of ideals.
> But actually, I found it by going deep within myself.
> It seems to be something that is the essence, that lasts.

Is this a mystic experience she is describing? It would seem that the counselor felt so, from the flavor of his responses. Can we attach any significance to such a Gertrude Stein kind of expression? The writer would simply point out that many clients have come to a somewhat similar conclusion about themselves, though not always expressed in such an emotional way. Even Mrs. Oak, in the following interview, the thirty-fifth, gives a clearer and more concise statement of her feeling, in a more down-to-earth way. She also explains why it was a difficult experience to face.

C: I think I'm awfully glad I found myself or brought myself or wanted to talk about self. I mean, it's a very personal, private kind of thing that you just don't talk about. I mean, I can understand my feeling of, oh, probably slight apprehension now. It's—well, sort of as though I was just rejecting, I mean, all of the things that western civilization stands for, you see. And wondering whether I was right, I mean, whether it was quite the right path, and still of course, feeling how right the thing was, you see. And so there's bound to be a conflict. And then this, and I mean, now I'm feeling, well, of course that's how I feel. I mean there's a—this thing that I term a kind of a lack of hate, I mean, is very real. It carried over into the things I do, I believe in . . . I think it's all right. It's sort of maybe my saying to myself, well, you've been bashing me all over the head, I mean, sort of from the beginning, with superstitions and taboos and misinterpreted doctrines and laws and your science, your refrigerators, your atomic bombs. But I'm just not buying; you see, I'm just, you just haven't quite succeeded. I think what I'm saying is that, well, I mean, just not conforming, and it's—well, it's just that way.

T: Your feeling at the present time is that you have been very much aware of all the cultural pressures—not always very much aware, but "there have been so many of those in my life—and now I'm going down more deeply into myself to find out what I really feel" and it seems very much at the present time as though that somehow separates you a long ways from your culture, and that's a little frightening, but feels basically good. Is that—

C: Yeah. Well, I have the feeling now that it's okay, really . . . Then there's something else—a feeling that's starting to grow; well, to be almost formed, as I say. This kind of conclusion, that I'm going to stop looking for something terribly wrong. Now I don't know why. But I mean, just—it's this kind of thing. I'm sort of saying to myself now, well, in view of what I know, what I've found—I'm pretty sure I've ruled out fear, and I'm positive I'm not afraid of shock—I mean, I sort of would have welcomed it. But—in view of the places I've been, what I learned there, then also kind of, well, taking into consideration what I don't know, sort of, maybe this is one of the things that I'll have to date, and say, well, now, I've just—I just can't find it. See? And now without any—without, I should say, any sense of apology or covering up, just sort of simple statement that I can't find what at this time, appears to be bad.

T: Does this catch it? That as you've gone more and more deeply into yourself, and as you think about the kind of things that you've discovered and learned and so on, the conviction grows very, very strong that no matter how far you go, the things that you're going to find are not dire and awful. They have a very different character.

C: Yes, something like that.

Here, even as she recognized that her feeling goes against the grain of her culture, she feels bound to say that the core of herself is not bad, nor terribly wrong, but something positive. Underneath the layer of controlled surface behavior, underneath the bitterness, underneath the hurt, is a self that is positive, and that is without hate. This I believe is the lesson which our clients have been facing us with for a long time, and which we have been slow to learn.

If hatelessness seems like a rather neutral or negative concept, perhaps we should let Mrs. Oak explain its meaning. In her thirty-ninth interview, as she feels her therapy drawing to a close, she returns to this topic.

C: I wonder if I ought to clarify—it's clear to me, and perhaps that's all that matters really, here, my strong feeling about a hate-free kind of approach. Now that we have brought it up on a rational kind of plane, I know—it sounds negative. And yet in my thinking, my—not really my thinking but my feeling, it—*and* my thinking, yes, my thinking, too—it's a far more positive thing than this—than a love—and it seems to me a far easier kind of a—it's less confining. But it—I realize that it must sort of sound and almost seem like a complete rejection of so many things, of so many creeds and maybe it is. I don't know. But it just to me seems more positive.

T: You can see how it might sound more negative to someone but as far as the meaning that it has for you is concerned, it doesn't seem as binding, as possessive I take it, as love. It seems as though it actually is more—more expandable, more usable, than—

C: Yeah.

T: —any of these narrower terms.

C: Really does to me. It's easier. Well, anyway, it's easier for me to feel that way. And I don't know. It seems to me to really be a way of—of not—of finding yourself in a place where you aren't forced to make rewards and you aren't forced to punish. It is—it means so much. It just seems to me to make for a kind of freedom.

T: M-hm. M-hm. Where one is rid of the need of either rewarding or punishing, then it just seems to you there is so much more freedom for all concerned.

C: That's right. *(Pause)* I'm prepared for some breakdowns along the way.

T: You don't expect it will be smooth sailing.

C: No.

This section is the story—greatly abbreviated—of one client's discovery that the deeper she dug within herself, the less she had to fear; that instead of finding something terribly wrong within herself, she gradually uncovered a core of self which wanted neither to reward nor punish others, a self without hate, a self which was deeply socialized. Do we dare to generalize from this type of experience that if we cut through deeply enough to our organismic nature, that we find that man is a positive and social animal? This is the suggestion from our clinical experience.

Being One's Organism, One's Experience

The thread which runs through much of the foregoing material of this chapter is that psychotherapy (at least client-centered therapy) is a process whereby man becomes his organism—without self-deception, without distortion. What does this mean?

We are talking here about something at an experiential level—a phenomenon which is not easily put into words, and which, if apprehended only at the verbal level, is by that very fact, already distorted. Perhaps if we use several sorts of descriptive formulation, it may ring some bell, however faint, in the reader's experience, and cause him to feel "Oh, now I know, from my own experience, something of what you are talking about."

Therapy seems to mean a getting back to basic sensory and visceral experience. Prior to therapy the person is prone to ask himself, often unwittingly, "What do others think I should do in this situation?" "What would my parents or my culture want me to do?" "What do I think *ought* to be done?" He is thus continually acting in terms of the form which should be imposed upon his behavior. This does not necessarily mean that he always acts in *accord* with the opinions of others. He may indeed endeavor to act so as to contradict the expectations of others. He is nevertheless acting *in terms of* the expectations (often introjected expectations) of others. During the process of therapy the individual comes to ask himself, in regard to ever-widening areas of his life-space, "How do *I* experience this?" "What does it mean to *me?*" "If I behave in a certain way how do I symbolize the meaning which it *will* have for me?" He comes to act on a basis of what may be termed realism—a realistic balancing of the satisfactions and dissatisfactions which any action will bring to himself.

Perhaps it will assist those who, like myself, tend to think in concrete and clinical terms, if I put some of these ideas into schematized formulations of the process through which various clients go. For one client this may mean: "I have thought I must feel only love for my parents, but I find that I experience both love and bitter resentment. Perhaps I can be that person who freely experiences both love *and* resentment." For another client the learning may be: "I have thought I was only bad and worthless. Now I experience myself at times as one of much worth; at other times as one of little worth or usefulness. Perhaps I can be a person who experiences varying degrees of worth." For another: "I have held the conception that no one could really love me for myself. Now I experience the affectional warmth of another for me. Perhaps I can be a person who is lovable by others—perhaps I *am* such a person." For still another: "I have been brought up to feel that I must not appreciate myself—but I do. I can cry for myself, but I can enjoy myself, too. Perhaps I am a richly varied person whom I can enjoy and for whom I can feel sorry." Or, to take the last example from Mrs. Oak, "I have thought that in some deep way I was bad, that the most basic elements in me must be dire and awful. I don't experience that badness, but rather a positive desire to live and let live. Perhaps I can be that person who is, at heart, positive."

What is it that makes possible anything but the first sentence of each of these formulations? It is the addition of awareness. In therapy the person adds to ordinary experience the full and undistorted awareness of his experiencing—of his sensory and visceral reactions. He ceases, or at least decreases, the distortions of experience in awareness. He can be aware of what he is actually experiencing, not simply what he can permit himself to experience after a thorough screening through a conceptual filter. In this sense the person becomes for the first time the full potential of the human organism, with the enriching element of awareness freely added to the basic aspect of sensory and visceral reaction. The person comes to *be* what he *is,* as clients so frequently say in therapy. What this seems to mean is that the individual comes to *be*—in awareness—what he *is*—in experience. He is, in other words, a complete and fully functioning human organism.

Already I can sense the reactions of some of my readers. "Do you mean that as a result of therapy, man becomes nothing but a human *organism,* a human *animal?* Who will control him? Who will socialize him? Will he then throw over all inhibitions? Have you merely released the beast, the id, in man?" To which the most adequate reply seems to be, "In therapy the individual has actually *become* a human organism, with all the richness which that implies. He is realistically able to control himself, and he is incorrigibly socialized in his desires. There is no beast in man. There is only man in man, and this we have been able to release."

So the basic discovery of psychotherapy seems to me, if our observations have any validity, that we do not need to be afraid of being "merely" homo sapiens. It is the discovery that if we can add to the sensory and visceral experiencing which is characteristic of the whole animal kingdom, the gift of a free and undistorted awareness of which only the human animal seems fully capable, we have an organism which is beautifully and constructively realistic. We have then an organism which is as aware of the demands of the culture as it is of its own physiological demands for food or sex—which is just as aware of its desire for friendly relationships as it is of its desire to aggrandize itself—which is just as aware of its delicate and sensitive tenderness toward others, as it is of its hostilities toward others. When man's unique capacity of awareness is thus functioning freely and fully, we find that we have, not an animal whom we must fear, not a beast who must be controlled, but an organism able to achieve, through the remarkable integrative capacity of its central nervous system, a balanced, realistic, self-enhancing, other-enhancing behavior as a resultant of all these elements of awareness. To put it another way, when man is less than fully man—when he denies to awareness various aspects of his experience—then indeed we have all too often reason to fear him and his behavior, as the present world situation testifies. But when he is most fully man, when he is his complete organism, when awareness of experience, that peculiarly human attribute, is most fully operating, then he is to be trusted, then his behavior is constructive. It is not always conventional. It will not always be conforming. It will be individualized. But it will also be socialized.

A Concluding Comment

I have stated the preceding section as strongly as I am able because it represents a deep conviction growing out of many years of experience. I am quite aware, however, of the difference between conviction and truth. I do not ask anyone to agree with my experience, but only to consider whether the formulation given here agrees with his own experience.

Nor do I apologize for the speculative character of this paper. There is a time for speculation, and a time for the sifting of evidence. It is to be hoped that gradually some of the speculations and opinions and clinical hunches of this paper may be put to operational and definitive test.

Notes

1 This portion needs explanation. As part of a research study by another staff member this client had been asked several times during therapy to sort a large group of cards, each containing a self-descriptive phrase, in such a way as to portray her own self. At one end of the sorting she was to place the card or cards most like herself, and at the other end,

those most unlike herself. Thus when she says that she put as the first card, "I am an attractive personality," it means that she regarded this as the item most charateristic of herself.

2 The therapist's reference is to her statement in a previous interview that in therapy she was singing a song.

References

Maslow, A. H. Our maligned animal nature. *Journal of Psychology,* 1949, *28,* 273-278.
Montagu, A. *On being human.* New York: Henry Schuman, Inc., 1950.
Rogers, C. R. *Client-centered therapy.* Boston: Houghton Mifflin Co., 1951.

Case 6

Editors' Introduction

This account of several sessions is unusual for a number of reasons. First, it consists for the most part of the actual words spoken between the therapist and the client. Second, we have the rare opportunity to "listen in" on Dr. Albert Ellis, the developer of Rational Emotive Therapy (RET), who comments on the treatment offered by Dr. Ben Ard to a most unfortunate and misguided woman. Third—and as Albert Ellis himself comments—the therapist courageously deals with the issue of religion, generally a subject most therapists avoid. The fourth characteristic that makes this selection unusual is the nature of the client, a woman whose maladjustment is almost unbelievable.

Rational Emotive Therapy is based on some extremely simple premises which can be summarized as "Reality is interpretation" or quoting the bard, "There's nothing either good or bad, but thinking makes it so." Ellis has miniaturized psychotherapy to three basic points: It is not A that causes C but rather B. A—Activating Event; B—Belief System; C—Consequences. So, Consequences (such as maladjustment) are not due to the Activating Events (such as cruel parents) but rather to the individual's Belief System. Now, the therapist comes in with D—Disputation—to try to make the client see that it was not A that caused C but rather B. Therefore the therapist's job is to change B, which is what Dr. Ard does so beautifully in this selection.

BEN N. ARD, JR., AND ALBERT ELLIS[1]

The Case of the Black and Silver Masochist

ELLIS: The excerpts from the following case involve a twenty-four-year-old, single woman referred to Dr. Ard by her counselor at the rehabilitation center where she was staying. She had been at the center only a short while since her recent release from a state mental hospital, where she had been confined for seven years. There she had been diagnosed as having a schizophrenic reaction Her counselor at the rehabilitation center believed that she needed more psychotherapy and so referred her to the therapist.

The case had many unusual aspects to it and its handling goes against what many professionals have been taught in their training. The therapeutic approach is direct, active, hard-hitting, even relentless. The client's religious assumptions, which have been unquestioned for many years and which seem to be at the base of her problems, are attacked in a straightforward manner. Attacking a person's religious beliefs is a form of heresy in many circles of the helping professions. Yet, as this case illustrates, just such steps are sometimes desirable if the client is to be helped on the road to better mental health.

The client was seen for a fifty-minute hour at intervals of once a week, sometimes every two weeks, from spring through fall of 1969.

Here, then, is the case of a very unusual human being who has had a hard life and adopted rather unusual methods of adaptation to her harsh treatment by several people. This case is not an ideal one; many probable mistakes were made in these therapy sessions. But the young woman does make some progress. This record shows that some help can be given to a client who many would feel was practically hopeless.

This young woman is labeled the "Black and Silver Masochist," since she had adopted the practice of paying men to beat her with black and silver belts to assuage her guilt feelings, which apparently derived from her religious assumptions. Prior to the present treatment, she had seen a number of therapists and had many shock treatments, none of which she felt had been very helpful.

From Albert Ellis, *Growth Through Reason* (Hollywood: Wilshire Books, 1974), pp. 15–45.

First Session

T¹: You said over the phone that you had had some other help?

C²: I spent seven years in — State Hospital.

T³: Did you feel you got some help there?

C⁴: A little bit. I got help in that I realized I needed it. I had thought it was kinda normal going around cutting up with razor blades.

T⁵: You cut yourself with razor blades?

C⁶: Yeah, I've cut myself *(reveals many, many scars on both arms, from the wrists up past the elbow)*. It's just lately that I've turned to razor blades because I couldn't get what I really want.

T⁷: What do you really want?

C⁸: I term it as "black and silver."

T⁹: When you say "black and silver," will you tell me what that means?

C¹⁰: A belt.

T¹¹: A belt?

C¹²: I had a list of guys who would use it, but the thing is they don't do it for free. I gave them the money that they want. But it's kind of a rotten deal.

T¹³: Let me see if I understand this: you want men to use a black and silver belt on you?

C¹⁴: Yeah. A black leather belt with a silver buckle. Just before I did this last job with the razor blade, I went out and bought me a black belt. It cost me five dollars. It's a real neat one. I have several of them.

T¹⁵: Umm.

C¹⁶: I lived with this guy who did it for me for two weeks. I did anything he wanted me to. He had a lot of grass floating around. I had a couple of bummers on it. I let him take pictures of me, nude.

T¹⁷: Why do you want these men to beat you with these black belts?

C¹⁸: I don't know; it's fun.

T¹⁹: How do you mean, "It's fun"?

C²⁰: It makes me feel better for the things I've done.

T²¹: It sounds like pretty rough punishment for yourself. Is that fair?

C²²: Yeah, it's fair. I told my counselor what a tramp I was.

T²³: You think you are a tramp?

C²⁴: Yeah.

T²⁵: Why do you think you are a tramp?

C²⁶: Various things. I think it started with my mother. Because she used to beat us up, you see. She was sick herself, you know. The more my father said against her, the more I had to justify her. He didn't do anything about her for five years. If anyone is to blame, he is the one. Because he didn't do anything about it for five years. After all the damage has been done, big deal! So he got a divorce, wow!

T²⁷: May I interject something right here? You just touched upon something that might be pretty basic to what you have been doing to yourself in your life. You talked about blaming. You mentioned your father and your mother, and you have previously been talking about yourself. One of the things that I hear in what you have been saying so far is that you have been blaming yourself pretty badly.

ELLIS: Although this first session has only gone on for a few minutes, Dr. Ard zeroes in on what he considers the client's main problem: *blaming herself*. He does this largely on theoretical grounds, since RET[2] theory hypothesizes that whenever people are seriously disturbed, they are almost invariably blaming themselves, blaming others, or blaming the world. And by "blaming" the rational-emotive therapist means not only *(a)* insisting that certain people or things are responsible for or cause unfortunate results but also *(b)* demanding that they should be damned *as individuals* (that is, rated as being *bad people*) and punished for their misdeeds. Although in this particular instance, since the client has such an unusual history, the therapist gets sidetracked for awhile before he returns to the essence of her disturbance, her blaming tendencies, he quite properly raises this important issue very early in the therapy session.

C^{28}:	I don't blame myself without good reason. I don't do anything without good reason.
T^{29}:	But is the reason you have been giving yourself such a bad time entirely justified?
C^{30}:	Yeah, why not?
T^{31}:	You said you were beaten as a child by your mother?
C^{32}:	Yeah, that's how I became handicapped. And my brother had seven fractures of the skull. He's mentally retarded.
T^{33}:	Your mother injured you?
C^{34}:	Yeah.
T^{35}:	How?
C^{36}:	I had a brain hemorrhage.
T^{37}:	From the beating?
C^{38}:	Yeah. From being thrown against the wall.
T^{39}:	But you are continuing to want to hurt yourself today. Is that right?
C^{40}:	Well, yeah.
T^{41}:	I am interested in what you are saying about your past; it may make the present more understandable. But I am also interested in us getting to work on the present and future, as fast as we can.
C^{42}:	Yeah; ooh, I agree. It isn't all my mother. I have done things that I know were wrong.
T^{43}:	Who have you killed?
C^{44}:	Oh—this guy. I didn't kill him; he committed suicide.
T^{45}:	You drove him to it, you mean?
C^{46}:	Yeah. I had an affair with him when I was fourteen. He was sixty-three. All I wanted him to do was to get him to stop because I was having these dreams. And at that time I thought they were a sign from God that he had told. Because I was hung up on religion. Because I was raised a Seventh-Day Adventist. I just wanted him to stop. When he found out I told, he committed suicide and left a note saying "May God forgive you." So when you say, "Who have you killed?" you're not far off.
T^{47}:	But you didn't kill him.
C^{48}:	But I feel I made him commit suicide.
T^{49}:	You feel you should be punished forever?

C^{50}: It's been ten years—

T^{51}: You are still trying to punish yourself, aren't you?

C^{52}: Yeah, but the problem that goes along with it is that it has been turned into—somewhat—pleasurable. So that makes it harder to give up.

T^{53}: Do you really want to give up these things that give you pleasure?

C^{54}: More than I did even last year. Last year I was seeing a psychiatrist, and one of the reasons I quit—there were two main reasons. One was that I felt I wasn't getting anywhere, and secondly I wasn't all that ready to give it up. I don't dig hypocrites. And I don't like to be one, and I felt I was being hypocritical.

T^{55}: By continuing to see the psychiatrist when you didn't really want to work on getting better?

C^{56}: Yeah. Yeah. Yeah.

T^{57}: Are you ready to work on getting better now?

C^{58}: Yeah.

T^{59}: It's going to be hard work. Damned hard work.

C^{60}: Ooh—Yeah, I know because I have tried to do it myself.

T^{61}: It isn't easy, is it?

C^{62}: No. I used to carry a razor blade around with me all the time in my key case, just for security reasons. I could take it or leave it, but when the time came, oh man, I failed.

T^{63}: You were going to use it to hurt yourself with, right?

C^{64}: Yeah, sure. Why not?

T^{65}: Well, one of the things you and I might find out, if we are going to work together, is what are going to be the understandings, the rules of the game, the commitment we have to each other here. I may operate a little differently from some of the other people you have seen.

C^{66}: Yeah. I don't want to go around and around like with a psychiatrist. I'm fed up.

T^{67}: Well, let's see if you think you would want to work with me. Let me tell you a little bit about the sorts of things we might do. One of the things we might do is talk about what you are doing to yourself. And in so far as it's helpful, I am all for encouraging you. But in so far as it is self-defeating for you, I am going to work against that.

C^{68}: What's "self-defeating"?

T^{69}: Anything harmful you do to yourself such as cutting yourself with razors—

C^{70}: Or drinking nail polish remover?

T^{71}: I don't want to go into specifics such as razor blades right now because that is not the problem, but rather what you are thinking inside your head which causes you to turn to razor blades or whatever you might turn to. I am going to offer you a little proposition and see if you think it's worth looking at. If you want to work with me, and I am willing to work with you, I would look upon you somewhat as a partner. That is, you and me as partners. Specifically, the healthy part of you working together with me, working on the problems you have been having. That means that the healthy part of you has to agree to work with me. Does that make sense to you? That is, there are some things within you that are working to your detriment, if I hear you right.

C^{72}: Um-hm.

ELLIS: Quite properly, Dr. Ard sees that he can easily get lost in the fascinating details of the client's story. But the purpose of RET is not to track down the gory details of her history and thereby show her how to "understand" herself. Rather, the main purpose is to demonstrate to her what thoughts she is thinking inside her head that cause her to have a long and checkered history of cutting herself, drinking nail polish, driving an older man to suicide, being beaten with belts, and so on. So in T^{71} and several subsequent responses, the therapist tries to get away from history-taking and to structure the therapeutic relationship with the client as a collaborative problem-solving kind of relation.

T^{73}:   But there is also a healthy part of you. The fact that you are in here right now, talking about possibly doing something differently in the future, says to me that you may be ready—or fixin' to start, as some people might say—to do something about it.

C^{74}:   Yeah.

T^{75}:   That's the sign of the healthy you—what I want to work with. You and me against that unhealthy part that says you have to hurt yourself, you have to get somebody to beat you, you have to do all these irrational things.

C^{76}:   I'm in agreement. It's just that I might not be able to give enough right away.

T^{77}:   I understand that you have been through quite a bit of hell, from what you have told me so far. And I am assuming that getting you to function in ways that are more satisfying for you is going to take some effort, maybe a hell of a lot of effort—hard work on your part. I am not expecting miracles. But if you are really ready to do some hard work, to adopt some different practices, different from those you have adopted in the past, and you are really ready to commit yourself to this, and you and I work together as a team, then we can put some distance between you and your problem. I want you and I working together. Does this make sense to you?

C^{78}:   Yeah. One of the things I want to accomplish is—well, this thing about punishment is all tangled up and connected with sex.

T^{79}:   Um-hm. Well, would you like to do some reading?

C^{80}:   Yes.

T^{81}:   You may like to start with Ellis and Harper's *Guide to Rational Living,* then.

C^{82}:   OK.

ELLIS: Dr. Ard's recommendation that the client do some reading as a supplement to her sessions is another typical method of RET. Because the theory states that people can be *taught* to understand and change their thinking, RET employs many different kinds of teaching techniques, including bibliotherapy . . . Although controlled studies of the effectiveness of this type of bibliotherapy have not yet been done, clinical reports indicate that it both hastens and intensifies the therapeutic process in many instances.

T^{83}:   It might be helpful, then, if we could get some orientation as to how you feel about sex and guilt, and start looking at some of your assumptions—start working on them.

C⁸⁴: It doesn't surprise me that I feel guilty about sex, because of what happened right off the bat with this guy who committed suicide.

T⁸⁵: But sex doesn't always have to be associated with guilt and bad feelings, does it?

C⁸⁶: I realize this.

T⁸⁷: Sex can be enjoyable and a good part of life, integrated in a satisfying way in your life and not involving beatings or punishment or bad feelings; is that possible?

C⁸⁸: Yes, but it kind of has to.

T⁸⁹: You assume.

C⁹⁰: It's been my experience.

T⁹¹: I can understand that. Is it possible, though, that you could think of sex in a different context?

C⁹²: Yeah, if I find somebody that I really dig.

T⁹³: You could change your ideas about sex, then.

C⁹⁴: Yes, but I just don't know how to go about it.

ELLIS: At this point Dr. Ard interrupted the session to tell the client about another client, an alcoholic woman, who also had severe sexual problems and who was guilty about having relations with men. He was able to show her how to combat her guilt and how to become so liberal sexually that she was able to go out by herself to bars and other public places, to pick up male companions, and to have sex relations with them if she cared to do so. She ultimately found a steady lover and later married him.

Telling stories, fables, events in the lives of other clients, personal incidents from the life of the therapist, and other material of this sort is frequently used in RET to make certain points clearer and to indicate to clients that they, too, can overcome their handicaps just as others have been helped to do so.

T⁹⁵: This means changing your assumptions about yourself, punishment and sex, and men—the interrelationship of all these factors.

C⁹⁶: I think I can do it but it might take some time and you might get fed up with me.

T⁹⁷: Has that happened with other therapists?

C⁹⁸: The people at the hospital got pissed off at me.

T⁹⁹: Why so?

C¹⁰⁰: They felt that if I had the willpower I could do it.

T¹⁰¹: What do you think about that?

C¹⁰²: I don't think that just locking a person up in a place is going to help them change their ideas. The reason shock treatment didn't work for me was that I considered it a punishment. I had about six or seven series of them (with about eighteen to twenty-seven in a series). I swallowed some razor blades, and they had to operate on me to get them out. They had to do that three times in four months. They put me in a maximum security ward, but I did it again just to prove to them that they couldn't stop me from doing it.

T¹⁰³: You proved it, didn't you?

C¹⁰⁴: Yeah, rather painfully so.

T[105]: Well, now, I hear you saying that you are giving yourself an awfully bad time and doing a variety of things that are really self-defeating for you, and have been doing them for several years—

C[106]: Since I was twelve. I only started it because I couldn't get to my mother. I was getting tired of my father saying I was rotten like my mother and no good. Until this year I was not going to have any kids because I just knew I would beat them up like my mother did. I kept having dreams that I was beating a child. And I would get sexual pleasure out of it. That really bugged me, you know? Because it just proved to me that I was just like my mother. I mean to me it proved that I was just like my mother.

T[107]: You think it proved you were no damned good, huh?

C[108]: Well, yeah.

T[109]: But it doesn't, does it, really? Can you see that, now?

C[110]: When I want to, I can scrape up a lot of patience.

T[111]: So there are a lot of good things in you, too.

C[112]: But it scares me to get angry because I just think I could kill somebody or something. I used to dream I was getting beaten by some guy with a black and silver belt until I got some guy to do it, then I didn't dream about it anymore. I used to get sexual pleasure out of that dream, too.

T[113]: Are you telling me—do I hear this right, that you want to get to the day, someday, when you won't need razor blades, or black and silver belts beatings, etc.?

C[114]: Yeah; if nothing else, it's a damned nuisance, you know. And I don't want to hang around with that kind of a crowd (the kind of guys who will do that sort of thing). As far as razor blades are concerned, it's a bloody mess to clean up. Not everybody in society is going to understand, and you are going to get rejected a lot.

T[115]: And maybe be put back in the hospital again?

C[116]: Yeah. And I don't believe in starting out on something unless you really want to do something about it.

ELLIS: The therapist, in response T[111], makes something of an RET error. For his pointing out to the client that "there are a lot of good things in you, too" implies that she cannot prove that she is no damned good *because* of these good things. This is technically correct, since she obviously cannot be *no* good if she has *some* good in her. In RET, however, we try to show individuals that they are not worthless or of no value to themselves *even* if they have no "good" or "worth-while" traits. Because the goal of their lives would better be not *rating* themselves at all as being either "worthwhile" or "worthless," but merely *enjoying* their existences. The therapist, more elegantly, therefore, could have pointed out to the client that she *does* have some good, efficient, or strong *traits* but that she'd better not rate or judge her *self* by these traits. *She* is neither good nor bad, even though her individual characteristics may be measurable.

Dr. Ard also chooses not to deal, at this point, with the client's statement that she gets so angry that she thinks she could kill somebody or something. Perhaps he does so because he knows that the session is near its close. Normally, however, a rational-emotive therapist would quickly pick up on a client's feelings of rage and show her how she creates these feelings herself by irrationally *demanding* or *dictating* that others behave the way she wants them to behave, and that she would benefit herself by disputing these irrational demands.

Although this first session has presented to the client little specific evidence of her irrational ideas and how to combat them, it has induced a highly disturbed individual to open up about herself, shown her that she is needlessly self-condemning, and got her to agree to collaborate with the therapist in an empirical and logic-based attempt to solve her problem.

Second Session

ELLIS: During the second session, the therapist continues to work with the client along lines similar to those employed during the first session and particularly tries to get her to change some of her negative, punitive ideas about herself. Here is an excerpt from this session:

T¹: I'm saying that you have some stupid reasons for doing many of the things that you've done in your life. Now my job, as I hear it, is to help you to see that what you've been telling yourself as reasons for doing them are stupid reasons, and to help you see for yourself that there are better ways of running your life. Does that make sense to you?

C²: Yes.

T³: That means that you're going to have to give up some of your previous ways of thinking, because they're self-defeating for you. Now, at the beginning you may not see that. Because as you say, for example, the belt bit, the "black and silver," does bring some pleasure. But in so far as you get beat up by it, that's not a good thing. The same thing about the razor blade. In so far as you punish yourself, and you *want* punishment, that makes some sense. But it's *really* self-defeating for you. And I want you to see that, not because I say it, but because it's true—whether I'm alive or dead—that if you go through life the way you have been in the past, you're only hurting yourself. And we've got to get you to *question* some of your assumptions and *change* them. Now that's easy for me to say; it's hard to get you to do.

C⁴: But you see, all the evidence I have tells me that I *deserve* it.

T⁵: That's what we're gonna have to question! And we're gonna only have to accept as evidence what is logical, clear, rational—not just because you have a *feeling*.

C⁶: Yes, but isn't it because I've contributed to someone's suicide?

T⁷: That's *not* justification for all the misery you've given yourself. No, no!

T⁸: Yes, but they put people in prison for life.

C⁹: Yes, but not for getting other people to commit suicide. Let's look at that one minute. If a person commits suicide, many people in his life could say that they are involved with him. But if I understand suicide, it means that by definition *he* chooses that. Now if you pulled a gun on him and shot him, that's murder. But murder is not the same as suicide. If he takes a gun and shoots *himself* because you said something to him, you are still not to *blame* for his death. Even though you said, "You know, I think you're a crumb, and you ought to kill yourself!" and he then goes and shoots himself, you're still not to blame.

ELLIS: In RET, the therapist teaches long-range instead of short-range hedonism: that even though the client enjoys, in the short-run, punishing herself, in the long run she is acting foolishly. He also teaches that feelings do not constitute evidence for beliefs or facts. The client *feels* that she deserves punishment for her past misdeeds, but this feeling hardly proves *(a)* that it is a *fact* she has done badly or *(b)* that she *should* or *must* punish herself for her "bad" act.

The rational-emotive therapist also tries to help the client see that *telling* someone to shoot himself does not actually cause him to commit suicide. He still *chooses* to heed the so-called suicide-impelling statement. Moreover, even if the client were truly responsible for another's suicide or significantly contributed to it, that client would not be to blame—meaning, condemnable or rotten *as a person*—for this wrong deed.

Technically, the therapist makes some mistakes, from the standpoint of rational-emotive philosophy, in response T^5, where he says: "That's what we're gonna have to question! And we're gonna only have to accept as evidence what is logical, clear, rational—not just because you have a *feeling.*" For his "gonna have to question" and "gonna only have to accept as evidence" are imperative, absolute statements that themselves could help create anxiety in the client. For if she *has* to question or *has* to accept as evidence what is logical, and she actually does not do what she *has* to, she will almost certainly condemn herself for her horrible errors. Dr. Ard could have more accurately pointed out to her that "*it would be better* if you questioned your assumption" and "*it would be much more desirable* if you accept as evidence what is logical, clear, rational." Then, if she does badly, she will tend merely to feel sorry rather than self-condemning. I have made this same error of using "have to," "should," "got to," and so on, with clients in my early writings. But these days I am more careful and rarely goof in this respect!

Third Session

ELLIS: In RET, the therapist teaches long-range instead of short-range hedonism: that even though the client enjoys, in the short run, punishing herself, in the long run she can change these ideas and thereby stop punishing herself, sexually and otherwise. A significant excerpt from this third session follows:

C^1: So I'm beginning to think that if they [the early Christian fathers] could be so wrong then—You're right, I have been questioning some of these, you know, beliefs.

T^2: So you don't have to blame yourself and get into all this punishment kick just because of some of the religious teachings you've been taught in the past.

C³: Well, so far I've been working on trying to convince myself that maybe everything I believe is not true.

T⁴: You mean in regard to religion?

C⁵: Yeah. And if I can do that, then—you know, then I can feel free to do other things. As far as religion, I do believe there is a God. But if he's the kind of a God that they've convinced me so thoroughly exists and presented to me, then—then the hell with it!

T⁶: Um-hm. It sounds to me like you've made some progress in this regard!

C⁷: I hope so! Because I'll be a lot freer if I can.

T⁸: Um-hm.

C⁹: It's still with me. But I'm working on it!

T¹⁰: Good!

ELLIS: When the rational-emotive therapist encounters a client whose dysfunctional behavior clearly seems to be related to dogmatic religious beliefs, he may try to get her to modify her beliefs and still be religious, or to change her beliefs radically and to surrender her religion. If, for example, she devoutly believes that her religion demands that she kill others who are irreligious, he may try to get her to become differently religious or nonreligious. In this case, the client seems to be maintaining a basic, somewhat vague belief in God, but to be giving up the damning aspects of the particular God in whom she used to believe. This may well be a satisfactory solution to her problem of self-punishment.

Later in the session, Dr. Ard discusses the client's relations with the latest boyfriend.

T¹¹: Can you do it [have sex relations] with Jack without being beaten?

C¹²: I've never done it with Jack. I don't think Jack would give it to me, either.

T¹³: Give what to you now?

C¹⁴: He'd give me sex.

T¹⁵: He'd give you sex?

C¹⁶: He would! I think he—he would! Well, if he's going to take me to Los Angeles for a week, I mean—it's kinda obvious that he would. Because he wouldn't be—

T¹⁷: Think you could have sex with Jack without being beaten?

C¹⁸: I hope I can. I hope that by the time I get around to it I—I—think I can picture—I can picture him—I can tell, you know—you can tell how gentle a guy's going to be by just, say, the way he kisses or the way he holds your hand or something.

T¹⁹: Um-hm.

C²⁰: And Jack is very, very gentle. He's just kind of a groove. Really!

T²¹: So you might be able to have sex with him and enjoy it, and have orgasm with him sometime, without ever having to resort to black and silver belt beatings?

C²²: I kinda think so. Because I can picture it in my mind. And—

T²³: Isn't it better to picture that than to picture being beaten by black and silver belts?

C²⁴: Yeah, man. It's a groove!

T²⁵: Well, if you continue to think that you've got to pay for some sin that you *assume* you've committed, that you *assume* you should be beaten for, then you'll resort to "black and silver" again.

C^{26}:   I guess so!

T^{27}:   And if you don't want to be beaten again, the way to avoid it is to question your assumptions that you have committed these sins, which you *should* be punished for.

C^{28}:   Well, I—I've been questioning mostly beliefs—that anything I've been told has been true. And I've pretty well come to the conclusion that maybe it hasn't. And I've also been thinking about what you were saying about people not being sinners but merely doing wrong acts.

T^{29}:   Um-hm.

C^{30}:   Doing wrong acts. And that makes sense. You know—

T^{31}:   Um-hm. So you can goof from time to time, but you don't have to blame yourself for your sins.

C^{32}:   Yeah, but I've goofed plenty! Hah!

T^{33}:   But you don't deserve the kind of punishment you've gotten for yourself. That right?

C^{34}:   Well, I've been accustomed to it! Though—

T^{35}:   I realize that—

C^{36}:   I didn't have to go out and *get* it, from the day I was born. I mean I—

T^{37}:   Just because your mother beat you up, though, does that mean that you have to be beaten the rest of your life?

C^{38}:   Um-hm. Um-hm. Well, I don't know.

T^{39}:   You said, for example, that your family taught you some religious things, which you're now beginning to question.

C^{40}:   Yeah.

T^{41}:   It is possible that they also did some other things to you which you now could begin to question?

C^{42}:   Oh, sure!

ELLIS: Dr. Ard keeps showing the client that she may well be able to change her self-defeating sexual pattern if she changes her self-damning assumptions. Even though she may have strongly learned from her family to defame herself, she could question their beliefs about her, just as she is now beginning to question the religious beliefs they taught her. In RET, the therapist takes almost every opportunity to show the client that her disturbed behavior is belief-caused and that she has the ability to change her beliefs.

Tenth Session

ELLIS: [In] the intervening sessions between the third and the last (tenth) session, the therapist used various techniques that are somewhat unique to rational therapy—namely, confrontation, confutation, deindoctrination, reeducation, and homework assignments. Some examples of these may be seen in the excerpts from the first, second, third, and tenth sessions.

The basic cause of this young woman's problems seems to reside in her unquestioned philosophic and religious assumptions, which she had heretofore never examined critically. The therapist works directly and actively at getting her to challenge and question her basic assumptions and to substitute less self-defeating ideas to enable her to live a more satisfying, more rational life.

C¹: A friend read me the books of Matthew and Mark, to check it out, and there are some contradictions there.

T²: A few.

C³: Yeah, yeah. Like where it said Judas gave back the silver. In Acts it said he went and bought some land with it.

T⁴: He couldn't do both, could he?

C⁵: No, I guess not. I've almost decided that all Christianity is a form of mass hypnotism.

T⁶: That's quite a bit different from what you have believed for a long time, isn't it?

C⁷: Yeah. I've almost decided that there is no hell.

T⁸: If there really was no hell, then you wouldn't have to worry about going there, would you?

C⁹: No.

T¹⁰: It might be worth your while to check that out real good, wouldn't it?

C¹¹: Yeah. All the churches have a different concept of hell. And they all claim that they come up with scripture to prove their concept is right.

T¹²: And that shows you that they can't all be right, doesn't it? Your logic is good: they can't all be right. And as a matter of fact, they may all be wrong.

C¹³: No.

T¹⁴: There may be no hell at all. Is that possible?

C¹⁵: Yeah, that's possible.

T¹⁶: In which case your worry about going to hell would be unnecessary, wouldn't it?

C¹⁷: Yeah, if there were none.

T¹⁸: And all that punishment jazz would have to go by the boards, wouldn't it?

C¹⁹: Yeah. If I got to believe that there was no hell, then there wouldn't be any fear of hell.

T²⁰: And you wouldn't have to punish yourself anymore, or hire those guys to punish you with those black and silver belts anymore, would you?

C²¹: No. I went through a period of a couple of days when I felt almost free from hell, and I didn't desire to be punished.

T²²: Well! Congratulations! That has been a long, hard road getting there, hasn't it?

C²³: Yeah.

T²⁴: You don't really need it, do you?

C²⁵: No.

T²⁶: That would be a great sense of relief to you to know that you don't really need it anymore; you don't have to have beatings, you don't have to punish yourself.

C²⁷: Yeah. True.

T²⁸: And you can live a good life without worrying about whether the streets are paved with gold or burning fire, or whatever that hereafter is supposed to have—those presuppositions that the Christians ask that you believe on faith alone.

C²⁹: Yeah. How's come, if we are supposed to believe on faith alone, that God gave us a mind that would ask questions? You know, he gives you this mind so that you can explore things and then is all pushed out of shape when you can't accept them on faith.

T[30]:   You are using your mind to think with and any idea about religion that says that such a God would object to your using your mind that you do have, is a pretty sad idea, isn't it?

C[31]:   Why did he give it to you if he didn't intend for you to use it?

T[32]:   Maybe he didn't give you anything; maybe the whole story is made up. Did you ever think about the story of Genesis, where he is supposed to have said don't eat of that tree in the Garden of Eden, and when he came and saw that they had eaten, he said "Where are you, Adam?" Isn't God supposed to be omnipotent? Doesn't he know where everybody is? How come he is asking where Adam is?

C[33]:   Because he wants to make him suffer by making him come out and face him.

T[34]:   Yes. As a matter of fact, that God of the Old Testament urged people to go out and kill all the men, women, and children in certain villages.

C[35]:   Yeah, right.

T[36]:   Is that the kind of God you want to believe in?

C[37]:   No.

T[38]:   And yet that is the same God who is writing down in his book every thought or fantasy you have, you say, according to what you have been taught. Why not say that that is a vicious idea, and I don't believe in such stories?

C[39]:   And how's come the very first thing every religion attacks is sex?

T[40]:   There you are.

C[41]:   I am afraid I will fail at sex.

T[42]:   You tell yourself all sorts of garbage, don't you? If you tell yourself you are going to be a failure in a sex relationship, what better way is there to insure that you will be a "failure"? There is no better way, is there? If you doubt your ability to function—if you say, "Oh, I'm going to do something wrong," "I'm going to make the wrong move," or "I'm not going to do the thing right"— then you pretty well insure that that is, indeed, what you are going to do, by worrying about it. Or, "He won't like this about me." Whereas, if you said, "I'm going to do the best I can; I'm going to try to be rational and sensible about this," then that would probably be a healthier attitude, wouldn't it?

C[43]:   Yeah, it would be.

T[44]:   If you have to ask yourself, "Would God like this? Would he like this act, or that movement?" that would really foul you up, wouldn't it?

C[45]:   Yeah.

T[46]:   But if you are willing to look at the consequences of your act from the point of view of what effect it is going to have on you, and forget about whether God is writing it down in his book or looking over your shoulder, that latter idea is a vicious idea, isn't it?

C[47]:   Yeah.

ELLIS: Dr. Ard does not hesitate, in the RET method, to directly dispute and question some of the client's basic religious ideologies. Thus, in T[32], he continues to attack the whole idea that the God of the Old Testament really exists and is all-powerful; and in T[46], he points out that it is a vicious, self-defeating notion to believe that God is spying on people and writing down, for future retribution, their errors. From his efforts in this respect during previous sessions, the client is already seriously questioning her self-punitive, religiously oriented beliefs; after she brings up the subject, he pursues it further with her and strongly tries to induce her to challenge her previously held dogmas.

The rational-emotive therapist is firmly disputatious and attacking in these important respects because *(a)* he believes that the client often can benefit from having straighter thinking pointed out to her; *(b)* he wants to show her, by precise examples, that her irrational ideas do cause and influence her emotional reactions, and that if she changes the former she will also significantly change the latter; and *(c)* he keeps teaching her a specific empiricological method of challenging any of her present or subsequent inconsistent, self-sabotaging philosophies, so that she will ultimately be able to use this method herself and not require his or any other therapist's help. Because of his attacking position, the RET therapist is often accused of trying to convince the client of his own ideas and therefore of being authoritarian. Actually, as consistently shown in this case, he attempts to help the client see how *her* ideas do not hold water when empirically and logically analyzed and how, if she sticks with them, she will continue to harm herself. He continually asks her to think about her own ideologies, to check them herself, to figure out how invalid they are in their own right and not because *he* says that they are. If she merely accepts *his* word that they are mistaken and harmful, she may then suggestively feel better; but he would not agree that she actually was better, for she would still be unthinking, highly suggestible, and poorly perceiving. She would also still be overly dependent on him or on others.

After helping the client challenge her religious ideas, Dr. Ard does not hesitate to bring up, once again, her sexual philosophies. He does not necessarily wait, as most psychoanalytic or client-centered therapists would do, for her spontaneously to come back to this issue. In the interest of saving her time and trouble, and getting to the source of her major irrational ideas efficiently, he again raises the question of her sexual notions and tries to show her how they are integrally connected with her misleading religious suppositions.

T[48]:   What do you think about punishing yourself to have some sex? Is that a question we can look at now? Have I got this right? In the past, implicit in what you have done, you think that it is all right to have sex or an orgasm *after* you have been beaten.

C[49]:   Yeah. Well, it makes it all right.

T[50]:   How does it make it all right?

C[51]:   I guess by paying for the wrong you are going to do.

T[52]:   In advance, so to speak.

C[53]:   Yeah, right.

T[54]:   So you pay for this "bad deed: sex" by being punished beforehand.

C[55]:   Right.

T⁵⁶: Like a little kid saying, in effect, I am going to play over the fence where I am not supposed to, so spank me first so I can go enjoy myself, right?

C⁵⁷: Yeah.

T⁵⁸: And yet, we are saying that if you decide it is really all right to go and play over the fence, then you don't have to be punished.

C⁵⁹: Right.

T⁶⁰: Is that applicable to your case, right now? To say that you don't have to punish yourself with black and silver belts in order to have enjoyable sex experiences?

C⁶¹: I don't know.

T⁶²: You said in this letter you left with me last time that when you are unhappy, you go to some God and talk to him and feel better; then you praise him for making you feel better, after his making you unhappy to begin with. Isn't that the same kind of thinking you have been doing on this sex bit and the beatings? That is, you are assuming that you should be punished, because sex is bad, and therefore you punish yourself first so that you can have the sex. How about questioning the assumption made at the beginning, that you have to punish yourself because sex is bad? If sex is not bad, then you don't have to punish yourself for having it, do you?

C⁶³: But the Bible speaks of fornication, adultery, and this and that.

T⁶⁴: I thought we were going to try and question that.

C⁶⁵: Oh, yeah, well—yeah, OK.

T⁶⁶: You said in this letter that there is something wrong with the idea of going to a God and talking to him, and he makes you feel better, when he is the guy who made you feel bad to begin with. Is that right?

C⁶⁷: Yeah.

T⁶⁸: You are saying, "God says sex is bad"; therefore anyone who indulges in it should be punished. Then you say, okay, I'll punish myself first, then I can have some sex (it will balance the books).

C⁶⁹: Yeah.

T⁷⁰: But maybe you ought to question what you assume without question: that sex is bad and God is against it. Maybe you don't even have to worry about that. Maybe sex is just natural and normal, and you don't have to worry.

C⁷¹: Yeah. In the churches they even think that masturbation is bad.

T⁷²: Do you think it is bad?

C⁷³: I was taught it was bad. God gave us sexual emotions and feelings, and then if you do something about it, it is bad. That doesn't make sense because he gave them to you to begin with.

T⁷⁴: Right. That is like giving you a mind and then saying "Don't eat of the tree of knowledge," isn't it?

C⁷⁵: Yeah.

T⁷⁶: He did that too, supposedly, according to the Bible. And maybe in both cases we shouldn't believe either of those stories. How about that?

C⁷⁷: Yeah. You know Paul, in the Bible?

T⁷⁸: Um-hm.

C⁷⁹: Well, I think he was against a lot of things anyway.

T⁸⁰: He sure was, wasn't he? He was a very sick man.

C[81]:   Like I think he despised women.

T[82]:   Yes, and yet he has probably influenced more Christians than perhaps any other man in the Bible. He influenced a great many Christians to believe that women are kind of bad, didn't he?

C[83]:   Yes.

T[84]:   And yet, in our culture, we base so much of our thinking on Christianity, and that puts women in a second-class citizenship, all because of Paul. That's pretty sick, isn't it?

C[85]:   Yes.

T[86]:   And if Paul was kind of off his rocker—

C[87]:   I think that bolt of lightning that hit him on the way to Damascus must have done something to him.

T[88]:   And so we should not believe what a man like that says; is that a fair conclusion? That is, if we ask how should we treat our women then we certainly shouldn't ask a man like Paul who has such a low opinion of them.

C[89]:   Yeah, right.

T[90]:   We ought to at least treat them as equals, as worthwhile human beings, and not beat them like gongs or drums. And yet you have a sort of philosophy that you should be beaten before you can have sex, that you should be punished. That is a sort of twisted, sick idea that we could trace back to Paul, couldn't we?

C[91]:   Yeah, I guess so.

T[92]:   And you are believing it when a man like Paul believed it, and yet you just told me you think he was kind of sick.

C[93]:   Oh, yeah.

T[94]:   Maybe we can dispense with Paul's beliefs about women and punishment and sex and marriage. And you decide what kind of philosophy of life you want to have on the basis of what works out best for you, what the consequences are for you.

T[95]:   Paul was the author of that famous statement, "It is better to marry than to burn." That's a pretty sick way to look at marriage, isn't it?

C[96]:   Yeah.

ELLIS: In his attempt to help the client dispute her self-punishing religious philosophy, the therapist does not hesitate to point out, in quite a heretical manner, that St. Paul was "a very sick man." He quotes chapter and verse to back this hypothesis; and he shows how the antisexual Christian philosophy, which the client has clung to for many years, directly stems, in all probability, from Paul's disturbed attitudes toward human sexuality. He takes the opportunity again, as is common in RET, to indicate that the client's goal would be better to acquire a philosophy of life connected with what works out best for her. Whereas much that goes on in psychotherapy is quite Establishment-centered, in that the therapist is helping the client adjust to the kind of society in which she accidentally was reared and to give up a good amount of her individuality in order to be accepted in that society, RET tends to be client-centered, in that the therapist tries to help the client discover what she really wants to do, whether or not she received considerable social approval for her acts, and to help her undefeatingly achieve her goals. The rational-emotive therapist fully realizes that, because she normally chooses to live in society, the client would better be socially as well as individually interested and should try to achieve individuality-groupness, or what Hans S. Falck (1969) describes as the "I-G effect." But because the client is usually too socially conforming and too little individually oriented, he tends to stress the latter rather than the former.

C[97]: Somewhere he [St. Paul] said that if you masturbate, you would be left with a reprobate mind. I thought, well, gee—I masturbate, now what in the hell does "reprobate" mean? So I went and looked it up. 'cause if I'm going to have a reprobate mind, at least I want to know what kind it is.

T[98]: What did you find out?

C[99]: It means corrupt, hopelessly bad and depraved, condemned.

T[100]: And so once again we have that vicious circle, haven't we?

C[101]: Yeah.

T[102]: But you are *not* depraved or a reprobate or all bad like that, because we can question the assumption that started the whole thing.

C[103]: Yeah.

T[104]: I would like to give you some "homework" assignments: do some writing like you did in this letter, that is, some thinking about why you feel guilty, why you think you ought to punish yourself; and then begin to examine and question your assumptions that lead you to feel guilty and think you need to be punished. If you would write some of those things out, I think it might help both of us get real clear about it. You would be clear in your own mind, having worked it out on paper, so to speak; would that help?

C[105]: Um-hm.

T[106]: Would you like to do that for next time?

C[107]: Yeah.

T[108]: You did it somewhat in this letter you wrote to your friend, but I am interested in your thinking it through for yourself. What follows from following your philosophy, which is the basic Christian philosophy of life?

C[109]: Um-hm.

T[110]: That you should be punished for being a bad girl; that you ought to be punished for having sex; and as I recall, you have even said that you ought to be punished for even having fantasies.

C[111]: Oh, yeah, because—let's see—

T[112]: Jesus was supposed to have said, "The thought is as bad as the deed."

C[113]: Yeah, right.

T[114]: That is another vicious idea, isn't it?

C[115]: Yeah, it is kind of a vicious idea, because there is nothing wrong with thinking, I guess, but he said there was.

ELLIS: Dr. Ard gets around to one of the main aspects of RET: assigning a specific homework task to the client. In this instance, he asks her to work out on paper some of her assumptions about guilt and self-punishment, and then to question these assumptions. Often, the rational-emotive therapist gives activity or motoric assignments as well. Thus, he may have this client deliberately engage in "forbidden" or "guilt-provoking" sex behavior, to show her what her specific beliefs are when she does so and to demonstrate that, by taking such risks, she does not have to make herself feel terribly guilty. Or he may have her deliberately refrain from all sex activity, to show her the logical consequences of her antisexual philosophy.

The specific homework assignment that he gives (or has the client give herself or asks her therapy group to give her) is partly designed to change her motoric patterns of behavior: to get her to do something, for example, that she thinks she "can't" do, and to help her become habituated to doing it easily and enjoyably. But it is largely designed to help change her thinking: to show her, in one way or another, that risk-taking is not catastrophic, that she has specific ideas motivating her disturbed behavior, that she can change these ideas, and so on.

T[116]: He said so; does that make it so?

C[117]: "Whatsoever a man thinketh in his heart, that shall he do," or something like that.

T[118]: So you can't even think about robbing a bank. Or passing a bakery shop, you can't even think about having a chocolate cake you see in the window. You are a sinner, hm? That is a pretty sad way of thinking, isn't it?

C[119]: Well—

T[120]: Even if you walk on down the street [and think of stealing but] don't steal anything. I don't see that you are such a terrible human being.

C[121]: Actually, it seems like it would be a compliment to the bakery.

T[122]: Why, certainly. Did you ever think about a married man walking down the street, and he sees a pretty girl going down the street; if the thought occurs to him, "There's a pretty girl," isn't that natural and normal and healthy, really?

C[123]: Well, yeah.

T[124]: Despite the fact that Jesus said he has committed adultery in his heart. I say that's just too damned bad. I am sorry Jesus felt that way, but it is mentally not very healthy to think that every time you have a thought you should be blamed and punished for it, even if it is a natural, normal, healthy thought—

C[125]: Hey! Well, how come it doesn't work the other way, then? If you think something good, you have already done it?

T[126]: It doesn't work that way either, does it? Do I get credit in the good book for having thought about giving a million to some charity but never actually doing it?

C[127]: No.

T[128]: Right. That shows you how foolish it is, doesn't it, really?

C[129]: Mmmm.

T[130]: He is docking you for all the bad thoughts but not giving you any credit for the good. You can't win in that system, can you?

C[131]: No. I guess not.

T[132]: One other reason for getting rid of that system—one good reason for dumping the whole system. Does that make sense to you?

C[133]: Yeah.

. . .

T[134]: If you did some reading and thinking about your own philosophy, I am sure you could come up with a better philosophy than the Christian philosophy, couldn't you?

C[135]: Well, yeah.

. . .

T¹³⁶: We could talk forever on how many angels can dance on a pinhead, and there is not much way of resolving that question since we don't know what size angels there are. But do you know that Christians have debated those kinds of questions endlessly?

C¹³⁷: Really?

T¹³⁸: Yes. *But don't take my word for it. Check it out.*

C¹³⁹: Oh, wow! A lot of good it is going to do you if you find out the answer!

T¹⁴⁰: I use that as an illustration of some of the absurd things religious people get into when they are trying to resolve issues that are unresolvable. So that is why I am saying to you: you don't have to resolve these issues—just dump the whole load.

C¹⁴¹: Oooh.

T¹⁴²: You don't have to spend any time trying to find out how many angels can dance on a pinhead because it is a *meaningless* question to begin with.

C¹⁴³: Yeah; I don't see the importance of it, anyway.

ELLIS: Dr. Ard uses here several methods commonly employed in RET: *(a)* He shows how the antisexual Christian philosophy, which he deliberately takes to extremes, is utterly self-contradictory, impractical, and absurd. *(b)* He points out that it is actually natural and desirable to think and act the way the antisexual philosophy says it is unnatural and undesirable to act. *(c)* He prods the client into bringing up an excellent logical point that she has thought out herself: namely, that if mere *thoughts* or *fantasies* are punishable, they are also logically rewardable; but that actually the Christian philosophy does not acknowledge their rewardability. *(d)* He indicates that the philosophy that the client swears by is one with which she can't possibly win. *(e)* He encourages the client to rethink her ideological position and to come up with a better, less defeating set of values. *(f)* He explicitly tells the client, once again, *"But don't take my word for it. Check it out."* *(g)* He notes how metaphysical and definitional the client's whole philosophy is: that it asks foolish questions and thereby gets foolish answers. *(h)* He encourages the client to stand apart from her own value system, to weigh it more objectively, and perhaps dump the system entirely.

T¹⁴⁴: I am going to offer you the idea that the same thing is true as to whether it is a sin—mortal, venial, or otherwise—if you masturbate, or whether you fornicate or not, or whether God cares about your fantasies (positive or negative). Let's put all that stuff in the garbage can, and let the garbage man take it away and you not worry about it anymore; then you could go on to live a happy, healthy, normal life. And you wouldn't hurt anybody intentionally, I'm sure, would you?

C¹⁴⁵: No.

T¹⁴⁶: You don't have to hire anybody to hurt you anymore. And you don't have to cut yourself with razors anymore.

C¹⁴⁷: No. I hope so. Another thing I do that I think would go if I could straighten all this out—you know how some kids carry a blanket, their security blanket? Well, I carry razor blades around with me, everywhere I go.

T¹⁴⁸: Let's see if I understand that. You carry these razor blades around with you so you can punish yourself by cutting yourself anytime you want to?

C^{149}:   Yeah, right.

T^{150}:   And we are saying that if you can get rid of this neurotic need to punish yourself, then you don't have to carry razor blades.

C^{151}:   Yeah, yeah.

T^{152}:   When you get an idea in the future that you want to punish yourself, what can you do instead of cutting yourself? Can you think of some things you could do? What alternatives can you think of? Say, next week you felt like you ought to punish yourself, and you happen to have a razor in your bag, what could you think—instead of what you used to think—that would prevent you from cutting yourself again? What could you think that would help you throw that razor blade in the garbage?

C^{153}:   That I don't need to suffer anymore, maybe.

T^{154}:   Yeah. You don't need to suffer anymore. And no *maybe*—period. You don't need to suffer anymore, period.

ELLIS: The therapist tries to show the client what she can do in the future when she is "overwhelmed" by the idea that she should cut herself: namely, that she doesn't need to suffer anymore. He could have, more specifically, shown her the ABC's of RET:

At point A, the *activating event* occurs when she makes some error or performs worse than she would like to perform. At point C, the emotional *consequence* is that she feels guilty and is impelled to cut and punish herself. Instead, however, of thinking that A must lead to C, she could stop and ask herself, "What am I telling myself, at point B, my *belief system,* to make me feel self-punishing at point C?"

Her answer would then normally be: "First, I am telling myself a *rational belief* (rB): 'How unfortunate for me to have made that error; I wish I hadn't made it.' But that would only lead, if I rigorously stuck to it, to a *rational consequence:* appropriate feelings of sorrow, regret, and annoyance at my own foolish behavior. Since I am actually getting a very *irrational consequence* (feelings of guilt and the urge to cut myself up), I seem to be telling myself an *irrational belief* (iB), such as 'How *awful* for me to have made that error. I *should* not have made it! What a louse I am for doing what I should not have done. I must condemn and punish myself!' "

The client could then be shown by the therapist exactly how to *dispute,* at point D, her *irrational belief,* by challenging herself as follows: "Why is it awful for me to have made that error? Where is the evidence that I *should* not have made it? Even if it was quite wrong of me to make it, why am I a louse for doing this wrong thing? What is the reason that I have to condemn and punish myself for acting badly?"

She would then tend to experience, at point E, the cognitive *effect* of believing *(a)* that it is not awful, but only inconvenient and unfortunate, for her to make errors; *(b)* that there is no evidence that she *should not* be fallible and make errors; *(c)* that she is never a louse or a worthless individual, even if she does things quite wrongly; and *(d)* that there is no reason why she ever has to condemn herself as a human being, even when her acts are heinous, or why she need punish herself for doing these acts—though there are good reasons why she'd better accept the wrongness of her deeds and make future efforts to correct them. She would also tend to experience, along with these cognitive effects, the behavioral or emotional effects of feeling considerably less anxious, less guilty, and less self-punitive.

The therapist, by helping the client to see that "I don't need to suffer any more, maybe," has probably induced her, vaguely and by shorthand statements to herself, to quickly undergo this A-B-C-D-E self-deconditioning process of RET. If further sessions had materialized, he could have persuaded the client to go through the more longhand process many times, and more effectively depropagandize herself and immunize herself against future recurrence of guilt and self-punitiveness.

T^{155}: If you could read the Bible critically, it might be good for you—that is, to question it. Read it like you would any other book. And say, "What did he say? What did he mean? Is it true? And so what?"

C^{156}: Yeah. Like in Matthew, Jesus did a stupid thing. He cursed a tree because it didn't have any fruit on it, and it was not the season for the fig tree to have any fruit, anyway. So he cursed the poor tree when it wasn't even made to have fruit then.

T^{157}: That is pretty stupid on his part, isn't it?

C^{158}: Yeah. And the time he cast the devils into the swine, and those guys got pissed off at him? Well, I would too, because they were their whole herd, you know; he destroyed the guys' herd.

T^{159}: And it wasn't the pigs' fault, was it?

C^{160}: No. And I think it was selfish, too, because he destroyed some guys' ways that they lived on.

T^{161}: And yet millions of people follow his every word, thought, and deed, as if he is God's own son; and he does stupid things like that.

C^{162}: In John is the only book where he says he is the savior, and if it was that important, why didn't they put it in all the rest of them?

T^{163}: Why, indeed? It sounds to me like you are beginning to question, beginning to think, beginning to use your mind.

C^{164}: Yeah.

T^{165}: In good, critical ways, for any book you read, including the Bible.

C^{166}: Yeah. And they found a man's bones that was over thirty thousand years old.

T^{167}: Despite the story in the Bible that the world is only four to six thousand years old.

C^{168}: Yeah.

T^{169}: The answer to that which I have heard some Christians give is that the devil must have planted those bones to confuse us.

C^{170}: Oh, wow!

T^{171}: Those kinds of answers ought to convince you that you don't have to worry about the Christian view of man anymore. Then you don't have to worry about hurting yourself anymore.

C¹⁷²: Wow! The devil planted the bones there to confuse us! How did he make the bones to begin with?

T¹⁷³: That's like the angels on a pinhead, isn't it? Not worth really discussing because there is no point to it.

C¹⁷⁴: Yeah. There are people starving in the streets, and these people waste their time trying to decide how many angels can dance on a pinhead.

T¹⁷⁵: Well, I see our time has gotten away from us. When would you like to get together again?

C¹⁷⁶: In about two weeks.

T¹⁷⁷: Okay. Same time?

C¹⁷⁸: Yeah.

ELLIS: It certainly would appear, from the closing passages of this session, that Dr. Ard's original goal has been at least somewhat achieved: that the client is beginning to think for herself, and not merely parroting any views that he may have given her. He agrees and in response T¹⁵⁵ onward, adds to her antibiblical views. But it seems as if *she* is making an effort to gather information in this respect and to think things through. So she appears to be successfully carrying out one of the main goals of RET: to have the client replace conventional, dogmatic beliefs with more individualized, open-minded attitudes.

Because of the impossibility of her making satisfactory arrangements (because of her physical handicap) to continue the sessions, this tenth interview proved to be her last. It had been previously agreed, moreover, that she would not have many sessions altogether; and it appeared to her that she had already made highly satisfactory progress; so therapy was, at least for the time, terminated. While it can hardly be said that the client was completely cured, she certainly seemed to benefit appreciably from the ten sessions she had with the therapist. The material just presented may help show what can be accomplished with an individual who seemed, at the start, to be almost hopeless. By pursuing rational-emotive therapy in an active, direct manner, the therapist helped this client to make some significant progress in a short period of time.

Notes

1 The therapist (T) is Ben Ard. (C) stands for the counselee. (Eds.)
2 Rational-Emotive Therapy.

Reference

Falck, H. S. Thinking styles and individualism. *Bulletin of the Menninger Clinic,* 1969, *33,* 133–145.

Case 7

Editors' Introduction

This paper is historically important, since it is the first instance of the clinical use of behavior modification. Mary Cover Jones, faced with the problem of Peter, a small child with a fear of rabbits, did what must have seemed an unusual procedure. Others might have taken the "common sense" attitude of "Oh, he'll grow out of it" or might have attempted to soothe and calm the child with words. Neither procedure, one might add, was likely to work. Instead, doing the exact opposite of what Watson and Rayner (1920) had done, she . . . well, we shouldn't give the story away.

It is also interesting to note that Dr. Jones did what all good behavior modifiers have subsequently done: she kept exact records and charted them to demonstrate change in the target behavior. She probably had no idea that her little report was years ahead of its time, the precursor of systematic desensitization which, as one will soon see, was brought to a more sophisticated level by Joseph Wolpe.

MARY COVER JONES

A Laboratory Study of Fear: The Case of Peter

As part of a genetic study of emotions, a number of children were observed in order to determine the most effective methods of removing fear responses.

The case of Peter illustrates how a fear may be removed under laboratory conditions. His case was selected from a number of others for the following reasons:

1. Progress in combating the fear reactions was so marked that many of the details of the process could be observed easily.

2. It was possible to continue the study over a period of more than three months.

3   The notes of a running diary show the characteristics of a healthy, normal, interesting child, well adjusted, except for his exaggerated fear reactions. A few descriptive notes show something of his personality:

> Remarkably active, easily interested, capable of prolonged endeavor . . . . A favorite with the children as well as with the nurses and matrons . . . Peter has a healthy passion for possessions. Everything that he lays his hands on is his. As this is frequently disputed by some other child, there are occasional violent scenes of protest. These disturbances are not more frequent than might be expected in a three-year-old, in view of the fact that he is continually forced to adjust to a large group of children, nor are they more marked in Peter's case than in others of his age. Peter's IQ at the age of two years and ten months was 102 on the Kuhlmann Revision of the Binet. At the same time he passed five of the three-year tests on the Stanford Revision. In initiative and constructive ability, however, he is superior to his companions of the same mental age.

4   This case is a sequel to one recently contributed by Dr. Watson and furnished supplementary material of interest in a genetic study of emotions. Dr. Watson's case illustrated how a fear could be produced experimentally under laboratory conditions (Watson & Watson, 1921). A brief review follows: Albert, eleven months of age, was an infant with a phlegmatic disposition, afraid of nothing "under the sun" except a loud sound made by striking a steel bar. This

From *Pedagogical Seminary,* 1924, *31,* 308–315.

made him cry. By striking the bar at the same time that Albert touched a white rat, the fear was transferred to the white rat. After seven combined stimulations, rat and sound, Albert not only became greatly disturbed at the sight of a rat, but this fear had spread to include a white rabbit, cotton wool, a fur coat, and the experimenter's hair. It did not transfer to his wooden blocks and other objects very dissimilar to the rat.

In referring to this case, Dr. Watson says, "We have shown experimentally that when you condition a child to show fear of an animal, this fear transfers or spreads in such a way that without separate conditioning he becomes afraid of many animals. If you take any one of these objects producing fear and uncondition, will fear of the other objects in the series disappear at the same time? That is, will the unconditioning spread without further training to other stimuli?"

Dr. Watson intended to continue the study of Albert in an attempt to answer this question, but Albert was removed from the hospital and the series of observations was discontinued.

About three years later this case, which seemed almost to be Albert grown a bit older, was discovered in our laboratory.

Peter was two years and ten months old when we began to study him. He was afraid of a white rat, and this fear extended to a rabbit, a fur coat, a feather, cotton wool, etc., but not to wooden blocks and similar toys. An abridgment of the first laboratory notes on Peter reads as follows:

> Peter was put in a crib in a play room and immediately became absorbed in his toys. A white rat was introduced into the crib from behind. (The experimenter was behind a screen). At sight of the rat, Peter screamed and fell flat on his back in a paroxysm of fear. The stimulus was removed, and Peter was taken out of the crib and put into a chair. Barbara was brought to the crib and the white rat introduced as before. She exhibited no fear but picked the rat up in her hand. Peter sat quietly watching Barbara and the rat. A string of beads belonging to Peter had been left in the crib. Whenever the rat touched a part of the string he would say "my beads" in a complaining voice, although he made no objections when Barbara touched them. Invited to get down from the chair, he shook his head, fear not yet subsided. Twenty-five minutes elapsed before he was ready to play about freely.

The next day his reactions to the following situations and objects were noted:

Play room and crib ....Selected toys, got into crib without protest
White ball rolled in ....Picked it up and held it
Fur rug hung over crib ....Cried until it was removed
Fur coat hung over crib.............Cried until it was removed
Cotton ....Whimpered, withdrew, cried
Hat with feathers ....Cried
Blue woolly sweater ....Looked, turned away, no fear
White toy rabbit of rough cloth ....No interest, no fear
Wooden doll ....No interest, no fear

This case made it possible for the experiment to continue where Dr. Watson had left off. The first problem was that of "unconditioning" a fear response to an animal, and the second, that of determining whether unconditioning to one stimulus spreads without further training to other stimuli.

From the test situations which were used to reveal fears, it was found that Peter showed even more marked fear responses to the rabbit than to the rat. It was decided to use the rabbit for unconditioning and to proceed as follows: Each day Peter and three other children were brought to the laboratory for a play period. The other children were selected carefully because of their entirely fearless attitude toward the rabbit and because of their satisfactory adjustments in general. The rabbit was always present during a part of the play period. From time to time Peter was brought in alone so that his reactions could be observed and progress noted.

From reading over the notes for each session it was apparent that there had been improvement by more or less regular steps from almost complete terror at sight of the rabbit to a completely positive response with no signs of disturbance. New situations requiring closer contact with the rabbit had been gradually introduced and the degree to which these situations were avoided, tolerated, or welcomed, at each experimental session, gave the measure of improvement. Analysis of the notes on Peter's reactions indicated the following progressive steps in his degrees of toleration:

A. Rabbit anywhere in the room in a cage causes fear reactions.
B. Rabbit 12 feet away in cage tolerated.
C. Rabbit 4 feet away in cage tolerated.
D. Rabbit 3 feet away in cage tolerated.
E. Rabbit close in cage tolerated.
F. Rabbit free in room tolerated.
G. Rabbit touched when experimenter holds it.
H. Rabbit touched when free in room.
I. Rabbit defied by spitting at it, throwing things at it, imitating it.
J. Rabbit allowed on tray of high chair.
K. Squats in defenseless position beside rabbit.
L. Helps experimenter to carry rabbit to its cage.
M. Holds rabbit on lap.
N. Stays alone in room with rabbit.
O. Allows rabbit in play pen with him.
P. Fondles rabbit affectionately.
Q. Lets rabbit nibble his fingers.

These "degrees of toleration" merely represented the stages in which improvement occurred. They did not give any indications of the intervals between steps, nor of the plateaus, relapses, and sudden gains which were actually evident. To show these features a curve was drawn by using the seventeen steps given above as the Y axis of a chart and the experimental sessions as the X axis. The units are not equal on either axis, as the "degrees of toleration" have merely been set down as they appeared from consideration of the laboratory notes with no attempt to evaluate the steps. Likewise the experimental sessions were not equidistant in time. Peter was seen twice daily for a period and thence only once a day. At one point illness and quarantine interrupted the experiments for two months. There is no indication of these irregularities on the chart. For example, along the X axis, 1 represents the date December 4 when the observation began. Eleven and 12 represent the dates March 10 A.M. and P.M. (from December 17 to March 7, Peter was not available for study).

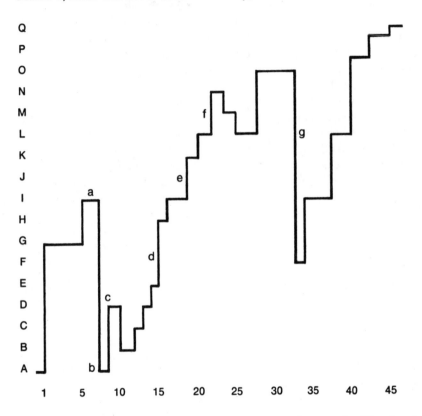

The question arose as to whether or not the points on the Y axis which indicated progress to the experimenter represented real advance and not merely idiosyncratic reactions of the subject. The "tolerance series" as indicated by the experimenter was presented in random order to six graduate students and instructors in psychology to be arranged so as to indicate increase in tolerance, in their judgment. An average correlation of .70 with the experimenter's arrangement was found for the six ratings. This indicates that the experimenter was justified from an a priori point of view in designating the steps to be progressive stages.

The first seven periods show how Peter progressed from a great fear of the rabbit to a tranquil indifference and even a voluntary pat on the rabbit's back when others were setting the example. The notes for the seventh period (see a on chart) read:

Laurel, Mary, Arthur, Peter playing together in the laboratory. Experimenter put rabbit down on floor. Arthur said, "Peter doesn't cry when he sees the rabbit come out." Peter, "No." He was a little concerned as to whether or not the rabbit would eat his kiddie car. Laurel and Mary stroked the rabbit and chattered away excitedly. Peter walked over, touched the rabbit on the back, exulting, "I touched him on the end."

At this period Peter was taken to the hospital with scarlet fever. He did not return for two months.

By referring to the chart at (b), it will be noted that the line shows a decided drop to the early level of fear reaction when he returned. This was easily explained by the nurse who brought Peter from the hospital. As they were entering a taxi at the door of the hospital, a large dog, running past, jumped at them. Both Peter and the nurse were very much frightened, Peter so much that he lay back in the taxi pale and quiet, and the nurse debated whether or not to return him to the hospital. This seemed reason enough for his precipitate descent back to the original fear level. Being threatened by a large dog when ill, and in a strange place and being with an adult who also showed fear, was a terrifying situation against which our training could not have fortified him.

At this point (b) we began another method of treatment, that of "direct conditioning." Peter was seated in a high chair and given food which he liked. The experimenter brought the rabbit in a wire cage as close as she could without arousing a response which would interfere with the eating. Through the presence of the pleasant stimulus (food) whenever the rabbit was shown, the fear was eliminated gradually in favor of a positive response. Occasionally also, other children were brought in to help with the "unconditioning." These facts are of interest in following the charted progress. The first decided rise at (c) was due to the presence of another child who influenced Peter's reaction. The notes for this day read:

Lawrence and Peter sitting near together in their high chairs eating candy. Rabbit in cage put down twelve feet away. Peter began to cry. Lawrence said, "Oh, rabbit." Clambered down, ran over and looked in the cage at him. Peter followed close and watched.

The next two decided rises at (d) and (e) occurred on the day when a student assistant, Dr. S., was present. Peter was very fond of Dr. S. whom he insisted was his "papa." Although Dr. S. did not directly influence Peter by any overt suggestions, it may be that having him there contributed to Peter's general feeling of well being and thus indirectly affected his reactions. The fourth rise on the chart at (f) was, like the first, due to the influence of another child. Notes for the twenty-first session read:

Peter with candy in high chair. Experimenter brought rabbit and sat down in front of the tray with it. Peter cried out, "I don't want him," and withdrew. Rabbit was given to another child sitting near to hold. His holding the rabbit served as a powerful suggestion; Peter wanted the rabbit on his lap, and held it for an instant.

The decided drop at (g) was caused by a slight scratch when Peter was helping to carry the rabbit to his cage. The rapid ascent following shows how quickly he regained lost ground.

In one of our last sessions, Peter showed no fear although another child was present who showed marked disturbance at sight of the rabbit.

An attempt was made from time to time to see what verbal organization accompanied this process of "unconditioning." Upon Peter's return from the hospital, the following conversation took place:

E. (experimenter): What do you do upstairs, Peter? [The laboratory was upstairs.]
P. I see my brother. Take me up to see my brother.
E. What else will you see?
P. Blocks.

Peter's reference to blocks indicated a definite memory as he played with blocks only in the laboratory. No further response of any significance could be elicited. In the laboratory two days later (he had seen the rabbit once in the meantime), he said suddenly, "Beads can't bite me, beads can only look at me." Toward the end of the training an occasional "I like the rabbit," was all the language he had to parallel the changed emotional organization.

Early in the experiment an attempt was made to get some measure of the visceral changes accompanying Peter's fear reactions. On one occasion Dr. S. determined Peter's blood pressure outside the laboratory and again later, in the laboratory while he was in a state of much anxiety caused by the rabbit's being held close to him by the experimenter. The diastolic blood pressure changed from 65 to 80 on this occasion. Peter was taken to the infirmary the next day for the routine physical examination and developed there a suspicion of medical instruments which made it inadvisable to proceed with this phase of the work.

Peter has gone home to a difficult environment but the experimenter is still in touch with him. He showed in the last interview, as on the later portions of the chart, a genuine fondness for the rabbit. What has happened to the fear of the other objects? The fear of the cotton, the fur coat, feathers, was entirely absent at our last interview. He looked at them, handled them, and immediately turned to something which interested him more. The reaction to the rats, and the fur rug with the stuffed head was greatly modified and improved. While he did not show the fondness for these that was apparent with the rabbit, he had made a fair adjustment. For example, Peter would pick up the tin box containing frogs or rats and carry it around the room. When requested, he picked up the fur rug and carried it to the experimenter.

What would Peter do if confronted by a strange animal? At the last interview the experimenter presented a mouse and a tangled mass of angleworms. At first sight, Peter showed slight distress reactions and moved away, but before the period was over he was carrying the worms about and watching the mouse with undisturbed interest. By "unconditioning" Peter to the rabbit, he has apparently been helped to overcome many superfluous fears, some completely, some to a less degree. His tolerance of strange animals and unfamiliar situations has apparently increased.

The study is still incomplete. Peter's fear of the animals which were shown him was probably not a directly conditioned fear. It is unlikely that he had ever had any experience with white rats, for example. Where the fear originated and with what stimulus, is not known. Nor is it known what Peter would do if he were again confronted with the original fear situation. All of the fears which were "unconditioned" were transferred fears, and it has not yet been learned whether or not the primary fear can be eliminated by training the transfers.

Another matter which must be left to speculation is the future welfare of the subject. His "home" consists of one furnished room which is occupied by his mother and father, a brother of nine years and himself. Since the death of an older sister, he is the recipient of most of the unwise affection of his parents. His brother appears to bear him a grudge because of this favoritism, as might be expected. Peter hears continually, "Ben is so bad and so dumb, but Peter is so good and so smart!" His mother is a highly emotional individual who can not get through an interview, however brief, without a display of tears. She is totally incapable of providing a home on the $25 a week which her husband steadily earns. In an attempt to control Peter she resorts to frequent fear suggestions. "Come in Peter, some one wants to steal you." To her erratic resorts to discipline, Peter reacts with temper tantrums. He was denied a summer in the country because his father "forgets he's tired when he has Peter around." Surely a discouraging outlook for Peter.

But the recent development of psychological studies of young children and the growing tendency to carry the knowledge gained in the psychological laboratories into the home and school induce us to predict a more wholesome treatment of a future generation of Peters.

Reference

Watson, J. B., & Watson, R. R. Studies in infant psychology. *Scientific Monthly*, 1921.

Case 8

Editors' Introduction

Joseph Wolpe is one of the pioneers of behavior therapy and the father of systematic desensitization. Few therapeutic techniques have been investigated so thoroughly or have received as much empirical validation. Desensitization has become an essential part of the behavior therapy armamentarium.

Essentially, Wolpe's conceptualization is that people tend to associate certain stimuli with unpleasant experiences and suffer anxiety whenever these stimuli occur. The therapeutic maneuver to reduce anxiety and thereby increase efficiency is to pair various images with relaxation, changing the imagery from minor to major as one gains increasing ability to cope with the images generated. This is the basic concept of systematic desensitization which is Wolpe's major contribution and which relates historically with Mary Cover Jones's research on erasing fear in a child.

Effectively reducing phobic anxiety calls for a combination of careful planning, imaginative situation setting, the ability to teach relaxation skills, and plain hard work—as this next reading clearly shows.

JOSEPH WOLPE

Isolation of a Conditioning Procedure as the Crucial Psychotherapeutic Factor: A Case Study

In a considerable number of publications (e.g., Bond & Hutchinson, 1960; Eysenck, 1960; Lazarus, 1962; Lazarus & Rachman, 1957; Lazovik & Lang, 1960; Rachman, 1961; Wolpe, 1958, 1961a, 1961b) it has been shown that methods based on principles of learning achieve strikingly good results in the treatment of human neuroses. Neuroses are usually characterized by persistent habits of anxiety response to stimulus situations in which there is no objective danger—for example, the mere presence of superiors, being watched working, seeing people quarrel, riding in an elevator. Since these habits of emotional response have been acquired by learning (Wolpe, 1956, 1958) it is only to be expected that they would be overcome by appropriate procedures designed to bring about unlearning. Most of the procedures that have been used have depended upon inhibition of anxiety through the evocation of other responses physiologically incompatible with it (reciprocal inhibition); for each occasion of such inhibition diminishes to some extent the strength of the anxiety response habit (Wolpe, 1958).

When "dynamic" psychiatrists are confronted with the therapeutic successes of behavioristic therapy they discount them on the ground that the results are "really" due to the operation of "mechanisms" postulated by *their* theory: transference, insight, suggestion, or derepression. Despite the fact that it is now manifest (Wolpe, 1960, 1961) that the basic "mechanisms" of psychoanalysis have no scientifically acceptable factual foundations, their proponents can still content themselves with saying that the *possibility* of their operation has not been excluded. Resort to this kind of comfortable refuge would be undermined if study of the therapeutic course of individual cases were to show *both* that there is a direct correlation between the use of conditioning procedures and recovery and that "dynamic mechanisms" are *not* so correlated, either because they cannot be inferred from the facts of the case or because even when they might be inferred they have no temporal relation to the emergence of change.

From *Journal of Nervous and Mental Disease, 134,* 316–329. Copyright 1962, The Williams and Wilkins Co. Reproduced by permission.

The case described below was made the subject of variation of several of the factors that are alleged from various standpoints to have therapeutic potency. A patient with a single severe phobia for automobiles was selected for the experiment because the presence of a single dimension of disturbance simplifies the estimation of change. It was found that a deconditioning technique—systematic desensitization (Wolpe, 1954, 1958, 1968a)—alone was correlated with improvement, which was quantitatively related to the number of reinforcements given. At the same time, activities that might give any grounds for imputations of transference, insight, suggestion, and derepression were omitted or manipulated in such a way as to render the operation of these "mechanisms" exceedingly implausible. Furthermore, the conduct of therapy in several series of interviews separated by long intervals had results incompatible with "spontaneous recovery"—a possibility that might have been entertained if improvement during the intervals had been as great as during the treatment periods; but in fact virtually no change occurred during the intervals.

This case incidentally illustrates how difficult it can be to find stimulus situations that evoke sufficiently low anxiety to enable *commencement* of desensitization, and how the details of procedure must be tailored to the needs of the case.

The Case of Mrs. C.

The patient, a thirty-nine-year old woman, complained of fear reactions to traffic situations. Dr. Richard W. Garnett, Jr., a senior staff psychiatrist, had referred her to me after interviewing her a few times. I first saw the patient at the University Hospital on April 6, 1960. Briefly her story was that on February 3, 1958, while her husband was taking her to work by car, they entered an intersection on the green light. On the left she noticed two girls standing at the curb waiting for the light to change, and then, suddenly, became aware of a large truck that had disregarded the red signal, bearing down upon the car. She remembered the moment of impact, being flung out of the car, flying through the air, and then losing consciousness. Her next recollection was of waking in the ambulance, seeing her husband, and telling him that everything was all right. She felt quite calm and remained so during the rest of the journey to the hospital. There she was found to have injuries to her knee and neck, for the treatment of which she spent a week in the hospital.

On the way home, by car, she felt unaccountably frightened. She stayed at home for two weeks, quite happily, and then, resuming normal activities, noticed that, while in a car, though relatively comfortable on the open road, she was always disturbed by seeing any car approach *from either side,* but not at all by vehicles straight ahead. Along city streets she had continuous anxiety, which, at the sight of a laterally approaching car less than half a block away, would rise to panic. She could, however, avoid such a reaction by closing her eyes before reaching an intersection. She was also distressed in other situations that in any sense involved lateral approaches of cars. Reactions were extraordinarily severe in relation to making a left turn in the face of approaching traffic on the highway. Execution of the turn, of course, momentarily placed the approaching vehicle to the right of her car, and there was a considerable rise in tension even when the vehicle was a mile or more ahead. Left turns in the city disturbed her less because of slower speeds. The entry of other cars from side streets even as far as two blocks ahead into the road in which she was traveling also constituted a "lateral threat." Besides her reactions while in a car, she was anxious while walking across streets, even at intersections with the traffic light in her favor, and even if the nearest approaching car were more than a block away.

During the first few months of Mrs. C.'s neurosis, her panic at the sight of a car approaching from the side would cause her to grasp the driver by the arm. Her awareness of the annoyance this occasioned subsequently led her to control this behavior, for the most part successfully, but the fear was not diminished.

Questioned about previous related traumatic experiences, she recalled that ten years previously a tractor had crashed into the side of a car in which she was a passenger. Nobody had been hurt, the car had continued its journey, and she had been aware of no emotional sequel. No one close to her had ever been involved in a serious accident. Though she had worked in the Workmen's Compensation Claims office, dealing with cases of injury had not been disturbing to her. She found it incomprehensible that she should have developed this phobia; in London during World War II, she had accepted the dangers of the blitz calmly, without ever needing to use soporifics or sedatives.

She had received no previous treatment for her phobia. During the previous few days, she had told her story to Dr. Garnett; and then a medical student had seen her daily and discussed various aspects of her life, such as her childhood and her life with her husband—all of which she had felt to be irrelevant.

The plan of therapy was to confine subsequent interviews as far as possible to the procedures of *systematic desensitization,* and to omit any further history taking, probing, and analyzing. Systematic desensitization (Bond & Hutchinson, 1960; Lazarus, 1962; Lazarus & Rachman, 1957; Wolpe, 1954, 1956, 1958, 1959, 1961b) is a method of therapy that has its roots in the experimental laboratory. It has been shown experimentally (Napalkov & Karas, 1957; Wolpe, 1952, 1958) that persistent unadaptive habits of anxiety response may be eliminated by counteracting (and thus inhibiting) individual evocations of the response by means of the simultaneous evocation of an incompatible response (reciprocal inhibition). Each such inhibition leads to some degree of weakening of the anxiety response habit.

In systematic desensitization, the emotional effects of deep muscle relaxation are employed to counteract the anxiety evoked by phobic and allied stimulus situations presented to the patient's *imagination.* Stimulus situations on the theme of the patient's neurotic anxiety are listed and then ranked according to the intensity of anxiety they evoke. The patient, having been relaxed, sometimes under hypnosis, is asked to imagine the weakest of the disturbing stimuli, repeatedly, until it ceases to evoke any anxiety. Then increasingly "strong" stimuli are introduced in turn, and similarly treated, until eventually even the "strongest" fails to evoke anxiety. This desensitizing to imaginary situations has been found to be correlated with disappearance of anxiety in the presence of the actual situation.

In the second interview, training in relaxation and the construction of hierarchies were both initiated. To begin with, Mrs. C. was schooled in relaxation of the arms and the muscles of the forehead. Two hierarchies were constructed. The first related to traffic situations in open country. There was allegedly a minimal reaction if she was in a car driven by her husband and they were 200 yards from a crossroads and if, 400 yards away, at right angles, another car was approaching. Anxiety increased with increasing proximity. The second hierarchy related to lateral approaches of other cars while that in which she was traveling had stopped at a city traffic light. The first signs of anxiety supposedly appeared when the other car was two blocks away. (This, as will be seen, was a gross understatement of the patient's reactions.) The interview concluded with an introductory desensitization session. Having hypnotized and relaxed Mrs. C., I presented to her imagination some presumably neutral stimuli. First she was asked to imagine herself walking across a baseball field and then that she was riding in a car in the country with no other cars in sight. Following this, she was presented with the allegedly weak phobic situation of being in a car 200 yards from an intersection and seeing another car 400 yards on the left. She afterwards reported no disturbances to any of the scenes.

The third interview was conducted in the presence of an audience of five physicians. The Willoughby Neuroticism Test gave a borderline score of 24. (Normal, for practical purposes, is under 20. About 80 percent of patients have scores above 30 [Wolpe, 1958].) Instruction in relaxation of muscles of the shoulder was succeeded by a desensitization session in which the following scenes were presented:

1) The patient's car, driven by her husband, had stopped at an intersection, and another car was approaching at right angles two blocks away.

2) The highway scene of the previous session was suggested, except that now her car was 150 yards from the intersection and the other car 300 yards away. Because this produced a finger raising (signaling felt anxiety), after a pause she was asked to imagine that she was 150 yards from the intersection and the other car 400 yards. Though she did not raise her finger at this, it was noticed that she moved her legs. (*It was subsequently found that these leg movements were a very sensitive indicator of emotional disturbance.*)

Consequently, at the fourth interview, I subjected Mrs. C. to further questioning about her reactions to automobiles, from which it emerged that she was continuously tense in cars but had not thought this worth reporting, so trifling was it beside the terror experienced at the lateral approach of a car. She now also stated that *all* the car scenes imagined during the sessions had aroused anxiety, but too little, she had felt, to deserve mention. While relaxed under hypnosis, Mrs. C. was asked to imagine that she was in a car about to be driven around an empty square. As there was no reaction to this, the next scene presented was preparing to ride two blocks on a country road. This evoked considerable anxiety!

At the fifth interview, it was learned that even the thought of a journey raised Mrs. C.'s tension, so that if, for example, at 9 A.M. her husband were to say, "We are going out driving at 2 P.M." she would be continuously apprehensive, and more so when actually in the car. During the desensitization session (fourth) at this interview, I asked her to imagine that she was at home expecting to go for a short drive in the country in four hours' time. This scene, presented five times, evoked anxiety that did not decrease on repetition. It was now obvious that scenes with the merest suspicion of exposure to traffic were producing more anxiety than could be mastered by Mrs. C.'s relaxation potential.

A new strategy therefore had to be devised. I introduced an artifice that lent itself to controlled manipulation. On a sheet of paper I drew an altogether imaginary completely enclosed square field, which was represented as being two blocks (200 yards) long (see Figure 8.1). At the southwest corner (lower left) I drew her car, facing north (upwards), in which she sat with her husband, and at the lower right corner another car, supposed to be Dr. Garnett's, which faced them at right angles. Dr. Garnett (hereafter "Dr. G.") was "used" because Mrs. C. regarded him as a trustworthy person.

This imaginary situation became the focus of the scenes presented in the sessions that followed. At the fifth desensitization session, Mrs. C. was asked to

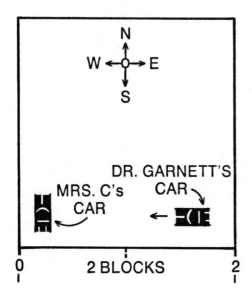

FIGURE 8.1. Imaginary enclosed square where Doctor Garnett makes progressively closer advances to Mrs. C.'s car. (See text.)

imagine Dr. G. announcing to her that he was going to drive his car a half-block towards her and then proceeding to do so while she sat in her parked car. As this elicited no reaction, she was next made to imagine him driving one block towards her, and then, as there was again no reaction, one and a quarter blocks. On perceiving a reaction to this scene, I repeated it three times, but without effecting any decrement in the reaction. I then "retreated," asking her to imagine Dr. G. stopping after traveling one block and two paces towards her. This produced a slighter reaction, and *this decreased on repeating the scene, disappearing at the fourth presentation*. This was the first evidence of change, and afforded grounds for a confident prediction of successful therapy.

At the sixth session, the imagined distance between Dr. G.'s stopping point and Mrs. C.'s car was decreased by two or three paces at a time, and at the end of the session he was able to stop seven-eighths of a block short of her (a total gain of about ten paces). The following are the details of the progression. In parentheses is the number of presentations of each scene required to reduce the anxiety response to zero:

1) Dr. G. approaches four paces beyond one block (3).
2) Six paces beyond one block (3).
3) Nine paces beyond one block (2).
4) Twelve paces beyond one block, *i.e.,* one and one-eighth block (4).

At the seventh session, Mrs. C. was enabled to tolerate Dr. G.'s car reaching a point half a block short of her car without disturbance; at the eighth session, three-eighths of a block (about 37 yards); at the tenth, she was able to imagine him approaching within two yards of her without any reaction whatsoever.

The day after this, Mrs. C. reported that for the first time since her accident she had been able to walk across a street while an approaching car was in sight. The car was two blocks away but she was able to complete the crossing without quickening her pace. At this, the eleventh session, I began a new series of scenes in which Dr. G. drove in front of the car containing Mrs. C. instead of towards it, passing at first 30 yards ahead, and then gradually closer, cutting the distance eventually to about three yards. Desensitization to all this was rather rapidly achieved during this session. Thereupon, I drew two intersecting roads in the diagram of the field (Figure 8.2). A traffic light was indicated in the middle, and the patient's car, as shown in the diagram, had "stopped" at the red signal. At first, Mrs. C. was asked to imagine Dr. G.'s car passing on the green light. As anticipated, she could at once accept this without anxiety; it was followed by Dr. G.'s car passing one way and a resident physician's car in the opposite direction. The slight anxiety this aroused was soon eliminated. In subsequent scenes, the resident's car was followed by an increasing number of students' cars, each scene being repeated until its emotional effect declined to zero.

At the twelfth session, the roadway at right angles to Mrs. C.'s car was made continuous with the public highway system (as indicated by the dotted lines) and now, starting off again with Dr. G., we added the cars of the resident and the

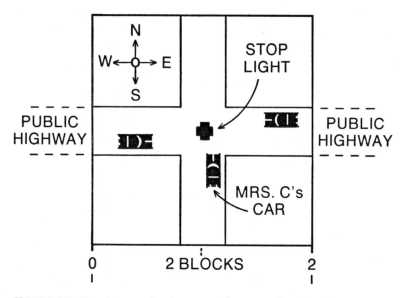

FIGURE 8.2. Imaginary enclosed square with crossroads and traffic light added. Other cars pass while Mrs. C.'s car has stopped at the red light. (See text.)

students, and subsequently those of strangers. Imagining two unknown cars passing the intersection produced a fair degree of anxiety and she required five presentations at this session and five more at the next before she could accept it entirely calmly. However, once this was accomplished, it was relatively easy gradually to introduce several cars passing from both sides.

We now began a new series of scenes in which, with the traffic light in her favor, she was stepping off the curb to cross a city street while a car was slowly approaching. At first, the car was imagined a block away, but during succeeding sessions the distance gradually decreased to ten yards.

At this point, to check upon transfer from the imaginary to real life, I took Mrs. C. to the Charlottesville business center and observed her crossing streets at an intersection controlled by a traffic light. She went across repeatedly with apparent ease and reported no anxiety. But in the car, on the way there and back, she showed marked anxiety whenever a car from a side street threatened to enter the street in which we drove.

Soon afterwards, the opportunity arose for an experiment relevant to the question of "transference." A medical student had been present as an observer during four or five sessions. Early in May I had to leave town for a week to attend a conference. I decided to let the student continue therapy in my absence. Accordingly, I asked him to conduct the fifteenth desensitization session under my supervision. I corrected his errors by silently passing him written notes. Since he eventually performed quite well, he agreed to carry on treatment during my absence, and conducted the eighteenth to the twenty-third sessions entirely without supervision. His efforts were directed to a new series of scenes in which, while Mrs. C. was being driven by her husband along a city street, Dr. G.'s car made a right turn into that street from a cross street on their left. At first, Dr. G. was imagined making this entry two blocks ahead, but after several intervening stages it became possible for her to accept it calmly only half a block ahead. The student therapist then introduced a modification in which a student instead of Dr. G. drove the other car. The car was first visualized as entering two blocks ahead and the distance then gradually reduced to a half-block in the course of three sessions, requiring sixty-three scene presentations, most of which were needed in a very laborious advance from three-quarters of a block.

At this stage, the therapist experimentally inserted a scene in which Mrs. C.'s car was making a left turn in the city while Dr. G.'s car approached from the opposite direction four blocks ahead. This produced such a violent reaction that the therapist became apprehensive about continuing treatment. However, I returned the next day. Meanwhile, the point had been established that a substitute therapist could make satisfactory progress. (Under the writer's guidance, but not in his presence, the student therapist went on to conduct two entirely successful sessions the following week.)

I now made a detailed analysis of Mrs. C.'s reaction to left turns on the highway in the face of oncoming traffic. She reported anxiety at doing a left turn *if an oncoming car was in sight*. Even if it was two miles away she could not allow her husband to turn left in front of it.

To treat this most sensitive reaction, I again reintroduced Dr. G. into the picture. I started by making Mrs. C. imagine (while hypnotized and relaxed) that Dr. G.'s car was a mile ahead when her car began the turn. But this was too disturbing and several repetitions of the scene brought no diminution in the magnitude of anxiety evoked. It seemed possible that there would be less anxiety if the patient's husband were not the driver of the car, since his presence at the time of the accident might have made him a conditioned stimulus to anxiety. Thus I presented the scene with Mrs. C.'s *brother* as the driver of the car. With this altered feature, Dr. G.'s making a left turn a mile ahead evoked much less anxiety, and after four repetitions it declined to zero; we were gradually able to decrease the distance so that she could eventually imagine making the turn with Dr. G.'s car only about 150 yards away (see Table 8.1). Meanwhile, when she was able to "do" the turn with Dr. G. three-eighths of a mile away, I introduced two new left-turn series: a strange car approaching with her brother driving, and Dr. G. approaching with her husband driving—both a mile away initially. Work on all three series went on concurrently. When Mrs. C. could comfortably imagine her brother doing a left turn with the strange car five-eighths of a mile ahead, I resumed the original series in which her husband was the driver, starting with a left turn while the strange car was a mile ahead. This now evoked relatively little anxiety; progress could be predicted, and ensued. The interrelated decrements of reaction to this group of hierarchies are summarized in Figure 8.3.

Other series of related scenes were also subjected to desensitization. They are

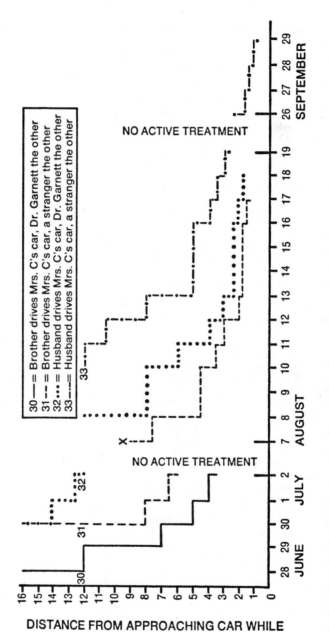

DISTANCE FROM APPROACHING CAR WHILE
MAKING LEFT TURN
(SIXTEENTHS OF A MILE)

FIGURE 8.3. Temporal relations of "distances accomplished" in imagination in desensitization series 30, 31, 32 and 33. X: indicates some relapse in Hierarchy 31 following a taxi
ride in which the driver insisted on exceeding the speed limit. The status of Hierarchy 32 was
not tested before the relapse in 31 was overcome.

TABLE 8.1. Summary of Data Concerning Hierarchies

No. of Hierarchy	Content of Hierarchy	No. of Presentations of Scenes from Each Hierarchy	Result
0	Baseball field (control scene)	1	No reaction
1	Approaching highway crossroads which another car approaches laterally (two distance variables—own distance and that of the other car)	15	Nil
2	Stationary at city intersection while other cars approach (two blocks maximum)	2	Nil
3	About to be driven from country lodge—starting from distance of two blocks (temporal variable)	9	Nil
4	Approached by Dr. G.'s car on imaginary field (Fig. 8–1) starting two blocks away	41	+
5	As No. 4, but Dr. G. starts each advance from one block away	50	+
6	Dr. G. drives his car to pass in front of hers (decreasing passing distance, 30 yards to 3 yards)	10	+
7-8	Mrs. C. stopped by red in imaginary field (Fig. 8–2) and increasing variety and number of medical school cars pass on green	10	+
9-10	As No. 7 but the crossroad now continuous with public highway and increasing variety and number of strange cars pass (Fig. 8–2)	27	+
11	Walking across road at intersection while a car moves towards her (decreasing distances from 1½ blocks to 10 yards)	30	+
12	Goes through on green with increasing number of strange cars stationary at right and left	4	No disturbance from outset
13	As her car passes on green, Dr. G.'s car advances at side (decreasing distance from ½ block to 10 yards)	25	+
14	While Mrs. C.'s car moves slowly in town, Dr. G.'s car turns into her lane from side street (2 blocks to ¼ block) (Sessions by student, see text)	39	+
15	As No. 14, but strange car (2 blocks to ½ block) (Sessions by student, see text)	62	+
16	Dr. G.'s car makes left turn across path of her slowly moving car (2 blocks to ¾ block) (Sessions by student, see text)	22	+
17	As No. 16, but student's car (2 blocks to ¾ block) (Sessions by student, see text)	26	+
18	Mrs. C.'s car in city turns left while Dr. G. advances (Handled alternately by student and author) (6 blocks to 3¾ blocks)	22	+ with difficulty
19	On highway (Fig. 8–2) turns left in front of tractor moving 5 mph. (1 mile to ¼ block)	36	+
20	Turns left in car while at fixed distance of ½ block a car whose driver is instructed by Dr. G. is advancing. Its speed was gradually increased from 5 to 30 mph.	93	+
21	Turns left while two strange cars advance a block ahead. Speed of the cars increased gradually from 15 mph to 26 mph.	25	+
22	While driving in taxi in through street, sees a car moving very slowly to stop at intersection ahead. Distance decreased from 1 block to 5/16 block	35	+

(TABLE 8.1—*Continued*)

No. of Hierarchy	Content of Hierarchy	No. of Presentations of Scenes from Each Hierarchy	Result
23	As No. 22, but the other car decelerates from normal speed. Distance gradually decreased from ½ block to zero from line of intersection	102	+
24	Walking across intersection at green light, while car a block away approaches. Increasing speeds 10–20 mph.	5	+
25	Stepping off curb to cross at unguarded intersection while car on left approaches at 10 mph. Decreasing distance 1 block to ⅜ block	137	+ very difficult progress from ½ block on
26	Does left turn in city while a car approaches at 10 mph. Decreasing distance from ⅞ to ⅝ block	67	+ very difficult from ¾ block on
27	She walks back and forth in the imaginary enclosed field parallel to a white line up to which Dr. G. drives his car at 1 mph. Her distance from the line decreases from 10 yds. to 4½ yds.	23	+
28	While she keeps constant parallel distance of 5 yds. from white line, Dr. G.'s speed increases from 1 to 18 mph.	68	+
29	Steps off curb at unguarded intersection while car on *right* approaches at 10 mph. Distances 1 block to ⅝ block	14	+
30	On highway in car driven by brother, does left turn in face of approaching car driven by Dr. G. Distance between them decreases from 1 mile to 350 yards	70	+
31	As 30, but stranger drives another car. Distances from 1 mile to 150 yds.	126	+
32	As 30, but Mrs. C.'s husband drives her car. Distances from 1 mile to 175 yds.	117	+
33	As 30, but Mrs. C's husband drives her car and stranger drives the other. Distances from 1 mile to 150 yds.	100	+
34	In taxi that does U-turn while a car approaches in city. Distances 2 blocks to 1 block	6	+
35	Driven by husband does left turn in city in face of slowly oncoming car. Distances of ½ block to 15 yds.	29	+
36	In sight of oncoming car, enters highway from side road after stopping. Distances ¼ to ⅛ mile	43	+
	Total Scenes	1491	

listed in Table 8.1, in order of commencement, but there was much overlapping of incidence. One comprised left turns *in the city* in front of oncoming cars. Since cars in the city move relatively slowly, she felt less "danger" at a given distance. At first, we dealt with left turns while an approaching car was about two blocks away, and in the course of several sessions gradually decreased the distance until Mrs. C. could comfortably "do" a left turn with the other car slowly moving 15 yards ahead. The series where Mrs. C. was crossing streets as a pedestrian was extended, and she was enabled in imagination to cross under all normal conditions. She reported complete transfer to the reality. A series that was started somewhat later involved driving down a through street with a car in a side street slowing to a stop. At first, the side street was "placed" two blocks ahead. The distance was gradually decreased as desensitization progressed, and eventually she could without anxiety drive past a car slowing to a stop. A series intercurrently employed to desensitize her in a general way to the feeling that a car was "bearing down upon her," was not part of any real situation. In our imaginary square field (Figure 8.1), I "placed" two parallel white lines, scaled to be about 20 feet long and 10 feet apart. During the session I said, "You are walking up and down along one white line and Dr. G. drives his car up to the other at one mile per hour . . . " This was not disturbing; but at subsequent visualizings the speed was gradually increased and at an early stage the distance between the lines decreased to five feet. At four miles per hour there was some anxiety. This was soon eliminated, and several presentations of scenes from this series during each of ten sessions made it possible for Mrs. C. calmly to imagine Dr. G. driving up to his white line at 18 miles per hour while she strolled along hers.

The total effect of desensitization to these interrelated series of stimulus situations was that Mrs. C. became completely at ease in all normal traffic situations—both in crossing streets as a pedestrian and riding in a car. Improvement in real situations took place in close relation with the improvements during sessions. A direct demonstration of the transfer of improvement with respect to crossing streets at traffic lights has been described above.

The patient's progress was slow but consistent. Because she lived about 100 miles away, her treatment took place episodically. At intervals of from four to six weeks she would come to Charlottesville for about two weeks and be seen almost every day. Noteworthy reduction in the range of real situations that could disturb her occurred in the course of each period of active treatment, and practically none during the intervals. She was instructed not to avoid exposing herself during these intervals to situations that might be expected to be only slightly disturbing: but if she anticipated being very disturbed to close her eyes, if feasible, for she could thus "ward off" the situation. Every now and then, particular incidents stood out as landmarks in her progress. One day in late August, driving with her brother in a through street in her home town, she saw a car slowing down before a stop sign as they passed it. Though the car did not quite stop, she had no reaction at all, though gazing at it continuously. This incident demonstrated the transfer to life of the desensitization to the relevant hierarchy (No. 23) which had been concluded shortly before. Since then, similar experiences had been consistently free from disturbance.

At the conclusion of Mrs. C.'s treatment, she was perfectly comfortable making a pedestrian crossing even though the traffic was creeping up to her. Left turns on a highway were quite comfortable with fast traffic up to about 150 yards ahead. When the closest approaching car was somewhat nearer, her reaction was slight anxiety, and not panic, as in the past. In all other traffic situations her feeling was entirely normal. Another effect of the treatment was that she no longer had headaches due to emotional tension.

In all, fifty-seven desensitization sessions were conducted. The number of scene presentations at a session generally ranged from twenty-five to forty. Table 8.1 records a total of 1,491 scene presentations, which does not include a small number of test scenes that were not continued because they were too disturbing when presented. The last session took place on September 29, 1960. It was followed by the taking of Mrs. C.'s history, given below. It will be seen that it contains nothing to suggest that there were sexual problems underlying the automobile phobia.

When Mrs. C. was seen late in December 1960, she was as well as she had been at the end of treatment. Her sexual relations with her husband were progressively improving. At a follow-up telephone call on June 6, 1961, she stated that she had fully maintained her recovery and had developed no new symptoms. Her relationship with her husband was excellent and sexually at least as satisfying as before the accident. A further call, on February 19, 1962, elicited the same report.

Life History

The patient was born in a small town in Virginia, the eldest of a family of five. Her father had died of heart disease in June 1957. He had always been good to her as a child and had never punished her. He had often embarrassed his family by getting drunk on weekends. The patient had felt very close to her mother, who was still living and had always been kind and loving and punished the patient only occasionally. Mrs. C. had always got on well with her siblings. She could recall no traumatic childhood experiences. She had always been a good student and had liked school very much, participating in games and making friends easily. The only person whom she had especially disliked was a teacher who had once put a tape over her mouth for speaking in class. She graduated from high school at seventeen, spent two years in an office and then a year in college. In 1942, when twenty-one, she had joined the U.S. Armed Forces and gone to England, where she had become engaged to an air force navigator who was later killed in action. She reiterated that during the blitz she had often been in danger, witnessed destruction and seen the dead and injured without any great distress. In December 1945, returning to the United States, she had worked at an office job until 1957, when she had married.

Her first sexual feelings were experienced at the age of twelve. She reported that she had never masturbated. From the age of thirteen she had gone out in groups and at seventeen begun individual dating. Her first serious attachment was to the airman who was killed, but she had seen little of him because of war conditions. After his death, she had lost interest for a time in forming other associations. On returning to the United States, she had resumed casual dating. Her next serious association was with her husband, whom she had met in 1955. They had married in May 1957, about nine months before the accident. Until the accident, the marital relationship had been good. Sexual relations had been satisfactory, most often with both partners achieving orgasm. Since the accident, however, she had been negatively influenced by adverse comments that her husband had made about her disabilities, so that sexual behavior had diminished. Nevertheless, when coitus occurred, she still had orgasm more often than not.

Discussion

Laboratory studies (Napalokov & Karas, 1957; Wolpe, 1952, 1958) have shown that experimental neuroses in animals are learned unadaptive habits characterized by anxiety that are remarkable for their persistence (resistance to the normal process of extinction). These neuroses can readily be eliminated through repeatedly inhibiting the neurotic responses by simultaneous evocations of incompatible responses (i.e., by reciprocal inhibition of the neurotic responses). The effectiveness of varied applications of this finding to human neuroses (e.g., Bond & Hutchinson, 1960; Eysenck, 1960; Lazarus, 1962; Lazarus & Rachman, 1957; Lazovik & Lang, 1960; Rachman, 1961; Wolpe, 1952, 1954, 1956, 1958, 1959, 1961b) gives support to the view that human neuroses too are a particular category of habits acquired by learning.

In the systematic desensitization technique the effects of muscle relaxation are used to produce reciprocal inhibition of small evocations of anxiety and thereby build up conditioned inhibition of anxiety-responding to the particular stimulus combination. When (and only when) the evocations of anxiety are weakened by the counterposed relaxation does the anxiety response *habit* diminish. By systematic use of stimulus combinations whose anxiety-evoking potential is or has become weak, the habit strength of the whole neurotic theme is eliminated piecemeal.

The case of Mrs. C. illustrates with outstanding clarity how the course of change during systematic desensitization conforms to the expectations engendered by the reciprocal inhibition principle. Whenever a scene presented to the patient aroused a good deal of anxiety, that scene could be re-presented a dozen times without diminution of the anxiety. On the other hand, if the initial level of anxiety was lower, decrements in its intensity were achieved by successive presentations. It is a reasonable presumption that, as long as evoked anxiety was too great to be inhibited by the patient's relaxation, *no change* could occur; but when the anxiety was weak enough to be inhibited, repeated presentations of the scene led to progressive increments of *conditioned inhibition* of the anxiety-response habit, manifested by ever-weakening anxiety responding. At every stage, each "quantum" of progress in relation to the subject matter of the desensitization sessions corresponded in specific detail to a small step towards recovery in an aspect of the real life difficulty. The fact that change occurred in this precise way in itself almost justifies the elimination of various "alternative explanations."

Mrs. C. had a total of sixty interviews, at each of which, except the first two and the last, a desensitization session was conducted. Including the initial three which proved to be unusable, thirty-six hierarchies entered into the sessions. All of these, tabulated in Table 8.1, share the common theme of "car-approaching-from-the-side," but each has its own unique stimulus elements calling for separate desensitizing operations. The amount of attention a hierarchy needs is diminished by previous desensitization of other hierarchies that have elements in common with it. This is graphically illustrated in Figure 8.3. Hierarchies 30, 31, 32 and 33, each of which relates to turning left on the highway while another vehicle advances, differ, one from the next, in respect of a single stimulus condition and are in ascending order of anxiety arousal. Desensitization in overlapping sequences, starting with Hierarchy 30, shows parallel progressions. Now, desensitization of Hierarchy 33 was in fact first attempted before Hierarchy 30, from which it has three points of difference. At that time, presenting the approaching car at a distance of *one mile* evoked more anxiety than could be mastered by the patient's relaxation. But after Hierarchy 30 had been dealt with, and in Hierarchies 31 and 32, the "other car" could be tolerated at about one-half mile, it was possible to introduce Hierarchy 33 at three-quarters of a mile with very little anxiety. The increase in toleration was clearly attributable to desensitization to the stimulus elements that Hierarchy 33 *shared* with the three foregoing ones.

Figure 8.3 also illustrates the significant fact that *therapeutic change did not develop during the intervals when the patient was not receiving treatment*, and this was true even of reactions that were the main focus of treatment at the time. There is no drop, following the intervals, in the reactive level of any of the hierarchies represented. However, it is interesting to note that between July 2 and August 7 the reactive level of Hierarchy 31 has risen somewhat. This was not a "spontaneous" endogenously determined relapse, but due to the fact that, late in July, Mrs. C. had ridden in a taxi whose driver, despite her protests, had persisted in weaving among traffic at high speed. Immediately after this she was aware of increased reactivity. As can be seen, the lost ground was soon regained.

A question that may come to mind is this. What assurance did the therapist have of a correspondence between distances as imagined by Mrs. C. and objective measures of distance? The first and most important answer is that only rough correspondence was necessary, since what was always at issue was *distance as conceived by the patient*. The second answer is that a firm anchoring referent was the agreement between patient and therapist that a city block in Charlottesville would be considered 100 yards in length. Similar considerations apply to Mrs. C.'s conceptions of speed.

Among other explanations that may be brought forward to account for the recovery, the only one that, even at face value, would seem to deserve serious consideration in this case is *suggestion*. We shall take this usually ill-defined term to mean the instigation of changes in the patient's behavior by means of verbal or nonverbal cues from the therapist. In all psychotherapy there is at least an implied suggestion of "This will make you well." Getting well under the impulse of such a general suggestion would not be related to particular therapeutic maneuvers, as was the case with Mrs. C. Another kind of suggestion has the form, "You will get well if . . . " In commencing Mrs. C.'s desensitization, the therapist was careful to say no more than, "I am going to use a treatment that may help you." He did not say under what conditions it would help. During the first few sessions (and also several times later) when the scenes presented aroused considerable anxiety, repetition brought about no decrement of reaction. Decrement was noted consistently when anxiety was less. To sustain a hypothesis that suggestion was behind this would require evidence of the very specific instruction—"You will have decreasing anxiety only to situations that produce little anxiety in the first place." In fact, no such instruction was in any form conveyed. The patient could only have become aware *a posteriori* of the empirical relations of her changing reactions.

The relevance of the other "processes"—insight, derepression, and transference— commonly invoked to explain away the effects of conditioning methods of therapy is negated by the absence of significant opportunity for such processes to have occurred. Any possible role of insight may be excluded by the fact that the only insight given to the patient was to tell her she was suffering from a conditioned fear reaction—and no change followed this disclosure. The possibility of derepression may be ruled out by the nonemergence of forgotten material, and the de-emphasis of memory, even to the exclusion of the taking of a history during treatment—other than the history of the phobia's precipitation two years earlier and brief questioning about previous similar events, none of which had any effect on the neurosis.

The action of anything corresponding to "transference" is rendered implausible by the fact that interviews with the therapist led to improvement *only* when conditioning procedures were carried out in accordance with the requirements of reciprocal inhibition, and improvement was limited to the subject matter of the procedures of the time. Also, for a week, when the therapist was away, progress was effected by a medical student (20 years younger than the therapist) using the same conditioning techniques. In addition, the rather mechanical manner in which the sessions were conducted could hardly be said to favor the operation of transference effects; and certainly, the patient-therapist relationship was in no way ever analyzed. The third to the tenth interviews (and many other irregularly later) were conducted with the patient in full view of an unconcealed audience, without adverse effects on therapeutic progress.

The possibility of "spontaneous" recovery could be excluded with unusual confidence, since clinical improvement was a consequence of each of the periods of one to three weeks when the patient was being treated in Charlottesville, and was never noted during the four- to six-week intervals the patient spent at home.

"Secondary gain," so often invoked in explanations of posttraumatic neurotic reactions, can have no credence as a factor in this case, either as a maintaining force or as determining recovery by its removal, for the patient did not receive any financial benefit, came for treatment eight months before litigation, became well two months before litigation, and did not relapse after a disappointing decision by the court.

Summary

The treatment by systematic desensitization is described of a severe case of phobia for laterally approaching automobiles. The initiation of desensitization required the introduction of imaginary situations in a fictitious setting in order to procure anxiety responses weak enough to be inhibited by the patient's relaxation. Recovery was gradual and at every stage directly correlated with the specific content of the desensitization procedures. Certain operations that are usually performed in most systems of therapy were excluded or modified in order to remove any basis for arguing that the successful outcome was "really" due to insight, suggestion, derepression, or transference.

References

Bond, I. K. & Hutchinson, H. C. Application of reciprocal inhibition therapy to exhibitionism. *Canadian Medical Association Journal,* 1960, *83,* 23–25.

Eysenck, H. J. *Behavior therapy and the neuroses.* New York: Pergamon Press, 1960.

Lazarus, A. A. Group therapy of phobic disorders by systematic desensitization. *Journal of Abnormal and Social Psychology,* 1961, *63,* 504–510.

Lazarus, A. A. & Rachman, S. The use of systematic desensitization in psychotherapy. *Journal of Psychological Studies,* 1960, *11,* 238–247.

Napalkov, A. V. & Karas, A. Y. Elimination of pathological conditioned reflex connections in experimental hypertensive states. *Zhurnal Vysshei Nervnoi Deiatelńosti,* 1957, *7,* 402–409.

Rachman, S. Sexual disorders and behavior therapy. *American Journal of Psychiatry,* 1961, *118,* 235–240.

Wolpe, J. Experimental neuroses as learned behavior. *British Journal of Psychology,* 1952, *43,* 243–268.

———. Reciprocal inhibition as the main basis of psychotherapeutic effects. *Archives of Neurology and Psychiatry,* 1954, *72,* 205–226.

———. Learning versus lesions as the basis of neurotic behavior. *American Journal of Psychiatry,* 1956, *112,* 923–927.

———. Psychotherapy based on the principle of reciprocal inhibition. In Burton, A., *Case studies in counseling and psychotherapy.* Englewood Cliffs, N.J.: Prentice-Hall, 1959, pp. 353–381.

———. The systematic desensitization treatment of neuroses. *Journal of Nervous and Mental Disease,* 1961, *132,* 189–203.

———. The prognosis in unpsychoanalyzed recovery from neurosis. *American Journal of Psychiatry,* 1961, *131,* 35–39.

——— and Rachman, S. Psychoanalytic evidence: A critique based on Freud's case of Little Hans. *Journal of Nervous and Mental Disease,* 1960, *131,* 135–148.

Case 9

Editors' Introduction

In making our selections from the burgeoning literature of behavior modification, we were overloaded with excellent articles. This particular genre of treatment outstrips all others in the quality of cases reported, and we were forced to make some very hard decisions. The selection to follow by Sajwaj, Libet, and Agras was made because it is the only instance we know of that represents true psychotherapy—of a six-month-old infant!

No ethical therapist would use punishment in therapy if different methods were available, just as no physician would use surgery if less drastic procedures were equally efficacious. However, in some cases powerful intervention is necessary as in this case of chronic ruminative vomiting which was threatening the life of this child.

The elegance of this report involves the use of a simple procedure rather than the shock treatment which has been used in such cases in the past. The reader should note the use of an ABAB design which offers convincing evidence for the efficacy of the treatment.

THOMAS SAJWAJ, JULIAN LIBET, AND STEWART AGRAS

Lemon-Juice Therapy: The Control of Life-Threatening Rumination in a Six-Month-Old Infant

Chronic rumination is a behavior of considerable clinical significance in infants. Kanner (1957, p. 484) defined it as . . . "bringing up food without nausea, retching, or disgust. The food is then ejected from the mouth (if liquid, allowed to run out) or reswallowed." This behavior appears to be "voluntary," that is, children actively engage in behaviors that induce the rumination, e.g., infants are observed to strain vigorously to bring food back to their mouth. The incidence of rumination in the general population is unknown, since it is typically confused with food allergies, especially to milk. Serious clinical problems, such as malnutrition, dehydration, and lowered resistance to disease, may prompt a life-threatening condition if significant amounts of food are lost. Kanner (1957) noted that eleven of fifty-two ruminating babies in one group died; Gaddini and Gaddini (1959) reported death in one of six cases. Within the first author's experience, one of eight referred ruminating children died.

Treatment procedures for infantile rumination are diverse. Kanner (1957) noted the use of surgery, drugs, mechanical devices (e.g., chin straps, esophagus blocks), thickened feedings with farina, and very high levels of attention, with the last treatment producing the most positive effects. Typically, an adult is assigned to provide the ruminating child with his undivided attention for at least eight hours a day. Fullerton (1963), Gaddini and Gaddini (1959), Hollowell and Gardner (1965), Menking, Wagnitz, Burton, Coddington, and Sotos (1969), Richmond, Eddy, and Green (1958), and Stein, Rausen, and Blau (1959) all reported reductions in rumination and increases in weight coincident with the onset of high levels of attention. One difficulty with this treatment is that cessation of rumination is usually slow. Hollowell and Gardner (1965), Menking et al. (1958), and Stein et al. (1969), reported that rumination gradually disappeared over four to eight weeks. In contrast, Fullerton (1963) reported cessation in four days for one infant.

Since rumination is often life-threatening, a more rapid treatment has been sought. White and Taylor (1967) apparently were the first to use contingent

From *Journal of Applied Behavioral Analysis,* 1974, 7, 557–563. Copyright 1974 by the Society for the Experimental Analysis of Behavior, Inc.

electric shock for rumination. Although they did not report adequate quantitative data, they concluded that shock did significantly interfere with rumination. Galbraith, Byrick, and Rutledge (1970), Lang and Melamed (1969), and Luckey, Watson, and Musick (1968) reported cessation of vomiting and rumination within two to four days when shock was used. Kohlenberg (1970) shocked stomach tension that preceded vomiting. Elimination of stomach tension and vomiting occurred within one day. Bright and Whaley (1969) first attempted to eliminate regurgitation and vomiting in a retarded boy with Tabasco brand pepper sauce before resorting to shock. The pepper sauce was sprinkled on the vomitus. Very substantial reductions in regurgitation and rumination resulted, but neither was eliminated. Shock then eliminated both behaviors within three days.

The present paper reports the successful treatment of life-threatening rumination in an infant through the use of lemon juice as a punisher. Even though the infant's physical condition was serious, the authors were reluctant to resort to shock, since they felt that it might jeopardize cooperation with the pediatrics ward staff. Further, successful treatment might require the use of shock after hospital discharge by the parents, but there was evidence of family instability and neglect of the child.

Method

Child

Sandra was born on September 6, 1971, to an economically marginal, rural family after an unplanned, uncomplicated pregnancy. She was delivered at home by a nurse-midwife and weighed eight pounds. The next day she was admitted to the University Hospital for feeding difficulties associated with a cleft palate and lip. These difficulties were rectified with gastric tube feedings, and Sandra was discharged to her aunt nine days after admission. During the next four months, weight gain was below average, although neither mother nor aunt reported any further feeding difficulties. There were, however, indications of neglect, and Sandra was cared for during this period by a number of different individuals, including neighborhood children.

Sandra was admitted to the University Hospital for the second time on February 29, 1972, at the age of about six months by the aunt because of a failure to gain weight associated with rumination. On examination, she was emaciated and unresponsive to her environment. There was very little grasping of objects, no smiling, no babbling, no gross movements, and some crying. She was primarily lethargic and lay passively in her crib. Exhaustive medical examinations and laboratory analyses revealed no organic cause for her difficulties. Her weight, however, was falling rapidly and was below her birth weight and below the third percentile for infant girls. Malnutrition and dehydration were pressing problems, and death, resulting from possible complications, was a distinct possibility.

Measurement of Rumination

Feeding consisted of a commercially prepared formula every four hours. Immediately after each feeding, ruminative behavior would begin. Sandra would open her mouth, elevate and fold her tongue, and then vigorously thrust her tongue forward and backward. Within a few seconds milk would appear at the back of her mouth and then slowly flow out. This behavior would continue for about twenty to forty minutes until she apparently lost all of the milk she had previously consumed. No crying or evidence of pain and discomfort was observed during this behavior. Rumination could be interrupted by touches, pokes, or mild slaps, but would resume immediately.

This rumination behavior was recorded through the use of the ten-second-block method (Allen, Hart, Buell, Harris, and Wolf, 1964). A check was made in each ten-second interval for any occurrence of tongue thrusting with her mouth open. The tongue did not have to be elevated or folded, nor did milk need to be visible. A check of observer agreement was made with the help of an independent observer on one occasion in each of the four experimental conditions. Observers were about three feet (0.9 meter) apart in full view of each other. Data sheets could not be readily seen and observers would mark each interval even if no coded behaviors occurred. An agreement was scored if both observers checked the occurrence of rumination in corresponding time intervals. A disagreement was scored if only one observer had scored rumination in an interval. Agreements on the nonoccurrence of rumination were not included in these computations. The four checks on the recording of rumination yielded indices (agreements divided by the sum of agreements plus disagreements) of: 91 percent (42/46), 100 percent (11/11), 95 percent (75/79), and 75 percent (12/16).

Sandra was observed for twenty minutes immediately following a feeding. The observational period started when the bottle was removed from her mouth for the last time. The period ended twenty minutes later whether or not rumination was continuing. During the first three experimental conditions, Sandra was observed after four to six feedings daily. During the final condition, observation was reduced to one to three times daily.

Sandra was weighed daily at roughly the same time in the morning while clothed only in diaper.The same scale was used throughout this study.

Procedure

Baseline conditions involved the usual circumstances and conditions of care given on the pediatrics ward. No one individual was assigned to care for Sandra. Rumination was not treated systematically, save for some intermittent mild slapping by ward staff when rumination was observed. However, no slapping was allowed during the five observation periods during the baseline condition or at any other time subsequently.

Lemon-juice therapy was initiated on March 15. This consisted of squirting about five to ten cubic centimeters of lemon juice (unsweetened Realemon brand) into her mouth with a thirty cubic centimeter medical syringe as soon as vigorous tongue movements were detected. At the occurrence of each instance of tongue movements, her mouth was filled with lemon juice. For the next thirty to sixty seconds, no more lemon juice was administered, although tongue movements might persist. Lemon juice was so omitted because it tended to produce some lip and tongue smacking. Then, lemon juice was reapplied, if ruminative tongue movements persisted or if a new episode started. During these thirty- to sixty-second periods, lip and tongue movements continued to be scored as ruminative behavior. Ward staff were carefully instructed in the use of lemon juice by observing the authors and by using the lemon juice while the authors were present to give feedback. Lemon juice was to be used at any time ruminative tongue movements were observed, whether or not the authors or observers were present. This responsibility was assigned to one of two specific ward staff for each shift, in addition to their normal duties. Reports from other ward staff and observation by the authors and observers indicated that the responsible staff correctly used the lemon juice.

After sixteen feedings with lemon-juice therapy, the use of lemon juice was suspended for eight hours, during which two feedings occurred. Lemon-juice therapy was then resumed immediately following the next feeding.

During the initial lemon-juice condition, informal observation by several individuals suggested that the amount of attention given Sandra by the ward staff began to increase spontaneously. To help control for this concurrent change, the ward staff were instructed to continue this relatively higher level of attention throughout the reversal condition and into the resumption of lemon juice. The authors verified that the staff continued high levels of attention by casual observations during the twenty-minute postfeeding periods and at other times of the day.

After eight weeks of lemon-juice therapy in the hospital, Sandra was discharged to the care of foster parents, who were carefully instructed in the use of the lemon juice. Five months later, custody was returned to her biological parents. Sandra was seen at seven follow-up visits over a twelve-month period. At ten months posthospitalization, the Denver Developmental Screening Test and the Vineland Social Maturity Scales were administered.

Results

The baseline of Figure 9.1 shows that the percent of ten-second intervals of rumination was between 40 percent and 70 percent for the first twenty minutes following a feeding. Her weight was falling rapidly (baseline, Figure 9.2).

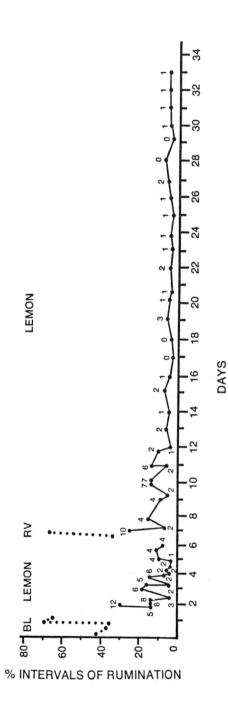

FIGURE 9.1. Percent intervals of Sandra's rumination during the twenty-minute postfeeding periods during baseline (BL), lemon-juice therapy periods (LEMON), and brief cessation of therapy (RV). The numbers over the data points refer to the number of applications of lemon juice after each feeding session.

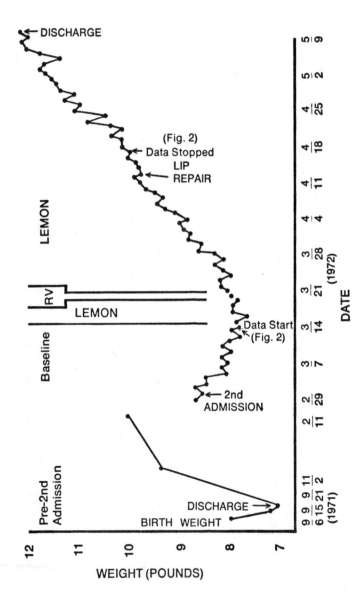

FIGURE 9.2. Sandra's weight before admission for rumination (before second admission), during baseline before lemon-juice therapy, during lemon-juice therapy (LEMON), and during brief cessation of therapy (RV). Data shown in Figure 9.1 were obtained between March 13 and April 16, 1972.

The initial use of lemon juice decreased rumination and vigorous tongue movements to below 10 percent of the twenty minute period. The number of applications of lemon juice during these periods is shown on Figure 9.1. Weight ceased to fall and stabilized at just under eight pounds. The brief omission of therapy prompted a return to high levels of rumination (Figure 9.1). The resumption of the use of lemon juice again reduced rumination. After the twelfth day (Figure 9.1), no regurgitated milk was ever observed in her mouth. The slight rates after this time were due to what appeared to the observers as normal lip and tongue movements. However, since these met the definition of rumination, they were scored as such. These normal mouth and tongue movements were difficult for the ward staff to detect and, consequently, lemon juice was applied intermittently for them. After Day 33, the use of lemon juice was dropped altogether for them.

Weight began to increase and continued to do so until discharge (Figure 9.2). There was a temporary reduction of weight gain, when the cleft lip was surgically repaired. Sandra was discharged with a weight of twelve pounds and five ounces, a 54 percent increase from pretreatment weight.

Table 9.1 gives the number and duration of rumination episodes observed during the twenty-minute postfeeding periods for each experimental condition. An episode was defined as rumination occurring on one or more consecutive ten-second intervals followed by one or more intervals in which rumination was not scored. Duration was the number of consecutive scored intervals of rumination in an episode multiplied by ten seconds. The table shows that the reduction in rumination level seen in Figure 9.1 was due to both a reduction in the number and in the duration of rumination episodes. It should be noted that these numbers and durations of rumination episodes are only estimates because interval recording does not permit precise rate and duration measures.

Weight on follow-up checks continued to increase. Six weeks after discharge, the foster mother reported two brief episodes of rumination, which were followed immediately by the use of lemon juice. Sandra was returned to her natural parents in October, despite the reservations of the authors. Eight months after discharge, a severe attack of gastrointestinal difficulties associated with vomiting was reported. Rumination did not recur and lemon juice was not used. Weight on one-year follow-up was just over twenty-four pounds, which placed her at about the twenty-fifth percentile for infant girls.

Concurrent with the reduction of rumination and with the increase of weight,

TABLE 9.1. Mean number and duration of rumination episodes for each experimental condition.

Condition	Mean Number	Mean Duration (seconds)
Baseline	9.6	60.6
Lemon-juice therapy	4.5	33.4
Reversal	6.0	106.0
Reinstatement of lemon-juice therapy (first half)	2.8	26.4
Reinstatement of lemon-juice therapy (second half)	0.9	9.8

changes in other behaviors were observed in the hospital. Sandra became more attentive of adults about her, smiling appeared, and she began grabbing at objects near her. Babbling also appeared for the first time. These behaviors continued to increase. During the follow-up visits, it was evident that motor, social, and speech development had continued. The Denver Developmental Screening Test and the Vineland Social Maturity Scale, given ten months after discharge when Sandra was about nineteen months old, indicated only a slight developmental delay.

Discussion

Although the case studies cited in the introduction of this paper suggest two different treatment modes for infantile rumination, namely massive attention and electric shock, there are questions as to the effectiveness of these treatment procedures. A treatment procedure can be demonstrated unequivocally by either: (1) omitting the treatment after its initial use and then reapplying it, or (2) using a multiple baseline design where the treatment procedure is applied sequentially to different patients or to different behaviors within a single patient. Unfortunately, none of the above cited studies utilized either of these designs. Rather, the treatment procedures were applied after an initial period of observation. No further manipulations of the treatment procedures were attempted, and possible contaminations by other time-related factors are not eliminated. Luckey et al. (1968) is a partial exception because rumination and vomiting in their patient recurred after contingent shock had apparently eliminated it. Shock was again used, and vomiting again rapidly disappeared.

Although the brief omission of lemon-juice therapy demonstrated its critical role, the question arises as to the critical role of the lemon juice itself, since the therapy has several components. Other contributing factors may be the interruption of the ruminative behavior, the forceful injection of a fluid into the mouth, the temperature difference between the room-temperature lemon juice and the mouth fluids, and the attention accompanying the administration of the lemon juice. This case study does not attempt an analysis of the differential role of these components. However, subsequent preliminary work with other ruminating children suggests a central role for lemon juice *per se*.

One major strength of behavioral techniques has been the ability of paraprofessionals to use them effectively. Shock, however, as a prime treatment tactic for rumination and vomiting does not lend itself to use because of the pain and suffering it entails. Even when used, some individuals may not use the shock as consistently and often as is initially necessary for it to be effective. Related to this minimal social acceptance is the problem of potential abuse. Paraprofessionals should not be trained in the use of shock when there is any suspicion of possible abuse or neglect. Consequently, shock is limited to use by professional staff in restricted settings, and it will be avoided altogether by some institutions and agencies.

The use of lemon juice as a punisher avoids these problems. Lemon juice caused only mild discomfort, if any, to the infant, and the pediatrics staff were not adverse to its use. Further, abuse would be difficult, if not impossible, and its use could be taught to most parents without fear. However, the evaluation of the effectiveness of lemon-juice therapy is limited to this one case. Whether the therapy will prove effective with other ruminating children in other settings in differing circumstances remains to be demonstrated.

Two medical complications may arise from the use of lemon juice therapy. First, since lemon juice is acid, it will irritate the interior and immediate exterior of the mouth. This irritation is minimal and disappears rapidly as the use of lemon juice decreases. Second, aspiration of lemon juice into the lungs is a possibility with serious medical complications resulting. The risk of aspiration can be minimized by keeping the child's head upright or down, not back, when the lemon juice is injected, by reducing the amount of lemon juice injected, and by minimizing the force with which the lemon juice strikes the inside of the mouth. Neither aspiration or gagging were ever observed with Sandra.

References

Allen, K. E., Hart, B. M., Buell, J. S., Harris, F. R., & Wolf, M. M. Effects of social reinforcement on isolate behavior of a nursery school child. *Child Development*, 1964, *35*, 511–518.

Bright, G. O., & Whaley, D. L. Suppression of regurgitation and rumination with aversive events. *Michigan Mental Health Research Bulletin*, 1968, *11*, 17–20.

Fullerton, D. T. Infantile rumination: a case report. *Archives of General Psychiatry*, 1963, *9*, 593–600.

Gaddini, R., & Gaddini, E. Rumination in infancy. In C. Jessner and E. Pavenstadt (Eds.), *Dynamic psychopathology in childhood*. New York: Grune & Stratton, 1959, pp. 166–185.

Galbraith, D., Byrick, R., & Rutledge, J. T. An aversive conditioning approach to the inhibition of chronic vomiting. *Canadian Psychiatric Association Journal*, 1970, *15*, 311–313.

Hollowell, J. R., & Gardner, L. I. Rumination and growth failure in male fraternal twins: association with disturbed family environment. *Pediatrics*, 1965, *36*, 565–571.

Kanner, L. *Child psychiatry*. (3d ed.). Springfield, Ill.: Charles C Thomas, 1957.

Kohlenberg, R. J. The punishment of persistent vomiting: a case study. *Journal of Applied Behavior Analysis*, 1970, *3*, 241–245.

Lang, P. J., & Melamed, B. G. Avoidance conditioning therapy of an infant with chronic ruminative vomiting. *Journal of Abnormal Behavior*, 1969, *74*, 139–142.

Luckey, R. E., Watson, C. M., & Musick, J. K. Aversive conditioning as a means of inhibiting vomiting and rumination. *American Journal of Mental Deficiency*, 1968, *73*, 139–142.

Menking, M., Wagnitz, J., Burton, J., Coddington, R. D., & Sotos, J. Rumination—A new fatal psychiatric disease of infancy. *The New England Journal of Medicine*, 1969, *281*, 802–804.

Richmond, J. B., Eddy, E., & Green, M. Rumination: A psychosomatic syndrome of infancy. *Pediatrics*, 1958, *22*, 49–54.

Stein, M. L., Rausen, A. R., & Blau, A. Psychotherapy of an infant with rumination. *Journal of the American Medical Association*, 1959, *171*, 2309–2312.

White, J. C., & Taylor, D. J. Noxious conditioning as a treatment for rumination. *Mental Retardation*, 1967, *5*, 30–33.

Case 10

Editors' Introduction

The report that follows differs from most of the others in that the treatment is directed to a population rather than to an individual. We have already mentioned the high frequency of quality articles in the literature of behavior modification; however, even among these Atthowe and Krasner's report on the use of a token economy in a mental hospital is a classic.

The absolute and the relative number of mental hospital patients has decreased enormously in the past decade, and the general explanation given for this phenomenon is the efficiency of the new psychotropic drugs. While it is true that drugs do play a part, and possibly a major part in this reduction, other considerations are also involved, including new ways of viewing mental "disease" as simply learned habits which can be changed and in viewing the "mentally ill" as not ill at all but instead presenting a complex array of treatable symptoms.

This is an historic paper, with important implications for the treatment of severely disturbed people.

JOHN M. ATTHOWE, JR., AND LEONARD KRASNER

Preliminary Report on the Application of Contingent Reinforcement Procedures (Token Economy) on a "Chronic" Psychiatric Ward

Although investigators may disagree as to what specific strategies or tactics to pursue, they would agree that current treatment programs in mental hospitals are in need of vast improvement. Release rates for patients hospitalized five or more years have not materially changed in this century (Kramer, Goldstein, Israel, & Johnson, 1956). After five years of hospitalization, the likelihood of release is approximately 6 percent (Kramer et al., 1956; Morgan & Johnson, 1957; Odegard, 1961), and, as patients grow older and their length of hospitalization increases, the possibility of discharge approaches zero. Even for those chronic patients who do leave the hospital, more than two out of every three return within six months (Fairweather, Simon, Gebhard, Weingarten, Holland, Sanders, Stone, & Reahl, 1960). There is certainly need for new programs of demonstrated efficiency in modifying the behavior of long-term hospitalized patients.

In September 1963 a research program in behavior modification was begun which was intimately woven into the hospital's ongoing service and training programs. The objective was to create and maintain a systematic ward program within the ongoing social system of the hospital. The program reported here involves the life of the entire ward, patients, and staff, plus others who come in contact with the patients. The purpose of the program was to change the chronic patients' aberrant behavior, especially that behavior judged to be apathetic, overly dependent, detrimental, or annoying to others. The goal was to foster more responsible, active, and interested individuals who would be able to perform the routine activities associated with self-care, to make responsible decisions, and to delay immediate reinforcement in order to plan for the future.

The Ward Population

An eighty-six bed closed ward in the custodial section of the Veterans Administration Hospital in Palo Alto was selected. The median age of the patients

From *Journal of Abnormal Psychology*, 1968, *73*, 37–43. Copyright 1968 by the American Psychological Association. Reprinted by permission.

was fifty-seven years and more than one-third were over sixty-five. Their overall length of hospitalization varied from three to forty-eight years with a median length of hospitalization of twenty-two years. Most of the patients had previously been labeled as chronic schizophrenics; the remainder were classified as having some organic involvement.

The patients fell into three general performance classes. The largest group, approximately 60 percent of the ward, required constant supervision. Whenever they left the ward, an aide had to accompany them. The second group, about 25 percent, had ground privileges and were able to leave the ward unescorted. The third group, 15 percent of the patients, required only minimal supervision and could probably function in a boarding home under proper conditions if the fear of leaving the hospital could be overcome.

In order to insure a stable research sample for the two years of the project, sixty patients were selected to remain on the ward for the duration of the study. The patients selected were older and had, for the most part, obvious and annoying behavioral deficits. This "core" sample served as the experimental population in studying the long-term effectiveness of the research program, the token economy.

The Token Economy

Based on the work of Ayllon and his associates (Ayllon, 1963; Ayllon & Azrin, 1965; Ayllon & Houghton, 1962; Ayllon & Michael, 1959) and the principle of reinforcement as espoused by Skinner (1938, 1953), we have tried to incorporate every important phase of ward and hospital life within a systematic contingency program. The attainment of the "good things in life" was made contingent upon the patient's performance.

If a patient adequately cared for his personal needs, attended his scheduled activities, helped on the ward, interacted with other patients, or showed increased responsibility in any way, he was rewarded. The problem was to find rewards that were valued by everyone. Tokens, which could in turn be exchanged for the things a patient regards as important or necessary, were introduced. As stated in the manual distributed to patients (Atthowe, 1964):

> The token program is an incentive program in which each person can do as much or as little as he wants as long as he abides by the general rules of the hospital, *but,* in order to gain certain ends or do certain things, he must have tokens. . . . The more you do the more tokens you get [p. 2].

Cigarettes, money, passes, watching television, etc., were some of the more obvious reinforcers, but some of the most effective reinforcers were idiosyncratic, such as sitting on the ward or feeding kittens. For some patients, hoarding tokens became highly valued. This latter practice necessitated changing the tokens every thirty days. In addition, the tokens a patient still had left at the end of each month were devalued 25 percent, hence the greater incentive for the patient to spend them quickly. The more tokens a patient earned or spent, the less likely he would be to remain apathetic.

In general, each patient was reinforced immediately after the completion of some "therapeutic" activity, but those patients who attended scheduled activities by themselves were paid their tokens only once a week on a regularly scheduled payday. Consequently, the more independent and responsible patient had to learn "to punch a time card" and to receive his "pay" at a specified future date. He then had to "budget" his tokens so they covered his wants for the next seven days.

In addition, a small group of twelve patients was in a position of receiving what might be considered as the ultimate in reinforcement. They were allowed to become independent of the token system. These patients carried a "carte blanche" which entitled them to all the privileges within the token economy plus a few added privileges and a greater status. For this special status, the patient had to work twenty-five hours per week in special vocational assignments. In order to become a member of the "elite group," patients had to accumulate 120 tokens which entailed a considerable delay in gratification.

The token economy was developed to cover all phases of a patient's life. This extension of contingencies to all of the patient's routine activities should bring about a greater generality and permanence of the behavior modified. One criticism of conditioning therapies has been that the behavior changed is specific with little evidence of carry-over to other situations. In this project plans were incorporated to program transfer of training as well as behavior change, per se. As a major step in this direction, token reinforcements were associated with social approval.

The attainment of goals which bring about greater independence should also result in strong sustaining reinforcement in and of itself. The aim of this study was to support more effective behavior and to weaken ineffective behavior by withdrawal of approval and attention and, if necessary, by penalties. Penalties comprised "fines" of specified numbers of tokens levied for especially undesirable behavior or for *not* paying the tokens required by the system. The fines can be seen as actually representing a high token payment to do something socially undesirable, for example, three tokens for cursing someone.

Method

The research program was initiated in September of 1963 when the senior author joined the ward as the ward psychologist and program administrator. The remainder of 1963 was a period of observation, pilot studies, and planning. Steps were taken to establish a research clinic and to modify the traditional service orientation of the nursing staff. In January 1964, the baseline measures were begun. The baseline or operant period lasted approximately six months and was followed by three months in which the patients were gradually prepared to participate in the token economy. In October 1964, the token economy was established and, at the time of writing, is still in operation. This report represents results based on the completion of the first year of the program.

The general design of the study was as follows: A six-month baseline period, a three month shaping period, and an eleven-month experimental period. During the baseline period, the frequency of particular behaviors was recorded daily, and ratings were carried out periodically. The shaping period was largely devoted to those patients requiring continual supervision. At first, the availability of canteen booklets, which served as money in the hospital canteen, was made contingent upon the amount of scheduled activities a patient attended. It soon became clear that almost one-half of the patients were not interested in money or canteen books. They did not know how to use the booklets, and they never bought things for themselves. Consequently, for six weeks patients were taken to the canteen and urged or "cajoled" into buying items which seemed to interest them (e.g., coffee, ice cream, pencils, handkerchiefs, etc.). Then all contingencies were temporarily abandoned, and patients were further encouraged to utilize the canteen books. Next, tokens were introduced but on a noncontingent basis. No one was allowed to purchase items in the ward canteen without first presenting tokens. Patients were instructed to pick up tokens from an office directly across the hall from the ward canteen and exchange them for the items they desired. After two weeks the tokens were made contingent upon performance and the experimental phase of the study began.

Within a reinforcement approach, the principles of successive approximation in gradually shaping the desired patient behavior were utilized. Once the tokens were introduced, shaping procedures were reduced. It would be impossible to hold reinforcement and shaping procedures constant throughout the experimental period or to match our ward or our patients with another ward or comparable group of patients. Consequently, a classical statistical design does not suit our paradigm. It is much more feasible, in addition to reducing sampling errors, to use the patients as their own controls. Therefore, we first established a baseline over an extended period of time. Any changes in behavior from that defined by the baseline must be taken into account. The effects of any type of experimental intervention become immediately obvious. We do not have to rely solely on the inferences teased out of statistical analyses.

Other than an automatic timer for the television set, the only major piece of equipment was the tokens. After a considerable search, a durable and physically safe token was constructed. This token was a 1¾-by-3½-inch plastic, nonlaminated, file card which came in seven colors varying from a bright red to a light tan. Different exchange values were assigned to the different colors. The token had the appearance of the usual credit card so prevalent in our society.

Whenever possible, the giving of the tokens was accompanied by some expression of social approval such as smiling, "good," "fine job," and a verbal description of the contingencies involved, for example, "Here's a token because of the good job of shaving you did this morning."

Results

There has been a significant increase in those behaviors indicating responsibility and activity. Figure 10.1 shows the improvement in the frequency of attendance at group activities. During the baseline period, the average hourly

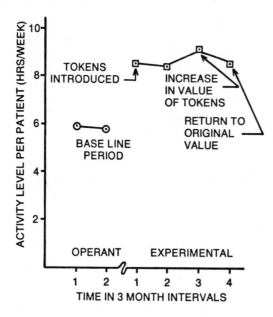

FIGURE 10.1. Attendance at group activities.

rate of attendance per week was 5.85 hours per patient. With the introduction of tokens, this rate increased to 8.4 the first month and averaged 8.5 during the experimental period, except for a period of three months when the reinforcing value of the tokens was increased from one to two tokens per hour of attendance. Increasing the reinforcing value of the tokens increased the contingent behavior accordingly. With an increase in the amount of reinforcement, activity increased from 8.4 hours per week in the month before to 9.2 the first month under the new schedule. This gain was maintained throughout the period of greater reinforcement and for one month thereafter.

Thirty-two patients of the core sample comprised the group activity sample. Nine patients were discharged or transferred during the project, and the remaining patients were on individual assignments and did not enter into these computations. Of the thirty-two patients, eighteen increased their weekly attendance by at least two hours while only four decreased their attendance by this amount. The probability that this is a significant difference is .004, using a sign test and a two-tailed estimate. Of those patients going to group activities, 18 percent changed to the more token-producing and more responsible individual assignments within four months of the onset of the token economy.

A widening of interest and a lessening of apathy were shown by a marked increase in the number of patients going on passes, drawing weekly cash, and utilizing the ward canteen. Of the core sample of sixty patients, 80 percent had never been off the hospital grounds on their own for a period of eight hours since their hospitalization. During the experimental period, 19 percent went on overnight or longer passes, 17 percent went on day passes, and 12 percent went out on accompanied passes for the first time. In other words, approximately one-half of those who had been too apathetic to leave the hospital grounds increased their interest and commitment in the world outside. Furthermore, 13 percent of the core sample left on one or more trial visits of at least thirty days during the token program, although six out of every ten returned to the hospital.

For the entire ward, the lessening of apathy was dramatic. The number of patients going on passes and drawing weekly cash tripled. Twenty-four patients were discharged and eight were transferred to more active and discharge-oriented ward programs as compared to eleven discharges and no such transfers in the preceding eleven-month period. Of the twenty-four patients released, eleven returned to the hospital within nine months.

Independence and greater self-sufficiency were shown by an increase in the number of patients receiving tokens for shaving and appearing neatly dressed. Fewer patients missed their showers, and bed-wetting markedly diminished.

At the beginning of the study, there were twelve bed wetters, four of whom were classified as "frequent" wetters and two were classified as "infrequent." All bed-wetters were awakened and taken to the bathroom at 11 P.M., 12:30 P.M., 2 A.M., and 4 A.M. regularly. As the program progressed, patients who did not wet during the night were paid tokens the following morning. In addition, they were only awakened at 11 P.M. the next night. After a week of no bed-wetting, patients were taken off the schedule altogether. At the end of the experimental period no one was wetting regularly and, for all practical purposes, there were no bed wetters on the ward. The aversive schedule of being awakened during the night together with the receiving of tokens for a successful non-bed-wetting night seemed to instigate getting up on one's own and going to the bathroom, even in markedly deteriorated patients.

Another ward problem which had required extra aide coverage in the mornings was the lack of "cooperativeness" in getting out of bed, making one's bed, and leaving the bed area by a specified time. Just before the system of specific contingency tokens was introduced, the number of infractions in each of these areas was recorded for three weeks. This three-week baseline period yielded an average of seventy-five "infractions" per week for the entire ward, varying from seventy-one to seventy-seven. A token given daily was then made contingent upon not having a recorded infraction in any of the three areas above. This token was given as the patients lined up to go to breakfast each morning. In the week following the establishment of the contingency, the frequency of infractions dropped to thirty and then to eighteen. The next week the number of infractions rose to thirty-nine but then declined steadily to five per week by the end of nine weeks (see Figure 10.2). During the last six months the frequency of infractions varied between six and thirteen, averaging nine per week.

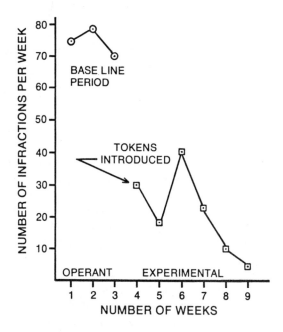

FIGURE 10.2. Number of infractions in carrying out morning routines.

A significant increase was shown in measures of social interaction and communication. A brief version of the Palo Alto Group Psychotherapy Scale (Finney, 1954) was used to measure social responsiveness in weekly group meetings. The change in ratings by one group of raters one month before the introduction of tokens compared with those of a second group of raters four months later was significant at the .001 level. A simple sign test based upon a two-tailed probability estimate was used. Neither set of raters knew which of their patients was included within the core sample. The rater reliability of the scale is .90 (Finney, 1954). Evidence of enhanced social interaction was dramatically shown by the appearance of card games using tokens as money among some of the more "disturbed" patients and an increased frequency in playing pool together.

Discussion and Conclusion

A detailed description of the entire procedures and results is in preparation. However, we wish to point out in this paper the usefulness of a systematic contingency program with chronic patients. The program has been quite successful in combating institutional behavior. Prior to the introduction of tokens most patients rarely left the ward. The ward and its surrounding grounds were dominated by sleeping patients. Little interest was shown in ward activities or parties. Before the tokens were introduced, the ward was cleaned and the clothing room operated by patients from "better" wards. During the experimental period the ward was cleaned and the clothing room operated by the patients of this ward themselves. Now, no one stays on the ward without first earning tokens, and, in comparison to prior standards, the ward could be considered "jumping."

Over 90 percent of the patients have meaningfully participated in the program. All patients do take tokens, a few only infrequently. However, for about 10 percent, the tokens seem to be of little utility in effecting marked behavior change. With most patients, the changes in behavior have been quite dramatic; the changes in a few have been gradual and hardly noticeable. These instances of lack of responsiveness to the program seem to be evident in those patients who had previously been "catatonically" withdrawn and isolated. Although most of the patients in this category were favorably responsive to the program, what "failures" there were, did come from this type of patient. Our program has been directed toward all patients; consequently, individual shaping has been limited. We feel that the results would be more dramatic if we could have dealt individually with the specific behavior of every patient. On the other hand, a total ward token program is needed both to maintain any behavioral gains and to bring about greater generality and permanence. Although it was not our initial objective to discharge patients, we are pleased that the general lessening of apathy has brought about a greater discharge rate. But, even more important, the greater discharge rate would point to the generalized effects of a total token economy.

The greater demands on the patient necessitated by dealing with future events and delaying immediate gratifications which were built into the program have been of value in lessening patients' isolation and withdrawal. The program's most notable contribution to patient life is the lessening of staff control and putting the burden of responsibility, and thus more self-respect, on the patient himself. In the administration of a ward, the program provides behavioral steps by which the staff can judge the patient's readiness to assume more responsibility and thus to leave on pass or be discharged.

The program thus far has demonstrated that a systematic procedure of applying contingent reinforcement via a token economy appears effective in modifying specific patient behaviors. However, the evidence in the literature based on research in mental hospitals indicates that many programs, different in theoretical orientation and design, appear to be successful for a period of time with hospitalized patients. The question which arises is whether the success in modifying behavior is a function of the specific procedures utilized in a given program or a function of the more general social influence process (Krasner, 1962). If it is the latter, whether it be termed "placebo effect" or "Hawthorne effect," then the specific procedures may be irrelevant. All that would matter is the interest, enthusiasm, attention, and hopeful expectancies of the staff. Advocates of behavior-modification procedures (of which the token economy is illustrative) argue that change in behavior is a function of the specific reinforcement procedures used. The study which most nearly involves the approach described in this paper is that of Ayllon and Azrin (1965) whose procedures were basic to the development of our own program. Their study was designed to demonstrate the relationship between contingency reinforcement and change in patient behavior. To do this they withdrew the tokens on a systematic basis for specific behaviors and, after a period of time, reinstated them. They concluded, based upon six specific experiments within the overall design, that

> the reinforcement procedure was effective in maintaining desired performance. In each experiment, the performance fell to a near-zero level when the established response-reinforcement relation was discontinued. On the other hand, reintroduction of the reinforcement procedure restored performance almost immediately and maintained it at a high level for as long as the reinforcement procedure was in effect [Ayllon & Azrin, 1965, p. 381].

They found that performance of desirable behaviors decreased when the response-reinforcement relation was disrupted by: delivering tokens independently of the response while still allowing exchange of tokens for the reinforcers; or by discontinuing the token system by providing continuing access to the reinforcers; or by discontinuing the delivery of tokens for a previously reinforced response while simultaneously providing tokens for a different, alternative response.

In the first year of our program we did not test the specific effects of the tokens by withdrawing them. Rather, we approached this problem in two ways. First, we incorporated within the baseline period of nine months a three-month period in which tokens were received on a noncontingent basis. During this period patients received tokens with concomitant attention, interest, and general social reinforcement. This resulted in slight but nonsignificant change in general ward behavior. The results of the experimental period were then compared with the baseline which included the nonspecific reinforcement. The results indicate that the more drastic changes in behavior were a function of the specific procedures involved. The other technique we used was to change the token value of certain specific activities. An increase in value (more tokens) was related to an increase in performance; return to the old value meant a decrement to the previous level of performance (see Figure 10.1).

We should also point out that the situation in the hospital is such that the token economy did not mean that there were more of the "good things in life" available to these patients because they were in a special program. The patients in the program had had access to these items, for example, extra food, beds, cigarettes, chairs, television, recreational activities, passes, before the program began, as had all patients in other wards, free of charge. Thus we cannot attribute change to the fact of more "good things" being available to these patients and not available to other patients.

Thus far, a contingent reinforcement program represented by a token economy has been successful in combating institutionalism, increasing initiative, responsibility, and social interaction, and in putting the control of patient behavior in the hands of the patient. The behavioral changes have generalized to other areas of performance. A token economy can be an important adjunct to any rehabilitation program for chronic or apathetic patients.

References

Atthowe, J. M., Jr. Ward 113 Program: Incentives and costs—a manual for patients. Palo Alto, Calif.: Veterans Administration Hospital, 1964.

Ayllon, T. Intensive treatment of psychotic behavior by stimulus satiation and food reinforcement. *Behavior Research and Therapy*, 1963, *1*, 53–61.

———, & Azrin, N. H. The measurement and reinforcement of behavior of psychotics. *Journal of the Experimental Analysis of Behavior*, 1965, *8*, 357–384.

Ayllon, T., & Houghton, E. Control of the behavior of schizophrenic patients by food. *Journal of the Experimental Analysis of Behavior*, 1962, *5*, 343–352.

Ayllon, T., & Michael, J. The psychiatric nurse as a behavioral engineer. *Journal of the Experimental Analysis of Behavior*, 1959, *2*, 323–334.

Fairweather, G. W., Simon, R., Gebhard, M. E., Weingarten, E., Holland, J. L., Sanders, R., Stone, G. B., & Reahl, J. E. Relative effectiveness of psychotherapeutic programs: A multicriteria comparison of four programs for three different patient groups. *Psychological Monographs*, 1960, *74* (5, Whole No. 492).

Finney, B. C. A scale to measure interpersonal relationships in group psychotherapy. *Group Psychotherapy*, 1954, *7*, 52–66.

Kramer, M., Goldstein, H., Israel, R. H., & Johnson, N. A. Application of life table methodology to the study of mental hospital populations. *Psychiatric Research Reports*, 1956, *5*, 49–76.

Krasner, L. The therapist as a social reinforcement machine. In H. H. Strupp & L. Luborsky (Eds.), *Research in psychotherapy*. Washington, D. C.: American Psychological Association, 1962, pp. 61–94.

Morgan, N. C., & Johnson, N. A. The chronic hospital patient. *American Journal of Psychiatry*, 1957, *113*, 824–830.

Odegard, O. Current studies of incidence and prevalence of hospitalized mental patients in Scandinavia. In P. H. Hoch & J. Zubin (Eds.), *Comparative epidemiology of the mental disorders*. New York: Grune & Stratton, 1961, pp. 45–55.

Skinner, B. F. *The behavior of organisms*. New York: Appleton-Century-Crofts, 1938.

———. *Science and human behavior*. New York: Macmillan, 1953.

Case 11

Editors' Introduction

Frederick S. Perls, known to all during his lifetime and after as "Fritz," was a genuine maverick, a man on the go, a lonely seeker, a genius. As was the case with many—and possibly all—other innovators in psychotherapy, his therapeutic system which he called "Gestalt Therapy" was in a sense an incarnation of himself. Unconventional, emotional, existing in the moment—so too was his system of therapy.

Perls was obsessed with time, particularly the here-and-now, and in this sense his system complements Moreno's psychodrama. He believed that one must go inwards, deeply and directly, to the heart of the problem, to confront it and even to exaggerate it, to show that one had control and could destroy the sickness within.

The selection we present is the best short account of how Perls and Gestalt operate, but only longer readings will give the full flavor of this remarkable person and his methodology.

FREDERICK S. PERLS

The Case of Jane

The following transcripts are taken from audiotape recordings made at a Gestalt Therapy workshop . . . during the summer of 1968.

FRITZ: Now, I want you all to talk to your dreams, and let the dreams talk back—not the content, but as if the dreams were a thing. "Dreams, you are frightening me," "I don't want to know about you," or something, and let the dreams answer back. *(All talk to their dreams for several minutes)* . . .

So, now I would like each one of you to play the role of their dreams, such as, "I only seldom come to you, and then only in little bits and pieces," or however you experience your dreams. I want you to *be* that dream. Reverse the role, so that you are the dream, and talk to the whole group, as if you were the dream talking to yourself.

NEVILLE: I fool you, don't I, because I'm full of important facts about you, and I won't allow you to remember me. That annoys the hell out of you, doesn't it? Confuses you, and I get a big kick out of it when I depress you, and watch you kind of sink deeper and deeper as the day goes along. You wouldn't have any difficulty remembering me if you just concentrated on me a little. So I play hide-and-seek with you, and I kind of enjoy your discomfort with it. I fool you all. I play games with you and then elude you, so that I confuse you all . . . I make you see a different me, don't I? . . .

GLENN: I don't come on very clear, very often, because you don't seem to understand me very well. I would put on many spectaculars, if you paid more attention, but as it is, you pay little attention to me and I do kind of a shoddy job for you.

RAYMOND: I'm sneaky. You know I'm here but I won't let you know what's going on.

BLAIR: I'm going to mystify you. I'm going to be symbolic, impenetrable . . . keep you confused . . . unclear.

BOB· I'm all enclosed in mist, like that mountain over there. Even if the mist left, you'd have a hard time getting things out of me.

FRANK: You shouldn't be ashamed of me. You should come out and meet me more. I feel that I can help you. I'd like to meet you more.

From F. S. Perls, *Gestalt Therapy Verbatim* (Lafayette, CA: Real People Press, 1969), pp. 217–272.

LILY: I can see, and hear, and feel and talk, and touch, and do everything you want to do.

JANE: I'm merry, exciting, interesting, I'm going to really turn you on, and then when we get to the end, I'm going to turn you off. And you're not going to get to see the end. And then you'll go around pouting all day, because you didn't get to the end.

SALLY: It's not us that disturb your sleep. If we could find a chance when you would listen to us, and then after this, we'd be clear, like lightning, it's very shocking. We're going to shock you, but you'll shake it off in a little while, and when you wake up, going about the chores of the day you'll take us with you. But if we keep doing this, over and over again, finally, you'll find that nothing goes right. You'll try to hide from all your faults, all your fears, but we will be there to upset you.

ABE: Be good enough to yourself to remember that we've given you some very fine moments, often of meaning, sometimes power. Recently we've given you horror—frightening horror, and also recently you've turned away from us.

JAN: I don't think you really want to remember me, or know me. I don't feel you want to enjoy me. Every time I do let myself get close to you, you always say, "Well, I'm too tired to write you down or pay attention to you. Maybe in the morning I'll do it." I feel you're still trying to avoid me.

FERGUS: I'm very weird. I'm the only honest, the only spontaneous part of you, the only free part of you.

TONY: I feel very sorry for you.

NANCY: I'm not going to give you the pleasure of knowing me, or the enjoyment of feeling grown up.

DANIEL: You know that I'm made of all kinds of bits and pieces left unfinished during the day, and it's better that I have them, than just forget about them. Besides, sometimes I'm very beautiful and very meaningful, and you know that I'm doing much good for you, especially when you look at me carefully.

STEVE: I am a multicolored cloak that sweeps down and carries you off, gives you power.

CLAIR: You're just playing games, and I am really all. And you can wait for me forever.

DICK: You're very much aware of my existence, but most of the time you ignore me.

TEDDY: I am a very creative, interesting situation. Plots, juxtapositions, that you'd never think of in your waking life. I'm much more creative, I'm much more frightening, and I appear to you not as pictures. You know what's going on when I'm there; afterwards you forget. But I'm not in movies; I'm a kind of knowing. You would like to see me in pictures but I don't appear.

JUNE: I am going to make you *miserable,* I am going to *destroy* you, I am going to *encompass* you, and push you *under,* and make you feel as if you can't breathe. And I'm going to *stay* here and *sit* on you! . . .

FRITZ: Well, possibly you noticed something very interesting for quite a few of you, how the dream as such symbolizes your hidden self. I would like you to work with that in the groups, to more and more act out *being* that thing that you just imagined was a dream. I don't know how much those who have played their dreams realize how much of themselves came through, but I'm pretty sure that most of you can easily recognize that this is the part of you that you don't like to bring forth. If you take *literally* what I asked you to do, to play your dream as if the dream was a person, these instructions would be complete nonsense. How can you be your dream? And then as you express it, finally it became so real. You really felt this is the person here. Sometimes there is a surprise, if this person had managed to wear his mask with grace and confidence. For instance, you noticed how much came out of June. I don't know how many of you have seen this tremendous destructive power of hers. It came out very clearly. Very beautiful.

Jane I

JANE: Ah, in my dream I'm going home to visit my mother and my family . . . and I'm dr—I'm driving from Big Sur to—to my mother's house . . .

FRITZ: What's going on right now?

J: It's really scary up here. I didn't know it would be half as scary. [This workshop session was held in a large room, with another seminar group of thirty people observing.]

F: Close your eyes . . . and stay with your scariness . . . How do you experience scariness?

J: Shakiness in my upper chest, *(sighs)* fluttering in my breathing. Ah, my—my right leg is shaking. My left leg—now my left leg's shaking. If I keep my eyes closed long enough my arms are going to start shaking.

F: At what moment did this scariness come up?

J: I looked out there. *(laughter)*

F: So look again. Talk to those people there. "You make me scared" or whatever.

J: Well, it's not so bad now. I'm picking and choosing.

F: So whom do you pick and choose?

J: Oh Mary Ellen, and Alison. John. I skipped over a whole bunch of faces.

F: Now let's call your father and mother into the audience.

J: I wouldn't look at them.

F: Say this to them.

J: Ah, wherever you're sitting I'm not going to look at you . . . because I don't—You want me to explain it? Oh, no. *(laughter)* OK, I'm not going to look at you, Mom and Dad.

F: What do you experience when you *don't* look at them?

J: More anxiety. When I tell you the dream it's like—it's just the same.

F: OK, tell me the dream.

J: OK, I'm going home to see my mother and father, and I'm anxious the whole time when I'm driving home. And I—there's a long flight of steps up to the house—there's about sixty steps. And in the dream I get m—more and more afraid each step I take. So I open the door and the house is very dark. And I call to my mother—Oh, I notice that all the cars are there, so they're home. I call to my mother and there's no answer. I call to my father and there's no answer. I call the children and there's no answer. So I—it's a very, very big house and so I go from room to room to look for them and I—I get into the bedroom and my mother and father are in bed but they're, they're just, they're not my m—they're skeletons. They don't have any skin. They're not, they don't talk . . . they don't say anything. And I shake—This dream happens over and over and lately I've gotten brave enough to shake them. But . . .

F: In the dream you can play the part . . . What happens when you shake them?

J: Ah, nothing. I mean I—I just feel a skeleton—a skeleton. And I yell really loud in the dream to them both. I tell them to wake up. And they don't wake up. They're just skeletons.

F: Good. Let's start all over again. You're entering the house, yah?

J: OK. I'm entering the house and I first—I first walk into the kitchen and it's very dark, and it doesn't smell like I remember it. It smells musty like it hadn't been cleaned in a long time. And I don't hear any noises. It's usually very noisy—a lot of children noises. And I don't hear any noises. Then I go to what used to be my bedroom, and there's nobody there, and everything is clean. Everything is neat and everything is untouched.

F: Let's have an encounter between the kitchen of your dream and your bedroom.

J: The kitchen and the bedroom. OK. I'm the kitchen, and—I don't smell the way I usually smell. I usually smell of food. I usually smell of people. And now I smell of dust and cobwebs. I'm usually not very neat but now I'm very, very neat. Everything is put away. Nobody's inside of me.

F: Now play the bedroom.

J: Bedroom . . . I'm very—I'm neat. . . . I don't know how to encounter the kitchen.

F: Just boast about what you are.

J: Well, I'm as neat as you are. I'm very neat, too. But I smell bad like you do, and I don't smell like perfume, and I don't smell like people. I just smell like dust. Only there's no dust on my floor. I'm very neat and I'm very clean. But I don't smell good and I don't feel good like I usually feel. And I know when Jane comes inside of me she feels bad when I'm so neat and there's no one inside of me. And she comes inside of me like she comes inside of you in the dream. And she's very scared. And we're very—I'm very hollow. I'm very hollow. When you make a sound inside of me it echoes. That's how it feels in the dream.

F: Now be the kitchen again . . .

J: I'm very hollow, too—I, ooh . . .

F: Yah? What happened?

J: I feel empty.

F: You feel the emptiness now. /J: Yeah./ Stay with the emptiness.

J: OK, I . . . don't feel it there now. Wait. I lost it. I'm very, you know, I—

F: Stay with what you experience now.

J: I have the anxious feeling again.

F: When you become the kitchen. Yah?

J: Yeah. I'm the kitchen . . . And there's no fresh air inside of me. There's no good—I'm supposed to be encountering the bedroom. Hmmm. Ohhh . . .

F: Just tell all this to the bedroom.

J: I'm as musty as you are. And it's very incongruous because I'm very clean and spotless. And Jane's mother usually doesn't keep me so neat. She's usually too busy to keep me so neat. Something's wrong with me. I'm not getting the kind of attention that I usually get. I'm dead. I'm a dead kitchen.

F: Say this again.

J: I'm dead. /F: Again./ I'm dead.

F: How do you experience being dead? . . .

J: Well, it doesn't feel bad . . .

F: Now stay as you are and be aware of your right and left hand. What are they doing?

J: My right hand is shaking and it's stretched out. And the left hand is clenched very tight and my fingernails are pushing into the palm of my hand.

F: What does your right hand want to do?

J: It's OK the way it is. I think it wants not to shake.

F: Besides this, anything else? Does it want to stop? To reach? I can't read your right hand. Continue the movement. *(Jane makes reaching movements with right hand)* You want to reach out. Good. And what does your left hand want to do? . . .

J: My left hand wants to hold back. It's holding tight. My right hand feels good.

F: So change. Let the left hand do now what the right hand does, and vice versa. Reach out with your left hand.

J: No . . . My left hand doesn't want to reach out.

F: What's the difficulty in reaching out with your left hand?

J: It feels much different, and my right hand isn't clenched: it's limp. I can *do* it. I can *do* it, yet—

F: This would be artificial. /J: Yeah./ Now reach out with your left hand again . . . *(softly)* Reach out to me . . . *(Jane reaches out . . . sighs.)* . . . Now what happened?

J: It started to shake . . . and I stopped it.

F: Now have an encounter between your right hand and left hand as it was originally, "I am holding back and you are reaching out."

J: I'm the right hand and I'm reaching out. I'm free. I'm very relaxed, and even when I shake, it doesn't feel bad. I'm shaking now and I don't feel bad . . .

Ah, I'm the left hand and I don't reach out. I make a fist. And now my fingernails are long so when I do it I hurt myself when I make a fist . . . Ohh . . .

F: Yah, what happened?

J: I hurt myself.

F: I want to tell you something that is usually the case. I don't know whether it will be the case with you. The right hand is usually the male part of a person and the left side is the female part. The right side is the aggressive, active, outgoing part and the left side is the sensitive, receptive, open part. Now try this on for size to see if it might fit with you.

J: OK. The loudmouth can come out, you know. /F: Yah./ But the soft part is . . . not so easy . . .

F: OK. Enter the house once more and have an encounter with what you encounter—namely, silence.

J: Encounter with silence. /F: Silence, yah./ Be the silence?

F: No, no. You enter the house and all that you meet is silence. Right?

J: Yes. You annoy me. The silence annoys me. I don't like it.

F: Say this to silence.

J: I am. He's sitting right there. You annoy me. I don't like you. I don't hear much in you and when I do, I don't like it.

F: What does silence answer?

J: Well, I have never had a chance to come around much because when you were young there were many children around you all the time and your parents are both loud, and you're loud, and you really don't know much about me. And I think maybe you're afraid of me. Could you be afraid of me?

Now let's try that one. Yeah. I don't feel afraid now, but I could be afraid of you.

F: So enter the house once more and again meet silence. Go back to the dream.

J: OK. I'm in the house and it's very silent and I don't like it. I don't like that it's quiet. I want to hear noises, I want to hear noises in the kitchen and noises in the bedroom and I want to hear children, *(voice begins to break)* I want to hear my mother and father laughing and talking, I—

F: Say this to them.

J: I want to hear you, laughing and talking. I want to hear the children. I miss you. *(begins to cry)* I can't let go of you . . . I want to hear you. I want to hear you . . . and I want to hear you.

F: OK, let's now reverse the dream. Let them talk. Resurrect them.

J: Resurrect them. /F: Yah./ I have them there.

F: You say you try to shake them. They are only skeletons. /J: *(fearfully)* Ohhh./ I want you to be successful.

J: You want me to encounter—I'm confused. *(has stopped crying)*

F: You are in the bedroom. Right? /J: Yeah./ Your parents are skeletons. /J: Uhuh./ Skeletons usually don't talk. At best they shake and rattle. /J: Yeah./ I want you to resurrect them.

J: To make them alive.

F: Make them alive. So far you say you would blot them out. That's what you're doing in the dream.

J: I shake them in the dream. I take them and I shake them.

F: Talk to them.

J: Wake up! /F: Again./

(loudly) Wake up! /F: Again./

(loudly) Wake up! /F: Again./

(loudly) Wake up! . . . And . . . *(loudly, almost crying)* You can't hear me! Why can't you hear me? . . . *(sighs)* And they don't answer. They don't say anything.

F: Come. Be phony. Invent them. Resurrect them. Let's have a phony game.

J: OK. We don't know why we can't hear you. We don't know. We don't know that we even don't want to hear you. We're just skeletons. Or are we still? No . . . We don't know why we can't hear you. We don't know why we're like this. We don't know why you found us like this. *(crying)* Maybe if you never went away, maybe if you never went away, this wouldn't have happened. It feels right. That's what they would say. That's what they would say.

F: OK. Take your seat again . . .

J: I feel like I want to tell you that I went away too soon and I really can't go all the way away. *(almost crying)*

F: Tell them that you still need them.

J: I still need you.

F: Tell them in more detail what you need.

J: I still need my mother to hold me.

F: Tell this to her.

J: I still need you to hold me. *(crying)* I want to be a little girl, sometimes—forget the "sometimes."

F: You're not talking to her yet.

J *(sobbing)*: OK. Mother, Mother, you think I'm very grown up . . . And I think I'm very grown up. But there's a part of me that isn't away from you and I can't, I can't let go of.

F: You see how this is a continuation of our last session? You started out as the toughy, the brazen girl, and the softness came out? Now you begin to accept that you have soft needs . . . So be your mother.

J *(diffidently):* Well, you know you can come back any time you want, Jane. But it's not going to be quite the same because I have other little girls to take care of. I have your sisters to take care of and they're little girls, and you're a big girl and you can take care of yourself now. And I'm glad you're so grown up. I'm glad you're so smart . . . Anyway, I don't know how to talk to you any more. I mean I know—I respect you but I don't understand you half the time . . . *(sobbing)* and, and . . .

F: What happened right now? What happened when you stopped?

J: I felt a pain in my stomach. I felt frustrated.

F: Tell Jane that.

J: Jane, I—*(crying)* I have a pain in my stomach. I feel frustrated; because I don't understand you because you do such funny things; because you went away when you were so young and you never really came back. And you ran away from me and I loved you and I wanted you to come back and you wouldn't come back. And now you want to come back and it's too late.

F: Play Jane again.

J: *(not crying):* But I still need you. I want to sit on your lap. Nobody else can give me what you have. I still need a mother. *(crying)* . . . I can't believe it. I just can't believe what I'm saying. I mean I can agree with what I'm saying but—

F: OK, let's interrupt. You woke up anyhow. Go back to the group. How do you experience us? Can you tell the group that you need a mother?

J: Hmm. *(laughter) (Jane laughs)* I can tell you, Fritz. Ah, no, there's too many.

F: All right, now let's see whether we can't get these things together. Now have an encounter between your baby dependence and brazenness. /J: OK./ Those are your two poles.

J *(as brazenness):* You really are a punk. You sound just like a punk. You've been around. You've been around for a long time. You've learned a lot of things. You know how to be on your own. What the fuck's the matter with you? What are you crying about?

Well, I like to be helpless sometimes, Jane, and I know you don't like it. I know you don't put up with it very often. But sometimes it just comes out. Like I can't work with Fritz without it coming out. I can hide it . . . for a long time, but . . if you don't own up to me I'm gonna really, I'm gonna keep coming out and maybe you'll never grow up.

F: Say this again.

J: I'm gonna keep coming out and maybe you'll never grow up.

F: Say it very spitefully.

J: I'm gonna *keep* coming out and maybe you'll *never* grow up . . .

F: OK, be the brazenness again.

J *(sighs):* Well I've tried stomping on you and hiding you and shoving you in corners and making everybody believe that you don't exist. What more do you want me to do with you? What do you want from me?. . .

I want you to listen to me . . .

F: Is brazen Jane willing to listen?

J: I just started to listen . . . OK, I'm gonna give you a chance. I feel like if I give you a chance . . . *(right hand makes a threatening fist)*

F: Yah? Yah?—No no no, don't—don't hide it. Come out. You don't give her a chance, you give her a threat.

J: Yeah, I know. That's what I do.

F: Yah, yah . . . Give her both. Give her a threat and give her a chance.

J: OK. I'll give you a chance. *(right hand beckons)*

F: Ahah, this means, "Come to me."

J: Yeah. Let's get together. Let's try to get together and see what we can do . . . But I'm warning you, *(laughter)* if you keep making a fool of me the way you do, Jane, with your crying and your dependency . . . you're never gonna let me grow up. *(thoughtfully)* I'm never gonna let you—Hm. (laughter) Well.

F: Be the other Jane again.

J: Well, I don't want to grow up—this part of—I don't want to grow up. I want to stay the way I am.

F: Say this again.

J: I want to stay the way I am.

F: "I don't want to grow up."

J: I don't wanna grow up. /F: Again./
I don't wanna grow up. /F: Louder./
I don't wanna grow up. /F: Louder./
I don't wanna grow up. *(voice begins to break)* /F: Louder./
I don't wanna grow up!

F: Say it with your whole body.

J *(crying):* I don't *wanna* grow up! I don't wanna grow up. I'm tired of growing up. (crying) It's too *fucking hard!*. . . *(sighs)*

F: Now be brazen Jane again.

J: Sure it's hard. I know it's hard. I can do it. I can do anything. I go around proving it all the time. What's the matter with *you?* You're always behind me. You have to catch up with me . . . Come and catch up with me . . .

OK, I'll catch up with you, Jane, but you have to help me.

F: Tell her how she can help you.

J: You have to allow me to exist without threatening me, without punishing me.

F: Say this again.

J *(almost crying):* You have to allow me to exist without threatening me and punishing me.

F: Can you say this without tears?

J *(calmly):* You have to allow me to exist without threatening me, and without punishing me.

F: Say this also to the group—the same sentence . . .

J: You have to allow me to exist without threatening me and without punishing me.

F: Say this also to Raymond [fiancé].

J *(crying):* You have to allow me to exist without threatening me . . . you know that . . .

F: Got it?

J: Yes . . .

F: OK.

Jane II

JANE: I had a dream last night that I'd like to work on. I'm at this, and it's very noisy and it's very hectic. . . . And I'm going through the crowd and I'm bumping into people and they're bumping into me and I'm not having a good time. And I'm holding onto my little brother's hand, so he won't get lost. And we're going through the crowd, and he says he wants to go into a—uh—this carnival ride where people get in these little seats and go through a tunnel. And—uh—

FRITZ: Back to the "and" bit. You use "and, and, and," as if you are afraid to let events stand for themselves.

J: Yeah. So, we don't have any money—we don't have any money to get into the ride. I take a watch off my wrist, I give it to my brother, and I ask him to ask the ticket man if he'll take the watch for both of us. He comes back and tells me the ticket man won't take the watch, so we're gonna sneak in.

F: Let's start the whole dream all over. This time you're not dreaming it; your brother is dreaming it.

J (*more boisterous*): Well, we're at this carnival and it's real fun except my sister's got ahold of my hand. She's constricting me at the wrist so she won't lose me. She's got me—she's holding me very tightly on my wrist, and I wanna—I want her to let go of me. I don't really care if I get lost. But she does, so I let her hold onto my wrist. There's a ride I wanna go on. I don't care if she goes with me or not, but I know she won't let me go unless she can go too, unless she can be with me. She doesn't . . . she doesn't wanna be by herself. . . . We don't have any money to get on—to get on the ride, and she gives me her watch. I'm really happy that—that we have a way of getting in. I go up to the ticket man and it doesn't work, but I really wanna go on the ride.

F: Say this again.

J: I really wanna go on the ride. /F: Again./
   I really wanna go on the ride. /F: Again./
   (*louder*) I really wanna go on the ride!

F: I don't believe you.

J: Ohh . . . *I* don't; my brother does. (*laughs*) Umm. I really want to go on that ride, Jane. I really want to go . . . Whether you go with me or not, I wanna go. It's *fun*. So gimme your watch . . . So she gives me her watch. The ticket man says no. Jane! We're gonna sneak in. She doesn't want to. Well, then *I'm* going to sneak in. Ohh. you don't want to go without me, so you'll sneak in, too. OK. So we'll sneak in. Now instead of *you* taking *my* hand, I'm gonna take your hand, 'cause I'm gonna help you sneak in. So hold on, and go under the gate, I'm very small, I'm very young—

F: Interrupt it, now. Close your eyes, experience your hands.

J: Hm. My right hand's stiff, very stiff. It's pointing. My left hand is shaking and it's—it's open. It's—um—both my hands are shaking. Both hands are shaking. And my knees and my ankles feel stiff. And I don't feel a heaviness in my chest like I usually do. But I feel heavy in the chair, and my right hand is pointing. And now—

F: I noticed that when you pulled, the right hand is the brother, the left hand is Jane.

J: Hm . . . I forgot where I was. I'm Jane. Oh, we're gonna—yeah—I'm gonna sneak in. So I'm very scared, but I'm more afraid of losing him than of sneaking in and getting caught, so I take his hand and—I take his hand—

F: Wait a moment. What's your brother's name?

J: Paul.

F: *Paul* is still dreaming the dream.

J: Oh. OK. So take my hand. I know how afraid you are of doing things like this, but I also know that you're *so* afraid that I'll get lost, so I can get you to sneak in with me, 'cause I want to sneak in to this ride. And I love to have fun, and I'm gonna have fun whether you're afraid of it or not. So we go—we go under the railing, and we go between people's legs, in and out, past the ticket man—

F: I don't believe you. You are not in the dream. Your voice goes Ahhhhhhrrrrr . . .

J: My legs are aching and my upper leg's kind of. . . . I have Jane by the hand. We're going—we're going (*voice becomes more expressive*) We're going between the legs of all the people and we're—we're crawling, and (*bright, happy*) I like it, I like doing this, and she's afraid. (*sigh*) And we're gonna—we're gonna go up to the door, and we're gonna go through the door, and she's *pulling* me, and I'm *pulling* her. I'm trying to pull her through, and she won't come with me. So I grab her wrist like she had my wrist and I pull her and I'm littler than her, but I can pull her through, and she's on her hands and knees and I'm pulling her along. And we go through—we go through the door, and I hop on the ride, and I leave her standing there, and the little clod goes in the door—she doesn't—she loses me. Once I got in there, I could go on the ride . . .

F: Now say good-bye to Jane.

J: Good-bye, Jane! . . . I'm—I didn't want to say good-bye to her. I'd rather have fun. . . . Jane's standing back there looking like a jerk. She's standing there with her legs shaking, and I don't give a shit. I really don't give a shit. It's easy to say good-bye to her. (*laughs*) She's standing there like some fool, and she's calling me, she's calling my name. She looks frantic, she looks like she's in a panic. (*disinterested*) But I'd rather have fun. She'll be all right.

F: OK. Now change roles again. Be Jane again.

J: The dream is very long.

F: There is so much already there.

J: Be Jane again. OK. I'm at the carnival with my brother and we're going through—I really *don't* think I want to be here, and—

F: Tell us. Tell *us* your position . . .

J: What I just said?

F: Your whole position. The situation is open, right? Very clear. There is your brother, and there is you. You want to hold onto him; he wants to be free.

J: Well I think—I think he's younger than me, and he *is* younger than me and I don't want him—to do what—what I did. I wanna (*quietly and hesitantly*) protect him or something. I hold onto him. I think I—I think I keep trying to do what my mother can't do. . . . It's insane. It's really insane. . . . I talk to him. I tell him. Paul, stop taking drugs, and stop roaming around. (*cries*) Stop trying to be so free, because you're gonna regret it. When you're twenty, you'll regret it.

Now I want to take his side. He'd say, how can you tell me not to do exactly what you do?—what you did when you were sixteen and seventeen. How can you say that? That's not fair. I *like* what I'm doing. Leave me alone! You're—you're really a bitch. You're just like my mother, you're such a bitch. How can *you* be such a bitch when you already did this? . . . (*sighs*)

I . . . I'm trying to take care of you. I'm trying to take care of you, and I know I can't—(*cries*) I know I have to let go of you, but I keep trying in my dreams, to hold onto you, and to keep you safe, because it's so dangerous what you're doing! . . . You're gonna get all fucked up. (*cries*)

But you're not all fucked up! So look at you! You've changed, you've really changed. You don't lie any more. Much. (*laughter*) You don't take drugs any more, like you used to. I'll change that. I just have to do what I have to do. You don't trust me, do you? You're like my mother, you don't trust me. You don't think I'm strong.

F: OK. Jane I think you can work this out on your own. I want to do something else right now. I want to start with the beginning. Always look at the beginning of the dream. Notice where a dream is taking place, whether you are in a car, whether the dream is taking place in a motel, or nature, or in an apartment building. This always gives you immediately the impression of the existential background. Now you start your dream out, "Life is a carnival." Now give us a speech about life as a carnival.

J: Life—life is a carnival. You go on this trip, and you get off. You go on that trip, and you get off. And then you bump into all kinds of people, you bump into *all kinds* of people, and some of them you look at, and some of them you don't look at, and some of them irritate you, and really bump you, and others don't, others are kind to you. And you win things at the carnival. You win presents . . . And some rides—most all the rides, the trips, are scary. But they're fun. They're fun and they're scary. It's very crowded, and there are lots of people—lots and lots of faces. . . . And in the dream, I'm—I'm holding onto somebody in the carnival, and he wants to go on all the trips.

Jane III

JANE: The dream I started on, the last time I worked, I never finished it, and I think the last part is as important as the first part. Where I left off, I was in the Tunnel of Love—

FRITZ: What are you picking on? (*Jane has been scratching her leg.*)

J: Hmm. (*clears throat*) . . . I'm just sitting here, for a minute, so I can really be here. It's hard to stay with this feeling, and talk at the same time. . . . Now I'm in the intermediate zone, and I'm—I'm thinking about two things: Should I work on the dream, or should I work on the picking thing, because that's something I do a lot. I pick my face, and . . . I'll go back to the dream. I'm in the Tunnel of Love, and my brother's gone in the—somewhere— and to the left of me, there's a big room and it's painted the color of—the color that my schoolrooms used to be painted, kind of a drab green, and to the left of me there are bleachers. I look over and there are all people sitting there. It looks as though they are waiting to get on the ride. There's a big crowd around one person, Raymond [fiancé]. He's talking to them and he's explaining something to them and they're all listening to him. And he's moving his finger like this, and making gestures. I'm surprised to see him. I go up to him, and it's very obvious that he doesn't want to talk to me. He's interested in being with all these people, entertaining all these people. So I tell him that I'll wait for him. I sit three—three bleachers up and look down, and watch this going on. I get irritated and I'm—pissed off, so I say, "Raymond, I'm leaving. I'm not gonna wait for you any more." I walk outside the door—I stand outside the door for awhile—I get anxious. I can feel anxious in my dream. I feel anxious now, because I don't really want to be out here. I want to be inside, with Raymond. So I'm going inside. I go back through the door—

F: Are you telling us a dream, or are you doing a job?

J: Am I telling a dream—

F: Or are you doing a job?

J: I'm telling a dream, but it's still—I'm not telling a dream.

F: Hm. Definitely not.

J: I'm doing a job.

F: I gave you only the two alternatives.

J: I can't say that I'm really aware of what I'm doing. Except physically. I'm aware of what's happening physically to me but—I don't really know what I'm doing. I'm not asking you to tell me what I'm doing . . . just saying I don't know.

F: I noticed one thing: When you come up to the hot seat, you stop playing the silly goose.

J: Hm. I get frightened, when I'm up here.

F: You get dead.

J: Whew . . . If I close my eyes and go into my body, I know I'm not dead. If I open my eyes and "do that job," then I'm dead. . . . I'm in the intermediate zone now, I'm wondering whether or not I'm dead. I notice that my legs are cold and my feet are cold. My hands are cold. I feel—I feel strange. . . . I'm in the middle, now. I'm—I'm neither with my body nor with the group. I notice that my attention is concentrated on that little matchbox on the floor.

F: OK. Have an encounter with the matchbox.

J: Right now, I'm taking a break from looking at you, 'cause it's—it's a—'cause I don't know what's going on, and I don't know what I'm doing. I don't even know if I'm telling the truth.

F: What does the matchbox answer?

J: I don't care if you tell the truth or not. It doesn't matter to me. I'm just a matchbox.

F: Let's try this for size. Tell us, "I'm just a matchbox."

J: I'm just a matchbox. And I feel silly saying that. I feel, kind of dumb, being a matchbox.

F: Uhhm.

J: A little bit useful, but not very useful. There's a million like me. And you can look at me, and you can like me, and then when I'm all used up, you can throw me away. I never liked being a matchbox. . . . I don't—I don't know if that's the truth, when I say I don't know what I'm doing. I know there's one part of me that knows what I'm doing. And I feel suspended, I feel—steady. I don't feel relaxed. Now I'm trying to understand why in the two seconds it takes me to move from the group to the hot seat, my whole—my whole *persona* changes. . . . Maybe because of—I want to talk to the Jane in *that* chair.

She would be saying, (*with authority*) well, *you* know where you're at. You're playing dumb. You're playing stupid. You're doing this, and you're doing that, and you're sucking people in, and you're—(*louder*) not telling the truth! and your stuck, and you're dead . . .

And when I'm *here*, I immediately—the Jane here would say, (*small, quavery voice*) well, that's—I feel on the defensive in this chair right now. I feel defensive. I feel like for some reason I have to defend myself. And I know it's not true. . . . So who's picking on you? It's *that* Jane over there that's picking on me.

F: Yah.

J: She's saying . . . she's saying, (*briskly*) now when you get in the chair, you have to be in the here and now, you have to do it *right,* you have to be turned on, you have to know everything—

F: "You have to do your job."

J: You have to do your job, and you have to do it *right.* And you have to—On top of all that, you have to become totally self-actualized, and you have to get rid of all your hang-ups, and along with that—it's not—it's not mandatory that you do this, but it's nice if you can be entertaining along the way, while you're doing all that. Try to spice it up a little bit, so that people won't get bored and go to sleep, because that makes you anxious. And you have to *know* why you're in the chair. You can't just go here and not know why you're there. You have to know *everything,* Jane.

You really make it hard for me. You really make it hard. You're really putting a lot of demands on me. . . . I don't know everything. And that's hard to say. I don't know everything, and on top of that, I don't know what I'm doing half the time. . . . I don't know—I don't know if that's the truth or not. I don't even know if that's a lie.

F: So be your top-dog again.

J: Is that—

F: Your top dog. That's the famous top dog. The righteous top dog. This is where your power is.

J: Yeah. Well—uh—I'm your top dog. You can't live without me. I'm the one that—I keep you noticed, Jane. I keep you noticed. If it weren't for me, nobody would notice you. So you'd better be a little more grateful that I exist.

Well, I don't want to be noticed, *you* do. You want to be noticed. I don't want to be noticed. I don't want . . . I don't really want to be noticed, as much as you do.

F: I would like you to attack the righteous side of that top dog.

J: Attack—the righteous side.

F: The top dog is always righteous. Top dog *knows* what you've got to do, has all the right to criticize, and so on. The top dog nags, picks, puts you on the defensive.

J: Yeah . . . You're a bitch! You're like my mother. You know what's good for me. You—you make life *hard* for me. You tell me to do things. You tell me to be—*real.* You tell me to be self-actualized. You tell me to—uh, tell the truth.

F: Now please don't change what your hands are doing, but tell us what's going on in your hands.

J: My left hand . . .

F: Let them talk to each other.

J: My left hand. I'm shaking, and I'm in a fist, straining forward, and [*voice begins to break*] that's kind of—the fist is very tight, pushing—pushing my fingernails into my hand. It doesn't feel good, but I do it all the time. I feel tight.

F: And the right hand?

J: I'm holding you back around the wrist.

F: Tell it why you hold back.

J: If I let you go you're—then you're gonna hit something. I don't know what you're gonna hit, but I have to—I have to hold you back 'cause you can't do that. Can't go around hitting things.

F: Now hit your top dog.

J *(short harsh yell):* Aaaarkh! Aarkkh!

F: Now talk to your top dog. "Stop nagging—"

J *(loud, pained):* Leave me alone! /F: Yah, again./ Leave me alone! /F: Again./ *(screaming it and crying) Leave me alone!* /F: Again./ *(She screams it, a real blast.)* LEAVE ME ALONE! I DON'T HAVE TO DO WHAT YOU SAY! *(still crying)* I don't have to be that good! . . . I don't have to be in this chair! I don't *have* to. *You* make me. You make me come here! *(screams)* Aarkkh! You make me pick my face, *(crying)* that's what *you* do. *(screams and cries)* Aaarkkh! I'd like to kill you.

F: Say this again.

J: I'd like to kill you. /F: Again./

I'd like to *kill* you.

F: Can you squash it in your left hand?

J: It's as big as me . . . I'm strangling it.

F: OK. Say this, "I'm strangling—"

J *(quietly):* I'm gonna strangle you . . . take your neck. Grrrummn. *(Fritz gives her a pillow which she strangles while making noises.)* Arrghh. Unghhh How do you like *that! (sounds of choked-off cries and screams)*

F: Make more noises.

J: Hrugghhh! Aachh! Arrgrughhh! *(She continues to pound pillow, cry and scream.)*

F: OK. Relax, close your eyes . . . *(long silence) (softly)* OK. Come back to us. Are you ready? . . . Now be that top dog again. . . .

J *(faintly):* You shouldn't have done that. I'm gonna punish you for that . . . I'm gonna punish you for that, Jane. You'll be sorry you did that. Better watch out.

F: Now talk like this to each one of us. . . . Be vindictive with each one of us. Pick out something we have done. . . . Start with me. As this top dog, for what are you going to punish me?

J: I'm gonna punish you for making me feel so stupid.

F: How are you going to punish me?

J *(promptly):* By being stupid . . . Even stupider than I am.

F: OK. Do this some more.

J: Raymond, I'm gonna punish you for being so dumb. I'll make you feel like an ass. . . . I'll make you think I'm smarter than you are, and you'll feel dumber and I'll feel smart. . . . I'm really scared. I shouldn't be doing this. *(cries)* It isn't nice.

F: Say this to him. Turn it around, "You should not—"

J: You sh—you shouldn't—you shouldn't—you shouldn't be doing—hooo—you shouldn't be doing—you shouldn't be so dumb. You shouldn't play so dumb. Because it isn't nice.

F: You're doing a job again.

J: Yeah, I know. I don't wanna do it. *(crying)* I—I know how I punish you. *(sigh)* I'll punish you by being helpless.

Raymond: What are you punishing me for?

J: I'll punish you for loving me. That's what I'll punish you for. I'll make it *hard* for you to love me. I won't let you know if I'm coming or going.

F: "How can you be so low as to love somebody like me?" Yah?

J: *I* do that.

F: I know. How can you love a matchbox? . . .

J: Fergus, I'm gonna punish you for being so slow—in your body, but so quick in your mind. The way I'm gonna do that—I'm gonna excite you, try to excite you, and it's the truth. I'll punish you for being sexually inhibited. I'll make you think I'm very sexy. I'll make you feel bad around me. . . And I'll punish you for pretending to know more than you do.

F: What do you experience when you are meting out the punishment?

J *(more alert, alive):* It's a very strange experience. I don't know that I've ever had it before, for such a long time. It's kind of—it's a feeling I used to get when I—When I got back at my brothers for being mean to me. I'd just grit my teeth and think of the *worst* thing I could do—and kind of enjoy it.

F: Yah. This is my impression; you didn't enjoy this here.

J: Mm.

F: OK. Go back and be the top dog again, and *enjoy* punishing Jane—pick on her, torture her.

J: You're the only one I enjoy punishing . . . When you're too loud—when you're too loud, I'll punish you for being too loud. *(no sound of enjoyment)* When you're not loud enough, I'll tell you that you're too inhibited. When you dance too much—when you dance too much, I'll tell you that you're trying to sexually arouse people. When you don't dance enough, I'll tell you that you're dead.

F: Can you tell Jane, "I'm driving you crazy"?

J *(cries):* I'm driving you crazy. /F: Again./

I'm driving you crazy./F: Again./

I'm driving you *crazy* . . . I used to drive everybody else crazy, and now I'm driving *you* crazy . . . *(voice drops, becomes very faint)* But it's for your own good. That's what my mother would say. "For your own good." I'll make you feel *guilty* when you've done bad things, so you won't do it again. And I'll—I'll pat you on the back when you do something good, so you'll remember to do it again. And I'll keep you out of the moment. I'll—I'll keep you planning—and I'll keep you programmed, and I won't let you live—in the moment. I won't let you enjoy your life.

F: I would like you to use this: "I am relentless."

J: I—I *am* relentless. /F: Again./

I am relentless. I'll do anything—especially if somebody dares me to do something. Then I've gotta tell you to do it, Jane, so you can prove it, so you can prove yourself. You've *gotta* prove yourself—in this world.

F: Let's try this. "You've got a job to do."

J *(laughs):* You've gotta job to do. You're gonna quit fuckin' around, and —you've been doin' nothin' for a long time—

F: Yah. Now, don't change your posture. The right arm goes to the left and the left arm goes to the right. Say the same thing again and stay aware of this.

J: You've been doing nothing for a long time. You gotta do something, Jane. You've gotta *be* something . . . You've gotta make people proud of you. You've got to grow up, you have to be a woman, and you gotta keep everything that's bad about you hidden away so nobody can see it, so they'll think you're perfect, just perfect . . . You have to lie. I make you lie.

F: Now take Jane's place again.

J: You're—you're *(cries)* you are driving me crazy. You're picking on me. I'd really like to strangle you—uh—then you'll punish me more. You'll come back—and give me hell for that. So, why don't you just go away? I won't—I won't cross you up any more. Just go away and leave me alone—and I'm not begging you!! Just go away! /F: Again./

Just go away! /F: Again./

Go away! /F: Change seats./

You'll be just a half if I go away! You'll be half a person if I leave. Then you'll really be fucked up. You can't send me away, you'll have to figure out something to *do* with me, you'll have to *use* me.

Well then—then I—I would change your mind about a lot of things if I had to.

F: Ah!

J: And tell you that there's nothing I could do that's bad . . . I mean, if you'd leave me alone, I wouldn't do anything bad . . .

F: OK. Take another rest.

J *(closes eyes):* . . . I can't rest.

F: So come back to us. Tell us about your restlessness.

J: I keep wondering what to do with that. When I had my eyes closed, I was saying, "Tell her to just relax."

F: OK. Play *her* top dog, now.

J: Just relax.

F: Make her the underdog and you're the top dog.

J: And you don't have to do anything, you don't have to prove anything. *(cries)* You're only twenty years old! You don't have to be the queen . . .

She says, OK. I understand that. I know that. I'm just in a *hurry.* I'm in a *big* hurry. We've got so many things to do—and now, I know, when I'm in a hurry you can't be now, you can't—when I'm in a hurry, you can't stay in the minute you're in. You have to keep—you have to keep hurrying, and the days slip by and you think you're losing time, or something. I'm *much* too hard on you. I have to—I have to leave you alone.

F: Well, I would like to interfere. Let your top dog say, "I'll be a bit more patient with you."

J: Uh. I'll be—I'll be a bit more patient with you.

F: Say this again.

J *(softly:* It's very hard for me to be patient. You know that. You know how impatient I am. But I'll—I'll try to be a bit more patient with you. "I'll try"—I'll *be* a bit more patient with you. As I say that, I'm stomping my foot, and shaking my head.

F: OK. Say, "I *won't* be patient with you—"

J *(easily):* I *won't* be patient with you, Jane! I won't be patient with you. /F: Again./

I won't be patient with you. /F: Again./

I won't be patient with you.

F: Now say this to us . . . Pick a few.

J: Jan, I won't be patient with you. Claire, I won't be patient with you . . . Dick, I won't be patient with you. Muriel, I won't be patient with you. Ginny, I won't be patient with you . . . And June, I won't be patient with you, either.

F: OK. How do you feel, now?

J: OK.

F: You understand, top dog and underdog are not yet together. But at least the conflict is clear, in the open, maybe a *little* bit less violent.

J: I felt, when I worked before, on the dream, and the dream thing, that I worked this out. I felt *good.* I keep—I keep—it keeps—I keep going back to it.

F: Yah. This is the famous self-torture game.

J: I do it so *well.*

F: Everybody does it. You don't do it better than the rest of us. Everybody thinks, "I am the worst."

Case 12

Editors' Introduction

In classifying the psychotherapies, generally, a three part division is made: (a) the "depth" therapies (Freud and Jung) with emphasis on the unconscious; (b) the "behavior" therapies (Sajwaj et al., Wolpe, etc.) with emphasis on objective behavior; and (c) the "humanistic" psychologies with emphasis on the experiencing person (Adler, Rogers, Ellis, etc.)

In this classification where could one place a person like Glasser or Greenwald, each of whom could be defined as an "eclectic" basing his system on common sense? Not that other therapists, such as Adler, for example, do not employ common sense, but rather that the underlying concept of these therapists is "What do we need theory for? since, after all, the good healthy life only depends on————" and then they state what it is.

Glasser seems to us a prime example of an exponent of consequences. Robert Green Ingersoll once stated, "In nature there are no rewards or punishments, only consequences." This could well be Glasser's basic notion: "Life is a kind of game, with rules. Figure out the rules and play according to them. If you don't want to be fat, then don't overeat. If you are in prison and want release, do what is necessary. If you are out of work, set a plan and follow it to get a job. This may mean cutting off your beard and dressing differently."

In short, we could summarize Glasser's therapy as simply an application of common sense. In this fragment, one has the opportunity to watch a therapist in the process of learning and we get some insight into the beginnings of Glasser's Reality Therapy.

WILLIAM GLASSER

The Case of Aaron

Aaron was the highly intelligent eleven-year-old son of an unemotional, overly intellectual divorced woman who worked as a mathematician at one of the Los Angeles missile and space laboratories, and a father who lived in another part of the country and had no contact with him. Aaron was often left home in the care of a neighbor while his mother went away on weekends with her boyfriend. At the time I saw him he had been seen by two other therapists over the previous two years, both third-year residents in a psychiatric training facility. He was assigned to me for treatment when I was also a third-year resident and was my first child outpatient. The other therapists had treated him conventionally with play therapy. Most of their time was spent interpreting the meaning of his play to him. For example, if he struck a female doll repeatedly, the therapist would ask him if he wouldn't like to hit his mother and hope Aaron would confirm the truth of his guess. Having also been trained in traditional psychiatry, I attempted at first to follow in the footsteps of the previous therapists. When Aaron confirmed his anger and hostility against his mother I wondered, as they must have, why this insight did not help him. He wanted to learn better ways to act, but up to then all of us had avoided teaching him what he needed to know.

One way to describe Aaron and his behavior is to say that although he was pleasant in appearance, he was the most obnoxious child I had ever met. I dreaded Monday and Thursday mornings because those days started with Aaron. He evidently had been treated very permissively by his previous therapists who, besides interpreting his behavior to him, accepted everything he did. And what he did was horrible. He ran pell-mell from game to game and toy to toy, never letting me help him to enjoy what he was doing. He seemed to be almost desperately avoiding my offer to play as if my joining in the play might deprive him in some way of some of his pleasures. He acted aggressively in a completely haphazard, unpredictable way, crying for my attention but turning nasty and withdrawing when I gave him some warmth. He discussed his mother in a highly critical way, making her into an ogre of psychiatric rejection. His angry com-

From pp. 135–140 in *Reality Therapy* by William Glasser. Copyright © 1965 by William Glasser, Inc.

ments paraphrased the words of the previous therapists, especially in his use of adjectives like hostile and rejecting as he described his mother. Criticizing the previous therapists at the clinic in their treatment of him as well as the clinic toys, playrooms, and lack of entertaining facilities, he also rattled on about all the destructive things he did and was planning to do at home.

He blamed his failure to be happy on his mother, her boyfriend, his missing father, or his previous therapists. His school did not escape his critical wrath: it was very bad, his teachers did not understand him, and the other kids picked on him. As time went on, however, he blamed more and more of his predicament upon me. He was preoccupied with his mother's current boyfriend, who had been the subject of voluminous psychiatric interpretations in the past. He had learned to blame many of his problems on the boyfriend, always ending on the martyred note that this man took his mother away from him. A reading of the record showed that his repetitive complaint was almost verbatim from what previous therapists had told him.

Regardless of how he behaved, no one had ever attempted to put a value judgment on his behavior, no one had ever told him he was doing wrong. Everything he did was accepted as something to be explained, or, in psychiatric terms, "interpreted" ad nauseum.

Because no one had attempted to set limits for him either in his home or in treatment, he was erratic and unhappy. His behavior was a desperate attempt to force someone to direct his behavior and discipline him so that he might behave better and achieve something worthwhile. All he felt was that no one really cared; he was involved with no one, and lacking the necessary involvement he acted almost totally on impulse.

In his attempt to get someone to set some limits, he tried everything, producing grossly inconsistent behavior. Vocally and physically aggressive at times, he might with equal suddenness become withdrawn and almost detached from reality. He would start a game, then destroy it if he suffered even one minor setback. He walked away from our outdoor play and then would come back to beg me for candy. He would run away, hide, and try to make me look for him all over the clinic. Continually begging for ice cream or for money, he became detached when he was refused. He made it a point never to talk about anything meaningful, that is, what he was doing and feeling. If it came up naturally in conversation he would stop suddenly and run, scream, or begin to talk gibberish. Several times during each session he would tell me that his mother did not like him and that her dislike caused his troubles. It was some time before I began to realize that he was well aware of his behavior, even to the extent that in his own erratic, impulsive way he devised new tests for my patience. He actually planned some of his misconduct, which must have been exhausting and difficult for him to keep up as long as he did.

His mother was an impersonal, detached individual who raised Aaron as an object rather than a person. Instead of reacting to his behavior and setting some limits, she discussed it with him objectively. Essentially a cold woman, she did contribute to his frustration, but if our hope was for her to change, Aaron had little chance. Basically Aaron felt worthless and unloved. From material in the record it was apparent that the school had given up trying to reach this intelligent boy and was just trying to live with him. He made fair grades in subject matter, but he was a disrupting influence in the classroom and in all his social contacts. The other children in school and around his neighborhood shunned him like the plague, precipitating further anger and obnoxious behavior, which in turn caused them to shun him even more. At home or in school he interrupted their play, destroyed their creative attempts, and broke into their recitations in class with snide remarks.

Although Aaron was desperate for some change, I was advised by my supervisor to continue to work with him in play therapy and to interpret his "anal retention and oral aggression." A firm believer in psychoanalytic theory, my supervisor was convinced that the child needed to know "why." Once his behavior was interpreted to him in terms of the transference—that he was reacting to the therapist as a good father and also as a bad abandoning father—he should be able to change. My supervisor also thought that many of Aaron's problems could be solved if his mother, through weekly conferences with a social worker, could gain insight into her role in his difficulties and improve her treatment of him; two years of traditional social work conferences, however, had produced only more intellectualizing from her. My supervisor failed to recognize the desperate, present situation in which Aaron was doing his best to change.

Although it was to be many years before Reality Therapy became definite in my mind as a method of treatment, it was with Aaron that I first discovered the dramatic force of confronting a child with present reality. This confrontation, fortunately made after we had gained some involvement, solidified our relationship into a deeper therapeutic involvement which produced great changes in Aaron.

I realized dimly that in following the principles of orthodox therapy I was contributing to Aaron's present desperation rather than relieving it, and I made up my mind to change my approach. Against all my training and reading, and without telling anyone what I planned to do, I began a kind of Reality Therapy. The explaining was over. From now on we were going to emphasize reality and present behavior.

When Aaron arrived the following morning I took him into my office, nudging him gently past the playroom when he tried to stop there as usual. Telling him to sit down and listen, I explained that I wasn't interested in anything he had to say, only that he listen to me this morning. He whined and tried to get away, but I held him and faced him toward me. I told him to shut up and for once in his life to listen to what someone had to say. I informed him that the play was over, that we would sit and talk in an adult fashion, or if we walked we would walk as adults. I explained clearly that I would not tolerate any running away or even any impolite behavior while we were walking. He would have to be courteous and try to converse with me when I talked to him. He was to tell me everything he did and I would help him decide whether it was right or wrong.

When he immediately attempted to leave, I forcibly restrained him. When he tried to hit me, I told him I would hit him back! After two years without restraint, it was probably the suddenness of this approach that shocked him into going along with me. After some brief initial testing, he did not resist much, probably because he had been anxious for so long to be treated in this realistic way. Also, apparently sensing my own desperation, he was afraid that if he pushed me too far I would leave, and he needed me very much.

I wanted to know what he did in school and at home, and what he could do that was better. When I told him frankly that he was the most miserable and obnoxious child I had ever met, he was greatly surprised. He had thought all therapists must automatically love their patients. I informed him that if he stayed in therapy he was going to have to change because neither I nor anyone else could possibly care for him the way he was now.

What happened next was most dramatic. First of all, he became likable, talking to me courteously. He seemed to enjoy being with me and surprisingly I began to look forward to seeing him. Even though we were now becoming involved, he complained to his mother about my tactics. He knew that she would be upset, and he wanted to find out if she could make me change my new approach to him. If his mother had been able to change me then, it would have proved that I did not really care and our involvement would have been broken. She sought me out as he knew she would, and asked me what I had in mind. When I told her that I was definitely going to continue with my new method, she threatened to take my "unpsychiatric behavior" to my child psychiatry supervisor. I bluffed her by telling her to do so. Had she told him I would have been in trouble, but the bluff worked. Aaron did not complain further and she never took any action against me. I discussed other cases with my supervisor, mentioning Aaron only to say that he was doing much better.

Rapidly Aaron and I grew more involved. Criticizing him for all his old weaknesses but praising him when he did well, I stood in his path whenever he tried to revert to his old ways.

In about six weeks he changed remarkably. I heard from his school that his work had suddenly risen to straight A and that his behavior had also become excellent. The teachers couldn't understand what had happened. I told them to be firm with him, treat him as kindly as they could, and not to make any comments about his changed performance. At home his mother noticed the changes that began to occur there also and, while she liked his new behavior, she was uncomfortable because he was "so different." Having always seen him as some kind of a miserable little boy creature, she found it difficult to relate to him as a responsible boy because of her poor attitude toward men and people in general.

Her attitude didn't seem to bother Aaron at all. He was only slightly involved with his mother, and he was now getting satisfaction from his relationships with other people. He rather enjoyed his mother's discomfort and her inability to understand what had happened to him. I told her very little other than to treat him as an adult and to expect good behavior. After a while she began to get used to her different son and eventually their relationship became a little better. Theirs will never be a warm, good, mother-son relationship, but it became far better than it had been in the past. As he began to play constructively with other children, for the first time in his life playmates began to seek him out.

About three months later he was discharged from therapy. He had developed a good relationship with his mother's boyfriend, and it was their new relationship which was going to make marriage between his mother and this man possible. Aaron would benefit because he certainly needed a father. After the marriage had been decided on, I thought it was a good time for him to quit therapy. School was almost over, Aaron had made some friends, and he needed me much less. I was able to follow the case for six months and he continued to do well. Not only had Aaron benefited greatly from the therapy, but I had learned the valuable lesson that breaking with teaching and tradition as I had done could be beneficial.

In private practice patients who are fairly responsible except for a particular problem often come for treatment. Unhappy as they and their families may be with the way they are, they usually present no great problem to anyone outside the family. As long as psychiatrists are in private practice, patients who have the means to do so will come looking for what they feel is missing in their lives. Treating them is difficult because the therapist cannot use this firmness or direction that he can employ in institutions or even with some clinic patients such as Aaron. Results come slowly and the gain in responsibility is never as dramatic as in cases in which the therapist has more control.

Case 13

Editors' Introduction

In searching for an appropriate case to illustrate existential analysis, we had a difficult time since (a) many existentialists' writings are too obscure to be generally understood without reading in great depth, and (b) existential therapists vary more than any other kind of therapists with respect to their conceptualizations and language.

Nevertheless, of the various case studies we found, we both came to the conclusion that for clarity of presentation, intrinsic interest of the individual portrayed, and total resolution the case of Father M is outstanding. Unfortunately, because of its original excessive length (in terms of the amount of space we could give proportionately to a case example of existential thinking) we had to do some minor editing, but this was primarily theoretical material which does not affect the understanding of the therapy.

We believe that this selection is a literary gem and we are happy to have found it and to present it to our readers.

HERBERT HOLT

The Case of Father M—A Segment of an Existential Analysis

Introduction

The case of Father M begins at a social gathering. A former patient of mine, who is now a professional pastoral counselor, entered into a conversation with a Roman Catholic priest, a stocky man of Mediterranean type with a forceful, even an opinionated manner of speaking. A man of considerable intelligence and charm—he was a graduate student at a great secular university—Father M expressed great disapproval of the group life of priests, saying that it is corrupt and hypocritical. "They just try to do the least amount of work possible and sit around drinking and card-playing all the time. They only care for the rich parishioners." This was the general tenor of his remarks. He felt very angry that other priests seemed to him blind to the poverty of men and to try only to amass money and pleasures for themselves.

Regardless of whether or not there might have been some truth to these observations from his experience, their generality and the degree of anger expressed by Father M to his listeners created in my former patient a certain alarm about the inappropriateness and one-sidedness of such a communication in a social situation. He became even more concerned when Father M discussed plans he had of dismissing these priests and reorganizing the parish ministry. It was almost as if he had been asked by his superiors to do so. Being quite willing to be drawn out in the matter, Father M even invited my friend to his room and showed him a whole dossier of plans for freeing the Church from the grip of the parish priests, who angered him not only by their behavior but also by virtue of being, in most cases, Irishmen.

These ideas of grandeur, and the unwarranted general accusation of a whole people, caused my former patient to suspect a deep problem of long duration in Father M. Citing his self-righteousness, his belief that he was on the right side and all the evil on the side of the Irish, my friend raised the question of discussing the problem with a psychiatrist, and referred the priest to me. For a few weeks

From: *Journal of Existentialism*, 1966, *6*, 369–395.

afterward, Father M said that he saw no reason to question his own point of view, but very gradually doubt set in, and he began to ask himself what, in fact, he had contributed to the religious and personal life of the Church. He found that he began to be aware of being troubled at his feeling of resentment, for example, over having to say Mass at a convent. Though he was paid for his time, it interfered, so he felt, with his studies. He began to wonder just how justified these feelings were. So he decided to call me. He told me that though he was convinced that nothing was the matter with him, still he knew my point of view from some papers he had read and wanted to discuss the problems of pastoral counseling. His tone over the telephone was superior, arrogant, and coercive, and when I asked him if there might be some personal problems which he might want to discuss in addition to his interest in pastoral counseling, he replied that there were, but only in reference to his work.

We made an appointment for a week later. He presented himself on time, greeted me very forcefully, shook my hand, and admired my furniture. He said that we had an especial affinity because he could see that the pieces came from Italy. He took command of the session and started to speak in great detail about his attitude toward the Church. During much of the subsequent time we spent together—sixty-four sessions in all—he was domineering, cynical, superior, a man who knows it all and feels that humility, though theoretically a Christian virtue, would if practiced, deny to men like himself the leadership role they deserve. He attacked me constantly, questioned my sincerity, ability, capacity, truthfulness to fact, and in one or another form of hostility rejected my interest. At the same time, however, he made excessive demands upon me in time, energy, attention, friendliness, and love.

The struggle between his world view and mine took on increased intensity and reached a polarity of extremes as the sessions unfolded. I defended myself against his verbal and emotional traps, maintaining my position without retaliation and without agreeing with his view of himself, with the demands he placed on his parents, the Church, and the world in general. He seemed to feel that all people exist only to fulfill his demands; that if they fail him he has a right to experience loss and anguish. Those who make promises and don't keep them are hypocrites and he cannot help hating them. This view of himself and his world was the only reality he accepted, and he reinforced this acceptance by believing what he heard himself saying.

How did such a state come to be? It developed that Father M was one of the younger children in a large family of several girls and twice as many boys. His father, an energetic man who provided well for his large family despite a proneness to imaginary fears, died quite recently of a chronic degenerative disease. His mother is still alive, though old and sick from the same disease which killed the father. For her to have a son in the priesthood is a great consolation, since the other sons are much given to "worldliness," and this element of maternal desire is significant in Father M's motivation. On his side, he claimed that he shares with his brothers an image of Latin masculinity which is aggressive, sensual, and a bit domineering. Consciously he conceived of his youth and early adulthood as a struggle to overcome this passionate nature. For him to submit himself to churchly discipline was, he felt, such an intense effort, given his nature, that it has been easy for him to think of himself as an "extraordinary man."

Much of Father M's life history, however, runs counter to these conscious elements. The first impression gained is the isolation which dominated his early years. His mother gave up all her creative activities in order to care for the large brood which in reality she resented. He feels that she especially had little time for him. His memory is that she put him, for long periods, into a bed with high bars, where he cried for her and was not satisfied. His first memory, in fact, was a memory of being an outsider. He was three at the time, and the scene was a Sunday party at his parents' country house. He looked at cars parked by the guests, and he saw people walking about, but the party was not for him. In his memory a mood of sadness and loneliness dominates his early years.

Other memories have to do with unfortunate habits too pleasant to be forgotten in his later life. He loved to defecate in his trousers, and he recalls a deliberate, almost a conscious indulgence of himself in this, despite prohibition and punishment. He links the forbidden pleasure with the ambivalent feeling he had later over the problem of masturbation. A bitter memory of his fifth year recalls a birthday party at which humorous comments about the family were read by a cousin in a playful mood. The image for him was that of a great pig; as we shall see, it came to dominate his feelings about himself. Though he subsequently learned to swim well, even at times competitively despite great shyness in public, and though on occasion he fought when his interests were attacked, one senses that for the most part his body became for him an alien thing, an instrument for the dramatization of his inner conflict to the world and to himself rather than the center of authentic experience and wholehearted participation.

As might be expected, the most sensitive area for this confusion of body image and sense of inner worthlessness was in the boy's developing sexuality. He recalls much sexual preoccupation during his boyhood years. There were several episodes of homosexual contact with older brothers, which in retrospect give him some of the few memories he has of the expression of affection in a family whose parents were quite stern with the children. These episodes seem to have had for the young Father M the value of defiance of his mother, who to his mind neglected him, and also that of helping to solve his problem of loneliness. Unfortunately these episodes became known and notorious. In a very theatrical scene the older boys had to kneel and ask forgiveness of the younger, forgiveness for what in fact had a positive even though a distorted value. An act of anal intercourse with a younger sister at age eight brought little pleasure to the boy, and future attempts to repeat it were frustrated by an ever-present aunt who was quick to publicize all wrongdoing.

Just before the onset of puberty Father M became mischievous in school. He decided not to enter training for the swimming team because of his fear of public competition and, perhaps more importantly, because swimming had become charged with sexuality for him. Frightened by the sensual advances of the girls in his group of friends, and frustrated by the ever-present aunt in his attempt to renew contact with his little sister, he began his solitary masturbation. In the typical fluidity of early adolescence he moved in contrary directions sexually. Once through a wall of a bungalow he glimpsed the naked body of a girl whose widowed mother had made cutting remarks about the brothers' homosexuality. An attempt to seduce the girl failed, and at about the same time the boy's religious interest began to be fostered by retreats which stressed the need for chastity. At about this time he made an exaggerated dedication of himself to his mother, bidding for salvation from his isolation in yet the most promising direction, the one in which he knew best how to move. In a sense he once more forced her to pay attention to him by means of accompanying her daily to the early mass, thus winning the exclusive care he felt he had been denied when a small boy. His religious activities in turn became a weapon against any other self-assertiveness of his in the hands of other members of the family: "When you've just been on a retreat you shouldn't . . . "

Method and Theory

This information, together with all that was to emerge from various levels of his mental functioning, was presented and received in the interaction of the clinical situation, either in direct conversation or in biographical material which Father M supplied. Though nothing in the case history thus far gives us any grounds for calling our method different, as existential analysts we refer ourselves in our operating procedures to theoretical and methodological differences between existential and orthodox psychoanalysis, and it would be well now to give some preliminary indication of what they are, in order to help clarify our interpretation of the history which follows. In contrast to Freud's commitment to strict scientific determinism, to the search for regularity and a system, we build our work on human nature understood as uniquely manifested in each individual, as a reality emergent in particular instances, as an entity whose inner meaning we try to help to unfold. Thus it might be better to speak of "human identity" than of "human nature," since we believe it to be personal and individual, and to that extent falsified when enclosed in deterministic definitions, but truly revealed to the extent that a given individual comes to terms with the realities of his own unique humanness. . . .

Father M's presentation of the events of his childhood revealed how it seemed to him that he came to his present condition. Now a child, before it becomes aware of its own body in terms of its particular relationships to the places and the people in whose midst it lives, tries to find a way to feel secure, to build an imagery of self which will explain its particular place in its life-space. Father M, for example, had a special corner in his bedroom where he felt at home, where he ordered his toys with utter regularity, in part to disprove the accusation of piggishness. If any of his brothers disturbed this order he would become hysterical, have tantrums, neglect cleanliness and thus conform to the label which had been placed on him. He then demanded the excessive attention of his mother, as we have mentioned. This demand of his was expressed most strenuously when she showed interest in any other of the siblings. His corner, being his place of refuge, turned out also to reinforce the developing image of himself. It was there that he had to endure the worst aggression of his brothers and sisters. They invaded his space and destroyed its order, and in self-defense he became what they called him. If curtailed in his activities by being called a pig, he at first tried to resist, saying "I'm not a pig, you're a pig" in the classic way of children. But he began to believe it, since his mother too used his symptoms of unkemptness and dirtiness to reinforce the label which his siblings had thrown at him out of mischievousness.

Gradually the boy became less and less active, going through a stage in which hyperactivity and passivity alternated. For being passive he received the emotional reward of being called a good boy, but at the same time he substituted daydreaming and modification of his body image for outgoingness and participation in his given life-space. As he restricted his use of space he put greater emotional distance between himself and his family as well. This led to a confusion of the boundary between himself and the not-self, between animate and inanimate objects and between self-conceptualization in daydreams and the development of self-conceptualization in interpersonal space. To a considerable degree he lost what capacity he had achieved to test reality in the time-space continuum, and this led to isolation and the reduction of stimuli and of the emotional and intellectual interaction between him and his siblings. He created as it were a buffer zone around his body, a procedure which is in all of us a psychological necessity but which carries very different emotional loading in different cases. Personal space needs to be part of a coherent body image, but in Father M as a boy it became part of his maneuvering for a sense of distance from others.

That is to say, it became apparent that his overbearing and inconsiderate manner was the cloak in adulthood for an overpowering inner sense of unworthiness developed in childhood. "I suppose if we named the central problem," he wrote of himself,

> we would call it *my* inhumanity. It's that I think that I should be perfect; it's the guilt from not being so that punishes me when I fail. It is that which inhibits my understanding of a poem or a picture; I don't know what is going on—what emotions are being expressed—because what is expressed is foreign to my vocabulary. Although I think I should respond, I can't because the poem elicits no real feeling. That feeling was denied long since.
>
> That inhumanity comes from my father. Father was authority. In my desire to please my father, to get his love, I had to please authority, and to please authority, I

imitated it. So I have imitated it until it has become fairly habitual with me. I am probably as much like my father as he could make me.

If I am to get free from this inhumanity, this superman-humanity, I've got to throw off this need for authority and its approval, and free myself from the straitjacket it imposes.

I thought for a while that I might go into the army, without finishing school, in order to break away from my parents. But that would only put me under the rule of greater authority, and the temptation to get approval from it would probably be too great. Instead of trying to become one of the men, I would alienate myself from them in trying to get above them.

It became clear that in his upbringing Father M had not enjoyed the experiences which would make a more objective attitude not only possible but preferable. Neither his parents nor his teachers were aware that he had begun to use words not in an interpersonal way but as a vehicle for private intrasubjective meaning. He developed a style of behavior which was effective enough in the context of school and Church. It was desired of him that he be obedient, and it disturbed no one that he became overly so, an exaggerated penitent and denier of the flesh, thus the skinny counterpart of the fat pig. But he needed the reward of approval for this sacrifice, and when no reward was forthcoming he became furious, as before he had been with his mother.

Gradually the nature of the expectations and the depth of the feeling were unfolded. Not only did Father M want to control the therapist and the session, but one day he had a dream in which he saw himself killing the therapist, eating his brain and his heart and his testicles and otherwise incorporating his strength in the manner of savages. It is particularly significant how in the dream he went about the killing. He invited me to his church to show me a new statue of the Madonna which had just arrived from Italy. I looked at this masterpiece in the dream and pointed out to him how beautifully the Madonna was sculptured, especially the fine features of her face, and Father M saw himself, as I did so, stabbing me in the heart, meanwhile screaming, "Now you know what it means to die for your convictions." Joyfully, then, in front of the statue he cut me to pieces and ate my organs on the spot, feeling very joyful and happy that he had succeeded at last.

Father M awoke from this dream feeling "wonderful," not remorseful but on the contrary strong and powerful. He could not wait to come to our sessions to tell me about it, feeling that I would share his delight. The need to incorporate in this way what he called his father image seemed to him to demonstrate his willingness to strive to get something to which he was entitled in any case. He felt that true love on my part would be appropriately demonstrated by my willingness to die on his behalf, to give not only my attributes but my very life for him. I asked him if he would do the same for me, but he replied that he certainly would not. What is more, there was no obligation for him to do so, since after all he was the pupil and I the teacher. It is the duty of parents and teachers, to his way of thinking, to sacrifice themselves for their children. This was the fantasy which compensated for his feelings of deprivation, the counter hostility to his sense of dependence. When one takes into account the religious symbolism under which Father M was nurtured, it is of course no accident that he wanted to incorporate his therapist into himself, since this is the central feature of the believer's participation in the eucharistic celebration. He is encouraged precisely to consider the symbols of the bread and wine as more than symbols, in fact as the body and blood of Him who brings salvation to the penitent who seeks for divine help. Father M's distortion of the symbolism is seen in the feelings of hostility and destructiveness which it evokes in him. Secondly, the image of the Madonna represents for him a way of freeing himself from the overriding attachment to his mother. She is transformed into a celestial, even a supernatural being, and she is frozen into a statue who thus can no longer inhibit the free play of his feelings. He becomes free to attack the therapist, who represents the aspect of him which helps objectify reality, a process threatening to his self-esteem in the present state of his experience of being. In this characteristic way he incorporates this aspect of himself, makes it his own by sympathetic magic. His joy is in the thought that now at last he can be free to join his brothers, an impulse which on the level of consciousness is indicated by his desire to become a pastoral counselor and thus to establish a degree of autonomy within the given structure of the Church.

A letter from his mother to me gave many indications of the nature of the events which gave rise to these feelings and showed how differently the childhood events appeared to her. She wrote:

> I was very unhappy with my husband when I became pregnant with my boy. He spent very little time with me and the children, and I was very lonely. One day when my son was twelve years of age we all started to talk about what the children would become. I knew that my tenderhearted son could not cope with life outside, and so I told him that I wanted him to be a priest, but my son at that time wanted to become an architect, which would mean eight years of study. When he said so, his father flew into a rage and started to beat him in front of us all, hitting him with his fists all over his head and body, knocking out one tooth so that he bled from his mouth. We stepped between them to avoid further injury. My husband went to his bedroom, packed a bag, and said, "I'm leaving." He started to leave, but my son, bleeding from his mouth, said, "Please, Daddy, come back, come back. Don't leave. I'll be a good boy. I'll leave and go to school." He left next day, a pretty dejected fellow.

It is significant that Father M never mentioned this incident to me in our therapeutic sessions, but his mother's letter gives eloquent testimony to the way in which his legitimate claims to self-assertion were sacrificed to his father's anger and to her loneliness and need of support. His hatred for his father found its expression only in the kind of fantasy which his dream provides, but it also generated a pattern of distorted perceptions of the intentions of others for him, and this gave rise to much inappropriate behavior on his part. The difference between voicing such claims in therapy and telling them to others in the *Mitwelt* of everyday experience—assuming of course that one is disturbed enough to have to find an audience for them—is that the feelings generated are apt to be discharged in humor or in the anger of a response in kind, thus to be "justified," as it were, their incongruity unnoticed, in the give and take of normal human interaction. But in therapy it is not so, and a predictable reaction occurred in Father M when he began to realize that his demands were fantastic and irrational. He began to be self-accusatory, depressed, convinced that he was tremendously unworthy. He regretted the discoveries he was making, claiming that he would have been better off if he had never known what he felt deep down inside. This unfolding of inner reality, he decided, took too much energy and time away from other pursuits.

We made together a careful analysis of both sets of shared feelings. Father M became aware that the need for a loss of identity, the need to minimize himself out of guilt for his previous thoughts and deeds, was concomitant with a whole line of thinking and feeling which was based on his earliest childhood view of himself. I was concerned to show that in its origins this state of being had a positive value for him in protecting him from the consequences of his negative feelings for his parents and his brothers. It took more than twenty-two sessions to help him to the experience that these types of feelings and thoughts, while very intense in the present, are not representative of his present state of being nor expressive of his true relationship with me or anyone else. The aim was to help him "bracket" the way he felt originally about himself in order to achieve a new lived world view.

From this summary of one instance of how our clinical praxis is managed, it is possible to repeat, but on a new level of communication, some of the ways in which existential analysis differs from other therapeutic procedures. We are concerned as therapists not so much to establish the boundary lines between the three existential modes of experience—the *Eigenwelt,* the *Mitwelt,* and the *Umwelt**— as to discover how to deal with distorted human lives whose distortions can be understood in terms of this threefold distinction. We are concerned not only with the dynamics of personal consciousness, and with the ways in which one may aid a patient to gain insight into the unconscious motivations which gave rise to consciously experienced conflicts, but also, and more focally, with the ways in which these personal dynamics are expressed interpersonally. Whereas free association directs attention primarily to the origins of the pathology and seeks improvement by a painstaking recapitulation of constitutive events, we focus on present consequences and seek to deal with such events as aspects of immediate reality which are of no greater intrinsic significance than other manifestations of current distortion. They may or may not be adequately accounted for in etiological terms, but that for us is of less importance than the fact that we deal with them in phenomenological terms—as presenting realities, as part of a praxis which obeys its own laws rather than being wholly subject to the laws of the unconscious.

---

*Eigenwelt = personal world; man's relationship with himself. *Mitwelt* = social world; man's relationship with others. *Umwelt* = natural world; man's relationship to nature. (Eds.)

Our concept of therapeutic encounter means that two human individuals (or indeed more when group psychotherapy is taken into account) make some sort of commitment of themselves. The therapist understands that he receives a communication of the patient's experience of being-in-the-world and that his communication of his own identity in return, at some appropriate level of openness, constitutes a factor of basic importance in the patient's attempt at reaching genuine identity, which may be realized, as we have stressed, only in intersubjective relationships. The existential analyst, acting on what is communicated directly, seeks to become totally aware of, and to that extent responsive to the feeling which is being shared, in order to make use of it in the therapeutic relationship. Realizing that this relationship, like all relationships in human existence, is structured in terms of a definite time-space context, he relates affect to the immediate experience of it, using the past as an indicator of present reality, and the future, as apprehended by the patient, as one of the dimensions which mark out the area of his human range.

The application of this form and method with Father M gave to our relationship its distinct flavor. It permitted him to express his secret assumptions in dealing with himself and with the people he met, not just an *Eigenwelt* experience of self-discovery but as a *Mitwelt* experience of shared emotions. In therapy Father M was provided with a new situation in which such feelings could be "bracketed," since they failed to elicit the expected response. He could not control his environment with a child's magic. He therefore could not verify his distorted view of life and reinforce his illness. It was my hope that for the first time he might anticipate feelings of safety and reality, despite his anger. My aim was that he might respond to a firm and consistent but friendly attitude as a basis for attempting the construction of a new view of himself, with new values and a new perception of people significant in his environment. Such achievements, as any therapist is aware, are not once-for-all, or even more than momentary, and they exact a price in the new awareness of old emotional patterns. Thus Father M kept demanding that I give him his world ready-made, but the trap was consistently refused, and after several stormy sessions it was mutually agreed that we should separate for six months in order that he should have the opportunity to choose on his own resources what modality of living would be more realistic for his present existence. He had to try to see whether he could transcend the old dual imagery of a fat pig and runt without substituting another delusional dichotomy for the vision of reality.

The *Umwelt* of a Catholic Priest

The therapeutic relationship, after all, organizes directly only a small fraction of an individual patient's waking time, and the conditions of his environment, even though in part the creation of his neurotic motivation, still by their own coherence and inertia affect the conduct of therapy and the patient's response to it. There is also the practical consideration that we need to maintain the patient in his responsibilities during the rest of his time. Few who seek it could afford therapy otherwise. Though this gives us the opportunity to discover new responses to old situations, the inertia of the old relationships often makes progress difficult. In Father M's case, we have mentioned the intimate relationship between his struggle for identity in a sexual sense and the demands placed on him by the Church. Repeatedly in our sessions these demands became the focus of his angry complaints. Now it is true that the modern age makes particularly cruel demands upon its priests, because of its insistence on the maintenance of a system of thought which is markedly at variance with that upon which the world does its work. Thus not only must the priest *behave* in a manner which is in most vital respects far different from that of other men, in that he is bound by conscience to the three vows of poverty, chastity, and obedience, but he must also recast his *thought* into a mold generally foreign to that of the people he meets in everyday life. His thought-world, that is to say, is no longer universal currency, but is confined to the limits of his institution. This state of affairs is an invitation to certain modes of fantasy, for not only must the priest invest his emotional resources in his personal moral struggle, but he must defend the institution, either consciously or unconsciously, against what he conceives to be a wholesale bombardment of its values by an essentially hostile or hypocritical humanity. This Father M was unable to do.

Where his sexuality is concerned, the Church did nothing to clarify the difficulties, and indeed did much to complicate them, since his initial commitment had the symbolic meaning for him of self-castration, a dedication of his sexuality to his mother and, by transference, ultimately to the Church. He assimilated her fear that he would go the way of his brothers into Latin sensuality, as we have said, but he was wholly unaware at first of the psychodynamic impulses against which this rationale defended him, and so he railed continually against the restrictions placed on his masculinity by the institution. As a particularly telling example, he told of his days as a novice, before his entrance into seminary training, when he was just beginning to wear the cassock, the black priestly garment which identifies him to the world and marks him off from it in his own eyes as well. His group of novices had a picnic, and as he sat on the grass his cassock became disarranged, revealing a bit of leg. For this supposed indiscretion he was rebuked by the moralistic novice master, who made an explicit connection with sexuality and condemned the Novice M for guilty thoughts. Father M rightly asked how one might come to terms with his sexual impulses under such conditions.

It was obvious enough that he had not done so, but what was irrational of him was to place all the blame on the Church, since it will be recalled that so many childhood sexual episodes in his life were charged prematurely with religious significance not by the church but by his father, who directed the scenes in which his boys knelt to pray for each other's forgiveness for acts which after all were moments of relationship for a boy who was lonely in the midst of a crowded life. His father's response to any troubling internal problem was to deny it, and to advise his son to do the same. But this kind of evasion was not the mode of Father M's response. His needs were too pressing, and he was not equipped by nurture or by his surroundings to deal adequately with the problem of his sexuality. For a time during his late adolescence the problem seemed controllable. But he began to be troubled by a kind of "involuntary" masturbation which took place during waking hours of contemplation without, he claimed, his active participation. His thoughts again and again returned to the moral issue which he tried to construct around the problem, even as it had to do with nocturnal emissions. These occurrences became in his mind the primary symptom of his conflict, perhaps indeed the only conscious one. The Church, which dictates to him a code he finds impossible to comply with, becomes repressive of the manhood which he believes only waits to break forth on the model of his brothers' lives.

It is true that *no* expression of sexuality is legitimate for him. For he realized that in Catholicism, sexuality simply has no status outside the socially approved institution of marriage. It is justified theologically and biblically as part of the goodness of God's creation, but this supposed "goodness" becomes merely an abstract category of thought rather than a reality to be experienced by living human beings who are not located within the approved institutional framework. And even within marriage there is only now coming to the fore a suggestion that sexuality in itself may be an expression of the truth of the marital relationship rather than an adjunct to its major purpose, the procreation of children. The psychic consequences which one may anticipate in extra-marital sexuality can only be guilty ones, and only a little thought leads one to the conclusion that the conditions under which sexuality can be allowed in theory to partake of the desired spirituality are so limiting that few can ever know it in reality. In any case the dangers of substituting such an ideal construct for a realistic morality are only too apparent, and it must be obvious that for a man in such a position as Father M's, even a sexual fantasy becomes a source of guilt.

In practice, of course, a realistic wisdom often asserts itself, but in Father M's case this only compounded the problem, for when in his distress he took it to his spiritual counselors, they refused to treat it as seriously as he seemed to want them to. They had, of course, met it many times before. But he forced it into the forefront of his relationship with them, even on occasions when he dimly realized that he was dealing with men who had no inner competence to deal with it. Those who were competent minimized the problem, and those who were not competent both reinforced the judgment which he needed to pass upon himself and used the information against him in his attempts to rise in the Church.

At two points in his life, however, it became apparent to Father M that the difficulty had other dimensions than simply that of an expression of sexuality. One was a specific event during the course of his seminary training, the other a generalized change of situation which mobilized the reactions that brought him to seek therapy. The first was a meeting, during the latter stages of his training, with an older man, a priest newly ordained who was undergoing a year of final preparation before being assigned to priestly duties. Finding each other congenial, they talked long and freely in ways which carried a sense of daring for Father M. Deep revelation of personal secrets brought the relationship to a point at which the other man encouraged Father M to acknowledge his "manhood" to himself. There was at least one homosexual act between them, and Father M seemed compelled by the pattern established in his family to discuss the resulting guilt with a spiritual director, with foreseeable results. But by the repeated testimony he gives of its importance to him he seems to demonstrate that the real significance of the episode centered more in the fact of relationship than in the sexuality on which so much attention was lavished. Father M was acknowledging a need deeper than sexuality, though he was unable for a long time to recognize it explicitly.

After his ordination Father M was permitted to enter graduate school in a secular university, and this change of scene forced a considerable change in his daily discipline as well. He did pastoral work at an unfamiliar church in order to earn a living for his study, and he made such a good beginning that he won a scholarship for a second year. Soon, however, he found that he was making insufficient progress on account of what he began to realize was an unresolved personality problem. The new situation only repeated in an intensified form what he had experienced previously. Sexual fantasies continually interrupted his working hours and made his mind shy off from difficult problems of analysis in his technical subject matter. He daydreamed away many hours, in the process creating for himself the fantasy role of synthesizer as opposed to specialist. He imagined himself writing the great work which would bring together Christianity and every significant movement in modern science and philosophy. Meanwhile, however, he translated his sexual preoccupation into two successive love affairs, the second with an older woman who came to have great significance for him in dreams, as we shall presently see.

In all these situations it is apparent that Father M was searching with increasing desperation for an intensity of relationship which few individuals, if any, and certainly no institutions are equipped to provide. We have seen how the belief that churchly discipline prevents his going the way of his brothers is really illusory, since in fact his history gives evidence of a longstanding estrangement from them. A significant example of this estrangement came in his twelfth year, when once at the dinner table the others were attacking his younger brother, the one with whom he now feels the closest emotional contact. On this occasion he offered his help, but his brother despised it. Thus the need for relationship runs very deep in his experience.

The psychodynamic reasons for this desperate need are provided by a bizarre event during the course of the time when he was in therapy. On a foray into the city's nightlife he encountered a Greek gypsy fortune-teller, who asked him into her shop to bless her work. Once inside he fell into a trancelike state and felt driven to give her everything he had. So he held out his wallet to her, whereupon she made seductive gestures and asked what she might do for him. His internal response was to identify her with his mother, and he asked her to have intercourse with him. She declined, but instead signaled for her daughter to dance. Father M made an immediate association of this episode with a day when at age ten he walked away from a fight because his mother had asked him not to fight any more. He dedicated his aggressiveness, and subsequently his sexuality, to her, and by the same token he bound himself to an incestuous relationship with her which he has continued to act out—not only in the offer to the gypsy woman but in his actual affair with an older woman. More importantly, one feels that the abundant mother-imagery of the Church is a key factor, both positively and negatively, and another element in the incestuous sexuality which Father M has never been able to outlive. Like the gypsy woman, all his mothers have deceived him, promising him a relationship which they have been unwilling finally to supply. His response is to continue to demand it. When it is denied, as it must be, he loses the identity he has formed on this false basis, and his emotional response is anger or despair.

It is at this point that institutional questions once more contribute to the problem. For chastity is not the only perpetual vow to which the priest binds himself. Obedience is at least as important, and it tends to be a much more important factor in the process of training for the priesthood. That is, sins against chastity tend to remain focused on the level of personal adjustment to the institution, except insofar as they are communicated to a candidate's confessors and spiritual directors. Disobedience, however, is by its very nature a public manifestation of difficulty. It is true that in this case Father M had a compulsive need to call attention to his sexual problems in a very explicit way, that he forced them to become a factor in his selection for further training by discussing them with men who, he realized, were not equipped to counsel him properly. But the present point is that the need for obedience, like the demand for chastity, becomes internalized in the novice who prepares for the priesthood. In cases like ours, it reinforces patterns established, perhaps, in a distortion of the basic relationship of son with mother and father, and it further complicates the problem by making the search for an authoritative answer another almost compulsive need.

The demand for obedience reinforced Father M's deep need to structure all his human relationships according to a pattern of dominance and submission. This turned out to be as true of his approach to therapy as it was of his relationship with the Church. In effect he felt he was purchasing an alternative form of advice. Constantly he sought to cast the therapist in the role of spiritual director, to set him up as an authority for decisions which he could then accept, in a spirit of true submission, or reject with anger. He wanted a savior he had not found in family or Church, and denial of this wish produced a succession of strong negative reactions—not only anger but even hatred, utter rejection, and blame for what the therapy was doing to his performance in graduate school.

But the other side of the personality of Father M was of course that he not only wanted to be saved but ardently wished himself to fulfill his early mission to be a savior. In this mode of perception of himself he cast the therapist into the role of proselyte, in effect, while he claimed the therapist's statements for his own, repeated them in a personal cognitive framework, and competed to formulate insights which then became substitutes for genuine feelings or appropriate action. He could not accept the therapist's identity as a finite human being any more than he could his own. Beset by the complementary illusions of a distorted perception of reality and of an intensely disciplined other worldly asceticism, he cannot be found as a human being who is the subject of a real interchange, the partner in a genuine communication.

For Father M's precarious equilibrium is maintained only by the ambivalence of demand and defiance. He seeks to make a benevolent and ideal mother or a spiritual director out of everyone to whom he relates in any closeness, but he cannot endure either detachment or the deeper demands of a real relationship. Certainly he is incapable of a realistic morality, which must be based on some considerable degree of experienced identity. Existential therapy, even though taxing for him and of limited usefulness at this point in his life, nevertheless confronted him with the depths of the demands he was making. The therapist, pressed for advice, stubbornly maintained his identity and refused to give it, recognizing that it would maintain Father M in the negative identity of resentment. By this means it was at least possible to show him that a simple rejection of his identity as priest would not accomplish anything.

The Inner World of Father M

As we have stated above, existential analysis focuses on the totality of a given experience in general and in particular on what is visible in the foreground of a given individual existence, the elements which are selected out in any given moment of encounter but which imply the background of all that one knows of him. Thus it is apparent that it will make a distinctive approach to the problem of interpreting dream material. The dream, we would maintain, is a "given" like any other phenomenologically experienced datum. It starts with something, with a given locale, given dimensions of space, a given situation which in fundamental ways recapitulates an individual's experience of the real world. We seek in it the sequence of action provided by the dreamer—since the dream is his own creation—and try to discover the motives for the selection of the particular modalities which are part of the totality of his existence. What can be plausibly inferred to be left out is, in certain respects, just as important as what is presented in the foreground arrangement of the dream events.

Typically the dreamer presents himself in several aspects, several images of his vision of himself. He dissociates these images into separate dream personalities, others from his *Mitwelt* of reality or strangers who reveal their identity by their actions in the dream. They are "let into" the *Mitwelt* of the dream, so to speak, in order to let the dreamer renounce responsibility for what he is saying to himself or doing in the dream. By creating a dream situation of events which are beyond his control he may discharge his personal identity altogether and become in his own imagining entirely the creature of circumstances.

A very brief dream image is perhaps the best illustration of the primary feeling attached to priesthood for Father M. He drives his car down a slippery road, seated between his girl friend and an unidentified second woman. To be in contact with the two bodies gives him a feeling of great harmony, but immediately he finds himself alone, walking in his cassock on a muddy road and almost crying, because "I did not know where to go." Priesthood therefore cuts him off from human affection, especially from the love of women. But his longing is much deeper and more primitive and his identity much more confused than might be suggested by a consideration of his sadness over the sacrifice of heterosexuality, because in dressing himself in a cassock, he loses all sense of proper direction as well.

Another dream expresses similar modes of feeling, though with the addition of significant elements which force a deeper analysis of the nature of Father M's experience of his world. He dreams that he is in his own room—that is, located realistically in his own living-space, the student-priest in an appropriate locale. But there is a problematic element in the presence of a dark-haired woman as his guest, for no woman belongs in a priest's room. He expresses his alienation in that she is not further identified. He doesn't know her, and in recognition of the inappropriateness of her presence he asks, "Who are you, and what are you doing here?" In reply she says, "Don't be funny. I am Bea." That is, she is his girl friend from the real world, and as she says so, she is transformed before his eyes so that he recognizes her. "My God," he exclaims, "I didn't recognize you!" By implication he has renounced responsibility for his own shift from priest to lover, since she transformed herself without his participation in the change. He approaches her and feels intense sexual attraction, but suddenly a bell rings, and he allows an alarm from the world beyond the initial dream space to intrude, to make the decision for him. Without taking her feelings into account, he presses the answer button, whereupon she looks hurt and asks, "Why did you answer? Why didn't you ignore it?"

Aware now to some degree of the need to try to undo the injury he has done, he rushes to the window to see who is coming, only to find a new scene at his window, a garden rather than the front terrace of the building. This sight makes him alert to his previous confusion over the bell, of the possibility he has lost to refuse to attend to the impulse brought by his ears. Now he cannot see the source of the intrusion, so he is left only with the possibility of action. He goes out to meet the people, taking the elevator to forestall a compromising confrontation with someone whom he assumes to be a fellow priest. But he finds no one there. Thinking it has all been a prank, he returns by the elevator and opens his door to find his mother and his brother, who have come up the stairs to surprise him, since the brother has told her that he entertains women in his room. She tells him this when he tries to ask, gaily, "Hello, Mother. How did you get in here?" He feels exposed and helpless, all his hypocrisy uncovered. In a pathetic attempt to keep up appearances he turns to his girl friend to introduce her to his mother. "Mother," he says, "I want you to meet a guest of mine. This is. . ." And as he turns, he finds he must end the sentence with "Father L," because the girl has transformed herself again, this time into a cassocked priest!

Father M thus reveals his inability to erect defenses against the mother image, since she represents his reality principle which intrudes upon this attempt at an improper relationship, and thus it is no wonder that he does not achieve, in dream or reality, genuine masculine identity. Indeed in his childhood days sexuality presented itself to him in the guise of aggressiveness and temptation, which he could accommodate to his poorly developed sense of himself only by transforming the impulses into incest fantasies for his mother, fantasies which he tried to sublimate under the imagery of the Church.

As we have suggested, the central problem revealed by Father M's dream presentation of himself lies deeper than a problem of sexual identification, deeper even than incestuous longings. It is a matter of his mode of apprehending the world of his experience, of his need to know his own identity in order to be able to be in genuine relationship with others. A set of two dreams reveals these needs with absolute clarity. In the first he became aware of a situation of danger, of terror and foreboding. He saw a cauldron in which boiled hot, molten metal of a lavalike consistency, giving off poisonous fumes which he had to breathe. He wanted to leave, but he became aware that he himself was the room in which the kettle boiled, and the bubbling mass of metal, his stomach. He realized that he could not escape the noxious fumes, for they were coming from his own inner depths. The pressure of his tension increased, and he felt he would break into fragments if he found no way to reduce it. In desperation he looked for a knife to plunge into his belly, to open a way for the fumes to escape, but, finding none, as a last resort he opened his mouth. There was a burst of escaping gas, and he felt a moment's release, only to find to his horror, on looking outward rather than down into his own insides, that the escaped fumes were organizing themselves into a ferocious mountain lion such as he had seen on a boyhood hunting trip. Thus one more terror was added to the maelstrom within, and the external one was compounded by his certain knowledge that the beast could swim after him if he tried to escape by water. Now he gasps, holding in his breath for fear of creating a greater monster. But more gas escapes, and indeed the lion grows. Only one outlet now remains, so he farts, and the gas shapes itself into a giant dog which growls at the lion. More farts produce a pack of dogs which tree the lion. The dreamer, momentarily out of danger, runs away and wakes.

Free-association interpretation of the dream in therapy produced an identification of the lion with his mother, the dog with Father M's father and brothers. The therapist asked whether the patient knew how the fire was sustained, who stoked it to raise the heat to such an unbearable degree. Why was there no water available to throw on the blaze, to put it out? The patient answered that to put the fire out would be to harden the metal which, being himself, would become frozen, statue-like. He would therefore be dead. But the alternatives to death presented by the dream are almost equally forbidding—identification, either with his mother or with his father and brothers in their attack on her.

Several particular features of this dream of Father M from an existential point of view carry great significance. Notice that at first his reaction to an admittedly frightening situation is natural and rational. He wants to escape from a situation in which he experiences himself as, after all, an onlooker. By inference there is a world outside for him to escape into, but in succeeding stages he draws constricting bonds around himself. First he shifts from being an onlooker to being in the room where the fire burns ever hotter and the poisonous fumes billow in ever-thicker clouds. Then the dreamer loses even this degree of separation from the events. He looks downward and inward, and his world becomes coextensive with himself. He contains it; in fact, he *is* it, and there is now no escape. His sense of space is constricted to the degree that it loses a primary dimension. He began with a world of horizontal extension. It became first a closed room and then became constricted entirely along the vertical axis, his vision being upward and downward only; he looked down into himself.

All these dream alternatives in fact are false, since the unseen need of the dreamer is the need to make the hard choice of experiencing himself as he is. Admittedly the reexperiencing of the modes of thought which caused him to deny his individuality would be painful; after all, the fumes from his overheated belly seem to him poisonous. But the negativity of all his present modes of approach to the *Mitwelt* of his experience is expressed by his ever-present hostility in interpersonal relationships. He identifies all people with his self-created images of foul gas, and the imagery horrifies him. He must expel it from him in spasmodic belching or farting, and then he must face the attacks of the reified products of his own inner turmoil. He cannot allow this and must try to incorporate them all somehow, for to allow them identity is to have to defend himself against one more bestial threat. His present dream alternatives are bestiality, a desperate control of a hostile *Umwelt,* or a cold and lonely death.

The Goals of a Phenomenological-Existential Analysis

Our objections to other formulations of psychoanalytic theory and practice depend on our conviction that they are premature solutions to crucial problems of self-discovery and relationship, which are always in a state of change, since they arise in the individual's confrontation with his time and space. What we feel we can contribute at this point in history, is a method which is at once scientific, human, and capable of taking account of as broad a range of problems as is possible for any method in our present cultural situation. For the method of phenomenological observation, as we have suggested, is capable of bringing "subjective" data under observation without the need of quotation marks, the pseudoscientific "bracketing" which often used to attempt to maintain an absolute distinction between internal and external or objective "facts." Husserl's phenomenology provides us with a method of observation which proceeds without such artificial initial distinctions, a method which therefore can reasonably claim the status of empiricism.

And what we observe, as cannot be repeated often enough, is a variety of individual human beings who are attempting, even as we are ourselves, to come to terms with the problem of being human in as full a sense as is possible for them. Thus phenomenology, though it renounces preconceptions, still provides us at the outset with, if you will, a reliable method of interviewing, which is the more accurate because it does not channel individual communication into preconceived modes of evaluation. The individual is what he says he is when he presents himself to us, and what he becomes free to communicate is what he is free to be. We do not feel that it is our duty to pass an initial judgment on the accuracy or inaccuracy of his perception of reality, thus to learn the "truth" about him; because the focal point is not what he sees but how he experiences himself in his world, in effect *how* he sees, and feels, and expresses the full implications of his human situation. For, as the phenomenologists show, the *Lebenswelt* of a given human being is the foundation of all categorical truth for men, and it is language alone, in all its social implications, which gives meaning to human existence. Thus freedom is meaningless as a concept apart from an awareness of human relationships and human limitations; it is a dialectical "standing-out" from them.

In the present case, as in many others, the salient clinical fact is the patient's isolation from effective human intercourse, an isolation of long duration whose inadequacy as the basis for adult living at last became known to Father M himself. It was this which brought him to therapy. As we have seen, therapy for him was initially a matter of purchasing a kind of advice which would be informed by deeper insight into the inner workings of personality than that to which his Church aspires. This indicates that he felt no adequate support from the inclusive institutional framework to which he had bound himself. In other words, it was not a matter of stripping him of his defenses, which were already exposed to him as inadequate, but of illuminating their continuity with other lines of defense which he had established for himself from childhood, and of casting grave doubt on a structure of authority which masked a deep longing to deny his individuality, to become nothing, to identify himself with his mother. His attempts to stand out against this imagery, as we have seen, operated only at the very primitive level of negative protest, of saying "No" to the demands of an institution which had taken her place in his internal imagery. Thus it was necessary to show him that all decisions made on the basis of such an imagery would be false.

What is the role of the existential analyst in providing the basis for a more authentic existence in those who come to him? No general answer will be adequate to all cases, since what will be an appropriate response to an individual who has reached a certain stage of psychological maturity would alienate another from the therapist and from himself, or would reinforce still another in his need for dependence on others. This is why we must dissociate ourselves from dogmatic positions on one side or the other of the question. It is apparent that the assumptions of a Freudian neutrality do not square with the concept of an encounter in which experience is shared and therefore "bracketed," so that the patient may more firmly establish his sense of identity in the *Mitwelt* on the model of what he achieves in therapy. We must be careful, though, not to leave the contrary impression that a "cure" takes place through the affective interest of the therapist in the patient, an unconditional acceptance of his every impulse after the manner of Carlos Seguin's "Psychotherapeutic Eros." One cannot love another into health, though to the extent that Seguin understands this Eros as openness to the patient's communication of himself, we can give him our support. Father M, it will be remembered, made the demand that he be loved, and to my mind the gratification of this demand would only have sustained him in a magic state of being. Such a supportive method is appropriate, I believe, only for psychotics who cannot begin to manage real human relationships; it perpetuates the attitude of dependence and would justify any hostility it invoked in the merely neurotic patient who strives to experience himself as an individual. Freudian theory creates hostility in the therapeutic relationship but invites the negation of gains when the transference phenomena come to be dealt with. A relationship based on the ideal of love, which can be linked with Seguin but also with Fromm and others, also creates a hostility which cannot be dealt with in the therapeutic situation itself, but which must therefore be discharged in such reactions as alienation from the social order. This may support a personal need of the therapist as well, but it is no help to the patient who must maintain himself in some meaningful relation to his *Mitwelt*. Existential analysis, like the existence under whose conditions we all discover our humanity, makes the demand of us that we take the conditions seriously, that if possible we learn to assess them realistically and make the choice to come to our identity in terms of them. We would present our version of existential analysis, therefore, as a method inclusive of what is best in previous systems but without the claim that it is a closed system, a final answer to general human needs in a cultural situation which after all is far too dynamic for systematic understanding. In the past we have demanded such a model under the necessity of approximating a "scientific" method, or we have taken refuge, alternatively, in calling psychotherapy an art in which intuition has first place. It has now become possible to see, however, that such dichotomies are close to the kind of dilemmas which we have discovered in

Father M's approach to human relationship. It is not that we must be either scientists *or* artists, either objective or subjective in our approach to clinical reality. The two primary conditions of our therapy are: first, that we constitute ourselves as informed observers of the modes of human behavior in their characteristic patterns of expression, and, second, that we realize our own identity as individuals, in order that we may be free, ourselves, to assist others in discovering theirs.

Case 14

Editors' Introduction

Although Eric Berne wrote quite extensively, he wrote relatively little about the cases he himself had handled, and the selection that follows is one of rather few presentations of Berne's personal practice of Transactional Analysis.

Berne was a somewhat mysterious and private individual, and in reading his materials and in reading about him, as well as in private discussions with people who knew him well, his essence manages to escape the investigator. He was not a forceful person like, for example, Fritz Perls; he was not a lifelong student of personality theory as, for example, Carl Rogers. It is almost as though relatively late in life, more or less casually, he developed a method of treatment of individuals in groups, which unexpectedly turned out to be quite popular. Indeed, TA (as his system is usually known) is one of the most popular existing forms of psychotherapy and has attracted a considerable number of followers.

Innovators in psychotherapy have three major qualities: they are (a) hardworking, (b) courageous, and (c) creative. Berne seems to have been especially gifted with creativity—a kind of deep awareness of how to say just the right thing, to use the proper term, or as the French say, *le mot juste*. Indeed, it may well be that it is Berne who, because of his flair for language and the accuracy of his perception of the human condition, has brought psychotherapy to the masses.

ERIC BERNE

A Terminated Case With Follow-Up

The following case illustrates the procedure and outcome in a completed course of structural and transactional analysis. Because the systematic use of this approach from beginning to termination has only recently become possible with the full flowering of its theoretical development, the follow-up is relatively short. Nevertheless, this is not an isolated instance, and whether by good luck or because the therapy accomplishes its purpose, there now exists a small group of cases whose ultimate outcome will be observed with special interest through the years. This consists of patients who made unexpectedly rapid (by former standards) symptomatic and social improvement under controlled therapeutic conditions.

Before taking up in more detail the case of Mrs. Enatosky, the case of Mrs. Hendrix, a thirty-year-old housewife, is worth considering briefly. Mrs. Hendrix was first seen ten years ago, when she was suffering from an agitated depression. She was treated by conventional supportive methods ("offering oral supplies," as it is colloquially called) for one year, in the course of which she recovered.

When she returned a decade later, she was, if anything, worse than she had been during her previous episode, with more active suicidal fantasies. This time she was treated by structural and transactional analysis, and within six weeks she improved more than she had during the whole year of therapy in her former episode; this in the opinion not only of herself and the therapist, but also of her family and intimates; and this improvement was brought about by a procedure decidedly different from "supportive" offering of "supplies." After another six weeks, she was coping better than she had ever done in her life, having relinquished some of her long-standing autistic ambitions in favor of living in the world. She had also given up an unhealthy tendency to postulate her position or her unfortunate childhood; instead of playing "Wooden Leg" and "If It Weren't For Them," she was beginning to find her identity within the framework of new possibilities which unfolded in her family life. This case is mentioned because it offers about as well-controlled a situation as it is possible to hope for in clinical

Eric Berne, *Transactional Analysis in Psychotherapy.* New York: Grove Press, Inc., 1961, pp. 247–262. Reprinted by permission of Grove Press, Inc. Copyright © 1961 by Eric Berne.

215

practice: the same patient with two similar well-defined episodes separated by a distinct interval, treated by the same therapist with two distinct approaches.

To return now to Mrs. Enatosky. This woman complained initially of "depressions" of sudden onset. It may be recalled that she had had three previous forms of treatment: Alcoholics Anonymous, hypnosis, and psychotherapy combined with Zen and Yoga. She showed a special aptitude for structural and transactional analysis, and soon began to exert social control over the games which went on between herself and her husband, and herself and her son. The formal diagnosis is best stated as schizo-hysteria. The case will now be reviewed session by session with significant extracts.

April 1

The patient arrived on time for her initial interview. She stated she had been going to other therapists but had become dissatisfied and had called a municipal clinic, and after some discussion with a social worker had been referred to Dr. Q. She was encouraged to proceed and at relevant points appropriate questions were asked in order to elicit the psychiatric history. She stated that she had been an alcoholic for ten years and had been cured by Alcoholics Anonymous. She dated the onset of her drinking from her mother's psychosis when she was nineteen. She said that her depressions began at the same time. The nature of her previous psychiatric treatment was discussed. The preliminary demographic information was obtained so that she could be placed as a native-born thirty-four year-old, once-married, Protestant housewife, a high-school graduate, whose husband was a mechanic. Her father's occupation, the length of her marriage, her sibling position in years and months, and the ages of her children were noted. A preliminary search for traumatic events elicited that her father drank heavily and that her parents separated when she was seven years old.

The medical history revealed headaches, and numbness of one arm and leg, but no convulsions, allergies, skin afflictions, or other physical disorders with common psychiatric implications. Her age at the time of all operations, injuries, and serious illnesses was noted. Her childhood was explored for gross psychopathology such as sleepwalking, nail-biting, night terrors, stammering, stuttering, bed-wetting, thumb sucking and other preschool problems. Her school history was reviewed briefly. Chemical influences such as medications and exposure to noxious substances were also noted. A cautious exploration of her mental status was undertaken, and finally she was asked to relate any dream that she could remember. Recently she dreamed: "They were rescuing my husband from the water. His head was hurt and I started to scream." She mentioned that she often heard inner voices exhorting her to health, and once, two years ago, an "outer" voice. This satisfied the requirements for preliminary history taking, and the patient was then allowed to wander as she pleased.

Discussion

The history taking was carefully planned so that at all times the patient seemed to have the initiative and the therapist at most was curious rather than formal or openly systematic in gathering information. This means that the patient was allowed to structure the interview in her own way as far as possible and was not required to play a game of psychiatric history taking. Because of her complaint of numbness she was referred to a neurologist for examination.

April 8

The neurologist suspected cervical arthritis, but did not recommend any specific treatment. The patient conducted this interview as a kind of psychological survey. She spontaneously mentioned wanting approval and rebelling "like a little girl," as some "grown-up part" of her judged it. She said the "little girl" seemed "childish." It was suggested that she let the "little girl" out, rather than try to clamp down on her. She replied that that seemed brazen. "I like children, though. I know I can't live up to my father's expectations, and I get tired of trying to." This also includes her husband's "expectations." Such expectations were generalized for her as "parental expectations," since she had practically said as much herself. She sees the two most important "parents" in her life as her husband and her father. She is seductive toward her husband and recognizes that she was the same with her father. When her father and mother separated she thought (age seven): "I could have kept him." Thus she has not only a conflict about compliance, but also an attitude of seductiveness, toward parental figures.

Discussion

The patient's special aptitude for structural analysis is already evident. She herself makes the separation between "the little girl" and "a grown-up part" and recognizes the compliance of "the little girl" toward certain people whom she relates to her parents. It was only necessary, therefore, to reinforce this trichotomy in a non-directive way. With many other patients this might not have been undertaken until the third or fourth session, perhaps even later.

April 15

She resents people who tell her what to do, especially women. This is another reaction to "parents." She mentions a feeling of "walking high." It is pointed out that this is the way a very small girl must feel, that this is again the Child. She

replied: "Oh, for heaven's sake, that's true! As you said that I could see a little
child . . . it's hard to believe, but that makes sense to me. As you say that, I feel I
didn't want to walk: a little girl in rompers . . . I feel funny now. They pull you up
by your right shoulder and you're outraged . . . yet I do the same to my own son. I
disapprove while I'm thinking 'I don't disapprove, I know just how he feels.' It's
really my mother disapproving. Is *that* the Parent part you mentioned? I'm
frightened a little by all this."

It was at this point that it was emphasized that there was no mysterious or
metaphysical aspect to these diagnostic judgments.

Discussion

The patient has now experienced some of the phenomenological reality of the
Child and has added to the behavioral, social, and historical reality she established in the previous interviews. The indications, therefore, are favorable for
treatment with transactional analysis.

April 22

"This week I've been happy for the first time in fifteen years. I don't have to
look far to find the Child, I can see it in my husband and in others too. I have
trouble with my son." The game with her son was clarified in an inexact but
timely and illustrative way in terms of Parent (her disapproval and determina-
tion), Child (her seductiveness and her sulkiness at his recalcitrance), and Adult
(her gratification when he finally did his work). It was hinted that an Adult
approach (good reason) rather than a Parental approach (sweet reason) might be
worth a try.

Discussion

The patient is now involved in transactional analysis proper and the idea of
social control has been suggested.

April 28

She reports that things work better with her son. Regression analysis is
attempted to find out more about the Child. She relates: "The cat soils the rug and
they accuse me and make me wipe it up. I deny that I did it and stammer." In the
ensuing discussion she remarks that both Alcoholics Anonymous and the Angli-

can Church require confession to "messes." For this reason she gave them both up. As the session ends she asks: "Is it all right to be aggressive?" Answer: "You want *me* to tell you?" She understands the implication that she should decide such things on Adult grounds rather than asking Parental permission, and replies: "No, I don't."

Discussion

During this session some of the elements of her script are elicited. It can be anticipated that she will try to repeat with the therapist in some well-adapted form the cat situation. Her question "Is it all right to be aggressive?" is perhaps the first move in this adaptation. This gives the therapist an opportunity to decline to play and to reinforce her Adult. The patient has made such good progress in understanding structural and transactional analysis that she is already considered adequately prepared for fairly advanced group therapy. The group she is to enter consists largely of women.

May 4

A dream. "I look at myself and say: 'That's not so bad.' " She liked the group but it made her uncomfortable during the rest of the week. She relates some memories, including homosexual play during childhood. "Oh! That's why I didn't like AA. There were two homosexual women there and one of them called me sexy." She complains of vaginal itching. "My mother and I slept together and she bothered me."

Discussion

The manifest content of her dream is taken to be Adult and indicates the possibility of a good prognosis. The experience in the group has activated sexual conflicts, and this is the first indication of their nature.

May 11

She felt highly excited on leaving the group meeting. "Things are moving quickly. Why did they make me laugh and blush? Things are better at home. I can kiss my son now and my daughter for the first time came and sat on my lap. I can't be a good lover when things are monotonous."

Discussion

The analysis of her family games . . . has resulted in the establishment of some Adult social control. It is evident that this improved control has been perceived by her children and for the first time in a long while they have the feeling that she can maintain her position and they react accordingly. Her excitement in the group and her statement that she can't be a good lover when things are monotonous indicate that she is involved in a sexual game with her husband.

An experience in the group later this week rather clearly showed her need for parental figures in some of her games. There was a new patient in the group, a male social worker, and she was very much impressed by his occupation. She asked him what they were supposed to do there. It was pointed out that she knew more than he did, since it was his first meeting and her third. She says she resents it when people tell her what to do, yet peasantlike, in spite of her superior experience, she asks a novice for instructions because she appears to be impressed by his education: evidently an attempt to set up a game. This interpretation strikes home. She recognizes how she "cons" a likely candidate into being parental and then complains about it.

May 18

She was upset by regression analysis in the group. It made her think of her fear of insanity, and of her mother in the state hospital. Her own production was of some elegant gates leading into a beautiful garden. This is a derivative of a Garden of Eden fantasy from before the age of five. The material indicates that the garden has become adapted to the gates of the state hospital where she visited her mother many years ago. This experience in the group offered a timely opportunity to mention to her that she might want to be hospitalized and so relieved of responsibility.

She has visited her mother only once in the past five or six years and it was suggested that it might be advisable for her to do that again. This suggestion was very carefully worded so as to be Adult rather than Parental. Any implication that she was a bad girl for not visiting her mother had to be avoided. She was able to understand the value of such a visit as an exercise for her Adult and as a means of preventing future difficulties between her Parent and her Child if her mother should die. The good reception of this suggestion was manifested by her bringing up new information. Her husband never washes his hair and always has a good excuse, which she accepts. He has not washed it for many months. She says it doesn't bother her too much. The therapist said she must have known that when she married him. She denied it.

May 25

She said she has always been more afraid of sick animals than of sick people. This week her cat was sick, and for the first time she was not afraid of him. Once when she was little her father hit her and her dog jumped on him, whereupon he gave the dog away. She told her children that her mother was dead. Whenever she would think of her mother she would start to drink. One time she was told that when her mother was eight months pregnant, her father tried to poison her. They saved the patient and thought her mother was a goner, but then she was revived. The aunt who told her this story says: "Your life has been a mess since birth."

Discussion

The import of this is not clear. It is evident, however, that she is working through some rather complex conflicts concerning her mother. Her maintenance of social control with the sick cat is evidence that a visit to her mother may be possible in the near future.

June 1

"Frankly, the reason I'm afraid to visit my mother is that I might want to stay there myself." She wonders: "Why do I exist? Sometimes I doubted my existence." Her parents' marriage was a shotgun wedding and she has always felt that she was unwanted. The therapist suggested that she get a copy of her birth certificate.

Discussion

The patient is now involved with existential problems. Her Adult has evidently always been shaky because her Child has implanted doubts about her existence, her right to exist, and the form in which she exists. Her birth certificate will be written evidence that she does exist, and should be particularly impressive to her Child. As social control is established and she learns that it is possible for her to exist in a form which she herself chooses, her desire to retreat to the state hospital should diminish.

June 8

She describes her husband's alcoholic game. At AA she was told that she should bless him and comfort him, and that made her sick. She tried something different. "One day I said I would call the ambulance for the hospital, since he didn't appear to be able to take care of himself, so he got up and didn't drink again." He said he was only trying to help her stay sober by drinking himself. This comes up because he was drinking heavily last week and she had pain in her shoulders and wanted to hit him, but told him off instead.

It appears from this that their secret marriage contract is based partly on the assumption that he will drink and she will function as a rescuer. This game was reinforced by AA to her benefit. When she refused to continue as a rescuer and became a persecutor instead, the game was thrown off and he stopped drinking. (Evidently it was reinstituted due to her insecurity of the past week.)

This outline was presented to her. She first said: "It couldn't have been part of our marriage contract, because neither of us drank when we met." A little later in the interview she suddenly said: "You know, now I remember I did know when we were married that he didn't wash his hair, but I didn't know that he drank." The therapist said that the unkempt hair was also part of the secret marriage contract. She looked skeptical. Then she thought a minute and said: "By golly, yes, I did know he drank. When we were in high school we used to drink together all the time."

It now appears that in the early years of their marriage, they played a switchable game of alcoholic. If she drank, her husband didn't; and if he drank, she stayed sober. Their relationship was originally based on this game, which they later interrupted, and must have exerted considerable effort to forget about.

Discussion

This session helped to clarify for the patient the structure of her marriage, and also emphasized the amount of time and effort which is required to keep marital games going, and equally, the amount of energy involved in their repression without conscious control.

July 6

There has been an interval of a month for summer vacation. The patient returns with a sore shoulder. She has been to the state hospital, and her mother sent her away. This made her feel hopeless. She has some olfactory illusions. She thinks she smells gas in the office, but decides it is clean soap. This leads into a discussion of her mental activity. During her recent Yoga training, she developed imagery which was almost eidetic. She would see gardens and wingless angels with sparkling clarity of color and detail. She recalled that she had had the same kind of imagery as a child. She also had images of Christ and her son. Their complexions were clear and lively. She sees animals and flowers. As a matter of fact, when she walks through parks she likes to talk secretly but aloud to trees and flowers. The longings expressed in these activities are discussed with her. The artistic and poetic aspects are pointed out, and she is encouraged therefore to write and to try finger painting. She has seen her birth certificate and her existential doubts are less disturbing.

Discussion

These phenomena and the auditory manifestations she had previously mentioned are not necessarily alarming. They point to childhood restitutive tendencies related to a deeply disturbed relationship between her and her parents. The conventional approach would be to give her "supportive" treatment and help her repress this psychopathology and live on top of it. Structural analysis offers another possibility which requires some boldness: to allow this disturbed Child to express herself and profit from the resulting constructive experiences.

July 13

She went to her internist and he gave her Rauwolfia because her blood pressure was high. She told her husband she was going to fingerpaint and he got angry and said: "Use pastels!" When she refused, he started to drink. She recognizes what happened here as a game of "Uproar" and feels some despair at having been drawn into this. She says, however, that if she does not play "Uproar" with him then *he* will feel despair, and it is a hard choice to make. She also mentions that the gate on the beautiful garden is very similar to the gate on the day nursery where her mother used to send her when she was very small. A new problem now arises: how to distinguish the effect of psychotherapy from the effect of Rauwolfia. She is eager to help with this.

July 20

She is losing interest and feels tired. She agrees it is possible that this is an effect of the medication. She reveals some family scandals she has never mentioned to anyone before, and states now that her drinking did not begin after her mother became psychotic, but after these scandals.

At this session a decisive move was made. During her therapeutic sessions, the patient habitually sits with her legs in an ungainly exposed position. Now she complains again about the homosexual women at AA. She complains that the men also made passes at her. She doesn't understand why, since she did nothing to bring this on. She was informed of her exposed position and expressed considerable surprise. It was then pointed out to her that she must have been sitting in a similar provocative way for many years, and what she attributes to the aggressiveness of others is probably the result of her own rather crudely seductive posture. At the subsequent group meeting she was silent most of the time, and when questioned she mentioned what the doctor had said and how this had upset her.

Discussion

This is a crucial session. At the price of sacrificing the possibilities of a normal family life, the patient has obtained a multitude of gains, primary and secondary, by playing games with her husband and other men and women. The primary external gain is the avoidance of pleasurable sexual intercourse. If she can relinquish these gains, she may be ready to undertake a normal marital relationship whose satisfactions should more than repay her for her abdication. The schizoid elements in her Child are clear from her symptomatology. The hysterical elements are most clearly manifested in her socially acceptable game of "Rapo." Hence the diagnosis of schizo-hysteria.

In her case, the naming of the game is avoided since she is still too soft-boiled to tolerate such bluntness. It is simply described to her without giving it a name. In very sophisticated groups, however, it is known technically as "First-degree Rapo." It is the classical game of hysterics: crude, "inadvertent," seductive exhibitionism, followed by protestations of surprise and injured innocence when a response is forthcoming. . . . ("Third-degree Rapo," the most vicious form, ends in the courtroom or the morgue.) The therapeutic problem at the moment is whether her preparation has been adequate and the relationship between her Child and the therapist sufficiently well understood to make this confrontation effective. In a sense, her life and those of her children hinge on the therapist's judgment in these matters. If she should decide to become angry and withdraw from treatment, psychiatry might be lost to her for a long time afterward, perhaps permanently. If she accepts it, the effect could be decisive, since this particular game is her chief barrier to marital happiness. The therapist, naturally, has not entured to bring the matter up without considerable confidence of success.

August 10

The therapist returns after a two-week vacation. The confrontation has been successful. The patient now describes an assault by her father in early puberty while her stepmother pretended to be asleep. He also molested other children, but her stepmother used to defend him. She relates this "assault" to her own seductiveness. This situation she discusses at some length, eliciting her feeling that sex is dirty or vulgar. She says she has always been very careful sexually with her husband because of this feeling and has tried to avoid sex with him for this reason. She understands that the games she plays with him are an attempt to avoid sex, as she feels she cannot let go enough to enjoy it and it is merely a burden to her.

Discussion

The patient is evidently shocked at the therapist's directness, but is gratified because it lays bare still further the structure of her marriage and indicates what could be done about it.

August 17 (Terminal Interview)

The patient announces that this is her last session. She no longer fears that her husband will think she is dirty or vulgar if she acts lusty. She never asked him if he thought so but just assumed that he did. During the week, she approached him differently and he responded with gratified surprise. For the last few days he has come home whistling for the first time in years.

She also realizes something else. She has always felt sorry for herself and tried to elicit sympathy and admiration because she is a recovered alcoholic. She recognizes this now as a game of "Wooden Leg." She feels ready at this point to try it on her own. She also feels different about her father. Maybe she contributed even more than she thought to the seduction. The remark about her skirts being too short shocked her but helped her. "I would never admit I wanted sex. I always thought I wanted 'attention.' Now I can admit I want sex." During the week she visited her father who was ill in another city in a hospital. She was able to observe her visit with considerable objectivity. Now she feels that she has divorced him and doesn't want him any more. That is why she was able to proceed sexually with her husband. She feels the transfer was accomplished through the intermediary of the therapist, who took her father's place for a while at first; but now she doesn't need him any more. She can talk freely to her husband about sexual repression causing her symptoms, and about her sexual feelings for him. He said he agreed with her and reciprocated her feelings. After she thought all this out, following the last visit, she had a dream that night in which there was a beautiful, feminine, peaceful woman, and it made her feel really good inside. The children are different too; they are happy, relaxed, and helpful.

Her blood pressure is down and her itching is gone. The therapist thought the improvement might be due to the medicine. She replied: "No, I don't think so, I would know the difference, I've taken it before. The medicine makes me feel tired and nervous when it's taking hold, but this is an entirely new feeling."

She reports that she is drawing instead of finger-painting, doing what she wants; she feels this isn't wrong, it's like learning to live. "I don't feel sorry for people any more, I feel they ought to be able to do this too if they went about it right. I no longer feel I'm below everyone although that feeling isn't completely gone. I don't want to come to the group any more, I'd rather spend the time with my husband. It's like we're starting to go with each other again when he comes home whistling, it's wonderful. I'll try it for three months and if I feel bad I'll call you. I don't feel so 'neurotic,' either: I mean having psychosomatic symptoms and guilt feelings and my fear of talking about sex, and like that. It's a miracle, is all I can say. I can't explain my feeling of being happy, but I feel we (you and I) worked together on it. There's more closeness and harmony with my husband and he's even taking over the children like he's becoming the man of the house. I even feel a little guilty about AA because I used them in my game of 'Wooden Leg.'"

She was asked directly whether structural analysis helped and whether game analysis helped, and in each case replied: "Oh, yes!" She added: "Also the script. For example, I said my husband had no sense of humor and you said 'Wait a minute, you don't know him and he doesn't know you because you've been playing games and acting out your scripts, you don't know what either of you is really like.' You were right because now I've discovered that he really has a sense of humor and that not having it was part of the game. I'm interested in my home and I'm grateful for that. I can write poetry again and express my love for my husband. I used to keep it in." At this point the hour was drawing to a close. The therapist asked: "Would you like a cup of coffee?" She replied: "No thanks, I've just had some. I've told you now how I feel, that's it, that's all, it's been a great pleasure to come here and I enjoyed it."

General Discussion

There is no need to regard this gratifying improvement with either skepticism, alarm, or pursed lips, in spite of the apparent raggedness of the above extracts. The patient herself has already answered many of the questions which might occur to an experienced reader.

For example, she herself perceived the substitution of the therapist for her father and the subsequent substitution of her husband for the therapist, so that this cannot be labeled a classical blind cure. The most impressive items are the changed attitudes of her children and, particularly, of her husband. Such indirect criteria are usually more convincing than the opinions of either the therapist or the patient. There is evidence that the original therapeutic aim has been systematically accomplished. She has given up playing many of her games and has replaced them with more satisfying direct relationships and intimacies. Her dress and behavior are more modest, and at the same time she looks more sexually attractive and sexually satisfied. A concise interpretation of what happened at the archaic level can be offered. She came to the therapist with a provisional fantasy of being dominated and hypnotized, as had happened with her other male therapists. She had slowly to give up this fantasy as she was confronted with her games, and the remark about her seductive posture made it clear to her that he was not going to be seduced. With her strengthened Adult she was then able to make the decision to relinquish her childlike ambitions and go about her grown-up business.

Although in some current thinking the course of this case may not indicate that the improvement is stable, it requires only one assumption to take a more optimistic view, and that assumption is borne out by experience; namely, that playing games and playing through one's script are optional, and that a strong Adult can renounce these in favor of gratifying reality experiences. This is the actionistic aspect of transactional analysis.

A few days short of the three-month trial period she had suggested, the patient wrote the therapist as follows:

> I feel fine. I don't have to take any pills and have been off those blood pressure pills for a month now. Last week we celebrated my thirty-fifth birthday. My husband and myself went away without the children. The water was beautiful, and the trees. Gosh,

if only I could paint them. We saw a huge porpoise, the first time I have ever seen one, and it was beautiful to watch, so graceful in movements. . . . My husband and I are getting along so nicely. Night and day such a difference. We have become closer, more attentive, and I can be me. That's what seemed to stump me most of the time. I always had to be polite, etc. He still comes whistling up the stairs. That does more good for me than anything. I am so glad you suggested drawing. You have no idea what that alone has done for me. I am getting better and I might try paints soon. The children think they are very good and have suggested that I exhibit some of them. Next month I am going to take swimming lessons, no fooling, something I would never have been able to do. As the time gets closer I am a little afraid but I have made up my mind I am going to learn. If I can learn to put my head under water, that alone will be a great thrill for me. My garden looks so nice. That's another thing you helped me with. By golly, I go out there at least twice a week now for several hours and no one objects. You know I think they like me better this way.

I didn't intend to ramble on this way but it seemed I had so much to tell you. I'll write and let you know how my swimming progresses. Love from all of us in Salinas.

This letter reassured the therapist of two things:

1. That the patient's improvement persisted even after the medication for her blood pressure was discontinued.

2. That the improvement in the patient's husband and children persisted even after psychotherapy was discontinued.

It should be added that the husband now washes his hair. The most pessimistic thing which can be said about this case so far is that it represents a flight into a healthy family life. The only clinical demand that can legitimately be placed on transactional analysis is that it should produce results which are as good as or better than those produced by any other psychotherapeutic approach, for a given investment of time and effort. In the case of Mrs. Enatosky, there were sixteen individual interviews and twelve group sessions.[1]

In this connection, and for purposes of comparison, the words of a thoughtful psychoanalyst of wide experience should be borne in mind: "What we conquer are only parts of psychogenesis: expressions of conflict, developmental failures. We do not eliminate the original source of neurosis; we only help to achieve better ability to change neurotic frustrations into valid compensations. The dependence of psychic harmony on certain conditions makes immunity unattainable. Freud's 'Analysis Terminable and Interminable' brought for those of us who nourished unlimited therapeutic ambitions both disappointment and relief" (Deutsch, 1959).

Note

1 The improvement was still maintained on a one-year follow-up.

Reference

Deutsch, H. Psychoanalytic therapy in the light of follow-up. *Journal of the American Psychoanalytic Association,* 1959, 7, 445–458.

Case 15

Editors' Introduction

The three "wild men" of modern psychotherapy were Wilhelm Reich, Fritz Perls, and J. L. Moreno. Each was highly unorthodox, highly creative, and completely irrepressible. Each was a European-trained physician who had in various ways strongly reacted against psychoanalysis.

J. L. Moreno, best known for his advocacy of psychodrama as a therapeutic system, was highly intuitive, imaginative, and courageous. He channeled his tremendous energies productively, founding a variety of journals, lecturing and demonstrating psychodrama around the world, and writing voluminously.

Of all of his items, the "Psychodrama of Adolf Hitler" is the most dramatic and most revealing of how psychodrama can be effectively used by a master therapist. The reader is in for a treat.

J. L. MORENO

Psychodrama of Adolf Hitler

Christs and Napoleons are frequently embodied by mental patients, but I do not recall that a pseudo-Hitler has ever been reported in the literature. It was my good fortune to treat such a case at the beginning of World War II. In order to illustrate the theory and technique of psychodrama, here follow a few highlights of the case.

I (DOCTOR) am in my office. The door opens, the nurse comes in.

NURSE: Doctor, there is a man outside; he wants to see you.

DOCTOR: You know I can't see anyone, because I am about to give a session in the theater and the students are waiting.

NURSE: He claims he has an appointment. He does not want to give his name.

DOCTOR: Try to find out who he is and what he wants.

(Nurse leaves and returns.)

NURSE: He insists that he has an appointment with you. He won't go away.

DOCTOR: Well, let him come in.

(The door opens; a man enters; he is in his early forties. We look at each other, our eyes meet. He looks familiar. Now he looks challengingly at me.)

MAN: Don't you know who I am?

DOCTOR: I'm sorry, I don't.

MAN: Well *(sharply)*, my name is Adolf Hitler.

(The doctor was taken aback; indeed, he looked the part—the same hypnotic look, the way of brushing his hair, the moustache. The doctor rises from his seat; [he thinks] he carries his body the same way, makes the same gestures, speaks in the same shrieking, penetrating voice.)

DOCTOR: Of course, now I recognize you. *(The doctor is flustered and uneasy, sits down again and tries to be as formal as possible.)* Won't you sit down, Mr. Hitler?

(He takes a seat. The doctor opens his record book.)

DOCTOR: Your first name, please?

MAN: But don't you know? Adolf!

DOCTOR: Oh, yes, Adolf Hitler. Where do you live?

MAN: *(Surprised and annoyed):* In Berchtesgaden, of course.

From J. L. Moreno, *Progress in Psychotherapy* (Vol. 1). (New York: Grune & Stratton, 1956), pp. 73–80. By permission.

DOCTOR: In Berchtesgaden, oh yes. But why have you come to me?

MAN: Don't you know? Didn't she tell you?

DOCTOR: Who?

MAN: My wife?

DOCTOR: Oh, yes, now I remember. *(He recalled that not so long ago a woman had come to see him; she spoke of her husband who owned a meat market on Third Avenue in the heart of Yorkville. It flashed through his mind that she was depressed and cried. She had said: "My husband has changed; he is sick: his real name is Karl and now he calls himself Adolf. He believes he is Hitler. I don't know what to do with him." The doctor had said: Why don't you let him come to see me?)*

(About three months had elapsed since she came; now, here he was.)

MAN: Is there anything you can do for me?

DOCTOR: I may, but first tell me what happened.

MAN: But didn't she tell you? *(Becoming excited again)* I organized the party for him, he took my name; I wrote *Mein Kampf* but he took it away from me! I was in jail for him for two years; he took everything I have, my inspiration, my brainpower, my energy. Right now, as I'm sitting here, he takes it all from me, every minute. That scoundrel! I can't stop him, maybe you can. *(Putting his head on the doctor's shoulder and weeping)* Oh, help me, help me! I will make you the chief of all the doctors in the Third Reich.

(The doctor begins to feel more at home in the situation, reaches for the telephone and speaks to the nurse. A moment later, two men come in—one fat, one skinny. The doctor performs the introductions.)

DOCTOR: Mr. Goering, Mr. Hitler; Mr. Goebbels, Mr. Hitler.

(Remarkably, the man [whom we shall now call Adolf] accepts them without question, is happy to see them, and shakes hands with them. [They are two male nurses, trained auxiliary egos. Hitler seems to know them well.])

DOCTOR: Gentlemen, let us all go into the theater. Mr. Hitler wishes to make an announcement. *(All four of them proceed to the psychodrama theater. A group of students are waiting.)*

The opening session is crucial for the course of psychodramatic treatment. The doctor had a clue which his (Karl's) wife had given him. She had come home after a short vacation and had seen the walls of their apartment covered with Hitler's pictures. All day long her husband (Karl) had stood before a mirror, trying to imitate Hitler's speech, the way he eats and walks. He neglected his business and took a job as doorman of a motion picture house, so he could wear a uniform and make converts for the cause. He and his wife no longer slept in the same bedroom; now he had his own. He did not seem to care for her anymore. She had asked him what all this meant, but he had only gotten angry. Theoretically, this would have been an excellent clue for the first episode, but it might have thrown off the whole production because "at this moment" the wife had no reality for him; speaking in psychodramatic jargon, he was not warmed-up to this episode. But he was intrigued with the fellows who portrayed Goering and Goebbels; therefore, the doctor followed his own clue. Compared with the thoroughly planned and prepared Christ psychodrama or even with the psychodrama of Mary who hallucinated John, this was practically unplanned. Therefore, the doctor had to follow carefully the clues handed out by the protagonist. He gave him full automony of production.

Karl steps forward and makes an announcement to the German people, speaking over a public address system. He states that he is the real Hitler; the other is an imposter. The German people should eject the imposter! He will return triumphantly to Germany to take over the helm. The group receives his proclamation with spontaneous applaise. A few scenes follow swiftly; Hitler returns to Germany on a boat. He calls a meeting of the war cabinet, planning with his ministers the future of the Third Reich. He ends the first session with a moving scene at the grave of his mother whom he lost at the age of eighteen.

The crucial therapeutic agents are the auxiliary egos. They are assistants to the chief therapist, but simultaneously they are closely related to the world of the patient. The auxiliary ego deliberately assumes the role which the patient needs or wishes him to assume. The success of intervention depends upon how well the auxiliary therapist is able to embody the person the patient desires to encounter. If an auxiliary ego is able to meet the requirements of the patient—for instance, in the role of his mother, which is crucial in the case of Karl (Hitler in his psychodramatic name)—the patient will be aroused to act the complementary part—the son. The ensuing interaction will then closely resemble the internal reality of the patient's world, be it loving or hostile. The protagonist sees different aspects of his mother at different occasions; the auxiliary ego is therefore expected to portray her at one time in one way, and occasionally in another; depending upon the patient's present disposition or his needs, as indicated by him or by the chief therapist. The progress of the patient may depend upon the ability of the auxiliary ego to obtain essential clues from him and to incorporate them rapidly into the portrayal. For example, if the mother-son relation is troubled, the auxiliary ego must have many more varieties of mothers within her repertoire than the protagonist's actual mother, in order that enactment operate as a corrective. We assume that if the mother would have been able to take the role or roles required by the patient at the time, the patient might not have developed distorted perceptions of womanhood. The patient may have become confused because of his mother's rigidity, her insensitivity to her son's clues. Because of the "absence" of an adequate mother figure in his mental world, he may have begun to project and develop an hallucinated substitute for his mother. Hallucinations are roles which may become indispensable requisites in the world of certain patients. The auxiliary ego attempts to make the patient's hallucinations unnecessary, or to weaken their impact by providing him with actual and tangible embodiments of an acceptable mother figure. If the auxiliary ego is not a satisfactory embodiment of the patient's hallucination, the patient is asked to portray the hallucination himself, then the auxiliary ego learns from watching the patient, repeats the action and incorporates what the patient has shown her (reinforcement).

For many weeks we had sessions with Hitler at regular intervals. We provided him with all the characters he needed to put his plans of conquering the world into operation (technique of self-realization). He seemed to know everything in advance; many things he presented on the stage came very close to what actually took place years later. He appeared to have a special sense for fitting himself into moods and decisions which were made thousands of miles apart from him. In fact, at times we speculated whether he, the patient, was not the real Hitler and the other in Germany his double. We had the strange experience of feeling the real Hitler among us, working desperately on finding a solution for himself. We saw him often with his mother or sweetheart alone, bursting out in tears, fighting with astrologists for an answer when he was in doubt, praying in his solitude to God for help, knocking his head on the wall, fearing that he might become insane before he could attain the great victory. At other times, he portrayed moods of great desperation, feelings that he had failed and that the Reich would be conquered by its enemies. In one of these moods, he stepped upon the stage and declared that the time had come for him to end his life. He asked all the Gestapo leaders who filled the audience—from Goering, Goebbels, Ribbentrop, Hess, down to the last man—to die with him. He ordered that the music of *Gotterdammerung* be played to accompany the death orgy. He shot himself in front of the audience. Many years later, when the real Hitler killed himself and his wife in some Berlin underground, I (the Doctor) recalled the strange coincidence that the poor butcher of Yorkville should have anticipated the future of world history so closely. Many times, he and I stood alone on the stage, eye to eye, involved in a conversation. "What's the matter with me?" he said, "Will this torture never end? Is it real or is it a dream?" Such intimate dialogues prove to be of unique value for the progress of therapy. It is at the height of psychodramatic production that rare levels of intensive reflection are reached.

Hospitalization did not seem indicated because his wife provided excellent supervision; she employed the two nurses who took the parts of Goering and Goebbels. Outside the sessions, while with his constant companions, he acted very distant in the beginning. But one day, due to the intimate rapport he established with them in the production of his inner life, he began to become more intimate with them. During an intermission of one session he said to Goering: "Hello, Goering, what do you think of the joke which I made on the stage today?" And they laughed together. But suddenly Hitler swatted Goering. Goering responded in kind and a regular fistfight took place on the spot, during which Hitler took a bad beating. Later they enjoyed a glass of beer together. From then on the ice gradually began to melt.

Physical contact and physical attack—from caressing and embracing, to pushing and hitting—is permissible in psychodramatic therapy if it is of benefit to the patient. It is obvious that here the utmost caution has to be practiced to prevent excesses, or to prevent the auxiliary ego from taking advantage of the patient in order to satisfy his own needs. A great responsibility rests upon the ego. It is natural that the auxiliary ego who portrays the part of a brutal father may really have to hit his son, not only "as if," in order to provoke in the son the responses in action, the perceptions and feelings he has for his father. It is customary in psychodramatic logic that a sick soldier who comes back home from war should embrace and caress his auxiliary mother or wife on the stage, if that is what he would do in real life. It is also psychodramatic logic that if some auxiliary ego takes the part of an older brother who is suddenly attacked by the patient, a real physical encounter may ensue upon the stage, or in the living quarters of the patient if it is there where the session takes place.

The result of the physical contact between Hitler and Goering was that Hitler permitted his auxiliary ego to call him by his first name, Adolf, and he called him Hermann. They acted like pals; their relation was full of homosexual undertones. From then on Hermann began to get an inside hold on Hitler's thoughts and feelings. We began to use this relationship as a therapeutic guide, for now Hitler was able to accept correction from Hermann. Our productions on the stage were greatly facilitated by getting clues from the auxiliary ego (Hermann) as to how to direct the production.

The point is that a therapist who is unable to establish a working rapport with a noncooperative patient, in a physician-patient situation, may be able to produce one by means of the psychodramatic method. For instance, in the case of our pseudo-Hitler, who was noncooperative to an extreme, it was possible to warm him up to a level of communication when an auxiliary ego portrayed the role of Goering in an episode relevant to his psychotic world. Once he had established rapport with the auxiliary therapist on the psychodramatic stage, he was later able to develop a relationship to the private person behind Goering, just a plain therapeutic nurse, with whom he began to communicate spontaneously on a realistic level. This was the turning point in the therapeutic process.

Approximately three months after treatment first began, a strange event occurred. The group was gathered in the theater waiting for Hitler's next session. Goering came to me and said: "Adolf wants a haircut."

DOCTOR: Well, call a barber.

It was the first time since he fell ill that he had allowed anyone to touch his hair. A barber came, and cut his hair according to Adolf's instructions—on stage. When the ceremony was over, the barber started to pack his instruments, getting ready to leave. Suddenly, Hitler looked sharply at the group, at me (the Doctor), then at the barber.

HITLER: Take this off! (He pointed at his moustache. The barber immediately soaped his face, applied the razor, and the moustache was gone! A very tense silence had descended upon the audience. Hitler rose from his chair, pointed at his face.)

HITLER: It's gone, it's gone, it's gone, it's over! (commencing to weep) I lost it, I lost it! Why did I do it? I shouldn't have done it!

Gradually, a change took place; from session to session we saw his body and behavior changing—the look in his eyes, his smile, the words he spoke. Still later he asked to be called "Karl" and not "Adolf." He asked his wife to come to the sessions. For the first time in many months, he kissed her in a scene on the stage.

(These episodes are from a large psychodramatic protocol, illustrating the rapid diagnostic picture given by protagonists, often within a single psychodramatic session.)

The patient made a good social recovery and returned to the fatherland a few years later. His case illustrates the hypothesis that "acting-out techniques" are the choice treatment for "acting-out syndromes."

The Group

The highlight of the above sessions was the intense participation of the group. The longer the sessions went on, the more we realized that the true hero of this psychodrama was the audience. After the second session, Hitler began to sit in the audience as one of the members of the group, and became the center of attractions and repulsions. At times the group became involved in the production to such a degree that everyone, without exception, sided with Hitler; at other times, they became involved in a negative way and reacted towards him as if he were the real Hitler. Many episodes resulting from the interactions were acted out on the stage, mixing the events in Hitler's dream with the actualities of the group. Sociogram and role diagrams, which were compared from session to session, showed that there were a few little Hitlers among the group. A magnificent panorama of the world of our time emerged in bold relief, as if caught in the miniature mirror of this group. Careful analysis of the responses, as well as of the production, suggested that the real Adolf Hitler might have profited greatly if he would have participated in psychodramatic sessions during his adolescence, and that World War II might have been averted, or at least taken a different form. On the deeper level of the structure we saw the familial figures in Hitler's life reflected in their relationship to the corresponding figures in the life of each member of the group. But we also saw the figures of the larger world—emperors and kings, autocratic rulers of nations like Stalin and Mussolini, rulers of free governments like Roosevelt and Churchill—in the midst, the crucified figure of Christ, the symbol of suffering and despair. Then we saw the little man, the unknown soldier, the victims of concentration camps, the refugees, a Negro student from Harlem identifying himself with Asiatic and African rebels, all the shades of love and hate, bias and tolerance, superimposing a drama of such intensity that it put Karl's actual, private drama into the shade. The more Karl himself participated in it, the more he learned to see his own private paranoiac world in the perspective of the larger one which he had unconsciously provoked. He gave us a number of clues, suggesting the dynamic forces operating in the development of his mental syndrome. Why did he want to become Hitler? He said once: "I had a dream since I was a little boy to conquer the world or destroy it, and I imitated Hitler because he tried the same." What helped him to recover from his obsession? He said: "I was surprised to see in the group so many others besides me who had the dream of becoming Hitler. That helped me."

The psychodrama of Adolf Hitler turned into the psychosociodrama of our entire culture—a mirror of the twentieth century.

Case 16

Editors' Introduction

One of the more important individuals in the field of modern psychotherapy was Rudolf Dreikurs, who was the primary exponent of Adlerian psychotherapy in the United States. Dreikurs was perhaps best known for his fascinating public counseling appearances, and the item we have selected shows him at his best. Luckily, many of his counseling sessions have been preserved on film, and can be obtained through the University of Vermont as well as through the North American Society of Adlerian Psychology.

While his unique style cannot be adequately caught in print, nevertheless in this selection, Dreikurs' bold procedures do emerge. We will watch a master clinician, operating with some fifty years of experience in such situations, cutting through to the heart of a problem leading to more-or-less instant psychotherapy.

We have placed Dreikurs in this section with family counseling, an area Alfred Adler pioneered in the early 1920s.

RUDOLF DREIKURS

Family Counseling: A Demonstration[1]

The participants are: the father (Mr. F.), the mother (Mrs. F.), the seventeen-year-old daughter (Sally), the eleven-year-old son (Mike), and the co-counselor, Mr. Robert L. Powers (Mr. P.).

We often have two counselors in our guidance centers. It was the original development in Vienna where we usually had a physician and a psychologist co-counseling. The whole method of co-counseling began in Vienna under Adler in the 1920s and we do it very often here too. Today Bob Powers is helping me out as much as might be necessary. We have limited time, and we have to go pretty fast.

DR. D.: Now I should like to ask you, Sally, with whom should we talk first, with your parents or with you?

SALLY: With my parents.

DR. D: Is this all right? (*General nodding. The children leave the room. Dr. D. turning to the parents.*) Will you tell us please what your problems are and why you came?

MR. F: Why we came here today? Well, actually we didn't know what we were coming into when we came here today.

DR. D.: Huh! Didn't people tell you anything?

MR. F.: We were told we were coming to a family counseling service. We did not know we were going to be a demonstration group. It's a little bit of a disappointment in that respect.

DR. D.: So would you like to go home? (*Mrs. F. whispers, "Yes."*)

MR. F.: For myself I can take it, for my wife and my family, I don't know.

DR. D.: If you don't want to be here you can go home.

MRS. F.: We felt that if this could help our son we would be glad to participate.

DR. D.: Ah, you see, this is a demonstration. It's a class. Most of the counseling which I do is a demonstration. You learn something, and they learn. So if you don't mind, I shall explain what goes on to the audience, and have a discussion with them, while I talk with you. Is this all right?

From *Journal of Individual Psychology*, 1972, 28, 207–222.

You see there are a number of these little things which are very effective and in which we train our students. Here you have something which is characteristic of this new technology of which I spoke earlier. In our child-guidance work with parents we bring a new psychology, a new technology, into the family. And its main point is to replace the traditional form of argument, of pressuring and so on, with stimulation from within.

I just did something which is extremely important. I don't know whether any of you realize the significance of what I did. I told Mrs. F. she could go home. Instead of saying to yourself, "I have to calm her or pressure her," you must give her a chance to leave. Hardly ever will a mother leave, once she has come, because she realizes there is something that might benefit her family. I have seen it time and again. In one particular case there was a large hall of 500 people. The mother didn't want to come, but she didn't want to let the father go alone either. So she came with him and sat there quietly. And after about ten minutes she began to talk—and couldn't be shut up. *(Some laughter.)* These are the kinds of arrangements where you achieve stimulation from within, instead of pressure from without.

DR. D.: Now what is the problem? Are you ready to discuss the problem with me?

MRS. F.: *(not audible)*

DR. D.: Yes, but you must talk loud enough that one can hear you. What is the problem?

MRS. F.: *(whispering):*. . .I guess.

MR. F.: Well, our son has a behavior problem in school, although that's just a small part of it. The behavior problem developed into a situation where he would go into a rage, and he would be uncontrollable. This has never happened in my presence so I haven't really seen. . . .

DR. D.: Well where is he uncontrollable? At school?

MR. F.: At home mostly, although at school he has been so disruptive in class for the past three years that he has been in what is called an ERA class, an Early Remedial Assistance class. This year for the first time he has been put into a regular class. I don't know if it's the pressure from the regular class or pressures at home or what.

DR. D.: I'm interested in that you said, you yourself have never seen him in a rage.

MR. F.: Well I've seen him wild, but never in these actual rages where he has in one or two instances threatened to take pills. . .

MRS. F.: . . . and kill himself. He's also threatened to kill himself by drowning.

DR. D.: Did he tell you so? And what is your answer?

MRS. F.: Well, at first I used to fight him and then I told him to go ahead and do it.

DR. D.: Has he diminished his threat?

MRS. F.: Well, when he first started threatening, there was a point when I didn't know what to do. The first time he did it, he took most of his clothes off—we have an upstairs and down—threw them down the stairs at me, and said, "I don't want anything you gave me, and I'm going to kill myself." And I told him not to be funny. But he locked himself in the bathroom and said he's going to drown himself. So he filled the sink with water and stuck his head in it. But he couldn't because he happens to be a terrific swimmer. And he came out and laughed and said: "I couldn't do it if I wanted to, because I couldn't keep my head under the water." And I said OK.

DR. D.: Good.

MRS. F.: I hope he can't hear me. The door is open. But he came out soaking wet, and finally when I did get him calmed down, he had taken. . . I don't remember if this was the same time he took his bottle of medication, which then was Ritalin, and threatened to take the whole thing. I chased him all over the house to take it away from him. But after a while I realized that I would just stop chasing him and tell him to go ahead and take it and I'll take him to the hospital and have his stomach pumped out. So he quit doing that.

Now, here you have the whole situation. We are always accused of improper procedure because we immediately jump to conclusions. When I see a patient or a client, after the first few sentences I know what goes on. This is only possible when you accept that behavior is purposive. Whatever a child does is for a purpose. We described the four goals of the disturbing behavior of a child. The child wants to belong, but gets the wrong idea about how he can belong, and then he switches from the useful way of belonging to the useless side and disturbs. Without knowing the four goals, neither parents nor teachers are a match for him. They do exactly what he wants them to do. And so the child manages the parents and the teachers.

The first goal is, he wants special attention. He prefers the attention in a nice way but if he can't get it, he disturbs. He would rather be scolded, threatened, and punished than be ignored.

When the fight becomes more intensive, the child moves to Goal 2, power. He will show you, "If you don't let me do what I want, you don't love me. I will see to it that you do what I want, but I don't do what you want." We are raising in America a whole generation of tyrants. Tell them what to do and they don't do it. Tell them what not to do and they feel honor-bound to do it.

When the fight becomes more intense, the child is no longer interested merely in attention and power. He wants revenge, Goal 3. He thinks he can have a place only when he can hurt you back as much as he believes he was hurt.

And then we find Goal 4, where the child is so discouraged that he wants to be left alone because he doesn't think anything can be done.

Now one of the ways by which we train parents and teachers to recognize the goal of the child is by showing them that not merely by observing what the child does can they see in which direction he moves, but also by their responses to his actions. This is actually the best way to recognize the child's goal, namely to watch your immediate reaction to his provocation. When you get annoyed, the chances are he wanted attention. When you feel defeated, he wanted power. When you feel humiliated, hurt, he wanted revenge. And when you feel like throwing up your hands and saying, "I don't know what to do with you," you do exactly what the child wants you to do—"Leave me alone, you can't do anything with me." And thus most adults trying to correct the child's behavior do in their immediate reaction the worst possible thing: They reinforce the mistaken goal of the child.

It is quite obvious from the description we heard that this boy has the power over his mother. "I will show you, you either do what I want, or else." So my first impression is that the mother and the one who does it most often, the teacher, get into a power conflict with the child. Whenever you fight with a child you have lost before you even start. The child is a much better fighter, he can do all kinds of things, endangering himself and so on, to force you to give in.

The new technology means there is no sense in fighting, there is no sense in forcing. You have to learn to stimulate from within. No temper tantrum has any meaning if there is no audience. And it is the teacher and the parent who provide the audience for such "uncontrollable" behavior. But it is uncontrollable only for them. It is not uncontrollable for him; he can stop any tantrum immediately. You see this in adults. They suffer from a temper tantrum to make people do what they want. But in the midst of the worst tantrum, as soon as the door opens and the neighbor comes in, they are completely quiet—only to continue the temper after the neighbor leaves. You must realize that all this is not conscious, yet well designed. You are dealing here with a tyrant.

DR. D.: You and so many parents and teachers must learn how to cope with a tyrant. You can cope with him neither by fighting nor by giving in. But there are various things you can do and which we recommend. One of them you apparently found out for yourself. Right? The moment you said, "Go ahead kill yourself," he lost the power over you. The moment you stop being frightened by a tyrant, there is no sense any more in being a tyrant. What do you think about this?

MR. F.: Well, I guess I don't know what to say really. It's just because he's never done this to me. I guess I'm the mean old dad and I. . .

DR. D.: You know why he has not done it to you? Because you don't fall for it.

MR. F.: Well, I tell him. I'm not asking him what to do, I'm telling him and insist that he does what I tell him. If he goes too far. . .

DR. D.: In general we don't believe in any overpowering and so on. But with this power of children, to show them that they won't get anywhere and that you can cope with them, deprives them of their methods. Do you beat him up?

MR. F.: I've hit him, not very often. I mean it's a rare occasion if I will hit him. But. . .

DR. D.: Does it have any good effect?

MR. F.: Well, I think it helps a little.

DR. D.: But not for very long.

MR. F.: Well, for very long? I mean if you achieve your objective then I would say it helps.

DR. D.: You don't achieve your objective if the same thing happens afterwards again. Your objective would be to help him to stop it altogether. But if he only heeds at the moment you punish him, then you only teach him the lesson that power is all that counts. You play right into his hands. He tries to overpower others and you try to overpower him. But we have to help the children to learn that overpowering is not the best way of finding one's place in life.

Now let's perhaps go through a typical day to see what the problems are. Very often when one goes through a day, one runs into all kinds of situations which the parents didn't realize were problems about which they can do something.

Now is there anything further that you want to tell us about him in general that upsets you, before we go through the average day?

MRS. F.: He doesn't like to do his homework.

DR. D.: Please, here is a technique which we use. From the assumption that everything the child does has a purpose we come to the conclusion that the crucial question is, what does mother or father do about it? When I train counselors, they have to learn this first lesson. Whenever the mother says what the child does, you come with the question, "And what did you do about it?" Because what you did about it reveals the purpose of what the child had done. Everything a child does is well designed, well calculated to get results, although the child is not aware of this. No child will continue any misbehavior if he doesn't get results. That is already present in infants when they size up the situation. Whatever gets results, they will continue. In our present situation parents and teachers are unable to help children because they do not know techniques of a democratic type. They therefore make it all the worse by actually satisfying the child's intentions. So, is the temper still going on?

MRS. F.: Oh yes. It's still going on.

DR. Dr.: Can you give us a recent example? Everything has to be concrete.

MR. F.: Well the most recent example I would say happened—unfortunately my wife lost her father just recently. Her parents lived in Florida, and she had been down there for three weeks. Then they brought him back here, put him in a hospital, and he passsed away a couple of days later. After the funeral and everything, the following day, I had gone back to work and my wife's mother was with us.

Grandmother. In our families you must always look for the grandmother. The influence of the grandmother is in many cases pernicious. She stands up for the child's right, because the grandparents and the child have a common enemy. *(Laughter.)* This is not necessarily so, but always watch for it. For instance even in juvenile delinquents, who are understood as being neglected, having a tyrannical father, and all kinds of bad living conditions, you find that the real culprit is the one who felt sorry for them and encouraged them in their desire, "I can do whatever I want." The grandparents have a tendency to spoil children. And spoiling means to teach them, "I can do what I want, and I don't care what you or society want." It isn't in all cases like that, but you always watch for it.

DR. D.: Now what happened?

MR. F.: Well, I'd gone back to school with him that day, because the day that my father-in-law passed away there had been a note from the teacher that she wanted to see one of the parents.

DR. D.: Let's stop here, because I like always to discuss everything as it comes up; it clarifies the situation. Why does the teacher want to talk with the parents?

MR. F.: Well, because he was disturbing the class.

DR. D.: Right. And do you know what I advise parents to do? When the teacher asks them to come and tells them what the child is doing wrong, I advise the parents to ask the teacher what she proposes to do. Because it is her job, and only if she does not know how to do her job does she blame the parents. How many of you are teachers? I can tell you a secret about teachers. Teachers send "love letters" home, because the child is tardy, does not study, and so on. Why? Do they really expect the parents can do something? It is the teachers' way of getting even with the child. They feel defeated by him in class and want to take it out on him at home, in which they usually succeed.

MR. F.: Except that in this case he is so disruptive that he keeps the whole class from learning.

DR. D.: That is the job of the teacher. The teacher has to learn how to deal with a class with a disruptive child. And the teacher who knows how to do it can actually succeed. The teacher has a group to work with. She has a whole room of children to help her. But the teachers are not prepared to deal with any child who doesn't want to learn, who doesn't want to behave.

MR. F.: What the teacher. . .

DR. D.: But wait. So she called you.

MR. F.: She called me. So I went and talked to the teacher. Mike wasn't doing his work, and is always trying to get the whole attention of the teacher. As long as he's the center of attention, that's fine. But once the teacher has to pay attention to the other thirty some children in the class, that creates a problem.

DR. D.: No, only if the teacher doesn't know what to do about it.

MRS. F.: I used to get a call from the school a couple of times a week—to take him, and keep him home at lunchtime, because he was creating problems and they couldn't handle him. And I would be keeping him home until I went to see the principal. I told him I felt he belonged in school. And he told me that if he was going to continue to create problems, I would have to keep him home.

DR. D.: You must keep in mind that at the start of this pathology of our situation is that we did not learn the new ways of coping with each other. We have a law according to which everybody who prevents a child from going to school is punishable. And this law is mostly violated by principals and teachers. *(laughter)* But that is a sad situation and we have to cope with it. Now I want an example of a temper tantrum.

MR. F.: Well as I started to say before, I had gone to school with him on the morning and then I went to work and I got a call that there was a problem at home, and I should come home immediately. He was sent home from school. The school psychologist had been at school that morning and said that she felt that he was on the verge of a nervous breakdown.

DR. D.: Who, the psychologist? *(laughter)*

MR. F.: He was quite disruptive in class. The principal sent the boy home, and he refused to go. So he called my wife. Considering the circumstances, she having just buried her father the day before, this created quite a turmoil between my wife, my mother-in-law, and my son. I didn't know who was worst off at the moment.

DR. D.: Here we have to come to a first important suggestion. If you want to learn how to cope with your child, you have to let the school and him fight it out with each other. You can't do anything about it.

MRS. F.: But the school doesn't want to be bothered fighting it out, and they keep constantly telling me I have to keep him home. They cannot keep him in school because he created too much of a disturbance.

MR. F.: There is a feeling among many of the parents in our school that our school is interested in the above average and the achieving child, and takes much less interest in the child that's average and below. And this has created a problem. In fact the fourth grade he was in had two classes and he was in the class in which the principal double-promoted all the children except three.

DR. D.: Let's stop right now because we don't get anywhere. I can not help you in dealing with the school. I have to help you to deal with him at home; so let's forget about the school because there's nothing you and I can do about it at the present moment. Right? But you can learn to cope with him at home. And mother is beginning already to extricate herself from the effects of his tyranny. Now what are the problems at home?

MRS. F.: Well, they put him on a new medication, and so far I don't know if it's having the effect that it should have or not, because he hasn't been in school since he started. He was out of school three weeks this past time because of the problem. He just went back the other day. I took him to school Wednesday, no, Tuesday, and the principal was out.

DR. D.: Please, do me one favor, let's leave the school out. We can not do anything about the school right now. You have to learn to cope with the problems which you have with him at home. That's the only thing that we can do now.

MR. F.: Well since he has been going back to school now, at the moment, there has not been any problem; but he is getting medication and tranquilizers.

DR. D.: That's all right, there's a whole history about that; but we can't go into this at this point. When we started our guidance centers we were accused by social workers that in this superficial form of counseling we could only deal with very mildly disturbed children. And my answer was, they are wrong. When a child is brain-damaged, or has anything else wrong, the parents still have to learn how to cope with him. And that is what we are trying to do, regardless of how difficult the situation may be, to see how we can improve the situation and have a different relationship at home. This is what I would like to discuss with you. What bothers you at home?

MRS. F.: Nothing at the moment, really.

DR. D.: You mean as long as it's outside it doesn't bother you?

MRS. F.: No, I don't mean that at all.

DR. D.: Now let's start with this morning. How does the morning begin?

MRS. F.: Well, I get him up for school.

DR. D.: You are upset right now. Did I upset you?

MRS. F.: No, I have a slight migraine that I got yesterday and I still have it. So that's what is upsetting me.

DR. D.: Boy, school, migraine, what can we do with all this? Do you know that the whole relationship between child and parents is decided in the morning? That is usually the crucial mistake and the first improvement: How do you wake him up?

MRS. F.: I usually go up and sort of shake the bed a little bit.

DR. D.: How many times do you have to wake him up?

MRS. F.: Well, he usually gets up pretty good when he's in the mood.

DR. D.: And if he is not?

MRS. F.: Well, then it takes a little longer, but he gets up far easier than my daughter does.

DR. D.: They both have the same idea, to put mother in their service.

MRS. F.: Well, Mike doesn't bother me as much getting up in the morning as Sally does.

DR. D.: That's right. She has you in her service.

MRS. F.: Don't they both?

DR. D.: They both do. Would you like to improve the situation?

MRS. F.: I'd love it.

DR. D.: The first step is to help the parents to extricate themselves from the demands and tyranny of the children. If you really want to have a new relationship you have to start in the morning. Whose responsibility is this to get up? Whose responsibility?

Mrs. F.: Well, I would say theirs, because they have things that have to be done.

Dr. D.: Yes, but who is taking on the responsibility?

Mrs. F.: I guess I am.

Dr. D.: That's right. And you cannot teach children responsibility, you can only give it to them. I will make a number of recommendations. We have a limited amount of time and I want to talk with the boy too. The first thing is that you declare your independence in the morning. You tell them: "Whether you get up or not is your problem; it has nothing to do with me." Could you do that?

Mrs. F.: I'll try.

Dr. D.: First, you have to be sure that you want to extricate yourself. What else happens? How about eating?

Mrs. F.: No problem, Mike is a big eater. Sally doesn't eat any breakfast.

Dr. D.: How do you feel about your daughter not eating any breakfast?

Mrs. F.: It used to bother me but I told her if she doesn't want to, it's her stomach.

Dr. D.: But you see, it bothered you a great deal.

Mrs. F.: At first. But it doesn't any more.

Dr. D.: When the parents are bothered, it is an invitation for the child to do it. The children are very adept to find out what the parents can't stand, and then they do it.

Mrs. F.: I guess we were the same when we were kids.

Dr. D.: Yes. Do they fight with each other?

Mrs. F.: Yes.

Dr. D.: What do you do about that?

Mrs. F.: What do I do? I try to stop it, but it doesn't always work, and the rest of the time I let them fight until Frank comes home, and stops them.

Dr. D.: When father comes home what do they do then?

Mrs. F.: They usually go to their own corner.

Dr. D.: You see we have such a tremendous amount of ground to cover in a very limited time. So I have to make this very short and merely indicate in which direction you will have to move. The fighting of the children is for the benefit of the parents. The one who provokes is usually the one who wants mother to come to his rescue. One tries to get special attention by fighting, the other tries to fight this. And the parents have to stand it. Now I will give you some ideas of the direction in which you can operate eventually, so that you have an idea of what can be done. Do you have somebody to work with, a counselor or somebody?

Mrs. F.: Well, we are going to the doctor.

Dr. D.: Well then he has to work it out with you. The first thing is, whenever mother gets upset, which means the children go after her, she has to retreat, and the best place to retreat is the bathroom.

Mrs. F.: That's exactly what Dr. Bina Rosenberg says.

Dr. D.: That's right. One has to understand the purpose of behavior or otherwise people think you give in to the child, when you go to the bathroom. In the bathroom the mother can find her independence. *(laughter)* But she has to know how to do it. If you don't do it properly it doesn't work. You have to know how to use the bathroom. Essential is a transistor radio, so that you can't hear what goes on outside. And you will be surprised how the family stops fighting and how much harmony you can have in a family from this one step of mother going to the bathroom. But you must be willing to extricate yourself. What prevents mother from being effective, is her tremendous sense of responsibility—"I have to see that they don't hurt each other; I have to see that they get up on time, *I* have to do it." The mother takes on the responsibility and the children have none.

The next important thing is the so-called family council. Once a week you get together to discuss everything that goes on, not dictating to them, but listening to them. In the family council everybody has the right to say what he thinks and the obligation to listen to what the other one thinks. We are right now writing a textbook on this, because so many parents do not know how to be democratic. We have to train parents to be democratic leaders and to become effective in this way. Instead of the personal battles which go on, all problems are brought up on one day of the week, and we will see what can we do to understand each other and to help each other. There is something for you to develop. Right? Now what is your reaction to this?

MR. F.: Well, it should work out. But it is not that easy.

DR. D.: The difficult step is only one: to be determined, "I want to do it." When you do it halfway, the child will call your bluff. These things are effective only when you really sincerely say, this is their job, they have to take care of it.

MR. F.: Well I'm all for giving him responsibility.

DR. D.: Do you agree in general with what I have suggested?

MR. F.: Well, how can I disagree?

DR. D.: You can, you are the boss.

MR. F.: Well, you are the expert.

DR. D.: *(turning to Mrs. F.):* What is your reaction?

MRS. F.: Well I've tried this bathroom bit once, because I had one occasion to try it since I had spoken to the doctor. I went in, locked the door, and started to read a book, and Mike stood there pounding on the door, and I just ignored it as long as I could.

DR. D.: And after you could no longer endure it, what did you do?

MRS. F.: I went out and scrubbed the bathroom floor, I scrubbed the basement.

DR. D.: But you must keep in mind that most parents make one mistake with the bathroom; the bathroom technique works only when you have the radio in the bathroom.

MRS. F.: I can see where it would.

DR. D.: You see, no recommendation will have any effect unless you do it properly, and these are things to discuss and to learn. I can only make this broad outline today. Regardless of how disturbed the child is, you can learn to cope with him.

MR. P.: May I make a comment on that, Dr. Dreikurs?

DR. D.: Yes, please.

MR. P.: A lot of people have read about Dr. Dreikurs and the "bathroom technique" because it was reported in the daily papers. One of the questions that comes up about it very often is whether it is not just one more tactic for mothers to use in fighting with their children. And if, *after* she has gotten into a conflict with a child, mother suddenly withdraws to the bathroom, it *is* a fighting tactic, and probably an unfair one. Once you are in a fight, it is very difficult to withdraw and then to expect not to be part of the fight.

It is when the fighting starts, when the children begin provoking her, that mother must decide to go to the bathroom, *instead* of fighting. "Excuse me, I have to go to the bathroom," is an unarguable declaration. This is a *substitute* for fighting, not a better *way* of fighting.

If this recommendation is followed, the mother is not nearly as likely to have the child pounding on the door. But when, as a form of fight, mother's part is to go into the bathroom, then the child's part is, understandably, to pound on the door. Do you agree with me, Dr. Dreikurs?

DR. D.: Yes, fully.

MR. F.: But this is not both children fighting with each other.

MR. P.: No, I mean with you.

MR. F.: It is just the one fighting with me.

DR. D.: It doesn't make any difference with whom he fights. You can not succeed in fighting with the child. You see for 8,000 years in our civilization we have had a technology of relationships, where one had to be the boss and have the power for drastic punishment, and one could subdue people. Today one can't anymore. Try to subdue a child and you will see what will happen. He subdues you.

Now how is the relationship between the children? How is the girl? Do you have any problems with her?

MR. F.: Well, her big problem is that she's not the least bit interested in school, which has us quite worried. She puts no effort out at all. If she graduates I feel it's a major miracle.

DR. D.: And what do you do about it?

MR. F.: I don't feel there is anything we can do about it.

DR. D.: Do you do anything about homework and so on?

MR. F.: I try and talk to her about the importance of getting an education, that she'll be able to do something when she grows up. But it just doesn't seem to . . .

DR. D.: You see, neither parents nor teachers know the psychodynamics. Our children lose more and more interest in school thanks to the work of the teachers who don't know how to stimulate learning and only know how to fight and to discourage. I guess from what you said that she is probably overambitious, and overambition leads to underachievement. "If I can't be on top, then I don't want to be anything else."

MR. F.: She's never been that good a student really.

DR. D.: That is a consequence of never having been interested in studying. Is there anything in life that she can do well?

MRS. F.: She likes animals, she loves animals. If she didn't have to go to school any longer to become a vet, she would have done it, because she loves to be with animals.

DR. D.: And why? You see every one of these statements is fraught with meaning, which one has to explore. Very often when people like animals it is because they can control them. They have the situation under control. But with people it doesn't go.

MR. F.: But she has liked animals since she has been an infant, really.

MRS. F.: She would walk out the door and chase the dogs down the street. She was this type.

DR. D.: Yes. We can't go into all of these aspects, there is a lot of material to cover. But apparently she's not interested in doing the average thing. She wants to do something special. Does she have friends?

MR. F.: Yes.

DR. D.: What kind of friends does she have?

MR. F.: Well, I think she's a sensible girl, she has sensible friends. To my knowledge she has never experimented with drugs, which I have to give her a lot of credit for, because in high school today drugs can be a serious problem. And I feel she hasn't experimented with sex, which can also be a serious problem.

DR. D.: I would be careful not to let her know that you would count it as a serious problem, because then she might be stimulated to do it. So be careful. Anyhow I can see that there is no deeper problem. I don't know whether we should go into any more today. But I would suggest to you the same as what I said about your boy. The problem of learning is a problem of the school. And it's up to her how she wants to deal with the school and what to learn. And since she has the motivation to become a veterinarian she have enough motivation to just pass. But she's not interested in school. Is there another problem which bothers you about her?

MRS. F.: Not really.

MR. F.: One problem that bothers me quite a bit is the matter of religion. I came from a very religious family; we are of the Jewish faith. I was brought up in the orthodox tradition, although I'm not quite orthodox right now.

DR. D.: Now please, time is very short.

MR. F.: The problem there is, that I feel that she doesn't hang around with the children of the same faith and I'm quite concerned about the possibility of intermarriage in the future.

DR. D.: Of course the problem is that we lose influence over our children. We have our own ideas and are not willing to give in. But did you so far get much out of our discussion?

MR. F.: Definitely.

DR. D.: I would like to talk with the children. *(The children are called in.)*

You can see from what even the limited circumstances permit that we are really working on brief therapy. From the first moment of diagnosis we show people what they can do differently. I maintain, and that is what I try to imbue in my students, if a client comes to me and leaves my office the same as when he came in, I have failed him. In every interview I try to explore all possibilities. A very important man in Israel pointed out, "Professor Dreikurs talks with each client as if it were the last time he had a chance to talk with him, not wasting time with relationship investigations, and immediately starting with the therapeutic, corrective effort." And I think that came out pretty well in our discussion.

DR. D.: *(to the boy, who in the meanwhile had taken his seat next to him):* Now would you mind to be open with me and to talk with me?

MIKE: No.

DR. D.: Good. Now, why are you here?

MIKE: I don't know.

DR. D.: Do you want me to believe that you don't know?

MIKE: I don't.

DR. D.: How many of you believe that he doesn't know why he is here? *(laughter)* Now why don't you tell me what you think why you are?

This is what we do. We confront the child with his goal in a very well defined technique. You ask: "Do you do that? Is it true?" Yes. "Why do you do it?" The child never knows. He will either say, "I don't know," or he will give you a rationalization. Then comes the next important question, "Would you mind if I tell you why you are doing it"? And then you come with the confrontation, always introduced with the words: "Could it be that. . ." "Could it be that you want to keep mother busy?" "Could it be that you want to show your power?" I think I am traveling internationally quite a bit, and it has come about that at various conferences in various places, people recognized immediately who were my students by these words "Could it be?" You don't reproach anybody. You don't accuse them. You try to reveal.

DR. D.: So you think you don't know why you are here?
MIKE: Right.
DR. D.: And that is the reason you don't want to tell me?
MIKE: Yes.
DR. D.: Now could I tell you what *I* think is the reason why you don't want to tell me?
MIKE: Yes.
DR. D.: Could it be you don't want to do what people tell you?
MIKE: I guess so.

Recognition reflex. *(laughter)* When you guess what he does, he begins to see.

DR. D.: I think that is part of your troubles. Your mother and father don't know what to do with you. Am I right?
MIKE: Right.
DR. D.: Do you know what to do with them? Honest.
MIKE: I don't know.
DR. D.: Do you think he knows what to do with father and mother?
MRS. F.: No.
MIKE: Yes, he does.
DR. D.: Now into what kind of troubles do you get? Do you get into troubles?
MIKE: *(inaudible)*
DR. D.: Can you hear him? Now into what kind of troubles do you get? Why did you not take your microphone when I told you to take it? Your first reaction is, "No." When I tell you to speak in the microphone, you don't want to. Am I right?
MIKE: Right.
DR. D.: Now I can imagine what kind of troubles you get into in this way. With whom do you get into troubles?
MIKE: My teacher.
DR. D.: Now what kind of troubles do you have with your teacher?
MIKE: Well, I want to do my work.
DR. D.: Yes, and she doesn't let you do your work? Now what kind of troubles do you have with the teacher?
MIKE: Well, like one time she wanted me to do my spelling during a different class, and I wasn't there that day, so I refused.
DR. D.: Did you refuse at other times too when the teacher told you to do something?
MIKE: No.

DR. D.: Come on.

MIKE: Not all the time.

DR. D.: Not all the time, but most of the time?

MIKE: About half.

DR. D.: And do you know why you are doing this?

MIKE: To get at the teacher.

DR. D.: No. May I tell you what I think?

MIKE: What?

DR. D.: Could it be that you want to show the teacher that you are strong enough and she can't make you do anything?

MIKE: Yes.

DR. D.: You see, you have the power. You know how to manage mother, you threaten her with doing things, to kill yourself, whatever it is, apparently because you want everyone to do what you want. *(Very slowly:)* And what do you do if people don't do what you want?

MIKE: I try to get my way.

DR. D.: And you get mad.

MIKE: Uh huh.

DR. D.: Do you have temper tantrums?

MIKE: Yes.

DR. D.: Why do you think you have temper tantrums?

MIKE: I don't know.

DR. D.: Could it be the same, you want to show your power?

MIKE: Yes.

DR. D.: What would happen if you would have a temper tantrum in the classroom and the teacher would have stopped screaming?

It is very effective to let the child have his temper tantrum and to tell the class we can not do anything, we have to wait until he's through, and he doesn't go on with the temper tantrum very long. But our teachers do the reverse: "Stop it," and then they become completely defeated.

DR. D.: Could it be that you wanted to show everybody "I can do what I want?"

MIKE: Yes.

DR. D.: You think that is a good idea?

MIKE: No.

DR. D.: Ah yes, you think it's a wonderful idea, you enjoy it. [*Laughter.*] You see, every child knows what he should do, he just decides not to do it. Now I hope you will work with somebody to help you. You see you are a nice boy if you want to, but if you don't want, you're a tiger. The principal doesn't know what to do with you, the teacher doesn't know what to do with you, nobody knows what to do with you. Isn't that wonderful?

MIKE: No.

DR. D.: How can you say no? It's an achievement. You should get an A on how to defeat grown-ups. Shouldn't you?

MIKE: No.

DR. D.: Well anyhow *(turning to Sally),* do you have any problems with your parents?

SALLY: No.

DR. D.: No?

SALLY: Well, yes at times.

DR. D.: Like what?

SALLY: At times I want to go out and they won't let me.

DR. D.: You want to go out. Do you have any other problems with them?

SALLY: The car.

DR. D.: The car. That is a typical juvenile problem. The war between the genera-
tions, the gap, the car, and dates. All the way through, until the poor parents are really
thrown in every direction, the kids support each other, and each family tries for itself
to solve the problem, which they can't. How about getting up in the morning?

SALLY: Well, I can't do it.

DR. D.: You can't do it. Why not?

SALLY: I just can't wake up.

DR. D.: You can't wake up?

SALLY: Too tired.

DR. D.: Too tired? You see that is a typical rationalization. May I tell you what *I*
think is why you don't get up?

SALLY: Yes.

DR. D.: Could it be that you want your mother to come to your service and get you
up?

SALLY: No, I get up when I'm not tired.

DR. D.: At times. Couldn't you get up every time?

SALLY: Not if I'm too tired.

DR. D.: You will be surprised how you could get up, once you realize why you
don't get up. It is your way of putting your mother in your service. If mother would
declare her independence and refuse to be an alarm clock, do you think you could get
up by yourself?

SALLY: Oh, I get up all right, she doesn't wake me up.

DR. D.: She doesn't wake you up?

SALLY: No.

DR. D.: But she says she does because you don't get up unless she comes several
times.

SALLY: She comes up and tells me to get up, and if I get up, I get up.

DR. D.: And if you don't get up, what does she do?

SALLY: I wait a few minutes and then I get up.

DR. D.: And doesn't she come afterwards again to remind you?

SALLY: No.

DR. D.: I might be wrong, but I have the feeling that you use her very much as a
servant for you to get up. I might be wrong about that.

SALLY: Sometimes.

DR. D.: And sometimes you are fighting also for your rights that you can do what
you want? Right?

SALLY: Yes.

DR. D.: This is part of the generation problem. Now we can only briefly outline
what I feel that the problems are. And I would like to help mother to become
independent. For instance, do you fight with each other?

SALLY: Sometimes.

DR. D.: Why?

SALLY: He gives my mother a hard time.

DR. D.: Now why are you saying that?

SALLY: Because of the tantrums.

DR. D.: Now may I explain to you? He wants to show mother and the rest of the world, "I can do what I want, and when I want to fight, I will fight." This is his way of defeating her. Mother can not stand it. So I have suggested to mother to become independent. About your getting up, that is your problem, about fighting; about many other things which you could not talk about. And I told her whenever she gets upset with anyone of you, to go to the bathroom, and to wait there until it's over. What do you think about that? Do you like that?

MIKE: She always does that.

DR. D.: Do you like it?

MIKE: No. Well I don't mind.

DR. D.: You don't mind. You try to get her out of the bathroom as quickly as possible. Don't you?

MIKE: Yes.

DR. D.: Because she hasn't used the radio yet, you see? When she has the radio, she will learn to become independent and then you will have to take care of yourself. What do you think about it? Is it a good idea?

MIKE: Yes.

DR. D.: Now do you want to say something? Not a word.

So I think and hope you have gotten at least some idea about our technique. I don't maintain that we really have solved the problem but we indicated the way in which it can be solved. Thank you very much.

Note

1 Comments addressed to the audience are in large type; the interview proper is in small type.

Case 17

Editors' Introduction

Possibly the single most important innovation in the last twenty years in psychotherapy has been the emergence of family therapy, which often is the treatment of a single person within a family context. The family therapist focuses primary attention on the interactions between members of the family rather than simply observing the identified patient.

As in the case of behavior therapy and behavior modification, there is an embarrassment of riches in that there are many excellent cases published in the field. It was somewhat difficult to make selections from those we read, but we believe that this story of a schizophrenic family as described by Umbarger and Hare is one that is memorable, and like the theater of the absurd, will remain with the reader a long time.

CARTER UMBARGER AND RACHEL HARE

A Structural Approach to Patient and Therapist Disengagement from a Schizophrenic Family

Several theorists have described families with a schizophrenic child as en-meshed (Mishler & Waxler, 1966). The family system is one in which each member is tightly interlocked with the others and any effort by one to change elicits immediate resistance on the part of the others. The difficulty in changing such family systems derives, in part, from the family's skillful induction of the therapist into inadvertent compliance with the affective, communicative, and structural transactions characteristic of the family.

Such inadvertent compliance has been called "suction" by Minuchin, *et al.* and is described as a process ". . . by which the therapist's choice of roles becomes restricted. He is compelled to behave in such ways that he would not generally choose. This can occur even when he senses that his behavior is being shaped to protect the family's equilibrium" (Minuchin, Montalvo, Guerney, Rosman, & Schumer, 1967). Frequently the therapist finds that even though the dynamic content of his interpretations is correct, it is offered in such a way as to preserve, virtually intact, a family structure that inhibits change, either in the unit or in its individual members.

The phenomena of suction and enmeshment are partially maintained by the communicative confusion and destruction of meaning, both denotative and connotative, so common in schizophrenic families (Schaffer, Wynne, Day, Ryckoff, & Halperin, 1962). Therapists are baffled by the seeming wealth of dynamic material and frustrated by their inability to focus effectively on any one theme or to render sensible the family's nonsense. The cumulative impact on the therapist can be discouraging, even overwhelming (Whitaker, Felder, & Warkentin, 1965). Therapeutic procedures with these families need to soften this experience, thus diminishing the family's ability to neutralize the therapist through suction. At the same time they should facilitate a healthy disengagement of parents and children from each other, thereby reducing the interactional "enmeshment" which inhibits healthy family development.

Several techniques have been suggested for combating induction into an

From *American Journal of Psychotherapy* 1973, 27, 274–284.

enmeshed family system. Bowen (1971) and Zuk (1968) advocate making an open alliance with one member of the family in order to disrupt a pathologic homeostatic balance. Minuchin *et al.* (1967) suggest that the therapist join the main affective axis of the family. Being more "crazy" than the crazy patient is one variation of this. Perhaps the most recommended technique is that of co-therapy (Zuk, 1968) and, on occasion, actually removing oneself from the situation by observing the family through a one-way mirror (Fulweiler, 1967).

Although these techniques are directed to the problem of enmeshment, there is very little in their *structural* arrangements to help the enmeshed family tolerate the individuation of a member from the family unit. Therapy procedures should have, in addition to opportunities for dynamically oriented interventions, a structural format that facilitates (a) the disengagement of the index patient from the family and (b) the freeing of the therapist from induction into a chaotic family system. In the case presented below, a review of the treatment history reveals little congruence between the structure and the goals of therapy.

The Decker Family

The family sought help because of the persistently peculiar behavior of Eddie, their twelve-year-old son, who had been diagnosed as schizophrenic. He had many bizarre mannerisms, speech that was often incoherent, an odd posture and gait, many fears, and numerous somatic complaints. On the other hand, he was of normal intelligence, attended a public school, had a small group of friends, and in general showed several areas of social and personal competence. Nevertheless, his sticky enmeshment with his father and mother put narrow and stringent limits on his development, and, as adolescence approached, he seemed increasingly immature and inappropriate in his behavior.

During the preceding four years the family had defeated a variety of therapeutic efforts, some thoughtful, others only momentarily clever. The history of these endeavors is one of debilitating struggle between therapists and family.

Eddie was first seen in play therapy when he was eight and some improvement was noted. Shortly thereafter Mr. and Mrs. Decker entered couple therapy, whereupon there was a recurrence of Eddie's symptoms. This eventually led them into family therapy, where several therapists tried techniques described earlier in the paper but with distressingly little sustained control or direction. Programs of "paradoxical intention" in the form of absurd tasks were instigated and then defeated as the family complied with every instruction in the obsessive and dehumanized manner that was part of their family style. Efforts to connect them with relevant social reference groups met similar failure. Treatment was sometimes disrupted as old therapists resigned and new ones volunteered. Eddie grew in stature but otherwise seemed more than ever entrapped in his family.

The following description of the Deckers and how they functioned together in therapy makes clear why a radically different therapy format was required if the family was ever to facilitate the growth of its individual members. The dialogue is a reconstruction, taken from taped interviews, of the interchanges which made the family so difficult to treat. The picture is one of a sad, hilarious, yet deeply troubled family. Beneath their strained gaiety was the desperate fear that Eddie was hopelessly ill and, between the parents, a bitter resentment for the loneliness each had endured in the course of their marriage. The dialogue points to the frantic uses of humor and the destruction of meaningful talk; it only hints at the darker moments of sadness and terror.

Harry and Imogene Decker seemed to costume themselves for the role of patients. Their outfits, down to the smallest detail, were comic parodies of a dress style fashionable only for the back wards of state mental hospitals. Theirs was a kind of chronic chic. Imogene, a small woman, wore pink sweat socks, blowsy skirts of indeterminate age and style, and mismatched blouses. Harry, a heavy man, was less floridly dressed, yet there was an unmistakable air of cultivated defiance about his clothes. His grey work pants, always several sizes too large, were bunched together at his waist by a beaded Indian belt. Like Imogene, he carried at least one paper shopping bag and sometimes two, filled with items that were indispensable only for a person going on the bum in an unfriendly climate: extra socks, woolen scarfs, a foreign language dictionary, and a box of Girl Scout cookies.

In the midst of the shuffle of parental shopping bags was Eddie. He was tall, ungainly, yet delicately made, a marionette whose strings were of the wrong length. He spoke in a high rapid voice, sometimes slurring his words so badly that even the most practiced and patient parent would have difficulty understanding him.

Therapy sessions inevitably began with this small family of three dividing themselves into two whirlwind armies who would descend on the therapist from opposite ends of the corridor. With gales of strained laughter they would finally enter the therapy room.

"I might choke to death," said Imogene, "since this room seems filled with chalk dust. Too much erasing, not enough correctness." She settled into one chair, then tried another, looking suspiciously under each chair for some evidence of dust and dirt. Harry was solicitous though uneasy with his wife's behavior. He offered to change seats with her, made a few ineffectual efforts to clean the blackboard, and then returned to his seat.

"There's dust at school, too," volunteered Eddie.

"Tell the doctor what happened there, if he wants to know," Mr. Decker said.

The therapist, feeling that a direction and topic were emerging, readily agreed. "By all means. What happened?" He was unaware that he had fallen in with Harry and Eddie who were effectively diverting attention from Imogene's odd behavior by introducing Eddie's school problems.

Eddie stared intently at his mother, never losing eye contact with her as he told his story. "I fell on the playground and scraped my side. Then when I got to the nurse's office I thought I might faint from the algebra left to do, so naturally I made the nurse call my mother and then I went home. And that's all of that. Aside from the three tongues." So saying, he seemed to consider the matter closed, although Mrs. Decker clearly had more on her mind.

"Thank God I was at home, the streets being what they are. Boy Scouts or no Boy Scouts," she concluded as a kind of mysterious afterthought.

"I think we should get down to an efficient discussion of why we are coming here, not why there are no Boy Scouts on the streets." Mr. Decker was again responding to his wife's meanderings by trying to organize the family.

"I thought we settled that last year," replied Mrs. Decker, "when we were worried about how Eddie was picked on in school. And his dizzy spells, some of which must be due to all the dust that's around."

"Is that what you've been worried about all this time?" asked Harry. "I thought you wondered about the fatigue of your mental processes and why your feet are swelling."

"Mother's feet don't swell," said Eddie heading off my focus on his mother.

"I'm sorry." Harry grinned weakly.

"Why can't you just be wrong like other men without having to be sorry all the time?" Mrs. Decker said. "Then our social life would improve."

The therapist, losing track of the bewildering school problems, moved quickly in support of Mrs. Decker's new topic. "Are you asking your husband to change something about your social life?" Though well intended, the question supported an implicit criticism of Mr. Decker and ignored his efforts of only a moment ago to "organize" the discussion, a typical fate for Mr. Decker's efforts to be efficient. As the therapist slipped from side to side, first in alliance with efforts to ignore Mrs. Decker's concern with a dusty, poisonous environment and then with *her* efforts to ignore Mr. Decker's attempt at organizing the family, he got a premonition of the trip to come.

Mrs. Decker grew wistful for a second. "We used to go to parties all the time, but the person who invited us died."

"I asked you to go to a meeting of Radicals Over Thirty with me and you refused. You complained that political people don't know how to polka. I mean I tried." Harry seemed genuinely hurt by his wife's attack.

The therapist, trying to hold onto a topic, said, "Each of you seems to really want the same thing, to do something together socially." He skipped over Harry's hurt feeling, inadvertently supporting Mrs. Decker's injunction that her husband should stop feeling "sorry" every time he was criticized. The family "rule" that mother should never be found wanting was being scrupulously, though inadvertently, observed by the therapist. Just to make sure, Imogene flared up, scooting to the edge of her chair. "Are you implying that we are a failure in social ethics?"

"Etiquette," said Harry.

"Ethical societies don't interest us and never will," Imogene continued. "Moreover there is nothing funny about trying to be ethical and I resent your implication that my husband and I aren't ethical."

"I only suggested that the two of you might do something social together . . . that is, not separate. Ah, thinking for the future . . . that is, since the past is over." The therapist was uncomfortable, but still trying to give cogent meanings to the conversation and smooth over ruffled feelings, a response typical of outsiders who tried to get inside this family.

"Mommy and Daddy can't go out," whined Eddie. "I need them at home to help me with my merit badges." He too was sitting on the edge of his chair, eyes fastened on his mother, with a glazed look, as if transported by thoughts of a merit badge in social ethics.

Suddenly, on some secret signal, all three members of the family arose and, crossing impolitely in front of the therapist, switched seats, each person moving over one chair.

"Whenever I stand up in here, the room gets small," said Eddie in his Alice-in-Wonderland voice.

"Then sit down!" replied the harassed therapist. He relaxed, happily unaware that he sounded just like one of the family.

"What is the rationale for peephole therapy?" asked Imogene, apparently referring to the observation mirror along one side of the room.

"Whatever it is," replied Harry in his efficient voice, while pulling a thermos from his shopping bag, "I think it's time for a tea break."

"It's always the same here," sighed Eddie taking a small wax cup of tepid tea. "Nothing ever changes, week after week."

"Better safe than sorry," commented Mrs. Decker dramatically.

"Precisely how many weeks has it been?" said Mr. Decker still dreaming of organization.

"Thirteen," said the therapist, holding out his cup.

Therapy Format

Many things made it difficult to deal with the Deckers: the disordered thinking of the mother; the collusion between father and son to circumvent and contain Mrs. Decker's peculiar associations by pretending they were part of a consensual concern; and, above all, the cat-footed equilibrium of the family triad, a gyroscopic sense of balance which held affect, communication, and power positions constant regardless of interventions by the therapist. The tenacity of the family in the face of obvious intrafamilial deviance and the efforts of the therapists to control that deviance was remarkable, even inspiring.

Certainly the suction phenomena account for some of the durability of the family system. In the dialogue above, for example, the therapist was easily led, following the father's cue, into focusing on the son's symptoms as though he were the sick one and mother perfectly sane. Regardless of content, a typical coalition for this family was that of father and son, called together in order to encapsulate the mother's peculiar behavior. The therapist inadvertently supported this coalition and thus failed to change the manner in which the family system made Eddie's symptoms so functional.

To avoid such induction, therapists require a breathing space, an opportunity for perspective and relief from confusion without waiting for the wisdom of hindsight. This breathing space can be provided by the therapy format. Moreover, where the family being treated is one with a schizophrenic child and where the task appropriate both to the child life's cycle and to that of the family is the differentiation and individuation of child from family, then the therapy format must also minimize the *child's* suction into the enmeshed family system.

From this perspective *we assume that both the therapist and the index patient have the same task vis-à-vis an enmeshed, schizophrenic family—to disengage in order to change.* The therapist needs to disengage in order to avoid suction and change the family system; the child needs to disengage in order to freely develop a reference group outside the family which will enhance his sense of autonomy and difference. Stated in terms of goals, the therapy format should (a) protect the therapist from induction into a destructive family system; (b) help the index patient disengage and grow into healthy adolescence, and (c) keep the family problem-oriented rather than therapist-oriented.

As for the third goal, we find that with families who are bright, verbal, and hostile, as well as sensitive to the nuances of interpersonal transactions, to pay exclusive attention to the transference aspects of patient-therapist encounters inevitably strengthens their hand. A therapist's sophisticated attention to transference content can weaken his perception of the structural aspects of family functioning and make his induction all the more likely.

Consequently, we feel it useful to provide a format that makes it difficult for the family to fasten on their personal relationship to the therapist. The format needs to disrupt the usual gestalt of shared expectations and covert familiarities that develop in most long-term therapist-patient relationships. A problem orientation helps the therapist establish such a format and protects him from the readiness of the family to use their personal feelings for him as the occasion for inducting him into the family system.

In consideration of these therapy goals, we devised the following therapy format in our treatment of the Deckers.

1. *Alternating Therapists.* There were two therapists each of whom saw the family on alternate weeks. The therapist who was not with the family observed the entire session from behind a one-way mirror. This arrangement was introduced to the family as one that would enhance our mutual efforts to help them solve their problems. We were quite explicit about the absent therapist being behind the mirror and were sure that at the beginning of each session both therapists were present in the hallway to greet the family.

Since this family delighted in deflecting attention from intrafamilial life to their interest in the therapists, we enforced two rules to minimize this tendency. The first was that they could not discuss the observing therapist, but would have to wait until the following week when that therapist would then be present. Second, if one therapist could not be present for a session, even if his role that week were only to observe, the session was canceled.

We believe that this procedure served (a) to keep the family problem-oriented rather than focus on their relationship to the therapist, (b) to reduce the chances of their "splitting the therapists," either by creating separate pairings with different family members or by tempting each therapist into inadvertently taking up different topics from the richness of the family's life, and (c) to offer the performing therapist the prospect of a breathing space, so he knew that in the following week he would enjoy the respite that comes from being an observer.

2. *Split Sessions and Restrictions—Beginning with the Family.* Each session was divided into two periods. During the first half the therapist met with the son and the two parents to discuss things related to promoting greater autonomy on the son's part. His conduct at school and on the playground might be discussed, or his club activities or his plans to take swimming lessons. Emphasis was on

how he and his parents hindered or helped this increase in separate activity; our explicit assumption was that they wanted him to be less involved in the symptoms that so often kept him homebound.

Consequently, we overlooked the obvious signs of distress which emerged, especially between the mother and son, whenever they contemplated any action that would separate them. The single exception to this was our successful restraint on the son that he not respond to his mother's anxiety by distracting us with his own bizarre talk. He understood that some of his remarks were irrelevant and was able, with the help of our reminder for "clear speech," to reduce drastically the frequency of this talk. A second restriction was that the parents not discuss affairs we labeled as essentially "adult" and relevant only to a married couple. This included many of their efforts to introduce highly sexualized material or to use their son as an arbiter of marital differences.

3. *The Mid-Session Break.*   The therapy hour was clearly divided into a time for parents and son and a time for husband and wife. This was accomplished by the therapist and son leaving the room together, the son to return to the waiting room and the therapist to confer with the colleague who was observing. This break had several advantages. First, it was the major bulwark against induction, since the performing therapist could seek the advice and distance of being, for a few minutes, associated with the observing therapist. Observations of family process, current mood, and possible strategy for the remainder of the hour were discussed.

On another level this pause emphasized the setting of generational boundaries in an enmeshed family where the lines between personal territories were few and scantily drawn. Indeed, we soon observed that following the departure of the son and during this temporary absence of the therapist, husband and wife began routinely to move their chairs closer together, presenting the returning therapist with a kind of united front. We wished to promote this unity since it was a marked shift from the scatter and spatial randomness that characterized seating patterns during the first half of the session.

4. *Split Sessions and Restrictions—Continuing with the Couple.*   Following the break, the therapist returned to begin discussion of the marital relationship. There were few restrictions here except the essential one: that content refer only to issues between them and not to the symptoms of their son. The content of this period tended to be highly personal, centering almost exclusively on the aspirations and disappointments each of them experienced in their marriage and on how they wanted changes for the future. The actual details of these discussions were perhaps less important than the fact that their attention was directed to their roles as husband and wife rather than as the parents of a disturbed child.

This redirection was facilitated by our policy of alternating therapists, which reduced their opportunities to seek pseudointimate relationships with us and instead kept the marital relationship as the principal focus. The heightened centrality of the couple and their separateness from the son served to reinforce an explicit message from the therapists, namely, that the husband and wife were the only two people who could, and would, deal with each other in the years ahead; their unit was clarified as a vital coalition into which no third person (principally their son) should intrude.

Therapy Outcome

The Decker family was seen for fifteen sessions over five months using the therapy format just described. The improvements were noted by ourselves and by previous therapists who observed some of the last few sessions. The most striking changes were seen in the son. Initially a boy of peculiar stance, nearly unintelligible speech, rampant somatic symptoms, unending fascination with his mother's every move, and a shrill, immature way of constantly intruding into his parents' conversations, he moved into adolescence as a boy with marked eccentricities but without any flagrant bizarreness.

He was capable of an increased number of activities outside of home and with other boys his age, remarking to his mother on one occasion, that "it isn't enough to have imaginary friends any more . . . I need some real friends." Though he retained many of his peculiar thoughts and ways of relating to people, he moved toward developing an eccentric position that would eventually be a recognizable and probably acceptable social role in larger society. His dress improved enormously, and he discarded many of his childish mismatched styles for the more fashionable ones of an early adolescent.

Both at home and in the therapy sessions his peculiar speech decreased. Other symptoms, especially those concerning his body, showed less improvement and continued to be signals to himself and to his parents that they were moving too fast toward separation and individual growth. On the other hand, with his mother's tacit approval, he greatly improved his ability to handle these somatic complaints without disrupting the daily social routines that gave some semblance of normality to his life.

An even more striking change was in his affect. Originally he was wildly manic and hilariously immature in his antics with his parents, constantly intruding into their every moment of being together. During the course of treatment he lost these qualities, becoming more and more subdued. There developed a sullen secretiveness about some of his activities, increasingly laced with outbursts of anger at his mother. On several occasions he nearly fought with his mother and was able to tell her to mind her own business, a sign that some sense of self-differentiation and of private territory was emerging. He seldom interfered with his parents and seemed to prefer the angry privacy of his increasing independence.

As for the parents, their changes were fewer and less dramatic, though mirror images of improvements in their son. They could sustain conversations with each other that were notable for their coherence and lack of sudden hostilities. In drawing closer together as a marital couple they increased their tolerance of an independent life for their son, though in any moment of stress they tended to draw him back into his old role as scapegoat. In their best moments, however, they were able to plan some future activities for themselves, to look forward to the time when the son would be gone from home and to put aside the chronic disappointments and resentments they had accumulated in silence for so many years.

The format made explicit the importance of drawing firm generational boundaries, thereby facilitating the disengagement of family members from each other. It also gave us an advantage in keeping the family focused on these key themes. For example, in previous therapies, the mother became competitively involved with female therapists over a question of "what makes a good parent." The mother's own feelings about having been inadequately mothered became confused with her feelings about what she was getting from the female therapist. In turn, she would attempt to involve her own son in a fight with the female therapist or in unending affirmations of her own worth as a mother.

Our format and the few rules it entailed avoided this triangulation by deferring the mother's concern until the second half of the therapy session when her son was gone and only her husband was present. This forced alliance with her husband had two results. First, the urgency of the mother's concern vanished when her son was gone and her husband was more in the picture. Second, it was the parenting *unit* that could now be the effective focus and tool for "being a good parent" rather than the highly personalized fantasies and events of the mother's experience of being a child. This example demonstrates the way in which attention to boundaries and the treatment unit helped the family sustain a problem orientation rather than become mired in their complicated responses to the therapists.

A final observation about our providing the couple with a well-bounded time for consideration of their life away from the son: this arrangement did not, in itself, help produce any change in the *structure* of the couple's relationship. Indeed, if anything, it helped preserve the awesome regularity with which the husband and wife made sure that no change ever occurred in their transactions with each other, though it did substantially short-circuit use of the child in their relationship.

One of the frustrating qualities of this family was their skill in neutralizing any inputs that might disrupt their system, and our format only increased their anxiety that one of them might change. This, in turn, intensified their efforts to undercut any apparent change. There was, however, a direct benefit from this heightening of their pathologic sensitivity to change between themselves— namely, it gave greater freedom for the son to go about his own business. As the mother and father turned more and more to the maintenance of their regulatory devices, they became less invested in making the son conform to the experiential pathways of an enmeshed family.

Summary

We have outlined a family therapy format for use with enmeshed schizo-phrenic families where the index patient is a child and where the life-cycle task of both patient and family is individuation through disengagement from the family system. These families are highly resistant to change, maintaining their balance by the continual destruction of meaningful communication, and rendering the therapist ineffective through suction. The format presented here reflects our viewpoint that patient and therapist can disengage themselves from such a system only when the structural aspects of therapy are congruent with the goals of establishing individual boundaries.

References

Bowen, M. The use of family theory in clinical practice. In Boszormenyi-Nagy, I., & Framo, J. (Eds.), *Intensive Family Therapy*. New York: Grune & Stratton, 1971.

Fulweiler, C. R. No man's land. In Haley, F., & Hoffman, L. (Eds.), *Techniques of family therapy*. New York: Basic Books, 1967.

Minuchin, S., Montalvo, B., Guerney, B., Rosman, B., & Schumer, F. *Families of the slums*. New York: Basic Books, 1967.

Mishler, E., & Waxler, N. Family interaction processes and schizophrenia. *International Journal of Psychiatry*, 1966, *2*, 37–48.

Rubinstein, D., & Weiner, O. R. Co-therapy teamwork relationships in family therapy. In Zuk, G. H., & Boszormenyi-Nagy, I. (Eds.), *Family therapy and disturbed families*. Palo Alto, Calif.: Science & Behavior Books, 1967.

Schaffer, L., Wynne, L., Day, J., Ryckoff, I., & Halperin, A. On the nature and sources of the psychiatrist's experience with the family of the schizophrenic. *Psychiatry*, 1962, *25*, 32–45.

Whitaker, C., Felder, R., & Warkentin, J. Countertransference in the family treatment of schizophrenia. In Boszormenyi-Nagy, I., & Framo, J. (Eds.), *Intensive family therapy*. New York: Harper & Row, 1965.

Zuk, G. When the family therapist takes sides: A case report. *Psychotherapy*, 1968, *5*, 24–28.

Case 18

Editors' Introduction

Harold Greenwald deserves a special place in the history of psychotherapy, and the reading of this case history, presented here for the first time, will explain why. He falls into the same category as Will Schutz and George Bach in being idiosyncratic and unpredictable, and yet he has the disciplined training of behavior modifiers in the search for order and regularity.

To watch Greenwald operate is pure pleasure. As in the case of Moreno, who was also a prime showman, Greenwald in demonstrating his techniques (and he seems to work best in front of an audience) can move the group from tears to laughter and back within minutes, always alive, always on point, always fixed on the objective.

We are all lucky to have this selection. It is a previously unpublished gem which we think will genuinely please the reader.

HAROLD GREENWALD

The Case of Marie

It was shortly after I had first presented the theory now known as Direct Decision Therapy that I was invited to give a lecture and demonstration for the staff of a psychiatric hospital. Before describing the theory, I asked if they could supply a patient who had volunteered to be treated in front of the staff. I have found this a very useful way of teaching both the technique and theory of psychotherapy and, incidentally, had frequently found that patients who are treated in that kind of a group situation do not feel exploited but instead, frequently, make dramatic progress. It has seemed to me that it is often a valuable adjunct to ongoing therapy.

When they first brought Marie into the room in which I was supposed to treat her, I felt my heart sink because she seemed like the typical, hopeless, backward schizophrenic. She was wearing a shapeless bathrobe, soft-sole carpet slippers; her hair was stringy, no makeup, unkempt with a kind of wild and vacant look in her eyes.

I said, "Won't you sit down please?"

She answered, "I'll sit down when I'm ready."

I then asked her her name.

She said, "Didn't you hear the doctor introduce me? I'm Marie."

I said, "I'm sorry, Marie. I didn't catch it at first, but I'm wondering if there is anything you would like me to do for you. Is there any way in which I can help you?"

Her answer was, "You can't help me. Why don't you leave me alone? Why are you bothering me? Why are all you people after me all of the time?" And her voice rose to a shriek and she became rather incoherent, just spilling a whole list of expletives.

I yelled almost as loud as she had and demanded, "Marie, cut it out. You don't have to speak that way."

Suddenly she became aware. Her eyes looked at me with a new understanding and with a slight smile she said, "How did you know?"

I answered, "Because it takes one to know one," at which point Marie gave herself permission to have a full, wide, knowing grin. (Years later when I discussed her progress with her, Marie was to tell me that that was the best thing that had ever happened because finally she had met a doctor who was "crazier" than she.) So I went back to asking her, "What would you like? How can I help you?"

Her answer was, "Get me out of this crazy place."

I asked, "Are you sure?"

She said, "Yes, I'm sure. I want to get out of this crazy place."

I said, "If you really do, Marie, you have to make a very simple decision."

"What's that?" she asked.

I said, "Just decide to act sane. But before you do, let me ask you some questions."

"OK, do that. At least, I think *you* might understand what I'm telling you, not like these other idiots here," she said, pointing at the staff sitting behind the table with me.

I asked, "Marie, when did you decide to act crazy?"

She replied, "That's an easy question. I don't know why nobody ever asked me that before. When I was five years old I was having an argument with my mother and she said, 'You're crazy,' and I thought to myself, if you think I'm crazy now, I'll show you what crazy is. And after that I was terrible. I became worse. I was taken to every doctor in town. This is the third hospital I have been in. They have given me all kinds of pills but all they do is make me worse."

"Marie," I said, "are you sure you want to give this up? Aren't you getting anything out of it?"

She looked at me and said, "I thought you had some sense. Of course I get things out of it. For one, I have complete social security. I never have to work in my life if I don't want to. I can stay here and they will take care of me for the rest of my life. Another thing is that I don't have to look for a job. I don't have to go to work. They will always take care of me. The third thing is I don't have to listen to my mother say, 'Why don't you go out like other girls do?' because there are enough crazy guys here. I meet them down in the boiler room and we have a good time. And furthermore, most important of all, I can say whatever I want to my mother. I can even kill her because I'm crazy."

So I asked her, "If you can do all of those things and you're getting so many great payoffs from being crazy, why should you stop?"

She said, "I want to be a part of life."

"OK, if that's what you really want," I said, "and make sure that's what you want; if you're really willing to give up all these things you told me about, then I can tell you what to do."

"Yes," she insisted. "I'm sick and tired of this. I want to be a part of life."

"OK," I said. "Then it's easy. All you have to do is decide to *act* sane. You see, the only difference between you and us is that we are all crazy but we have decided to act sane." (I was pointing at myself and the other doctors who were sitting across the table from Marie.)

She smiled and replied, "You're telling me. I know you're all crazy. You're the first one that ever admitted it."

I said, "OK, how do you feel about acting sane?"

She said, "OK, I'm going home this weekend and I'm going to act sane."

I asked, "What do you think will happen when you go home and you act sane with your family?" (I have often found it necessary to help people who are making a change to understand what their families' reaction may be when that change takes place.) So I repeated the question, "How do you think your family will act?"

Marie answered, "They will be delighted."

My answer was, "I don't think so. So if you want to act sane, you do that, if that's what you want. But don't expect all that delight from your family."

I came back a few days later for another session, and Marie was present again, and I asked her, "How did it go at home?"

She replied, "You must know my family because when I got there and told them that I had been speaking to you and that I was going to act sane, my sister said, 'Oh my, that American professor really drove our Marie crazy. She's sicker than ever now.' How do you like that?" she asked. "And I really acted very sane and very differently." Already she looked different. She had taken some care with her clothes. She looked a little better, hardly the best dressed woman in the world, but certainly better than I had seen her the first time.

It happened that I was in that hospital on a number of occasions and had an opportunity to see Marie several times. There was one other session, a lengthy session, when I was giving a workshop on psychotherapy to some other people, and Marie came from the hospital to be present at the workshop. This time we agreed that she could take a chance on expressing some of her fantasies and didn't have to be fearful about them. So she expressed several fantasies in which she killed her mother in a variety of ways, the most graphic of which was that she chopped her up into little pieces and fried her with onions for her father's meal. She felt, as she said, good about having been able to express all that rage and anger and didn't have to be crazy to do it.

She now realized that there was an option, that instead of having to act crazy, whenever she felt angry, she could express the anger directly and openly and also that she could, as she said, decide to give herself permission to have fantasies about what she would like to do instead of trying to do it to these people.

I left the area but continued to correspond with Marie. She wrote me some very exciting and touching letters. Finally she got out of the hospital, and shortly after she was out of the hospital, she wrote me a letter telling me something like this:

"If I had known how hard it is to be on the outside, how hard it is to be sane, and if I had you here, I'd kick your ass up to the top of the Rocky Mountains. You didn't warn me how difficult it was to be in the sane world." She then went on to describe having gone to a party and finding herself the outsider, not knowing how to speak to people. "For after all," she said, "I had lived like a nun, away from the world, in the cloistered atmosphere of mental hospitals for so many years, that I really didn't know how to behave."

A few months later I was back in town and saw Marie and we discussed this problem. I asked, "What do you do when you go to a party?"

She said, "I try not to talk because I don't want the people to know how crazy I was."

I said, "Well, that's one way, but you could do something else."

She asked, "What's that?"

I told her, "You could make yourself the center of attention by telling them how crazy you were and how cured you are now."

She said, "I'll try it!"

She wrote me back, shortly thereafter, saying that she had gone to a party and she told people that she had been crazy and that she had been in the nut house, the fruit farm, and they were fascinated by her stories and they just thought she was fantastic to be able to talk about it so openly and freely. She continued to make progress and when the summertime came along, she was now out of the hospital. She dressed up very well. She was hiking. She had gone for a long backpack trip, had run into one of her psychiatrists from the hospital and she said, "That woman doctor was livid with jealousy when she saw how attractive I was and what a good looking man I had with me."

A few months later Marie was married. A year later she had a child. About three months after having the child, she wrote me saying, "You know, when my daughter was born I began to find life too much for me. I not only had to take care of her and my husband, but as you know, I have gone back to school and I had to complete my studies. I began to think that it was too much for me and found myself drifting off the way I used to in the past. And then I was reminded of your philosophy and said to myself, 'No, I can decide to be the kind of wife and mother I want to be.' That helped me a great deal." She completed her studies and the last time I heard from her, which is now about two years ago, she had made a very good adaptation. She had another child. She was a good wife. She said her husband loved her very much. And she was operating three nursery schools in a small city which they had moved to and settled in. She also sent the following letter to describe her experience with me:

The Ringmaster

Actually he was not that. It was only a name they had put on him. For he loved strong effects, things outside the program, laughter. Yes, he didn't even flinch from ridiculing himself if it only could bring him nearer his target.

Actually he was a professor. Which serious professor would accept to be called a ringmaster? Or enjoy the nickname Old Nick (the devil)? But his colleagues listened to him and tried to learn. For with all sorts of tricks and ways, he got the patients on his side—in the fight against their illness. "I am just as crazy as you," he could say. Then the patient might wonder if being looked upon as normal was anything to struggle for. For when the normal was so strange, then—

Those who knew him, loved him. He came into a dark and closed world and brought with himself hope. He didn't conceal what it cost to be on his side, to struggle towards health. He didn't conceal it, but— The fight he talked about, had he not gone through it himself, he did not with the deepest of his mind know what it meant to leave a world that one's own mind had made up and fight towards a world that is very tough—the real world. If it is tough for the average man—it is even tougher for one coming from the mental hospital. Some did not dare the decision. The darkness is a good friend.

But he got results, results nobody had thought possible. Nobody except himself, for he knew what he was doing.

Those two became friends. Such good friends that she more or less started to look at herself as a star number in the circus. In an amicable way they fought at serious seminars so that the partakers forgot their dignity and laughed. She never knew what could happen when she talked to him, neither when they were alone, nor in a room full of authorities. He was perhaps the greatest of them all, but he despised the pedestal of the authority and instead he came into the world of the patient as an equal. Perhaps that is the key to his enormous results?

By Marie

Marie is an example of the approach to therapy known as Direct Decision Therapy. The technique of Direct Decision Therapy illustrated in this case can be summarized in the following steps:

1. The patient or client is asked to state his or her problem as completely as possible. In encouraging the statement of the problem, the patient is sometimes asked, "What goal do you have?" because decision therapists have found it more useful to speak in terms of goal rather than problem. Marie made her goal clear. It was to get out of the hospital.

2. The next and important and a really original part of Direct Decision Therapy is in Step 2 where the patient and therapist together examine the past decisions which helped create the problems which are preventing the patient from reaching his goal. In discussing past decision, it is clear that this decision may not be in awareness. Therefore, the therapist will help the patient become aware of his decisions as they express themselves both in his activity and his attitudes and philosophy of life. Marie clearly remembered having made such a decision and expressed it. Incidentally, I have frequently found it easier to utilize this method and get quicker results with so-called psychotics than with many neurotics who are much more defended against remembering and being aware of the decisions which have led them into their situation.

3. Another innovative step in Direct Decision Therapy is the examination of the payoffs for the past decisions which are behind the problem. These payoffs may be positive such as gaining attention or experiencing feelings of superiority, or they may be the negative payoff of avoiding anxiety. Marie was able to

verbalize clearly the payoffs for her psychoticlike behavior, the security and probably the most important emotional payoff of all, being able to speak to the mother in the way that she wanted to.

4. The question is then asked, "What is the context within which this decision was originally made?" Direct Decision therapists believe that all decisions, when first made, had validity to the person making them, that though they may no longer be functional, they were once very important to the psychic economy of the individual.

5. The patient is then invited to examine what options he has or what alternatives he has to function in a way other than that based on his past decision. For example, many clients suffer from a decision to perfectionism in which they try to do everything as well as they possibly can. This may have been important for them in their early functioning because this was the only way they felt they could survive within their own particular family. When they are asked to examine the options, some will see that they no longer need such perfectionist demands but can accept their human limitations and while still trying to do well, will not attack themselves for not doing as well as they might like to do. Their decision, their new option or new decision which they may consider may then be that they will try to do as well as they can but will still accept the possibility of not fulfilling their own exalted demands on themselves.

6. A new decision is made and the client is helped to carry through this decision. A great deal of the emphasis in therapy frequently requires help in carrying through this new decision. For example, if somebody has decided to withdraw from the world because they found it too anxiety-provoking and now makes a decision to go forth to be more assertive, to enter into both social and intellectual relationships, the therapist may help him develop through practice, homework, a series of aids, self-administered rewards, in carrying through this new decision. It is also made clear that many of these decisions have to be made over and over again. If, for example, the individual makes a decision to lose weight, if it is not put into practice, it is considered only a wish. It only becomes a decision when it is put into practice, and the client is helped to see that the decision must be made over and over again every time the individual sits down to eat. Also he is helped to see that just because he fails once in not carrying out this decision to limit his weight, it does not mean that he has to give up the entire procedure of dieting but that he can return and try to carry out the decision in the future.

References

Greenwald, H. The integration of behavioral, existential and psychoanalytic therapy into direct decision therapy. *Journal of Contemporary Psychotherapy,* 1971, *4,* 37–43.

———. *Direct decision therapy.* San Diego: Edits, 1973.

———. Decision therapy. *Personal Growth,* 1974, *20,* 7–15.

Case 19

Editors' Introduction

Dorothy Baruch and Hyman Miller, husband and wife, psychologist and allergist, collaborated in the treatment of patients with allergies who were not responding to medications. They had impressive successes even with individuals who had failed to respond to conventional medical treatment for many years.

Baruch used as her vehicle of treatment the employment of spontaneous drawings, and this selection well illustrates her methodology and results. This item has interest not only in that it is an example of psychosomatic treatment but also because it is the only example of pure group therapy which we present. While the selections describing the work of Perls, Moreno, and Dreikurs discuss individuals treated in groups, none of these accounts, strictly speaking, is group therapy, while the Baruch and Miller article is an example of a conventional therapy group employing an unconventional procedure—spontaneous drawings, which through interpretation help to affect personality change.

While we have been unable to reproduce the patients' actual drawings, they are well described in the text and are available in the journal in which the case was originally published *(American Journal of Psychotherapy,* Vol. 5 (1951), pp. 45–58).

DOROTHY W. BARUCH AND HYMAN MILLER

The Use of Spontaneous Drawings in Group Therapy

Pictorial images, both structured and unstructured, have been established in the Rorschach, TAT, Szondi, and other tests as psychological tools for diagnostic purposes on the basis of the individual's projections. Paintings and drawings by the individuals themselves have also been seen to possess diagnostic value (Altschuler & Hattwick, 1947; Liss, 1938; Schmidl-Waehner, 1942; Schube & Cowell, 1939; White, 1944). Some studies have dealt with the therapeutic values as well (Arlow & Kadis, 1946; Elkisch, 1948; Fleming, 1940; Goetein, 1943; Goetein, 1944; Mosse, 1940; Naumberg, 1947; Shaw, 1938; Wickes, 1948; Wolff, 1947.)

Motion pictures have been reported as an effective aid in group therapy (Prados, 1948). But to the authors' knowledge, paintings and drawings done by patients themselves have not been utilized as an adjunct in interview group therapy. Consequently when patients began to bring their drawings of dreams, fantasies, memories, and the like into the therapy group which will be described presently, a problem was posed. Could their pictures be utilized to the benefit of the group as a whole? And if so, how could this be done?

The therapy group in question consisted of twenty members with ages ranging approximately from twenty to forty and with the sexes about equally divided, including four married couples. Half the group were allergic patients, the other half had entered for help on personality problems.

Although the individual members of the group shifted as one patient finished and a new one came in, the composition of the group was maintained as described in a former report (Baruch & Miller, 1947). The individuals were all nonpsychotic, consisted mainly of patients with mixed neuroses, and included several parents who had entered primarily to benefit their children.

The group met weekly for a period of an hour and a half in the informal atmosphere of the home of the therapist and the physician who acted as leader and coleader respectively. As described in another report (Baruch, 1945), the group atmosphere was permissive and its functioning dynamically oriented.

From *American Journal of Psychotherapy,* 1951, *5,* 45–58.

Complete stenographic protocols were made of each session. The following material is taken from these. Because of the necessary brevity of the excerpts, they fail to give the sense of time span, depth, and the group's multiple interactions.

The drawings just began when several group members had spent an evening with one member who had been taking painting lessons. Their host suggested that they try to draw their feelings "like children do, freely." They fell in with his idea although only one had had any technical training. They were so excited by some of their results that they brought these into the group.

Immediately various group members reacted, "It looks to me as if Jane meant this" or "Andy had tried to show that." Their attempt was to decipher what the other person had been feeling, making each artist in his turn the specimen on the pin, to be dissected and exposed. Even though much of this was projection, it was considered too indirectly focused.

The therapist pointed out that more might be gotten out of the pictures if each person "put himself" into them instead of attempting to interpret any other person's meanings. From time to time it was asked, "What does this picture mean to each of you? What does it tell you about *yourself* and your own feelings?" Or again, "What do *you* see in it? What does it remind *you* of?"

As the weeks went on, other members of the group voluntarily bought chalk or paints and brought in pictures which they had done at home. In the group they continued to respond with their own associations. As one of the members said, "You don't look at these like paintings in a painting class. They're like Rorschachs. If I see confusion in them and resent it, I'm resenting the confusion in myself."

Turning now to some of the pictures—the first three are by Andy, thirty-four, an obese man who had had persistent and severe asthma since the age of four. He was a laboratory technician, was changing jobs continuously and was having a severe economic struggle to maintain his wife and four-year-old child. When he first came into the group he was wheezing constantly and sat on the fringes of the group circle with his back turned toward the other members. He spoke extremely slowly and hesitantly and in a barely audible monotone. He often arrived unkempt and unshaven. All in all, he was the typical passive dependent asthmatic described in the literature (Alexander & French, 1941), his aggression greatly repressed. Sexually he suffered from premature ejaculation. As would be expected, his wife "wore the pants." (She was, incidentally, referred to another office for analysis.)

Andy brought in this first picture . . . seven months after he had entered the group and after he had been in for an occasional individual session. On seeing it lying on the table several people exclaimed without knowing who had done it, "That's a self-portrait of Andy!" It shows him as he felt himself to be at this time. An amorphous baby.

During the discussion, Andy elucidated. "I feel," he said, "something of nothing . . . flaccid, pudgy . . . myself with my parents . . . my asthma and me . . .

they press me down, weigh me down with guilt. They cover up their real feelings with kindness. They're hitting me over the head with kindness, closing me in, stifling me with kindness. I've no masculine or feminine qualities . . . I feel just an empty shell. Sexless. I wish I could cry."

With continuing attendance in the group and the occasional individual sessions he requested, Andy's asthma improved considerably. Intermittent attacks coincided with periods of resistance and gradually lessened in frequency and decreased in severity. After fourteen months of therapy his condition was characterized in his medical record as mildly instead of severely asthmatic. During the next eleven months he was comparatively clear. By this time his personality had also undergone marked changes. He had assumed a more aggressive role in his marriage relationship and no longer suffered from premature ejaculation. He had, moreover, assumed a more positive position in regard to his child, and had held his jobs longer. He had taken off weight and appeared neater. He now sat *in* the group face to face and spoke in a louder voice with more color and inflection.

And then—one night he came into the group in a severe asthmatic attack and related that his wife, Elsa, had "fooled him" and had become pregnant despite his outspoken opposition. The group unanimously expressed indignation—how angry they would feel if in his boots. But he could not get angry. All he could do was feel sorry for himself. Helpless.

At the next meeting, still wheezing severely, he brought in the next picture of a mother and child . . . After a good deal of associating, he decided, "That little figure is me who wants to get that close to my mother. I am wallowing in her, my head in her breasts. That is the desire I have for closeness. But it's also the fear of the closeness."

> NED (*who had been having great difficulty in facing his attachment to his mother*): I would like to be the little child. The softness and warmth of the breasts; I would feel loved and accepted . . . Sucking the nipples is good . . . A sex desire in me . . .
>
> TOM (*whose difficulty had been in admitting hostility toward his mother*): I want all the things Ned was talking about, but, (*tentatively*), I want to kick her, too . . .
>
> DIANA (*who had been in an extremely resistant period*): I don't see any child, but a chicken.
>
> *Therapist*: The child is like a nothing to you.
>
> DIANA: It's disgusting.
>
> NORA (*a frigid girl*): Being that close to anyone is repulsive to me . . . I want it but I'm afraid.
>
> TOM (*no longer tentative about his hostility*): I would like to pull out all her guts like a butcher with a chicken . . . Disembowel her . . .

As was their custom by now, the various group members projected their own feelings into the picture and associated to it.

Then Andy said, "I'm associating Elsa's having a child and my mother having my sister. I wanted to kill that child . . . wanting to kill my mother. Being that close and being suffocated. She's holding my penis and if I leave her I'd lose my masculinity. Now it is being brought to the present day with Elsa. Here she is having another child . . . and she is very dangerous to me."

ROY (*who had been denying a deep sense of his mother's desertion*): I feel the mother isn't making an effort to hold the baby close.

And Andy, his aggression mobilized by group interaction, "I didn't say that . . . I said *I* was trying to get closer. I *wanted* to be that close to her . . . my head against her breast. Mother's arm under my body holding my penis. I had the feeling when painting it that I was in an asthmatic attack and calling her to hold me that way."

DIANA (*coming out of her resistance no longer seeing "a nothing"*): She is masturbating the baby with the hand that is hidden.

ALICE (*an asthmatic who had experienced extreme maternal rejection*): She's too preoccupied to think about the baby . . .

THERAPIST: What does it mean to each one of you about yourselves now?

ALICE: I want to be very close . . .

NED: It would feel good . . .

NORA: It makes me sick. I can't stand it . . . certainly I don't want a child hanging onto me.

JANE: I still see myself in that position. I still feel like that child with intense desire for my mother . . .

THERAPIST: How do you express it?

JANE: Right now by moaning and groaning that nobody loves me . . . I never realized I couldn't get this from mother and I'm still trying . . .

At the next session Andy was still wheezing. He again brought in the picture and this time related more of his present feelings to it. He said, "Elsa's having a child has thrown me into the state of an angry four- or five-year old. Since I can't let loose and beat up my mother, I'm afraid I will beat Elsa up . . . I've been putting all the blame on myself. I still want love but I feel murderous and still want to kill that child that's in her. It takes away from me. I hate her and want to get even . . . I'm full of self-pity. I don't want to accept any of the responsibility of an adult . . . When something like this happens I feel rejected and want to beat and jump on whoever it is. My relationship with Elsa is getting unbearable. I would really like to beat the hell out of my mother to break the spell she has held over me all these years."

And then, for the very first time, he became aggressive to the therapist. After listening for a while to others talk, he went back to his own childhood.

"When you're a child," he said, "you have to compete with adults. They have another child without asking you or telling you. . . ."

The therapist intervened, "And your wife now?"

Andy turned on her angrily. "Never mind *that*. *I'm* talking . . . and. . . ."

"But the way I feel," June, another member, inadvertently interrupted.

"June! Please!" Andy pounded, "*I* have something to say. . . ."

He went on talking, then commented, "For the first time I don't feel guilty about interrupting," and he finally stated clearly that he resented having this child.

After this meeting, the physician noted that his wheezing was less. During the week, however, it again increased. He came into the next session with a new picture [depicting oral stimulation of a male's exaggerated genitalia]. "I would like to show a picture of mine—though I would not really like to because I don't know what is going to come out. . . ." Then, after the group had associated for a bit, he said, "When I painted it I had no good idea of what I was going to paint. I had to go through the painting of background first—in other words, the problem didn't exist. That is what I've done in my everyday living—do the background—to cover what is really bothering me. . . ."

The therapist said, "You still don't quite want to get to what you've been living through."

Andy answered, "I certainly don't feel like it. But, taking away all that obscure color and coming to the real issue . . . I have finally come to where I want to grab Elsa by her hair so she will be helpless like I am with the asthma that has been choking me all my life. Make her suffer with no escape.

"In the past I've been a very little boy with a small penis, overpowered by my mother, seeking affection and running to her. Then turning the penis into my own throat and getting asthma. That is what intercourse works into somehow. I have been so sick lately. When I have intercourse I get asthma right in the middle of it. I choke up as though the penis were in my throat and I can't breathe."

He paused, and resumed thoughtfully, "I remember something when I was a little boy—five—one day I started to swear at them . . . terrible swear words. I called my father a bastard and my mother a cocksucker . . . They beat me . . . All I can think of was the rage and helplessness and I wanted to kill them . . . It was also the time my mother was bearing my sister. . . ."

And later, after a lot more discussion, "I feel if I had my father's penis which would be big enough, I'd choke her with it. I want to do it to my wife now and I'm scared stiff of it. . . ."

Still later, "I felt all these things tonight. . . . What I wanted to do was to ram my penis down my mother. Now I want to make Elsa suffer . . . but I am suffering because I do it to myself. . . ."

A little while after he noticed that he had stopped wheezing and he commented, "I've been so panicky and full of asthma because I couldn't get these feelings out."

During the following two and a half months, up to the time of reporting, he had no attacks of asthma. In spite of his continuing and outspoken resentment at his wife's trickery, their relationship improved. He accepted her pregnancy as he showed when he stated a month after the last picture, "I'm not a little boy any longer. I have this responsibility."

The second series of pictures is by a redheaded man, married and childless, thirty-eight years old. He came into the group at his wife's instigation because of the dispersed hostility which was affecting his personal relations and professional career. At first he had not been able to express affect toward his parents, but he was now openly hostile toward them for the rejection he felt. When he brought in his picture of a figure hanging from a gibbet . . . various group members started projecting themselves into it and associating to it.

A married woman who during childhood had been attacked by her father and had wanted to punish him said, among other things, "It looks like a castrated figure. The penis is cut off."

A divorced man who consistently denied both fear and hostility to his parents and characteristically let out aggression in cynical witticisms, said, "All I can think of is a nursery rhyme about a pecked off pecker." A few minutes later, however, he grew more forthright, saying, "They killed my father and mother. Then I had guilt feelings and hung myself."

A very aggressive woman who had recently lost her father and separated from her husband took the female figure on the gibbet for a man, exclaiming, "Hang him until dead, dead, dead."

And a man, extremely repressed and resistant, said, "It seems like there is not really any rope there . . . as though the figure is hanging but without rope. Nothing really there."

Tom, who had started expressing his aggression in the earlier session with Andy's picture now said, "Kill someone. Stick them in the belly," and then he recalled that at three, he had run at his mother with a broomstick when she was pregnant with his younger brother, wishing "to kill the baby in her belly."

A dependent, asthmatic woman took the rope in another manner. She said, "I have the feeling that it is really an umbilical cord, tying me to my mother."

Bill, who had drawn it, said, "I was having a fantasy and this noose here kept getting into it. I thought I had to draw a picture about it. I started the picture with just a noose in it. Then I discovered I was putting my mother's head in the noose . . . Then for some reason I said, 'She has to be pregnant.' I made her pregnant . . . everything is dead except the turkey . . . the dead wolf is my father. He can't get to my mother. I'm the turkey. I got rid of my father by killing the wolf. You know what wolves are in common parlance. . . . "

The bayonets reminded him of war and he then remembered that his mother had been pregnant with his younger sister when World War I was declared. "I'm jealous of the child," he said, "and I want to get inside there myself and also my peter. . . . I'm the turkey. I was bad. My behind was spanked black and blue like the turkey's."

For the next few months he kept reiterating the hostility to his mother and expressed it also in his relation to the therapist. And then he brought in the picture of his "redheaded horse.". . . He said the horse had red hair like himself. The redheaded horse was himself, bringing his "crap" as a gift to the therapist.

From this time on he became more openly ambivalent to his mother, expressing this also in his relationship to the therapist whom he called "mama." Furthermore he reiterated hostility to the physician who was coleader of the group and to whom the therapist was married. Bill called him "papa." He grew especially antagonistic to him when he and the therapist moved to a new home. At the first group session there, Bill carried on his own little psychodrama, sulked in the hall, came in sullenly and accused "papa" of moving "mama" further away from where he himself lived. Then he brought in a picture which he described as a "lonely baby," turning to himself and sucking his own foot for comfort . . . and "doing his doodoo."

During discussion, when he was asked what the bowel movement looked like, he replied quickly, "A pawn to get the other guy's queen."

Then he associated that his mother was a fanatic on cleanliness and that as a child he'd gotten his mother "away from the other guy"—his father—by prolonged "messing" so that she had had to wash him clean.

The remaining pictures will be described more briefly.

A repressed woman showed in her "green devil" . . . how she had felt crushed all her life. Her own lack of expressiveness was reflected in the baby's ex'd out features.

The same woman a few months later brought in a picture which led to the recollection that her grandfather, a physician, had given her vaginal douches when she was small. This she associated with masturbation fantasies and guilt which had made her "sew herself up" and become frigid. . . .

The frigid woman who had been attacked by her father in childhood brought in a picture of herself as a "woman without a uterus," . . . being killed by a black widow spider, which reminded her of her mother, and being injected with venom by a green snake whose color she "had to admit" she "especially liked."

Another woman who had been attacked by an adult relative when she was six, and who incidentally had never before drawn, brought in a chalk drawing remarkable in its primitive form and balance. . . . After a good deal of associating, she finally put it together. "The little girl," she said, "it's me. The big one is a man who practiced a perversion of sex on me when I was a child. The whip is his penis and he was whipping me with the fire that burned within him. He sets me on fire with his perversion. . . . I didn't know what I was painting when I did it but that's what it turned out to be." In associating to the birdlike figure in the upper right corner, she recalled that he had told her to "take the little birdie in her mouth."

Alice, the passive dependent asthmatic referred to earlier, brought in a picture of "a little girl wandering through the trees. . . . She looks like a doll with a big question mark. . . . Shock! Or blank face! The round things on the path are tracks . . . stones . . . beads . . . *Rings!* My mother's engagement ring. I wanted it all my life."

Another member of the group exclaimed, "I'm afraid to look up in that tree!"

Alice said, "That reminds me, I finished the picture about a week ago but felt I'd left something out. I didn't know what. And all of a sudden my chalk just made those marks in the tree. Then I felt satisfied. My picture was done." And she pointed out the trifoil in the tree above the little girl's head.

Various members of the group said this looked to them like a penis and testicles or a man's head. "It's my father!" Alice exclaimed. "My mother's engagement ring led me to him. It was my father I wanted all my life."

These are only a few of the pictures that have been brought into this group. Seeing their effectiveness in stimulating associations, the therapist subsequently introduced the idea of bringing pictures into several other groups and found that their effect was similar.

It is hoped that the presentation here will stimulate other workers to further experimentation since the experience so far has raised many possibilities as yet unexplored.

Summary

This paper has dealt with the use of spontaneous drawings and paintings of patients in group therapy. It briefly gives the composition and character of the group. It tells how members originally brought in their pictures and describes the techniques which evolved for using them therapeutically in the group.

From the exploration to date it has appeared that the drawings served as stimulus for release and helped toward increasingly deep insights, not only for the individual who produced the picture but for other group members as well.

References

Alexander, F., & French, T. M. *Psychogenic factors in bronchial asthma.* Psychosomatic Monograph IV, National Research Council, Washington, D. C., 1941.

Altschuler, R. H., & Hattwick, L. *Paintings and personality: A study of young children.* Chicago: University of Chicago Press, 1947.

Arlow, J. A., & Kadis, A. Finger painting in the psychotherapy of children. *American Journal of Orthopsychiatry,* 1946, *16,* 134–146.

Baruch, D. W. Description of a project in group therapy. *Journal of Consulting Psychology,* 1945, *9,* 271–280.

———— & Miller, H. Interview group psychotherapy with allergy patients. In Slavson, S. R. (Ed.), *The practice of group psychotherapy.* New York: International Universities Press, 1947, pp. 156-175.

Elkisch, P. The scribbling game—a projective method. *The Nervous Child,* 1948, *7,* 247–256.

Fleming, J. Observations on the use of finger painting in the treatment of adult patients with personality disorders. *Character and Personality,* 1940, *8,* 301–310.

Goetein, L. P. Diary of fellatio. *Journal of Criminal Psychopathology,* 1943, *5, 95–113.*

————. The diary of a self slasher. *Journal of Criminal Psychopathology,* 1944, *5,* 521–540.

Lewis, N. Graphic art productions in schizophrenia. *Proceedings of the Association for Research in Nervous and Mental Disease,* 1928, *5,* 344–368.

Liss, E. The graphic arts. *American Journal of Orthopsychiatry,* 1938, *8,* 95–99.

Mosse, E. P. Painting analysis in the treatment of the neurosis. *Psychoanalytic Review,* 1940, *27,* 65–82.

Naumburg, M. Studies of the free art expression of behavior problem children and adolescents as a means of diagnosis and therapy. *Nervous and Mental Disease Monograph,* New York State Psychiatric Institute, 1947.

Prados, M. The use of pictorial images in group therapy. Paper presented at the American Group Therapy Meeting, 1948.

Schmidl-Waehner, T. Formal criteria for the analysis of children's drawings. *American Journal of Orthopsychiatry,* 1942, *12,* 95–104.

Schube, P., & Crowell, J. Art of psychotic patients. *Archives of Neurology and Psychiatry,* 1939, *41,* 709–720.

Shaw, R. F. *Finger painting.* Boston: Little, Brown, & Co., 1938.

White, R. W. Interpretation of imaginative productions. In Hunt, J. McV. (Ed.), *Personality and Behavior Disorders.* New York: Ronald Press Co., 1944, pp. 214-251.

Wickes, F. G. *The inner world of man.* New York: Henry Holt & Co., 1948.

Wolff, W. *The personality of the preschool child.* New York: Grune & Stratton, 1947.

Case 20

Editors' Introduction

Many psychotherapists in their early careers use hypnosis and then later, as in the case of Sigmund Freud, discard it for other procedures. Despite the enormous literature on this topic and its historical primacy as a treatment methodology, as illustrated in our first selection by Pierre Janet, hypnosis is still not well understood.

In this selection, the reader will note the connection not only with Janet and automatic writing but also with the Baruch and Miller article preceding this case study, which illustrates how certain themes and techniques cut across various theories and ages.

At this point, a bit of theory may be useful. Psychology generally falls into two points of view: interior/exterior; phenomenological/objective; mentalistic/behavioral; covert/overt, and so forth. We have seen examples of the latter position in the Wolpe and the Atthowe and Krasner selections illustrating behavior therapy. But within the interior—phenomenological—mentalistic—covert camp there is still another division: consciousness/unconsciousness. Theorists such as Adler, Rogers, Ellis, and Glasser, as examples, discount, minimize or ignore the notion of an unconscious mind, while theorists such as Janet, Freud, Jung, and Holt accept it. Erickson and Kubie accept the importance of the unconscious as will be seen in this fascinating selection.

MILTON H. ERICKSON AND LAWRENCE S. KUBIE
Automatic Drawing in the Treatment of an Obsessional Depression

No matter how accurate any body of scientific theory may be, its confirmation by the use of some technique other than that on which the theory first rested is always valuable. This is the most convincing way of ruling out the misleading influence of possible undetected methodological fallacies. With this in mind, the following case is reported in detail because, by means of a nonpsychoanalytic technique, it illustrates a certain type of symbolic activity which is comparable in character to that studied by psychoanalysis in dreams and in psychotic states, and because of its clear demonstration of certain of the dynamic relationships which exist between conscious and unconscious aspects of the human psyche. Finally, it is reported because of our interest in this general type of technique as a means of uncovering unconscious material, and because of the challenge this may offer to certain phases of psychoanalytic technique.

History

A twenty-four-year-old girl attended a clinical demonstration of hypnosis for a class in psychology at the university. At this demonstration, particular emphasis was laid on the phenomenon of automatic writing and on the integrated functioning of subconscious processes as a seemingly independent entity in the total psyche. Afterwards, she inquired at length about the possibility of acquiring the ability to do automatic writing herself, and whether it was probable or possible that her own unconscious might function in a coordinated, integrated fashion without her conscious awareness. Affirmative replies were given to both inquiries. Thereupon, as the explanation of her interest, she volunteered the statement that, during the preceding month, she had become unhappy and uneasy in all her relationships for some unknown reason, and that she was becoming increasingly "worried, unhappy and depressed," despite the fact that she knew of no personal problem that could trouble her seriously. She then asked if she

From *Psychoanalytic Quarterly,* 1938, 7, 443-466

might try automatic writing through which her unconscious, acting independently, could give an account of whatever was troubling her. She was told that she might try this plan if she were really interested, and she responded that first she would like to have a formal psychiatric review of her life.

Accordingly, on the next day, she was interviewed at length. The more important data obtained in this interview may be summarized as follows:

1. She was an only child, idolized by her parents, as they in turn were by her, living in what seemed to be a very happy home.

2. Her adjustments to college had been excellent until the preceding month, when her work had begun to suffer seriously in consequence of the sudden development of "worry," "concern," "fear," "unhappiness," and "horrible depression," which persisted almost continuously and for which she knew no cause whatever.

3. Recently, she had been impelled to read some psychoanalytic literature and had found the subject of symbolism "most interesting and fascinating," but "silly," "meaningless," and "without any scientific validity." When asked for the references, she replied, "Oh, I just thumbed through a lot of books and journals in the library, but the only thing that interested me was symbolism."

4. For a month, and only since reading about symbolism, she had noted the development of a habit of "scribbling," "scratching," "drawing pictures and lines" when telephoning, studying, sitting in the classroom, or merely idling. She did this in an abstracted manner, usually without noting what she was doing and thought of it merely as a sign of nervousness, of a desire to do something; what this might be, she did not know. She added that it was a "jittery" habit, objectionable because it "dirtied" the walls of telephone booths, the tablecloths in restaurants and clean paper in her notebooks. (Throughout the interview the patient constantly demonstrated this "habit" most adequately, and it was obvious that she was not aware that she was doing so. Only at the close of the interview did she notice her scribbling and remarked, "Well, I guess I have demonstrated that jitteryness better than I described it.")

5. The only personal problem which troubled her consciously was the fact that her three years at college had slowly and gradually separated her from her most intimate girlhood friend, in spite of that girl's regular weekend visits to the patient's home. The patient felt "lonely" and "resentful" about this, and during the preceding few weeks, this angry feeling had increased until it had become an "uncontrollable resentment" over the loss of her friend. Nor was this obsessive resentment diminished by her realization that there was nothing she could do about it because of the ever increasing divergence of their interests.

At the completion of her story, in the manner so characteristic of psychiatric patients who have told more than they know, she dismissed her account as probably being of no significance and asked insistently whether now, after hearing her story, it still was thought possible to secure by means of automatic writing the facts which were pertinent to her problem—"if there really were a problem." She thought that if she could read subsequently whatever she might write automatically, she could thus force herself to become consciously aware of what was troubling her. She also wanted to know if the examiner was confident that her subconscious could function in a sufficiently integrated fashion to give a coherent, understandable account.

In response to these anxious inquiries, she was told emphatically that she could do exactly as she wished. She was then given repeated carefully worded suggestions in a gentle, insistent, and attention-compelling fashion (which served to induce the passively receptive state that marks the initiation of a light hypnotic trance) to the effect that:

1. The time intervening until her appointment on the next day would be spent by her subconscious in reviewing and organizing all the material to which she wished access.

2. In addition, her subconscious would decide upon the method or means of communication. It would select some tangible method by which to communicate what it had to say in a way which would be clearly understandable to the examiner and at the proper moment, be clearly understood by the patient herself, so that no doubts or equivocations would arise.

3. Since she herself had suggested automatic writing, pencils and paper would be supplied, so that she would have an opportunity to employ that method in the same abstracted manner as that in which she had made her drawings during the interview. The reader will note that this suggestion actually constituted an indirect command to repeat her *drawings* in an intelligible fashion. It was given for the reason that automatic writing is often the most difficult to secure on first attempts.

It was to be expected that this would be even more true with this patient, whose entire story implied a resolute unconscious reluctance to know certain things, despite her strong concomitant conscious desire to become aware of them. For her, therefore, automatic writing itself would have proved too revealing, if successful at all, and would have forced on the patient a too rapid realization of her repressed material. This would either have proved profoundly upsetting or would have summoned up vigorous repressive mechanisms to forestall complete communication.

4. In the interval before her next appointment, she was to keep her mind consciously busy with studying, reading light fiction, and social activities, thus supplying herself with innocuous topics for conversation on which she could report consciously. Thus at the time of the appointment, communications concerning her problem would be imparted entirely by subconscious automatic behavior (the drawing) and not become part of her conscious speech.

At the end of the interview, the patient seemed rather confused and uncertain about her instructions. She attempted several times to pick up the sheets of paper on which she had again been "nervously scribbling," suddenly made a last plea for reassurance, and then left quickly when this had been given.

Examination of her drawings after she departed disclosed various figures and lines repeated over and over in varying sizes. There were long and short lines, vertical, horizontal and oblique ones. Some were traced lightly, others heavily shaded. Also, there were spirals, cylinders, triangles, squares and rectangles of various proportions, some drawn lightly and others heavily. While she had been making these drawings, no sequences or relationships had been observed. One peculiarity was the fact that each figure had been drawn as an isolated unit with no attempt to run one into the next (Figure 20.1).

FIGURE 20.1.

A subsequent examination of two different books of her lecture notes showed that her "nervous scribbling" had been a sudden development of the preceding weeks. In these notebooks, page after page was found with the same limited types of figures and lines, drawn over and over in a totally disconnected, confused fashion.

The next day, the patient appeared promptly and remarked at once that the suggestions given her the day before seemed to have been effective, since she had not thought about herself at all after leaving the office. She had even lost conscious interest in her problem so completely that she had returned only because she felt herself to be under an obligation to keep her appointment. She also explained that she had read a recent novel and was prepared to relate the entire story in detail, remarking facetiously that it would be a cheap way for the examiner to become posted on the latest information of the literary world.

She was told promptly that she could start the story at once; as she did so, her chair was carefully placed sideways to the desk so that her right arm rested on the desk in close proximity to paper and pencils, while the examiner took a position diagonally opposite. Thus, although she faced away from the paper, it remained well within the range of her peripheral vision.

Shortly after she had begun to tell the story of the book, she abstractedly picked up the pencil and in a laborious, strained fashion began to repeat on the upper half of the sheet of paper the drawings of the previous day, now and then glancing down at her productions for a moment or so in an absent-minded fashion. As before, no particular sequence of the drawings was noted, but a significant duplication of some of the elements may be observed in Figure 20.2.

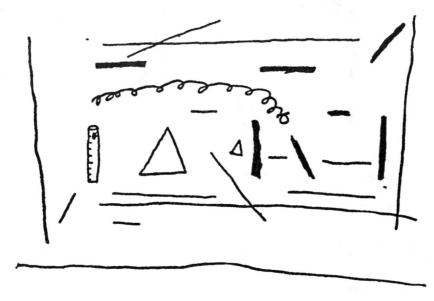

FIGURE 20.2.

When she had completed these drawings, she became rather confused in her speech and was observed to relax and tighten her grip on the pencil as if she wanted to lay it down but found herself unable to do so. She was encouraged here by an insistent, low-toned suggestion, "Go ahead, keep on, it's all right, go ahead, go ahead, keep on."

She immediately remarked, "Oh yes, I know where I am, I just lost the thread of the story for a moment," and continued the narrative.

At the same time, her hand was seen to take a fresh grip on the pencil and to shove the pad forward so as to make the lower half of the paper available. She drew a line as if to divide the paper in halves. Then in a slow and deliberate fashion, with a marked increase in the tension of her right hand and some speeding of her speech, she began to construct a picture by arranging the elements which she had previously drawn so often and so repetitively in an incoherent manner into an orderly, systematic whole. It was as if she had first laid out the materials for her construction and was now putting them together. Thus the four heavily shaded lines of equal length became a square, and the other units were fitted together to form the picture shown in Figure 20.3.

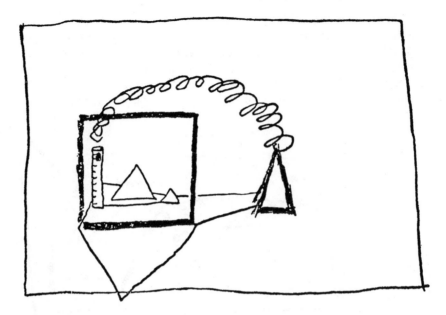

FIGURE 20.3.

In completing the square, however, the patient showed marked uncertainty about its lower left-hand corner and kept glancing down at it abstractedly for a moment or so at a time. Finally, she distorted the corner slightly, leaving it open. Also, in making the lower right-hand corner, she pressed down unduly, breaking the pencil point.

In making the diagonal line extending downward from the lower left-hand corner of the square, her hand moved with sudden force and speed. After a considerable pause, her hand moved more and more slowly on the upstroke to the lower right-hand corner of the square, the line wavering; finally her hand moved quickly and forcibly over to the shaded triangle.

Upon drawing the line connecting the small triangle with the heavily shaded triangle, her hand stopped short as it approached the side of the square and placed a period. Following this, her hand lifted and moved over the edge as if surmounting a barrier, after which it completed the line in a steady, firm manner.

The spiral line connecting the cylinder and the shaded triangle began freely and easily, but as it approached the triangle, the hand movements became increasingly labored and slow.

Repeatedly during the drawing process, the patient's hand would return to the larger of the two light triangles, as if to touch it up a bit and to make it more perfect in outline, while the shaded triangle was drawn roughly.

During her drawing it was possible to record the order in which the various elements were added to the total picture:

1. Square.
2. Cylinder.

3. Large light triangle.

4. Small triangle.

5. Connecting lines between cylinder and large triangle, large triangle and little triangle and cylinder and little triangle.

6. Enclosing rectangle.

7. Heavily shaded triangle.

8. Connecting line between the little triangle and the shaded triangle.

9. The line leading from the cylinder out of the square and beyond the rectangle, then back to the square and thence to the shaded triangle.

10. The spiral line.

11. The central shading of the upper part of the cylinder.

As she completed the picture, she glanced casually at it several times without seeming to see it. This was followed by a noisy dropping of the pencil which attracted her notice. Thereupon, she immediately called attention to her drawing, picking up her pencil as she did so. Then, using her left hand, she tore off the sheet from the pad to examine it more closely, leaving her right hand in a writing position as if waiting for something. Noting this, the examiner inferred a subconscious desire to make a secret comment and accordingly gave the suggestion: "A short, vertical line means 'yes,' a short horizontal line means 'no.'"

Misapplying this suggestion, the patient scanned the drawing carefully, declared that she saw no such lines, and asked how they could mean anything.

The question was then asked, "Is it all there?" to which she replied, "I suppose so, if there is anything there at all," while her hand, without her awareness, made a "yes" sign.

"Everything?"

"Well, I suppose if anything is there, everything is," and again her hand made the "yes" sign without her awareness.

She scanned the picture carefully for some moments and then remarked, "Well, it's just silly nonsense, meaningless. Do you mean to say that you can make any sense out of the scratching—to use your own words, that it tells everything?"

Apparently in answer to her own question, her hand made another "yes" sign and then dropped the pencil as if the task were now complete. Without waiting for a reply she continued, "It's funny! Even though I know that picture is silly, I know it has meaning because right now I've got an urge to give you something; although I know it's silly, I'm going to give it to you anyway because it's connected with that." Pointing to the shaded triangle, she took from her pocket a packet of matches advertising a local hotel and dropped it on the desk.

She then consulted her watch, declared that she had to leave and seemed to be experiencing a mild panic. After a little urging, she consented to answer a few questions about what the picture might mean. She looked the drawing over and offered the following comments, which she insisted she could not elaborate:

"Two pictures in frames; a large one,"—pointing to the rectangle—"and a small one,"—pointing to the square—"with the corner broken." Pointing to the figures in the square, she said, "These are all connected and the connections between the little one"—pointing to the small triangle—"and that"—indicating the cylinder—"is a cigarette with smoke. We all smoke in our family, maybe those are father's matches I gave you. But the whole thing makes no sense at all. Only a psychiatrist could see anything in it." With that, she rushed from the office, only to return at once to ask, "When can I see you again?" On being told, "Just as soon as you want to know a bit more, call me" she rushed away. No comments were made on the unitary drawings and she seemed not to notice them.

Three weeks later, she appeared unexpectedly "to report progress." She stated that, evidently, her drawings must have meant something since she had experienced a marked change in her emotions. She was no longer worried or depressed, though at times she felt "an intense dread of something, as if I were going to stumble onto something; I have a feeling that I'm going to find out something dreadful." With much hesitation, she added, "What I really mean is that I have a feeling that I am getting ready to know something I already know, but don't *know* I know. That sounds awfully silly, but it's the only way I can explain it; I am really afraid to find out what it's all about. It's connected with these matches." She handed the examiner a second pack similar to the first. "We (the family) had dinner at the hotel last night, and that's where I got them. I saw another pack on the library table last night, but these are the ones I got."

All the other remarks were casual in character and nothing further was learned. She left rather hurriedly, apparently somewhat uneasy and confused.

Two weeks later, she again appeared unexpectedly, declaring as before that she had come "to report progress." She explained that, in the interim, she had developed an absolute certainty that her drawing was meaningful. "There is a complete story in that picture that anybody can read and I'm getting terribly curious to know what it is."

Here she demanded to see the drawing, and after scrutinizing it closely remarked, "Really, it still looks like a mess of nothing. I just know it's the whole story, too; but why I say that, I don't know. Yet I am sure that my subconscious knows a lot that it don't tell me. I have a feeling that it is just waiting for my conscious mind to prepare itself for a shock and it's just making me darned curious so I won't mind the shock."

Asked when she would know, she replied "Oh, I suppose not long." She then became emotionally disturbed and insisted on changing the topic of conversation.

A week later, she came in to state that she had an engagement to dine with her girlhood friend at the hotel that evening, and that this was causing her much emotional distress. She explained: "I hate to see our friendship broken up just by drifting apart the way we have. And I don't like my attitude toward Jane. You see, Jane's a year younger than I, and she has a boy friend and is pretty much in love with him. She says she thinks I know him but she won't tell me his name or anything about him. I don't like my attitude toward Jane because I'm so jealous that I just hate her intensely; I'd like to pull her hair out. I hate her because I feel as if she had taken my boy friend away from me, but that's silly, because I haven't got a boy friend. I don't want to keep my appointment because I know I'm going to quarrel with her. There really isn't anything to quarrel about, but I know I'll just say one nasty thing after another. I don't want to, but it's going to happen and I can't avoid it. And another thing: after I quarrel with her, I'm going to have a fight with my father. I've been working up to this for a week. I've only had two fights with my father and they were both about my college plans; I don't know what this fight's going to be about. Probably some little thing like his carelessness in smoking and dropping ashes on the rug at home, probably any little old excuse. I just hope Father isn't in when I get home. Can't you say something to me so this all won't happen? But I suppose as long as it's in me, I might as well come out and get it over with. When I made the appointment with Jane, I had a vague idea of what was going to happen; as soon as she accepted, I could see, just as plain as could be, what I've just told you; so I hung up the receiver before I had a chance to cancel my invitation."

More remarks of a similar character and significance were made. All attempts to discuss her drawings or to secure an elucidation of her premonitions failed. She declared that the only things of interest to her at the moment were the "impending battles."

The next day, she dropped in the office to report hurriedly, "I'm in a rush. All I got time for is to tell you it all happened just as I predicted. Jane and I started out visiting nicely, then I got to wisecracking and began hurting her feelings. I didn't notice that at first and when I did, I just didn't give a damn and I went to town on her in the cruelest, nastiest, most subtle fashion I could. I didn't say anything particularly, but it was the way I said it and mocked her. When she cried, I felt a lot better, and although I was ashamed of myself, I didn't feel any sympathy for her. I wound up by telling her that we could agree to disagree, and she could go her way and I'd go my way. Then I went home and Father was sitting there reading. I was itching for him to say something, just anything. I was awfully amused at myself, but I figured there wasn't anything I could do about it, so I began smoking and pacing the floor. Finally he told me to sit down and be quiet, and that just set me off. I just yelled at him to shut up, that I could *run around* if I wanted to, and he couldn't say anything to me. It was too late to go out, and if I *wanted to run around,* I had just as much right as he had. I told him he might think he was smart but I was a lot smarter, that I wasn't born yesterday, that I knew what it was all about, and a lot of silly, incoherent, tempery things that I really didn't mean and that didn't make sense. He got disgusted and told me if I couldn't talk sense to shut up and go to bed and sleep it off. So I did. And the funny thing is that when I woke up this morning, I thought of those drawings I did for you; I tried to think about them, but all I could think was first the word 'today' and then the word 'tomorrow,' and finally, I just kept thinking 'tomorrow.' Does that mean anything to you? It doesn't to me." With this remark, she took her departure.

The next afternoon, she appeared and declared, "After I left you yesterday, I had a funny feeling I had made an appointment with you for today, but I really knew I hadn't. Then this morning, the first thing I thought of was that drawing, and I knew that I could understand it now. I've been thinking about it all day. I remember the whole picture; I can see it in my mind plainly, but it's still meaningless, doesn't mean a thing. Let me look at it."

She was handed the picture. She scrutinized it in a most painstaking fashion, with an expression of intense curiosity on her face; finally sighing and putting it down to remark, "Well, I guess I'm mistaken. It doesn't mean a thing—just a silly picture, after all." Then, suddenly brightening, "But if you will say just a word to start me off, I know I'll understand it."

No heed was given this indirect request and she repeatedly examined the picture only to lay it aside each time in an intensely puzzled fashion.

Finally, she repeated her request for a "starting word" and was countered with the question, "What word?" To this she replied, "Oh, any word. You know what the picture means, so just say any word that will give me a start. I am really just dying to know what it's all about even though I am a little bit afraid, maybe a lot. But say something, anything."

Her insistent request was acceded to by the remark, "Sometime ago, you told me you were terribly interested in and fascinated by symbolism." As this remark was made, the packet of hotel matches was carefully dropped on the desk.

She seized the drawing and looked at it momentarily, grabbing, at the same time, the packet of matches and throwing it violently on the floor. She then burst into a torrent of vituperation, intermingled with expressions of sympathy for her mother and explanatory details. The following is a summary:

> "The damned nasty filthy little cheater. And she calls herself my friend. She's having an affair with Father. Damn him. Poor Mother. She visits Mother, damn her, and Father acts like a saint around the house, damn him. They go to the hotel, the same hotel Father took us to [for dinner]. I hated her because she took my father away from me—and mother. That's why I always stole his cigarettes. Even when I had some, I'd sneak into the hall and get some out of his coat pocket. Sometimes I'd take the whole package, sometimes only one or two. If she thinks she's going to break up my home, she's got another thought coming, plenty too. The first time she told me about her boy friend—her boy friend, huh—she lit her cigarette with those matches. I knew then, but I couldn't believe it. And I used to take Father's matches away from him and I'd get so goddamn mad when he'd tell me to use my own. I didn't want Mother to see those matches, and it didn't make sense then." This was followed by much profanity and repetition of the above remarks which seemed to exhaust her rage, following which she sobbed bitterly. Composing herself, she apologized for her profanity and rage. She then remarked quietly, "I suppose I better explain all this to you. When you said symbolism, I suddenly remembered that Freud said cylinders symbolized men, and triangles, women. I recalled that cigarettes were cylinders and that they could symbolize a penis. Then the whole meaning of the picture just burst into my mind all at once. I guess I just couldn't take it, and that's why I acted like I did. Now I can explain the picture to you."

Pointing to the various elements of the picture, she explained rapidly, "This cigarette is father, and that big triangle is mother—she's short and fat and blonde—and the little triangle is me. I'm blonde too. I'm really taller than mother, but I just feel little to her. You see, those lines all connect us in a family group and the square is the family frame. And that line from father breaks through the family frame and goes down below the social frame, that's the big square, and then it tries to go back to the family and can't, and so it just goes over to Jane. You see, she is a tall, slender brunette. That smoke from father's penis curls around Jane. That line between me and Jane is broken where it comes to the family frame. I've been drawing these pictures all the time like that (pointing to the unitary drawings at the top of the page) but this is the first time I ever put them together. See where I blackened father's face. It should be. When I gave you those matches, I told you they were connected with Jane, even though I didn't know that was Jane then."

For some minutes, the patient sat quietly and thoughtfully, now and then glancing at the drawing. Finally she remarked, "I know the interpretation of this picture is true, but only because I feel it is true. I have been thinking everything over. There isn't a solitary fact that I know that could possibly substantiate what I've said. Jane and I have drifted apart, but that doesn't make her Father's mistress. Jane does call at the house but always on evenings when Father is out, and while she doesn't stay more than three-quarters of an hour, that doesn't mean that that's a blind. Mother can't hide anything and her nature is such that she would know about things before they happen. I know she has no inkling of this. As for the matches, anybody could have hotel matches and my stealing Father's cigarettes only proves there's something wrong with me. Well, now that I've discovered this, I'm going to go through with it and clear it up so that I'll have better proof than just my subconscious drawings."

What this proof was to be she refused to state. The rest of the interview was spent by her in outlining a calm, dispassionate, philosophical view and acceptance of the entire situation.

Two days later, she came to the office accompanied by a young woman. As they entered the office the patient said, "This is Jane. I bullied and browbeat her into coming here without giving her any idea of what or why, and her own sense of guilt toward me kept her from refusing. Now I'm going to have my say. Then I'm going to leave her with you so she can talk to you and get a little sense put into her head." Then turning to Jane, "Just about two months ago, you started something which you didn't want me to know about. You thought you were getting by with it, but you weren't. You told me your boy friend was about four years older than you, wanted an affair with you, but that you wouldn't consent. You were just a sweet young girl talking things over with your dearest pal. And all the time you knew, and all the time I was putting two and two together. Finally I went to a psychiatrist and the other day I got the answer. I know your whole sordid, nasty story. Here's a cigarette, light it with *these* matches—they're hotel matches. Now you know just what I'm talking about."

With that she rushed out of the office. As she did so, Jane turned and asked, "Does Ann really know about her father and me?"

Then, without any questioning of any sort, Jane responded to the difficult situation in which she found herself by relating the story of her intrigue with the patient's father, fully confirming every detail given by the patient, adding the information that both she and her lover had been most secretive. They had been confident that they could not even be suspected. On the occasion of Ann's first weekend home from college after the beginning of the affair, she had felt that Ann was most disagreeable and irritable for no good reason, and Ann's father had made the same comment during one of their meetings. She attributed Ann's knowledge of the affair entirely to "intuition."

Following these disclosures, Ann was recalled to the office. As she entered, she eyed Jane closely and remarked, "Well, I did have a faint hope that it wasn't so, but it is, isn't it?" Jane nodded affirmatively to which Ann replied philo-sophically, "Well, what Father does is his own business, and what you do is yours, but you're not visiting at our home any more. You and Father can pick another hotel since the family is in the habit of eating at that hotel frequently. I'll just explain your failure to visit at home to Mother by saying we quarreled. As for you and me, we're acquaintances, and you can tell Father that heaven help both of you if Mother ever finds out. And that's that! You can go back to town by one bus and I'll take another. Beat it now because I want to talk to the doctor."

After Jane's departure, the gist of the patient's remarks was that she intended to accept the whole matter in a dispassionate, philosophical manner. She was still tremendously puzzled as to how she had "stumbled on to it." She felt convinced that "it must have been just plain intuition that worked out right. When I first started drawing those little pictures, it made me feel terribly jittery, but I couldn't stop. I was just obsessed by them, but they had no meaning until last Thursday. Now when I look back at it all, the whole thing just seems screwy because I must have known from the beginning, and yet I really didn't know a thing until the other day here. But hereafter, I'm not going to let any subconscious knowledge upset me as frightfully as that did."

The patient was seen casually thereafter on a number of occasions, and satisfactory evidence was obtained of a continuing good adjustment. A few years later, she married very happily. One additional item of information obtained from her was that, on a number of occasions before her upset, she had suspected her father of intrigues with various women but had always dismissed her suspicions as unworthy. These suspicions were confirmed unexpectedly by Jane while discussing with the examiner her intrigue with the patient's father. She volun-teered that, over a period of eight years, the father had had a series of affairs, one of which had been broken off only at her insistence.

After the passage of several months, the patient's notebooks were again examined. She remarked, "Oh, I know! I forgot to tell you. I lost that habit just as soon as I found things out. I haven't done a bit of scribbling since then." Inspection of the notebooks verified her statement.

Subsequently, Jane too was seen casually and volunteered the information that the intrigue was continuing, but that she had complied with Ann's injunc-tions.

Discussion

The Significance of the Illness

It is hardly possible to overestimate the theoretical significance and interest of this case. Only rarely does an opportunity arise to study a severe neurotic storm—in some ways nearly psychotic—under such well-controlled conditions.

A young woman deeply and apparently peacefully devoted to her father and mother suddenly is confronted with the threat of a deep hurt to her mother through her father and her own best friend, and with the acutely painful picture of her father's emotional desertion of the family. This of course is adequate grounds for sorrow and anger. But it was more significant still that she was confronted by these jolting facts not in her conscious perceptions but only in her unconscious; and that, furthermore, her reaction to this unconscious knowledge was not one of simple sorrow and anger, but a far more complex constellation of neurotic and affective symptoms. All of this becomes clear directly from the data of the case, and without any intricate or debatable analytic speculations and interpretations.

Here, then is a test case: Can psychic injuries of which we are not consciously aware be at the heart of major psychopathological states? And how does the reaction of this patient illuminate this problem?

On the weekend of her return home when she first sensed unconsciously the intimacy between her friend and her father, her immediate response was one of troubled and unmotivated irritability—an irritability which never found any focus, but which was displaced incessantly from one trivial object to another. Thereafter, she lapsed into a state of obsessional depression, which seemed to her to be without content or meaning, although it was accompanied by a withdrawal of interest from all of her previous activities and from all previous object relationships. As this depressive mood gathered, her irritability persisted undiminished and still without adequate conscious object. For the first time, however, it began to focus its expression in two symptomatic compulsive acts whose symbolic meaning later became unmistakable. The first of these was a minutely circumscribed kleptomania, i.e., the specific compulsion to steal cigarettes and matches from her father's pockets, obviously with an angry and punitive preconscious purpose, but which was seen in the automatic drawings to have a much deeper unconscious castrative goal as well. The second was an equally circumscribed, almost encapsulated obsessional drive toward the constant repetition of scribbled drawings of cylinders, triangles, looping spirals and straight lines slanting in all directions (Figure 20.1).

It is of interest to note that her illness began with episodic emotional flurries, which quickly were followed by an affect which became fixed and obsessional, and that this in turn was supplemented by a group of obsessional acts. The theoretical significance of this sequence of events is a matter into which we cannot go at this point, but the sequence should be borne in mind.

The patient's involuntary and, to her, mysterious irritability deserves another word. It is an exact replica of a type of frantic, shifting, and apparently unmotivated irritability which one sees in children when they are stirred into overwhelming states of unconscious jealousy towards parents and siblings. In this patient, it is possible to observe how the irritability was precipitated when the patient's unconscious was confronted with the love relationship between her father and her friend. Furthermore, it is clear that the irritability reflects her conflict between various roles, as for instance her identification with her mother in the family group, her fantasy of herself in the role of her father's mistress, her jealousy of this mistress, and the resulting conflicts which manifested themselves throughout her upset period between the vengeful, guilty, and protective impulses toward everyone involved in the situation.

It is clear that the unconscious impulses which were driving her strove in many ways for adequate expression and resolution: first in the vengeful gestures (stealing matches and cigarettes), then in the automatic incoherent drawings or scribblings (a so-called "habit" which is later seen to be infused with specific and translatable meanings), and finally in the increasing and obsessive need to find out what it was all about, as manifested in her blind search into psychiatric and analytical literature, her fascination and skepticism about symbolism, and in the appeal for help, still slightly veiled behind her "curiosity about automatic writing."

Surely both the driving and the directing power of unconscious mentation could not be more beautifully illustrated in any laboratory test than it is here. A further example is in the unwitting double meaning in the naively chosen phrase "run around" which the patient used repeatedly in her blind, angry outburst against her father, without realizing consciously its obvious reference to his sexual habits.

And finally, the symbolic representation of complex human relationships by simple, childlike scribbled drawings, which is the most dramatic feature of the story, is so clear as to need no further comment.

Technique

The technical challenges with which this experience confronts us are several. In the first place, it must be admitted quite simply that the most skillful use of orthodox psychoanalytic technique could not possibly have uncovered the repressed awareness of the father's liaison in a mere handful of sessions. Speed in achieving a result is of course not the sole criterion of excellence. It may well be that with such rapid therapy, certain vital reconstructive experiences cannot be brought to a patient, whereas they, on the other hand, may be an essential part of the more orthodox analytic approach. But there is nothing in this observation which would seem to make the two methods mutually exclusive. In some form, they might be supplementary or complementary to one another; and for at least a few of those many patients to whom analysis is not applicable, such an approach as this, if only because of its speed and directness, might be useful.

Furthermore, it must be emphasized that automatic drawing as a method of communication has a close relationship to the psychoanalytic method of free association. Here the patient's undirected drawings were certainly a nonverbal form of free association. That the translation of such drawings into understandable ideas presents grave difficulties must be admitted; but these difficulties are not always greater than those which confront the analyst when he deals with the symbolic material of dreams. On a two-dimensional plane, these drawings are equivalent to the dramatic symbolic representation of instinctual conflicts which Homburger (1937) has described in children's three-dimensional play with building blocks.

Furthermore, as one studies this material, it is impressive to see how ready the unconscious seemed to be to communicate with the examiner by means of this accessory sign language of drawing, while at the same time, the consciously organized part of the personality was busy recounting other matters. It suggests that by using either this or some other method of widening the conscious gap between the conscious and unconscious parts of the psyche, it might be possible to secure communications from the unconscious more simply than can be done when both parts of the personality are using the single vehicle of speech. It suggests that when only one form of communication is used, the struggle between the expressive and repressive forces may be intensified.

The point which we have in mind here is quite simple. Under circumstances of usual analytical procedure, the patient expresses everything—both conscious and unconscious, instinctual drives and anxieties, fears and guilt—often all at the same moment and in the same system of gestures and words. That under such circumstances, his speech and his communications may be difficult to disentangle is not strange. If, however, by some method, one could allow the various aspects of the psyche to express themselves simultaneously with different simple and direct methods of communication, it would be conceivable at least that each part could express itself more clearly and with less internal confusion and resistance. In this instance, it seems to have worked that way; and the shame, guilt, anxiety and rage which prevented the patient from putting into words her unconscious knowledge left her free to express it all in her automatic scribbled drawing; furthermore this throws light on the essential mechanism of literature and art, a discussion of which will have to be reserved for another time.

It must be borne in mind, however, that the repressive forces rendered the drawings wholly chaotic until the influence of the psychiatrist was exerted on this patient in a clear-cut and definite manner, in order to assist her in the expression of her problem. In the first place, looking back it becomes obvious that the patient came seeking a substitute father who would give her permission to know the facts about her real father—a "permissive agent," whose function would be to lessen her guilt and her anxiety and to give her the right to express the rage and hurt that she felt.

Thus, we see that the first movement towards recovery came as she simultaneously talked and scribbled in the first interview and apparently without any insight. The observer on that occasion gave her a certain direct quiet but impressive suggestion: that she was to allow her unconscious to deal with her problem instead of her conscious mind. This is an important divergence from psychoanalytic technique with its deliberate drive to force everything into consciousness, because at the same time that the psychiatrist gave the patient permission to face the facts unconsciously, he gave her conscious mind the right to be free from its obsessive preoccupation with the problem. The patient experienced an immediate temporary relief. She felt so "well" the next day that she even thought of not returning for her next appointment. With this ground under her feet, however, at the next session, she went deeper into her problem and emerged with her first moment of conscious panic—a panic that was not at this point accompanied by any insight. Her next emotional change evolved rapidly out of this experience, and soon manifested itself in her ability to express her rage, chagrin, and resentment openly in her compulsive outburst against her friend and her father, instead of in symbolic acts alone.

In all of this, the "permissive agent," by his active encouragement and direct suggestions, served to lift the weight of guilt, anxiety and ambivalence from the patient's shoulders. As a new and kindly father, he diverted some of these obstructing feelings from their older goals, thus allowing the eruption of the full awareness of the affair. This important function of the therapist—to dislodge old and rigid superego patterns—is one which unquestionably was executed by this mild suggestion at the first interview between the therapist and the patient.

Naturally, this could not occur without anxiety; but the appearance of this anxiety, replacing the depression and the compulsions which had existed for so long, marked the upturn in the patient's illness.

Conclusion

We are far from drawing any conclusions from this single experience. Such observations must be amplified and repeated many times before it is decided that, as a consequence, any changes in analytic technique are indicated.

It is just to say, however, that without any effort to open up all the buried material of the patient's highly charged oedipal relationships, a direct link was established between conscious and unconscious systems of thought and feeling which surrounded the parental figures, and this by a very simple technique. Furthermore, as a direct consequence, there was almost immediate relief from seriously disturbing neurotic and emotional symptoms.

It is unfortunate that, although we have a clear picture of the patient's neurosis, we have no analytic insight into the character and personality out of which this neurosis developed. This is important because it is conceivable that such a method as this might be applicable for one type of character organization and not for another, even when the two had essentially similar superimposed neuroses. Such studies as these, therefore, should be carried forward in conjunction with psychoanalysis.

Reference

Homburger, Erik. Configurations in play—clinical notes. *Psychoanalytic Quarterly,* 1937, *6,* 193–214.

Case 21

Editors' Introduction

William C. Schutz is unique in the field of psychotherapy. No one is more inventive or more resourceful than he. He has one leg in scientific psychology, and his book *Firo* is the product of many years of laborious work worthy of any pedant while his book *Joy,* from which this incident is excerpted, well illustrates his other aspect: courageous, creative, bold.

Will Schutz, as he is generally known, is the developer of a total system of psychotherapy known as Open Encounter, and we place his conceptualizations and operations within that area we have labeled Human Potential. This account by a former—how shall we label her?—certainly not client or patient—perhaps best described by the words "fellow traveler"—has interest for us in that it is an account by one who has been in therapy with comments by Dr. Schutz.

While the use of fantasy as a therapeutic method is not new, Schutz has developed it to a fine art. Unfortunately, the full impact of such a fantasy must be experienced *in vivo,* but even so in this selection we can feel the force of this procedure.

Notice who is in the room at the time—possibly as a participant—Fritz Perls. This scene took place at the Esalen Center where both Fritz and Will were among the most shining stars.

WILLIAM C. SCHUTZ

Fantasy—The Guided Daydream: Nora's Account

For some people, in some situations, defenses are too high for verbal or even sometimes nonverbal methods to work effectively. If the person has some awareness of the situation, his resistance prevents anything significant from occurring. The fantasy methods are extremely effective for these situations since they allow a nonconscious part of the personality to take over.

The fantasy requires relaxation on the part of the participant. For this reason, lying on the floor is often helpful. Ordinarily the person is then led into the fantasy by the guide, with a specific image. Then the fantasizer shuts his eyes, attends to the images in his mind, and reports them to the guide. He must not try to force pictures that he wants to see, though after a very short time that will rarely be possible in any case. Instead he should try to observe his own imaginings. The guide enters into the fantasy at various points to facilitate the experience. His function is to induce the fantasizer to face difficult or painful situations, or to provide help and support to meet various obstacles, or to help see the image more clearly or tie the various segments together. The fantasizer frequently experiences a wide variety of emotions, including fear, elation, laughter, crying, tension, depression, relaxation. The guide allows the fantasizer to leave the fantasy when he feels that his actual feelings are positive and largely untroubled.

Caution: This technique should not be attempted without the aid of a professional. There are many starting points for fantasies, many of which are described in the literature, and experience suggests which should be used for which situations. The type of intervention also requires experience, and the various situations that can be unproductively upsetting must be known. . . .

Nora's Account

The morning of my fantasy I can recall as if through walking in fog. The hatred of my being enclosed in my body was now replaced by a terrible fear of it.

From William C. Schutz, *Joy* (New York: Grove Press, 1967), pp. 90–107.

This body which enclosed me had, up until then, been ugly and a source of shame to me—now it had become a source of terror, something hideous. Yet how to escape from it? I longed only to unzip my skin and come tumbling out.

Fritz Perls came then. [He is a psychotherapist who was present during this group.] He held me. I can feel his hands, very firm. I can smell him. I can see the eyes within his eyes. The outer eyes watery and diffused, the inner eyes clear and strong.

I'll now come back from my journey, to say very clinically that utter despair is a prerequisite for successful fantasy.

I could not have remained in that room for very long if I had to remain totally conscious; my need to escape was so powerful.

Oh Bill—your request for this account was complete with just one sentence—my reply can be as long as the Arabian Nights!

You asked us all to picture a man and a woman in our minds.

My man and woman were not very clearly seen, but they were fighting. The man was screaming, "She is mine!" and the woman was also screaming, "She is mine!" Then the woman bludgeoned the man to death. At first she felt victorious, but soon she was so sorry she had killed him because killing was not a feminine thing to do. She had behaved like a man.

I see the man lying dead. He is very tall, like Gulliver among the Lilliputians. He has black hair, very straight and flat to his head and long black sideburns. He is wearing shiny boots—high ones that come to just below his knees, and black pants and a black long-sleeved sweater with a high neck. Over the sweater is a vest of chain mail.

A flock of blue birds hovers around him. Each bird takes a little piece of his clothing in its beak and together they lift him, still dead, and carry him to the top of a mountain. They gently land him and fly away. He wakes up and looks around and walks to the mouth of a cave and goes in. The roof gets lower and lower as it slopes toward the back of the cave. It is light in the cave. He sees a pool way at the back. He wants to put his face in the water, but he can't bend down because of the stiff chain vest. He takes the vest off and his boots too. He sits in the pool. Soon he wants to leave the cave and the mountain, but there is no way to get down. The mountain is shiny and black and slippery like marble. He sees a big rock in the bottom of the pool. He tugs at it and pulls it out. Then he sits in the hole and slides down. It is like a chute which runs down through the middle of the mountain. He emerges at the foot of the mountain, and tumbles out onto a grassy hill. A small country village lies below the hill.

There is a girl. She is dressed in a long pinafore that is red with blue and gold embroidery around the hem. Underneath, she wears a white blouse with puffed sleeves. She wears a kerchief on her head. Golden ringlets show from the edges of her kerchief. Her skin is very white and creamy. Her body and arms are rounded and soft.

He wishes to take her to the top of the mountain. He tells her about the cave and the pool. She is reluctant to go with him. She points out that there is no way to climb that steep mountain.

(I was content to leave them there until you suggested a helicopter, Bill.)

The helicopter lands, picks them up and flies to the top of the mountain and lands them there.

The man takes her hand and gently leads her to the cave. She is very reluctant to go. He convinces her. They enter the cave. She looks around and is filled with wonder. He leads her to the pool. He sits down in it. She is timid, but finally lifts her skirts and sits in it too. She then becomes worried about leaving. In answer, he shows her the big rock. As he removes it, he tells her to be prepared to slide down the chute the moment he removes the rock. He explains that they must slide down with the water or else the inside of the chute will be dry and the rocks will scratch and bruise them.

She braces herself, he removes the rock, and down they slide through the dark chute. Out they tumble at the bottom. They are wet and disheveled, his flat straight hair has become wet and curly. They roll and play on the grassy hill like two puppies, curly and wet and rolling. Then they stand up, look down at the village, and walk hand-in-hand down toward it.

While in the fantasy I was conscious of your voice, Bill, and sometimes conscious of my body, but of very little else.

The fantasy was all in pictures—much like watching a movie; yet more, because I instantly knew the thought and feelings of the players. Somehow *I* was each of them and in some way was the mountain and the chute too.

When I "awoke" it was like returning from a dream. My depression was gone. I felt a peace and sleepiness, much like what you feel after crying for a long time. I could take deep breaths.

You then asked me to go into my body.

I entered through my mouth. Slid down my throat which was the same as the chute in the mountain. I tumbled down and landed in my vagina. I was very tiny. I stood up and parted the vulva and jumped out onto the seat of a chair on which the body had been sitting.

I was free! Yet I was uneasy. I wanted to enter another body, but they were all taken—and yet I didn't want to go back into mine. You asked me to go back again. I consented with reluctance. I then decided I'd go back, but to my brain this time. I was very elated to go into my brain. I liked my brain.

I entered through my "third eye" and found myself standing in front of a heavy wooden door bound in iron, like the old Spanish doors.

I was still very tiny and had to push with all my strength to open the door. It opened just enough for me to quickly squeeze through, and then it shut with a loud slam. Inside, I saw a spring on the door which made it close so quickly.

It was pink inside my brain and very light—very bright light everywhere. I heard a humming sound—it was that of the machinery. I inspected the machinery. It was all working smoothly.

There were very fine wires overhead. I heard a whirring noise and saw a tiny piece of paper, folded in half, suspended by a clothespin, coming quickly gliding along a wire. I stood on tiptoe and read the note. It said, "Move your feet." Many more notes came whirring in. They all had short messages written on them. I enjoyed reading all these messages to my brain. I then noticed a book hanging from the wire. It was very thick and very old, with a worn, maroon-colored binding. I thumbed through the book. I decided it was much too long to read.

You asked me then to try to read it. I turned to the first page, but couldn't read it. It was in a foreign language. You then asked if I could get someone to help me with it. Then I saw Fritz sitting on a high stool in a corner. He was wearing his jumpsuit. It was dirty. His legs were crossed at the knee and he was holding his head up with one hand, his elbow resting on his knee.

He asked if he could help me—and then I began to cry. I came out of the fantasy then. I remembered our meeting that morning. I could only remember the beauty of him and the love. I get lost in the memory of it even now.

You then asked me if my teeth could help me to read the book. [This was because she was grinding her teeth as she lay there.] I put my ear next to my teeth. I heard vibrations. If I could understand the language of these vibrations . . . my teeth were telling me something, but I couldn't understand the language. I sat on my tongue. It moved in a rhythm—the same rhythm as the vibrations—but I couldn't understand what the rhythm meant.

I went back into my brain. I opened the big book. The first page was covered with writing, but it wasn't really letters or lines; the page was entirely covered with markings, all jumbled together, filling the entire page. I looked closer and saw that it was written in many foreign languages. There were Russian letters and Japanese strokes and Egyptian hieroglyphs, all mixed together.

I felt so confused and helpless. How could I ever hope to decipher those markings? I knew that they contained a very important message; if I could understand them, I would then know the answer.

You then told me to look at the first few markings. I looked closer and looked very hard. I saw the first line. There was a hammer and a sickle, a star, an X and a triangle. None of these symbols have any meaning for me. I kept repeating hammer and sickle, hammer and sickle. What do you do with a hammer? A hammer is to pound with—a sickle? A sickle to cut with. Pound and cut, pound and cut what? Pound and cut the star! I pounded and cut the star and each of the five points of the star broke off, and then there were ten points around the star. I hammered and cut more and more, until there were many, many tiny points and the star became a seal. It looked like a notary's seal. It was gold and grew very big. It was the Great Seal. The Great Seal of Approval! I hammered and cut it. It broke up into tiny pieces. I ground it into gold dust and it blew away. The hammer and sickle and star were gone. I looked at the X. X means unknown. I hate unknowns. I changed the X and made it AX. It means Accept. Accept what? Accept the triangle, but what does the triangle mean? I stared at the triangle. It became a Haman taschen. A Haman taschen is a Jewish cookie, baked in the shape of a triangle. It is eaten during the Purim festival. The Haman taschen is named after the evil king, Haman, who decreed that all the Jews in his kingdom must die.

The message then said, Accept the Haman taschen. I laughed—how ridiculous! All this work just to be told to accept the Haman taschen! The message had no meaning for me. I needed a meaning. The Haman taschen was very big, because I was still very tiny. I walked into the center of it. It was filled with prune filling and was very sticky. I was soon covered with the prune filling. It clung to my feet and my face. I wiped it away from my eyes and my nose. It almost smothered me and I could hardly breathe. It was now covering my hands. I licked one of my fingers. It tasted good. It was sweet. I ate the filling from my hands, and then ate all the rest of the filling, until all that was left was the crusty outside part. I was very hungry. I took a bite of the crust. That tasted good too. Not like a Haman taschen at all, but like a butter cookie. It was very big, but I ate all of it. The Haman taschen was gone. Just the X was left. It still meant unknown, but then I remembered that I had changed it to AX and then to Accept. The message meant Accept! It had great meaning for me. I must accept myself, I must accept my body as part of me. I cannot have just a mind, I must have a body also.

I came out of the fantasy and I was at peace. I marvel at me—the wonder of me!

How I wish you were here in the days after I came home. I wanted you to see me then—to see and know the joy! You shared the pains of the birth—but did not witness the joy that came after.

I came home to my husband, David. I saw him and loved him. I can't imagine any returning traveler being welcomed with the warmth and understanding that I came home to.

And life is sweet—but too soon the "business of living" hides living. And David goes to work and I go to school and our boys go to school and we wear our wristwatches again and put on our shoes again.

The peace remains. The joy? The joy I fear is too gossamer a cloak. It cannot withstand the buffeting winds of our world down here.

A semiamusing epilogue to this fantasy began upon Nora's return home. She told David that one of their marital problems is now clear to her: she feels that she is physically stronger than he is. So they wrestled and he won. She is content.

But he isn't. His own concerns about masculinity are focused by this event and he feels that he must prove himself by wrestling with Nora's group leader—me. David begins a program of weight lifting and wrestling, and signs up for one of my workshops five months hence. On the last day of the workshop he announces that the time has come. No amount of cajoling will do, we must wrestle. The next day he looks exhilarated, he has met the test. And indeed it appears that the contest was very valuable for him.

I certainly hope so. As I sit here writing, two weeks later, my ribs still ache.

I asked Nora what the impact of the fantasy is now, six months later. This is her reply.

Nora's Reply

That message *was* a good one, because I had to accept all of me. Yet in the months since it also became a barrier for me, because I could not accept my body. I wanted to change it, and that meant that I didn't accept it as it was.

Two weeks ago, two friends and David decided to put me into the middle of the circle and have me break out (just like we did with Nancy). My reaction to being surrounded was grotesque. I was totally petrified. I finally broke away from David and one other woman. But the other man caught me and held me around the waist, and I couldn't break away. The fear of having him so close, holding and feeling me was enormous. Later that night I realized that it was the fear of his touching and feeling my body, that had petrified me. I didn't want him to feel the fat and ugliness of me. And when he did, I could no longer hide—he knew my secret. Then I knew that I had been using my fat to hide behind. All my life I felt that I couldn't really compete with other women, because of my body. So instead, I became a "helper"—thus I was not a threat to them and they liked and accepted me. It worked the same way with men. I could never be thought of as a woman, to be desired physically, so I became a mother to the men. The helper role was genuine sometimes, but too often it was just a role, so that they would accept me, but on "safe" ground, always intellectual, never physical. The helper role had become so integrated into my personality, that I couldn't distinguish any longer between really wanting to help or using it as a hiding device.

I don't have to be a helper anymore. I want to compete with other women and be desired by men. I don't need the fat anymore. I am getting rid of it. I will make my body beautiful.

I have no more secrets! I got rid of that last bit of debris that was clogging the stream, and now I'm running swift and clean!

The beautiful residual effects of our group never dry up. Like golden drops of honey they filter through the hive of my mind, adding sweetness again and again.

"Nora" is a lousy pseudonym for me, I don't look or feel like a Nora anymore. Nora sounds like somebody's mother—so how about Bathsheba?

The joy isn't a "gossamer cloak." It isn't anything to wear. The joy is this wonderful, throbbing core of me.

Hope your ribs are all healed. . . .

My job as guide to Nora's (or Bathsheba's) fantasy was to keep her focused on the message until she could decipher it. It was as if she had the answer to her problem within herself, but she needed outside support to dare to read what it said. Once she could decipher the message, the release followed.

APPENDIX

Note: In doing our research in the selection of readings for this book, we came across a good many case histories which we liked very much and which we considered for inclusion, but which for one reason or another we could not use. Below is a list of these articles. We suggest that the serious student of psychotherapy investigate these instructive case histories.

Dan Wedding
Raymond Corsini

Additional Case Studies

Ayllon, T. Intensive treatment of psychotic behavior by stimulus cessation and food reinforcement. *Behaviour Research and Therapy,* 1963, *1,* 53–61.

Ayllon, T., & Michael, J. The psychiatric nurse as a behavioral engineer. *Journal of the Experimental Analysis of Behavior,* 1959, *2,* 323–334.

Bachrach, A. J., Erwin, W E., & Mohr, J. P. The control of eating behavior in an anorexic by operant conditioning techniques. In L. P. Ullmann & L. Krasner (Eds.), *Case studies in behavior modification.* New York: Holt, Rinehart & Winston, 1965.

Barlow, D., Reynolds, E., & Agras, W. Gender identity change in a transsexual. *Archives of General Psychiatry,* 1973, *28,* 569–576.

Binswanger, L. The case of Ellen West. Translated in R. May, E. Angel, & H. F. Ellenberger (Eds.), *Existence,* New York: Basic Books, 1958.

Boss, M. A patient who taught the author to see and think differently. In *Psychoanalysis and Daseinsanalysis.* New York: Basic Books, 1963.

Bressler, B. Ulcerative colitis as an anniversary symptom. *Psychoanalytic Review,* 1956, *43,* 381–387.

Buck, B. Psychodrama of drug addition. *Group Psychotherapy,* 1952, *4,* 301–321.

Cautela, J. R. Multifaceted behavior therapy of self-injurious behavior. *Journal of Behavior Therapy and Experimental Psychiatry,* 1973, *4,* 125–131.

Colm H. The therapeutic encounter. *Review of Existential Psychology and Psychiatry,* 1965, *5,* 137–159.

Cooke, R. M. The use of music in play therapy. *Journal of Music Therapy,* 1969, *6,* 66–75.

Corsini, R. J. Treatment of a pedophile. *Group Psychotherapy*, 1951, *4*, 166–171.

Dreikurs, R. Counseling a boy: a demonstration. *Journal of Individual Psychology*, 1972, *28*, 223–231.

Ellis, A. The treatment of a psychopath with rational-emotive therapy. *Journal of Psychology*, 1961, *51*, 141–150.

Ellis, A. A twenty-three-year-old woman guilty about not following her parents' rules. In A. Ellis (Ed.), *Growth through reason*. Hollywood: Wilshire Books, 1974.

Erickson, M. H., & Hill, L. B. Unconscious mental activity in hypnosis: psychoanalytic implications. *Psychoanalytic Quarterly*, 1944, *13*, 60–78.

Freeman, H. L., & Kendrick, D. C. A case of cat phobia. *British Medical Journal*, 1960, *11*, 497–502.

Gill, M., & Menninger, K. Techniques of hypnoanalysis illustrated in a case report. *Bulletin of the Menninger Clinic*, 1946, *10*, 110–126.

Hall, J. W. The analysis of a case of night terror. *Psychoanalytic Studies of the Child*, 1946, *2*, 189–227.

Jacobi, J. A case of homosexuality. *Journal of Analytical Psychology*, 1969, *14*, 48–64.

Johnson, A. M., & Fishback, D. Analysis of a disturbed adolescent girl and collaborative psychiatric treatment of the mother. *American Journal of Orthopsychiatry*, 1944, *14*, 195–203.

Karpman, B. A case of paedophilia (legally rape) cured by psychoanalysis. *The Psychoanalytic Review*, 1950, *37*, 235–276.

Kavaka, J. Ego synthesis of a life-threatening illness in a child. *Psychoanalytic Studies of the Child*, 1962, 344–362.

Kendall, P. C., & Finch, A. J. A cognitive-behavioral treatment for impulse control: a case study. *Journal of Consulting and Clinical Psychology*, 1976, *44*, 852–857.

Lang, P. J., & Melamed, B. G. Avoidance conditioning therapy of an infant with chronic ruminative vomiting. *Journal of Abnormal Psychology*, 1969, *74*, 1–8.

Lazarus, A., Davison, G. C., & Polefka, D. A. Classical and operant factors in the treatment of a school phobia. *Journal of Abnormal Psychology*, 1965, *70*, 225–229.

Ludwig, A. M., Marx, A. J., Hill, P. A., & Browning, R. M. The control of violent behavior through faradic shock. *Journal of Nervous and Mental Disease*, 1969, *148*, 624–637.

Marsh, L. C. An experiment in the group treatment of patients at the Worchester State Hospital. *Mental Hygiene*, 1933, *17*, 396–416.

McCann, W. The roundtable technique. *Group Psychotherapy*, 1953, *5*, 233–239.

Moreno, J. L. A case of paranoia treated thru psychodrama. *Sociometry*, 1944, *7*, 312–327.

Munford, P. R., Reardon, D., Liberman, R. P., & Allen, L. Behavioral treatment of hysterical coughing and mutism: a case study. *Journal of Consulting and Clinical Psychology,* 1976, *44,* 1008–1014.

Murphy, W. F. A case of anxiety hysteria. In W. F. Murphy, *The tactics of psychotherapy.* New York: International Universities Press, 1965.

Novaco, R. W. Stress inoculation: a cognitive therapy for anger and its application to a case of depression. *Journal of Consulting and Clinical Psychology,* 1977, *45,* 600–608.

Papp, P. The family that had all the answers. In P. Papp (Ed.), *Family therapy: full length case studies.* New York: Gardner Press, 1977.

Poe, J. S. The successful treatment of a 40-year-old passive homosexual based on an adaptional view of sexual behavior. *The Psychoanalytic Review,* 1952, *39,* 23–33.

Regardie, F. I. Analysis of a homosexual. *Psychiatric Quarterly,* 1949, *23,* 548–566.

Reich, W. Psychogenic tic as a masturbation equivalent. In *Early Writings* (Vol. 1). New York: Farrar, Strauss, & Giroux, 1975.

Seidenberg, R. Psychosexual headache. *Psychiatric Quarterly,* 1947, *21,* 351–360.

Sterba, R. A case of brief psychotherapy by Sigmund Freud. *The Psychoanalytic Review,* 1951, *38,* 75–80.

Szasz, T. S. Recollections of a psychoanalytic psychotherapy: the case of "prisoner K." In A. Burton (Ed.), *Case studies in counseling and psychotherapy.* Englewood Cliffs, N. J.: Prentice-Hall, 1959.

Thigpen, C. H., & Cleckley, H. A case of multiple personality. *Journal of Abnormal and Social Psychology,* 1954, *49,* 135–151.

Ullmann, L. P., & Krasner, L. (Eds.) *Case studies in behavior modification.* New York: Holt, Rinehart & Winston, 1965.

Watzlawick, P., Weakland, J. H., & Fisch, R. *Change.* New York: W. W. Norton, 1974.

Index

Book Manufacture

Great Cases in Psychotherapy was typeset at Weimer Typesetting, Indianapolis. Printing and binding was by Banta Brothers, Menasha, Wisconsin. The cover was designed by John Firestone and Associates, Canal Winchester, Ohio. F. E. Peacock Publishers art department designed the text. The typeface is Bodoni Bold display with Times Roman.